About Island Press

Island Press is the only nonprofit organization in the United States whose principal purpose is the publication of books on environmental issues and natural resource management. We provide solutions-oriented information to professionals, public officials, business and community leaders, and concerned citizens who are shaping responses to environmental problems.

In 1999, Island Press celebrates its fifteenth anniversary as the leading provider of timely and practical books that take a multidisciplinary approach to critical environmental concerns. Our growing list of titles reflects our commitment to bringing the best of an expanding body of literature to the environmental community throughout North America and the world.

Support for Island Press is provided by The Jenifer Altman Foundation, The Bullitt Foundation, The Mary Flagler Cary Charitable Trust, The Nathan Cummings Foundation, The Geraldine R. Dodge Foundation, The Charles Engelhard Foundation, The Ford Foundation, The Vira I. Heinz Endowment, The W. Alton Jones Foundation, The John D. and Catherine T. MacArthur Foundation, The Andrew W. Mellon Foundation, The Charles Stewart Mott Foundation, The Curtis and Edith Munson Foundation, The National Fish and Wildlife Foundation, The National Science Foundation, The New-Land Foundation, The David and Lucile Packard Foundation, The Pew Charitable Trusts, The Surdna Foundation, The Winslow Foundation, and individual donors.

RESHAPING THE BUILT ENVIRONMENT

Reshaping the Built Environment

Ecology, Ethics, and Economics

Edited by Charles J. Kibert
Foreword by Alex Wilson

ISLAND PRESS
Washington, D.C. • Covelo, California

Library of Congress Cataloging-in-Publication Data
Reshaping the built environment : ecology, ethics, and economics / edited by Charles J. Kibert.
    p. cm.
  Includes bibliographical references.
  ISBN 1-55963-701-3
  ISBN 1-55963-702-1
  1. Real estate development—Environmental aspects—United States.
  2. Construction industry—Environmental aspects—United States. I. Kibert, Charles J.
  HD255.R47 1999   99-12892
  333.73'15—dc21   CIP

Printed on recycled, acid-free paper

Manufactured in the United States of America
10 9 8 7 6 5 4 3 2 1

This volume is dedicated to

JOHN TILLMAN LYLE,
whose final words of encouragement to
respect nature and live within its bounty
are contained within these pages.

Contents

Foreword

That our buildings and our process of building are having profound negative impacts on the environment will become abundantly clear as you read this book. Indeed, considering the resource consumption associated with building, or the global climate change our profligate consumption of fossil fuels is causing, or the patterns of development that threaten both environment and community throughout America, one might almost give up. The environmental indicators seem so bad and the challenges before us so great as to be almost unachievable.

Yet, there is cause for hope. The chapters that Charles Kibert has assembled here, while certainly not shirking from describing the monumental difficulties ahead, offer a sense of hope and optimism. Yes, the challenges are great, but so too are the minds and ideas of those visionaries and practitioners who are leading our building industry in the direction of sustainability. Sooner or later, the mainstream design and construction industries—and the clients they serve—will recognize that fundamental changes are needed in the way we create buildings, landscapes, and communities. This will probably happen fairly early in the twenty-first century. That so many answers and solutions have already been found, as evidenced here, bodes very well for our society's ability to find a way to live within our environmental means.

For centuries, building has been seen mostly as a way to live apart from the environment—our homes have sheltered us from the elements and protected us from lurking dangers. Indeed, real estate development has been a form of dominion over nature, modifying the environment to suit our every need. The forests were cut down by early colonial settlers on the East Coast of America to open the way for agriculture and towns. Swamps were drained and estuaries filled throughout the Southeast to produce habitable land. Species perceived as threatening, from wolves to prairie dogs, were exterminated to "reclaim the land."

In recent decades, the environmental movement has focused a significant amount of its effort on the ills of real estate development—trying to stem the flow of suburban sprawl, trying to protect islands of wild in a growing tangle of asphalt, trying to save a free-flowing river, or a vital aquifer, or an endangered songbird from

the ravages of development. For many in the environmental community development is evil and developers are the enemy.

But I believe all this may change. *Reshaping the Built Environment* shows that
real estate development and the process of building can not only be less damaging
to the environment but can actually be the vehicle to improve our collective environment. Some of the projects and ideas described in this book demonstrate that
development—the right kind of development—can not only help to protect but
also help to restore ecosystems, biodiversity, water supplies, and even our global
climate. When the building industry begins to adopt the ideas in this book widely,
we just might find that the environmental villains of the twentieth century become
the environmental heroes of the twenty-first. Real estate development and our
building industry have produced some of our most challenging environmental
problems; now it is time to use the tremendous power of this industry in reshaping
our built environment and protecting our environment.

Alex Wilson
Executive Editor and Publisher
Environmental Building News
Brattleboro, Vermont
October 1998

Preface

The built environment of the future will hopefully be significantly different than the version being produced today. Rapid deterioration of resources and ecological systems coupled with negative global environmental impacts have motivated many professionals and academics to rethink the fundamental premises that underlie how we design and produce buildings and infrastructure. Although the roots of this shift in thinking can be traced back many years, the past decade has witnessed an especially strong upsurge in research, publications, and demonstration projects that are laying the groundwork for a major reshaping of human habitat. This new movement resembles, in many respects, the energy conservation movement spurred by the oil shortages of the 1970s, but with the addition of a host of other resource, environmental, and human concerns. Ecological systems are being examined for the lessons they hold for human systems. Producing a built environment that mimics and complements rather than conflicts with nature is emerging as the Holy Grail of this movement.

Beneath the technical effort to reshape the built environment lies the concept of sustainable development or sustainability. An acknowledgment of human responsibility to do better than we have in the past, with respect for both natural systems and future human generations, is creating a new interest in the ethical quandaries we have created for ourselves and the articulation of responsibilities that may help us emerge into a new era. New economic visions, such as those being spelled out in the rapidly emerging field of ecological economics, are providing new meanings for words such as *cost* and *value*.

This book contains the thoughts on this reshaping of a group of eminent scholars and practitioners who were invited to the University of Florida during the winter and spring of 1998 as part of the Rinker Eminent Scholar Series, "Sustainability in the Built Environment." Eighteen lectures were delivered to faculty, students, and staff of the University of Florida and to the local community during the period January–April 1998. In addition to the chapters in this volume, a set of videotapes capturing the lectures was produced.

The chapters in this book are organized into three parts to provide a logical delivery of the thoughts of the participants in this series. Part I, "Foundations," provides the underlying framework for thinking about how the built environment should be reshaped and considers the ecological, ethical, and economic underpinnings for sustainability in the built environment. Part II, "Content," considers the energy, water, materials, land, and landscape resources that are the "stuff" of the built environment. Part III, "Process," provides insights into how we can organize and design our structures in a fashion that carries out this reshaping to the benefit of both human and natural systems.

As is usually the case with a series and publication of this complexity, many people were involved and contributed to the success of this project. We are grateful for the participation and patience of the eminent scholars and practitioners who not only invested their time in coming to the University of Florida to present their ideas but also participated in many other activities that greatly enriched the experience of our faculty, students, staff, and the local community. I would like to thank my fellow faculty members in the M.E. Rinker Sr. School of Building Construction in the College of Architecture at the University of Florida for electing to devote resources from the Rinker Eminent Scholar Fund to this lecture series. The funds were provided by the late "Doc" Rinker and give the school an unparalleled opportunity to create new visions for the construction industry. We are fortunate that Doc chose to invest in the future of the school and are indebted to both him and the Rinker family. We would also like to express our appreciation to Wayne Drummond, dean of the College of Architecture, for affirming the decision of the faculty and for providing continuous moral support for the concept underlying both the Rinker Eminent Scholar Series and this volume. Thanks also to Jimmie Hinze, director of the M.E. Rinker Sr. School of Building Construction, for his support and encouragement throughout the entire process.

I would also like to acknowledge and thank the staff of the Center for Construction and Environment for making this dream a reality. Gisela Bosch was the chief organizer of the speakers and logistics for the Rinker Eminent Scholar Series, and she was ably assisted by Brad Guy in her many coordination tasks. Pegeen Hanrahan provided noteworthy support by carefully editing several of the chapters. Many of our student assistants handled the bulk of the logistics for this effort, especially Falynn Schmidt and Stephen Schell. Dottie Beaupied provided her usual excellent administrative skills, keeping information to and from all parties flowing smoothly.

Funding for the Rinker Eminent Scholar Series was provided by the Marshall E. Rinker, Sr. Foundation, Inc. and the Marshall and Vera Lea Rinker Foundation, Inc.

We gratefully acknowledge and thank Island Press, especially Heather Boyer, our editor, for her confidence in our concept for this volume and her hard work in helping bring together the wide range of ideas presented here into a coherent book.

Chapter 1

Introduction

Charles J. Kibert

The emergence of sustainable development as a major paradigm for human society brings with it numerous intellectual and operational challenges. The Brundtland Report definition of *sustainable development,* ". . . meeting the needs of the present without compromising the ability of future generations to meet their needs . . . ," provides a complex direction that juxtaposes current behavior with long-term survival. Needs of both present and future generations must be based on two fundamental concepts: (1) the fair and just intergenerational allocation and use of natural resources, and (2) the preservation of biological systems function across time. The construct of human society designed to allocate and provide resources to people is the economy, which, at least for the production of material goods, depends almost entirely on nature for its energy and physical inputs. The built environment is a major sector of the economy, and to be sustainable it, like every other sector of activity, must examine its behavior in light of the imperatives and constraints dictated by sustainability. The unsustainable use of land, energy, water, and materials that is characteristic of construction industry must be changed from the present-day open-loop, cradle-to-grave model to a closed-loop system integrated with an overall industrial system that focuses on dematerialization, deenergization, decarbonization, and detoxification. This shift provides abundant challenges to the wide range of professionals engaged in producing homes, commercial and institutional buildings, industrial complexes, and the wide variety of systems comprising the infrastructure servicing and interconnecting the elements of the built environment. This volume describes some of the key current thinking of academics and professionals seeking to discover the path to sustainability in the built environment.

Insights

Construction industry, like other sectors of the economy, is at present an inefficient and wasteful activity that creates human habitat in a manner generally focused on profitability without consideration of its long-term impacts. In this volume, construction industry refers to the wide range of actors involved in the life cycle of the built environment: developers, planners, designers (including architects, landscape architects, and interior designers), engineers, builders, facility managers, supporting materials industries, and the demolition industry that removes the built environment at the end of its physical or economic useful life. The built environment consumes 40 percent of extracted resources in most industrial countries and 30 to 40 percent of generated energy and thus has a profound effect on the availability of natural resources for future generations. It has a particularly great responsibility to address its current behavior and change course to one that is sustainable.

The subject of sustainability or sustainable development is a complex one, and to explore it thoroughly requires a wide-ranging exploration of diverse subjects. Sustainability is about interconnections within and between several major systems: ecological, social, and economic. The subject becomes no less complex when the viewer is restricted to the subject of creating the built environment in which resource issues, environmental degradation, human health, building economics, community development, and many other issues are closely coupled and intertwined and must be at least partially unraveled for analysis and understanding.

Addressing the concept of sustainability in the creation of communities and buildings also entails dealing with a complex web of ecological, social, and economic issues. Humankind's habitat, as is the case with other species, is constructed by humans primarily for protection from the elements and for safety. Unlike species that rely on their endosomatic appendages (claws, teeth, tails) to build their habitat, man has the ability to make widespread use of exosomatic or human-made tools to create a wide variety of complex structures for habitat, work, play, and movement between the various locations for these activities: the built environment. The creation, maintenance, renovation, and exchange of elements of the built environment provide the economic element of the equation. In the United States the built environment creation process alone accounts for 7 to 10 percent of all economic activity, a significant portion of the total. Ecological interactions with the creation of the built environment are wide and deep. Nature provides all the goods and materials needed to create the fabric and working components; the land on which the buildings and infrastructure are located; the fuel to power the construction and run the resulting structures; the water for the occupants; and the mechanisms for absorbing, assimilating, and processing waste. In short, without nature and ecological systems there would be no resources for a built environment. The actual creation of the built environment has many negative impacts on the natural systems that are in fact so crucial to its existence: destruction of plants and wildlife habitat, solid waste generation, non-point source pollution, release of toxic materials, alteration of natural drainage systems, and water and air pollution. Building creation and operation is tied to power plant construction and operation; automobile access and use; connection of water, natural gas, and other utilities; solid waste generation; wastewater and stormwater processing and disposal; and many other human-made systems that impact natural systems.

Creating a *sustainable* built environment is a complex task requiring a far wider range of knowledge and experience than conventional practice. At its very roots, sustainability demands attention to the environmental and social contexts of the built environment. The interconnectedness of the built environment with the community and the health of its citizens can no longer be neglected by architects, engineers, building owners, and developers. Engaging a broad range of citizens and disciplines is the first order of business in this new movement, and the reshaping of the built environment based on sustainability depends on inclusion and interdisciplinary teamwork to succeed.

Organization

This volume addresses the broad range of complex issues connected to reshaping the process of creating the built environment. The roots of sustainable thinking and the reason for its rise in stature are environmental problems, damage to ecosystems, resource shortages, and social inequity; thus these topics must be thoroughly addressed for an understanding of alternative thinking to be uncovered. In addition, an attempt is made to deal with the peripheral issues in a manner proportional to their relative importance to the subject. To organize coverage of these concepts, this volume is divided into three parts.

Part I, "Foundations," provides essential background on creating a sustainable built environment.

The limits to sustainability are covered in Chapter 2 by Charles J. Kibert of the University of Florida. The physical and technical limits of nature and humankind's use of its abundant resources lead to the conclusion that sustainability is perhaps more a journey than a goal. Some of the frameworks for changing directions and the potential outcomes for redirecting the built environment onto a path of sustainable development are addressed.

Chapter 3 by Stephen R. Kellert of Yale University clearly articulates the looming crisis for the environment and its myriad ecological systems as they are impinged upon in an unsustainable manner by humankind. Human values themselves are being challenged as spiritual values come into conflict with human behavior in the form of irreversible destruction to natural systems

Ethics, the subject of Chapter 4 by Sarah van Gelder, editor of *Yes! A Journal of Positive Futures*, is an essential element required for understanding sustainability and the role of the built environment in embracing sustainability principles. At its core, sustainable development is questioning the right and wrong of various courses of action and their effects on natural systems and future human generations.

Economics are of crucial importance in dealing with the subject of sustainability, both to demonstrate the ultimate advantages of creating a sustainable built environment as well as to demonstrate the greatly undervalued role that natural systems play in our economic system. In Chapter 5, Herman E. Daly of the University of Maryland provides insights into the unsustainable behavior of the world's economic system and the dangers inherent in today's much ballyhooed movement toward globalization.

Part II, "Content," addresses the major resource issues pertinent to the built environment: land, energy, materials, and water.

Perhaps the key to resolving the dilemma of overdependence on limited fossil fuel resources is the shift to widespread use of renewable energy resources by the built environment. In Chapter 6, Stephen J. Strong of Stephen Strong & Associates provides a vision of a built environment that mimics natural systems by converting abundant solar energy into electrical power through the integration of photovoltaics into the building fabric. He also addresses the role of other forms of renewable energy in a future less dependent on rapidly depleting nonrenewable energy sources.

Building materials are the subject of Chapter 7 by Nadav Malin of *Environmental Building News*. Materials are perhaps the most difficult issue in creating a sustainable built environment because the industrial subsystem producing them has paid little or no attention to the impacts of extraction, waste, and the ultimate fate of their products. Insights into these problems, potential solutions, and a methodology for selecting materials for use in the built environment are provided.

Water resources and the processing of wastewater from human activities often are the limiting factor in the creation of human habitat. Lessons gleaned from nature are discussed by John Todd of Living Systems, Inc., in Chapter 8, which describes the evolution of wastewater processing systems inspired by natural systems. The chapter details the principles and lessons learned in creating Living Machines—ranging in size from household systems to industrial wastewater treatment plants—that adapt the technology inherent in natural systems to benefit humankind.

Chapter 9 by John Tillman Lyle of the University of California–Pomona covers the importance of landscape in the creation of the human environment. Lyle's notion of a regenerative landscape uses nature as the model for human-produced landscapes and envisions a shift from the industrial model of a one-way flow of resources from source to sink to landscapes that behave in a cyclical manner in their use of energy, water, and biomass.

In Chapter 10, Peter Yost of the National Association of Home Builders Research Center provides new insights into reusing and recycling the waste generated during the construction and demolition phases of the construction life cycle. He provides an overview of lessons learned and practical approaches the industry can use to reduce waste during construction and make better use of the remnants of buildings at the end of their useful lives. He also discusses the emerging trend of

Green Builder programs throughout the United States and how these programs can help stimulate the movement to a more resource efficient construction process.

Part III, "Process," describes the role of various actors involved in the life cycle of the built environment to include architects, planners, and the government.

Gail A. Lindsey of Harmony Design covers the subject of sustainable building design and the role of the architect in Chapter 11. In addition to ensuring that future buildings are resource efficient and healthy, architects need to reconsider their fundamental role in creating buildings that are inherently valuable and whose function and fabric contribute to a wholesome, human-oriented community that integrates with and respects nature.

In Chapter 12, David Orr of Oberlin College describes an essential character of buildings that is often ignored—that they can be instructive in their own right. This is especially true if they are designed to mimic natural processes and complement rather than destroy natural systems.

Daniel Williams of Florida International University views the built environment at large scale in Chapter 13 by addressing the need to consider its bioregional context. His thesis is that the planning of built environment elements should consider the model of natural systems functioning at large scale, where tasks such as water storage and purification, microclimatic control, and resource use and reuse are the result of natural forces that provide "free work." Applying these principles to infrastructure, utilities, and neighborhood patterns could free society from its dependence on conventional energy sources by taking advantage of the elegant designs provided by nature.

In Chapter 14, Randall Arendt describes the concept of conservation subdivision design. He argues for a fundamental shift in land development patterns that would not only provide for more green space in new developments but would also increase the profitability of developers and the quality of life of home owners. By reducing the size of individual land parcels and agglomerating the balance in land tracts that remain in their original condition, a wide variety of natural and farmland resources are retained to include mature woodlands, breeding/feeding grounds, and stream valleys. Cooperation among developers would result in larger contiguous tracts of land that enhance the natural and economic value of the resulting arrangement of built and natural land tracts.

In Chapter 15, Thomas E. Graedel of Yale University proposes the application of lessons learned from the emerging science of industrial ecology to the creation of "green" buildings. Using lessons learned from the automotive industry, he suggests a methodology for assessing the performance of buildings systems that would provide an easily understood picture of how building designs could be analyzed to determine those facets that are successful in terms of environmental performance as well as those that require additional measures to reduce their impacts.

Chapter 16 by Raymond J. Cole of the University of British Columbia describes progress in developing comprehensive building assessment systems that provide a scorecard for the environmental performance of individual buildings. He discusses the limitations inherent in first generation building assessment systems and how these shortcomings are being translated into newer methods that more closely link environmental performance with design criteria.

One of the key resources required to produce the built environment is land, and much of the land in urban areas has suffered from contamination due to industrial activities. In Chapter 17, William J. Trumbull of Chicago's Department of the Environment describes the city's innovative Brownfields Initiative, perhaps the most advanced program in the United States for recycling formerly contaminated industrial lands back into productive use. Using an approach informed by academic research, the Brownfields Initiative created a dialogue among government, business, and community representatives to develop public policy that is contributing to the revitalization of once blighted neighborhoods.

Ernest A. Lowe of Indigo Development describes the application of industrial ecology to the development of Sustainable New Towns in Chapter 18. Using first-hand experience gained in post-apartheid South Africa, he describes how new towns can be viewed as a whole system rather than a patchwork of individual initiatives and incremental developments. To accomplish this feat, environmental stewardship, self-governance, a strong and diverse economy, and lifelong learning must serve as the underpinnings of the entire planning process.

MOVING FROM THE PRESENT industrial-economic way of functioning to a more sustainable way will require all sectors of human activity to reconsider their behavior with respect to the environment, resource consumption, waste, processes, and society. As a major economic force, consumer of resources, and destroyer of ecological systems, the built environment has a particularly difficult path ahead if it is to alter course. Fortunately, natural systems provide abundant models for architecture, engineering, production, and waste conversion to use in rethinking the human habitat and its interconnections. Many efforts around the world have begun this process and the potential to make the shift relatively painless clearly exists. This volume provides numerous models for a new era that values nature and people while decreasing waste, inefficiency, and poor design. The ideas presented here form the basis of a new beginning and mark a new era in which the built environment will be reshaped to provide not only greatly improved human living conditions but also circumstances in which the life-support systems and resources provided by nature are respected and protected.

Part I

Foundations

Chapter 2

The Promises and
Limits of Sustainability

Charles J. Kibert

Numerous worldwide sustainability efforts and movements describe two distinct but potentially conflicting goals: (1) leaving adequate resources and environmental quality for future generations, and (2) providing support to developing countries to assist them in creating healthy economies that provide their populations a quality of life better than mere survival. Juxtaposing the needs of present and future generations forces the examination of whether natural systems and natural resources can meet the resulting enormous and complex intertemporal demands. Without rapid, large increases in resource efficiency, primary emphasis on renewable resources, huge reductions in waste and pollution production, stabilization of population, international accords limiting greenhouse gas emissions, and widespread protection of natural areas for their function and biodiversity, sustainable development will be nothing more than a grand illusion. This chapter examines these issues and provides some conclusions about sustainable development in general and, more specifically, about the impacts of sustainability on the future of the built environment.

Concepts and Outcomes

The concept of sustainable development is much in vogue and appears in the construction disciplines in various forms, such as sustainable construction, ecologically sustainable development (ESD), green building, sustainable architecture, and resource-efficient construction. The motivation for these activities is to reduce resource consumption and waste and protect the function and biodiversity of natural systems. The desired outcomes are national and international societies that consume energy, water, and materials at a replenishable rate—that is, one that can be maintained indefinitely while ensuring that natural systems are protected and healthy human habitats are created. The widespread implementation of the reduce–reuse–recycle philosophy and other pillars of this concept is implicitly understood and explicitly advertised to make the earth's finite quantity of materials presumably inexhaustible. Issues such as population growth, quality of life, and standard of living are tacitly assumed to be accounted for and addressed within the framework of sustainability.

The reality is that sustainability is and must be constrained by the very laws of nature that govern the natural systems that are the object of preservation and protection. These laws include those of physics, thermodynamics, and chemistry. Time and the underlying chaos present in nature also set limits on resource availability. The First Law of Thermodynamics establishes that a system can deliver no more energy output than the energy inputs to the system, while the Second Law states that we cannot even break even—that the fate of all systems is degradation in energy and quality. Thermodynamics also applies to materials and their degradation and thus establishes limits on recycling. The high degree of self-organization characteristic of nature is powered by the availability of solar energy, allowing the complexity found in natural systems to develop and evolve. Similarly, the complexity of human-made systems is permitted by the consumption of large quantities of high-quality energy that ultimately finds its way, via inefficiency and thermodynamic limitations, to low-temperature, largely useless thermal sinks. In addition to energy constraints, time is a governing variable that dictates what resources can be made available and when. Technology, which is nothing more than applied science, affects how resources can be extracted and utilized, and it can create both opportunities for more efficient resource use as well as negative environmental impacts.

Sustainability is a laudable and desirable goal, but the fundamental question is How close can it be approached, if at all? It should also be acknowledged that sustainable development is a highly complex issue with significant moral components: (1) the current generation must pass on its inheritance of natural wealth not unchanged but undiminished in potential to support future generations (Daily and Ehrlich 1992); and (2) all people have a right to their fair share of the earth's resources. Many of the problems encountered as the movement to sustainable behavior is explored have technical solutions but technical solutions are not always possible (Hardin 1968). People and institutions often have to intervene when market forces are unable to correct the behavior of economies that tend to deplete and destroy natural systems. Behavior can be an enormous obstacle to achieving sustainability. It is intertwined with technology because consumer demand for products of technology results in many of the problems affecting the environment: global warming, ozone depletion, threats to biodiversity, air and water pollution, and soil erosion, to name a few.

Clearly, human behavior may destroy the planet long before resource shortages cause widespread dislocation. However, the exploration of how many of us can survive on the planet in a sustainable manner, and for how long, will help determine the boundaries to sustainability. H.T. Odum, the eminent systems ecologist, maintains that sustainability is in fact unachievable and that humankind, as every other species, is constrained by the laws of nature. Consequently, humans can expect to grow in numbers, reach a maximum quantity or "climax," and then decline in numbers as the ability of the earth to support their consumption, sometimes referred to as *carrying capacity,* is exceeded. The question, according to Odum, is not whether humans can live sustainably, because they cannot, but how fast the population declines after it climaxes. By adopting what are termed sustainable styles of existence, the decline can be the equivalent of a soft landing as the population stabilizes at levels the earth can accommodate. Otherwise, the resulting crash landing will cause inevitable pain and suffering for the vast bulk of humanity.

Goals of Sustainable Development

Many international, national, regional, and local sustainability movements are seeking to reverse the course of destruction of natural systems, planetary pollution, the depletion of nonrenewable resources, and the unsustainable use of renewable resources. The fundamental unanswered question is whether it is feasible, under any realistic human population scenario, for a reasonable approximation to sustainability to actually be achieved. A reasonable sustainability scenario would be one in which a so-called "good" quality of life is maintained in the Organisation for Economic Cooperation and Development (OECD) countries while their economies are dematerialized and deenergized. At the same time, economic development in the lesser developed countries (LDC) must allow their vast populations to move beyond mere survival to a good quality of life. The question of what constitutes a good quality of life must, of course, be answered and quantified. It should include adequate nutrition; clean air, water, and land; a decent and universal education system; a just, equitable, and democratic system of government; a functional economic system operating within resource and environmental constraints to provide safe jobs with equitable wages; and protected natural systems.

Framing the Debate

There are clearly many sides to the debate over whether humans can continue to increase both their population and aggregate consumption at present rates. However, there are two readily identifiable extreme positions that can be reviewed to provide the limits of probable consequences for humans as a result of their lifestyle and behavior patterns. At one extreme, the *anthropocentric view,* are those who believe nature exists for human use and that human ingenuity can always find a new material, process, or system to replace whatever nature cannot provide. The other extreme, the *gaia view,* holds that the earth is itself a living system and that humankind is in fact destroying this system through land development, extractive industries, polluting transport and industry, throwaway attitudes, and a general disregard for nature (Lovelock 1988). The real truth is that both of these polar opposites exist simultaneously. Nature is in fact being ravaged by humankind, the survival of many species is in question, rainforests and fisheries all over the world are being destroyed at an accelerating rate, and the atmospheric concentrations of greenhouse warming gases continue to rise at an increasing pace. At the same time, humankind has proven to be clever and adaptable, with an incredible array of technologies being developed at an ever increasing rate, materials use per capita actually dropping in industrialized countries, and a significant swing in attitude and consciousness toward environment-friendly behavior occurring worldwide. Knowledge can indeed increase the productivity of natural resources by improving the efficiency with which they are used (Sagoff 1995). To assess the potential for humankind to live sustainably and explore the limits to sustainability, several major classifications of human impacts on the earth bear reviewing: (1) the alteration of planetary systems, (2) the depletion of nonrenewable resources, (3) the unsustainable use of renewable resources, and (4) the pollution of earth, land, and water systems by humankind's waste.

Alteration of Planetary Systems

The earth before the emergence of *Homo sapiens* was a complex, self-regulating system in which the waste of one species was food for another. There were no human-made synthetic substances, only materials made from geological, geochemical, and solar processes. There were no machines other than biological ones. All gases and substances entering the atmosphere were due to biological or geological activity. Mass movements of matter were totally the province of either geological forces or weather systems. The only sources of energy were solar or geological in origin. Water and other nutrient cycles were driven solely by geochemical and solar processes.

The period now known as the Industrial Revolution radically altered this picture. The emergence of fossil fuel–consuming energy systems, mechanized materials extraction and processing systems, synthetic materials manufacture, and the wastes from these activities have altered the planet in a dramatic manner. Humankind is disturbing complex, naturally evolved, and diverse natural systems and is doing so in a fashion that can only result in catastrophe (see Table 2.1).

The earth's total surface area of 510 million km^2 is comprised of a terrestrial component of 147 million km^2 and an aquatic component of 363 million km^2. The net primary production (NPP) of the terrestrial area is 132.1 billion metric tons (MT) and the NPP of the aquatic area is estimated to be 92.4 billion MT. Humans are coopting almost 40 percent of terrestrial NPP and almost 30 percent of aquatic NPP (Vitousek et al. 1986). It is likely that NPP cooption is proportional

Table 2.1. A general classification of human impacts on natural systems

Depletion	*Appropriation*	*Destruction*
• Soil	• Net primary production (NPP)	• Biodiversity
• Nonrenewables	- Terrestrial	• Renewable resource base
- Oil	- Aquatic	- Fisheries
- Coal	• Fresh water	- Forests
- Natural gas		• Waste assimilative capacity
		• Ozone Layer

Modification	*Pollution and Toxification*
• Agriculture	• Water: sewage; industrial, agricultural,
• Extractive industries	and marine wastes
• Built environment	• Air
	- Greenhouse warming gases
	- Ozone-depleting gases
	- Acidification gases
	- Toxic gases
	• Land: municipal solid waste;
	construction/demolition waste;
	industrial and agricultural waste

to population, so a doubling of world population from 1986 to 2026 (5 billion to 10 billion) would result in 80 percent of terrestrial and 60 percent of aquatic NPP being diverted to human use. Although the exact consequences of this doubling is unknown, it is probable that the result would be devastating for global ecosystems. The question is at what level of stress, if at all, will these natural life-support systems simply collapse to a level where human life itself is threatened. Interestingly enough, Vitousek noted (in 1986) that human cooption of marine productivity was rather small, only 2.2 percent, and that this small use was unlikely to dramatically alter ocean ecosystems. In 1998 fisheries in most oceans around the world are in crisis as numerous species are being severely depleted in an unsustainable fashion that is likely to lead to their extinction. The bottom line is that the cooption, destruction, and diversion of terrestrial and aquatic resources by humankind is contributing to a rapid and widespread extinction of species and genetically distinct populations, amounting to the loss of potentially useful species and the genetic impoverishment of others that may survive.

Humans are also appropriating a vast percentage of the natural flow of water for their own uses. Total sustainable fresh water available to the earth's land mass is about 110,000 km^3, comprised of 70,000 km^3 of evapotranspiration (ET) by plants and 40,000 km^3 of runoff (R). Of the R portion, only 12,500 km^3 is actually available (AR) for human use due to temporal and geographic factors. Humans currently appropriate about 26 percent of the ET and 54 percent of the AR for their own uses, or about 30 percent of all water powered by the natural solar cycle. Consumption or use of AR for human purposes, based on current trends, will probably rise to more than 70 percent by the year 2025. The consequences of this enormous increase in water appropriation will inevitably result in the further decline of fish populations and extinction of many species (Postel et al. 1996). Although world energy consumption and accompanying global warming are serious concerns, it could be humankind's need for water that ultimately may seriously limit local and global economic and human development. Not factored into the appropriation problem is the increasing pollution of world water bodies, particularly in light of the rapid growth of economies in Asia. China in particular is at risk, with damage to natural ecosystems so severe that the recovery of these systems, even with extreme shifts in policy and activity, is considered very unlikely.

Humans are clearly appropriating a massive proportion of ecosystem goods and services and dumping staggering quantities of waste to air, water, and land. Yet humans are just one of an estimated 30–60 million organisms. Edward O. Wilson, the renowned ecologist and Pulitzer Prize winner, has stated that the fossil record indicates there have been five major upheavals on earth that caused major extinctions of life on the planet: Ordovician (440 million years ago), Devonian (365 million years ago), Permian (245 million years ago), Triassic (210 million years ago), and Cretaceous (66 million years ago). The recovery of life to its pre-catastrophe diversity and quantity after each of these upheavals required 20–100 million years. Human activities of the present and probable future scales are creating conditions for another cataclysmic event, and, similar to the earlier upheavals, these actions stand a good chance of wiping out not only its cause, the human species, but much of life on earth (Wilson 1989, 1992).

The signs of planetary stress are clear. The planetary average land and water temperature in 1998 was the highest average annual temperature ever recorded. The ten warmest years in the last 130 years have occurred in the 1980s and 1990s. Insurance industry payouts for weather-related damage have climbed from US$16 billion in all of the 1980s to US$48 billion for 1990–1995 (Brown et al. 1996). Acid rain is threatening both freshwater fish and forests due to the emissions of sulfur and nitrous oxides from the combustion of fossil fuels in power plants and automobiles. Species extinction rates are 100 to 1,000 times higher than before the arrival of humankind, with a potential acceleration to 1,000 to 10,000 times higher if species now threatened become extinct in the next century (Brown et al. 1996). Far fewer species exist and the complex web of life created through billions of years of evolution is being unraveled in just a few hundred years. Logging, mining, agriculture, and grazing are degrading watersheds. Over 85 percent of U.S. inland waters are artificially controlled. Over half of U.S. wetlands, excluding Alaska, have been drained while only recently have their complex roles in stormwater control, biodiversity maintenance, and clean water become evident.

The alteration of planetary systems has potentially dire consequences for humankind because of the wide range of services that natural systems provide that benefit humans and human settlements (see Table 2.2).

A recent economic analysis was made of the ecosystem services shown in Table 2.3. The value of these services was estimated to be at least US$33 trillion annually, with a range $US16 trillion to $US54 trillion per year. World economic output is approximately $US18 trillion per year, giving an ecosystem-to-GNP ratio of about 1.8. Although placing a monetary value on natural systems is abhorrent to some, it is also true that decisions are often made on the financial consequences of an activity, whether in the public sector or private sector (Costanza et al. 1997). Pollination, one of many services provided by natural systems to the human economy, was estimated to be worth $100 billion in Europe in 1989, and high pesticide use on cotton crops that in the United States kills natural pollinators reduces annual yields by 20 percent, or $400 million dollars (Abramovitz 1998).

Table 2.2. Services provided by systems to human settlements

Air quality enhancement/maintenance
Soils for food, wood, and paper production
Ambient temperature enhancement/maintenance (hot weather moderation)
Dampening flood peaks
Filtering and recharging groundwater
Reduced urban-chimney effects
Erosion control (cover, slope component, rainfall, wind, and soil texture components)
Renewable energy sources (solar, wind, biomass, geothermal, tidal)
Tree, bush, and flower pollination
Albedo change forces (energy budget for plants and animals)
Providing evapotranspiration cooling and shade for animals, people, and buildings
Food and water for wildlife
Dampening vertebrate pest damage to crops and other land production
Recreational and tourism areas and area access
Grazing for domesticated animals
Providing noise barriers and separation
Natural fires (for secondary succession conditions)
Carbon, energy, and water storage
Hazard reductions of several types

Table 2.3. Ecosystem services and function

Ecosystem Service	Ecosystem Functions	Examples
1. Gas regulation	Regulation of atmospheric chemical composition	CO_2/O_2 balance, O_3 for UVB protection, SO_x levels
2. Climate regulation	Regulation of global temperature, precipitation, and other biologically mediated climate processes at global/local levels	Greenhouse gas regulation, DMS production affecting cloud formation
3. Disturbance regulation	Capacitance, damping and integrity of ecosystem response to environmental fluctuations	Storm protection, flood control, drought recovery, and other aspects of habitat response to environmental variability mainly controlled by vegetation structure
4. Water regulation	Regulation of hydrological flows	Provision of water for agricultural or industrial processes or transportation
5. Water supply	Storage and retention of water	Provision of water by watersheds, reservoirs, and aquifers
6. Erosion control and sediment retention	Retention of soil within an ecosystem	Prevention of soil loss by wind, runoff, or other removal processes, storage of silt in wetlands and lakes
7. Soil formation	Soil formation processes	Weathering of rock and accumulation of organic material
8. Nutrient cycling	Storage, internal cycling, processing and acquisition of nutrients	Nitrogen fixation; nitrogen, phosphorus, and other elemental or nutrient cycles
9. Waste treatment	Recovery of mobile nutrients and removal or breakdown of excess or xenic nutrients and compounds	Waste treatment, pollution control, detoxification

10. Pollination	Movement of floral gametes	Provision of pollinators for the reproduction of plant populations
11. Biological control	Trophic-dynamic regulation of populations	Keystone predator control of prey species, reduction of herbivory by top predators
12. Refugia	Habitat for resident and transient populations	Nurseries, habitat for migratory species, regional habitats for locally harvested species, or overwintering grounds
13. Food production	That portion of gross primary production extractable as food	Production of fish, game, crops, nuts, fruits by hunting, gathering, subsistence farming, or fishing
14. Raw materials	That portion of gross primary production extractable as raw materials	Production of lumber, fuel, or fodder
15. Genetic resources	Sources of unique biological materials and products	Medicine, products for materials science, genes for resistance to plant pathogens and crop pests, ornamental species
16. Recreation	Providing opportunities for recreational activities	Ecotourism, sport fishing, and other outdoor recreational activities
17. Cultural	Providing opportunities for noncommercial uses	Aesthetic, artistic, educational, spiritual, and/or scientific value of ecosystems

Source: Costanza et al. 1997.

Resource Depletion

At present, all signs point to rapid depletion of both renewable and nonrenewable resources. While economies are generally using materials and energy more efficiently than in the past, already huge and rapidly growing numbers of humans are causing aggregate materials and energy consumption to rapidly increase. Forests are being depleted at an accelerating rate, from 40 percent of the earth's land surface 1,000 years ago, to 30 percent in 1900, and only 20 percent at present (Bates 1990; Brown et al. 1996). In addition to the loss of 1 acre of rainforest per second, temperate forests are being destroyed at an equally astonishing rate. For example, each year 4 million hectares of forest in Siberia and 1 million hectares in Canada are being lost. World grain production per capita has already peaked, with 465 million tons in 1987 (adequate for 104 days' use) shrinking to just 229 million tons (adequate for 48 days' use) in 1996 (Brown et al. 1996). World fishery productivity has also peaked, growing from 22 million tons in 1950 to 100 million tons in 1987 and then falling to 90 million tons in 1995. Large numbers of ocean species are under threat of extinction, including sharks, orange roughy, blue fin tuna, beluga sturgeon, and grouper. Soil erosion worldwide is occurring at 25 billion tons/year, a rate far exceeding the ability of natural regeneration and thus essentially making it a nonrenewable resource (Brown and Wolf 1984).

In a finite world, resources cannot be consumed forever at the current rate, and especially not at the rate of the richer countries. Table 2.4 shows the estimated lifetimes of some key global resources in 1989 and in 2030, assuming a world population of 10 billion and world consumption at current U.S. levels. Reserves are quantities that can be extracted with current technology and resources are quantities thought to exist.

Clearly, technologies will be developed to aid in the extraction of nonrenewable materials from increasingly dilute resources. The terrestrial stocks of the most

Table 2.4. Estimated lifetimes of some global resources

	Current Consumption Rate		2030 Rates	
	Reserves	Resources	Reserves	Resources
Aluminum	256	805	124	407
Copper	41	277	4	26
Cobalt	109	429	10	40
Molybdenum	67	256	8	33
Nickel	66	163	7	16
Platinum group	225	413	21	39
Coal	206	3,226	29	457
Petroleum	35	83	3	7

Source: Frosch and Gallopoulos 1989.

highly concentrated minerals have already been exploited. As resources become more dilute, the quantity of earthen materials that must be processed and the energy needed for extraction and concentration will both increase proportionately. Damage to natural ecosystems is also proportional to the quantity of land disturbed and materials removed, resulting in accelerating negative effects on these systems as vast quantities of rock and soil are processed into mine tailings and other detritus.

Issues of Waste and Pollution

As noted by many authors, humans are the sole species whose waste is not food or a resource for other species. The quantity of waste generated by human activities is enormous. Municipal solid waste in the United States ranges from 125 to 200 million tons, depending on the source of the information. Construction and demolition (C&D) waste per capita in most OECD countries is about 0.5 tons, or approximately 125–130 million tons annually in the United States. Official estimates of U.S. C&D waste are 25 million tons per year, probably severely underestimating the actual quantity. Industrial waste in the United States amounts to 12 billion pounds on a net basis. Virtually all this waste is sent to engineered landfills with insignificant recycling or reuse.

It should be noted that materials extracted from the earth's crust do not simply disappear as a consequence of human activity because the earth's matter is essentially fixed. It is the dissipation of high-quality, concentrated materials that causes many of the world's environmental problems, including heavy metals that tend to build up in river bottom sediments. This dissipation effect corresponds to entropy in thermodynamics, a conversion from useful to useless (Ayres 1993; Georgescu-Roegen 1971).

Strategies for Sustainability

The goal of sustainability is to guide the economic and social forces of the earth's nations to live within the goods and services provided by ecosystems and naturally occurring sources of energy (solar, geothermal, tidal) without reducing the availability of these goods, services, and energy sources for future generations. Implicit in this notion is that pollution must also be limited to stabilized levels and types that can be assimilated by natural systems without compromising their function and human health. The arguments as to how to accomplish this are complex and wide ranging and center around the world economic system and the assumptions underlying its function and health.

Some economists from the new school of thinking known as *ecological economics* suggest that the world economy must attain a *steady-state* condition in which the matter–energy throughput reaches a sustainable level. The earth is a finite, nongrowing, essentially closed system (except to solar energy) and the world economy is merely a subsystem of this larger system. The physical reality of this finite system clearly collides with the scenario of uncontrolled growth as the *modus operandi* of profit-motivated companies (Daly and Cobb 1989). A steady-state economy assumes a good quality of life accompanied by a constant income level for individuals, a distributional system equitably allocating resources, and a relatively small, stable world population (Daly 1991). This alternative view clearly conflicts with the underlying assumption of sustainable growth of the economy. Another vision suggests that the economy can continue to grow if low resource-consuming sectors such as services, information, culture, education, and finance are the basis for growth rather than material-energy intensive industries (Sagoff 1995). To provide the bare essentials for the world's current population would require a tenfold increase in economic activity. Technology will then have to improve by a factor of twenty to maintain current levels of environmental burden (Hart 1997). Recent work by the Rocky Mountain Institute and the Wuppertal Institute provides evidence that an overall fourfold increase in resource efficiency is achievable with existing technologies, giving at least a modicum of hope that the world can move far closer to sustainability than it is currently (von Weiszäcker et al. 1997).

There are many strategies and frameworks that have been offered as approaches to achieving sustainability. Several of the most promising of these approaches are described in the following paragraphs: ISO 14000, The Natural Step, Social Accountability Standard 8000, Sustainability in Three Steps, and Industrial Ecology.

International Organization for Standardization: ISO 14000 Series

The ISO 14000 series of standards provides a potential framework for helping organizations and companies achieve at least a measure of sustainability (see Table 2.5). In the early 1990s, the British Standards Institution (BSI) developed BS 7750, Environmental Management Systems, as a companion to its BS 5750 standard on quality management systems. BS 5750 was the forerunner and template for the ISO 9000 quality management standards. These British Standards and ISO 9000 were the precursors to ISO 14000. The ISO 14000 series prescribes behavioral performance and auditing methods in the arena of Environmental Management Systems (EMS), mainly for commercial entities. ISO 14000 is a series of voluntary generic standards being developed by ISO that provides business management with the structure for managing environmental impacts. EMS is defined as a segment of an organization's overall management structure that addresses the immediate and long-term environmental impacts of its products, services, and processes. The standards include a broad range of environmental management disciplines, including the basic management system, auditing, performance evaluation, labeling, and life-cycle assessment. All the standards except ISO 14001 are

Table 2.5. The ISO 14000 Series of Environmental Management Systems Standards

ISO 14001:	Environmental Management Systems—Specification with Guidance for Use
ISO 14004:	Environmental Management Systems—Guidelines on Principles, Systems and Supporting Techniques
ISO 14020:	Environmental Labeling—General Principles
ISO 14031:	Evaluation of Environmental Performance
ISO 14040:	Environmental Management—Life-Cycle Assessment—Principles and Guidelines

guidance standards. This means that they are descriptive documents rather than prescriptive requirements. A company or organization does not register to ISO 14000 as a series but registers to ISO 14001, the specification standard that is a model for an environmental management system. Classified according to their focus, the standards fall into two categories: (1) organization or process standards—environmental management system (EMS), environmental auditing (EA), and environmental performance evaluation (EPE); and (2) product-oriented standards—life-cycle assessment (LCA), environmental labeling (EL), and environmental aspects in product standards (EAPS). The EMS and auditing standards became full international standards in September and October 1996, respectively. The other standards are in various stages of development.

The ISO standards provide at least some measure of support to the goals of sustainable development by creating environmental awareness throughout an organization, by incorporating environmental goals into the mission statement, and by setting measurable targets on waste reduction and pollution prevention. However, like many other standards, it has dual edges. Its main purpose is to improve the environmental performance of businesses. However, instead of improving environmental behavior, its main purpose may be to gain competitive advantage, "greenwash," and provide access to international markets. Although requiring measurable goals, the goals themselves may be very unambitious and merely meet the letter of the standards rather than directing the organization to truly clean, resource-efficient, and pollution-free operations.

The Natural Step

One of the strategies for achieving sustainability in organizations that is rapidly gaining popularity is The Natural Step, the brainchild of Karl-Henrik Robèrt. This framework was developed by Robèrt, a former cancer researcher in Sweden, in 1988 by virtue of his experience with cancer in his patients. He concluded that it was the destruction of the environment by human activities that was leading to terrible consequences for humankind (Robèrt 1995). In Sweden and in many other countries, including the United States, The Natural Step is widely acclaimed and it has been adopted by a vast array of businesses and municipalities as the basis for promoting sustainability. It is based on adhering to what seem to be four relatively simple system conditions that can be extraordinarily complex in their implementation.

1. Extracted substances from the earth's crust must not systematically increase in the biosphere.
2. Substances produced by human society must not systematically increase in the biosphere.
3. The productivity and biodiversity of the earth itself must not systematically be physically deteriorated.
4. Human needs must be met with a fair and efficient use of energy and other natural resources.

One of the key questions posed to businesses by proponents of this approach is, Are we systematically making ourselves more dependent on resources or practices that have no future? In the case of substances being mined, for example, the answer clearly is that eventually these substances will be depleted and the mining will have systematically accumulated them in the biosphere. At small scale, for some individual businesses, the shift to alternative practices such as using materials from renewable, natural resources is possible and the solutions are readily available. However, the vast quantities of minerals, ores, aggregates, and other substances being mined far outstrip the rather small quantities of materials being sustainably harvested. Even if there were natural substitutes for all currently available materials not in consonance with the system conditions, it is still questionable whether nature would be able to supply all the needed resources in a sustainable fashion. System condition 2 implies that artificial, nondegradable substances such as DDT, PCBs, and chlorofluorocarbon refrigerants must not be produced, another daunting step for industry and society. The vast quantities of plastics and human dependence on them makes an alternative scenario difficult to propose. Despite the difficulties in its application, The Natural Step can be used as a guiding framework for auditing organizations to assess how they are behaving relative to the natural environment and to systematically and logically determine the alternatives to their current practices.

Combining ISO 14001 and The Natural Step

Some organizations such as Mitsubishi Electric America (MEA) are finding that applying ISO 14001 and The Natural Step in tandem can help tie their environmental initiatives together. ISO 14001 requires that companies make their employees more aware of environmental issues within their organizations through training. The Natural Step provides a "natural" framework for providing this education and also helps organizations like MEA move beyond mere compliance to actually incorporating environmental perspectives in their company culture, ultimately directly affecting its bottom line. Rather than concentrating on preventing violations of environmental regulations, this combination shifts the focus to how to better provide the company's products and services while adhering to fundamentally sound environmental practices.

Social Accountability Standard 8000

A new global standard, Social Accountability Standard 8000 (SA 8000), that addresses perhaps the weakest link in sustainability frameworks, social awareness and justice was launched in early 1998. Its purpose is to provide an independent, third-party verified and certified framework for the ethical production of goods. SA 8000 defines specific requirements on child labor, forced labor, employee health and safety, union matters, discrimination, compensation and working hours, and management systems to accomplish these requirements. This standard was developed by the Council on Economic Priorities (CEP) and the Council on Economic Priorities Accounting Agency (CEPAA) based on conventions such as the International Labor Organization (ILO), the Universal Declaration of Human Rights, and the United Nations Convention on Rights of the Child. Pilot tests of the standard have been conducted in the United States, Europe, Honduras, and Mexico, and several companies such as Toys 'R Us and Avon Products have adopted the standard in their facilities. Combining ISO 14001 and SA 8000 provides a powerful and comprehensive set of tools for organizations to use to move strongly into the era of sustainability, both practically and philosophically.

Sustainability in Three Stages

The shift to sustainability will not occur overnight and will undoubtedly occur in phases as either organizations conclude it is the strategy for market position or future survival, governments move toward green taxes, or environmental conditions and resource shortages force sustainable behavior. One line of thinking is that companies can shift to a sustainability strategy in three stages. Stage one is a shift from pollution prevention to pollution control driven in part by new international standards such as ISO 14000. Stage two is product stewardship that emphasizes minimizing the life cycle environmental impacts of products using concepts such as design for the environment (DFE). Stage three is the development of clean technologies, changing the technology base from one that depends on unsustainable behavior to a base that is inherently in sync with natural systems. Table 2.6 is a framework developed to help companies assess where they are today and how they can shift from pollution prevention to product stewardship and ultimately to clean technologies. The very rapid growth of the world's economy, particularly in Asia, is creating substantial environmental problems but also an enormous opportunity to leap forward technologically to clean processes (Hart 1997).

The backdrop to a potential for a three-stage shift to sustainability in OECD

Table 2.6. Diagnostic tool to determine sustainability of a company's strategy

	Clean Technology	Sustainability Vision
Tomorrow	Is the environmental perform-ance of our products limited by our existing competency base?	Does our corporate vision direct us toward the solution of social and environmental problems?
	Is there potential to realize major improvements through new technology?	Does our vision guide the develop-ment of new technologies, markets, and products?
	Pollution Prevention	Product Stewardship
Today	Where are the most significant waste and emission streams from our current operations?	What are the implications for prod-uct design and development if we assume responsibility for a prod-uct's entire life cycle?
	Can we lower costs and risks by eliminating waste at the source or by using it as a useful input?	Can we add value or lower costs while simultaneously reducing the impact of our products?
	Internal	External

Source: Hart 1997.

countries is the condition of economies in poorer nations. Their economies often cause deforestation, soil erosion, desertification, and species extinction because survival has priority over the protection of valuable ecosystems. The need to sur-vive and the absence of economic growth are resulting in massive environmental impacts in countries whose populations represent 75 percent of the world's peo-ple (Myers 1993).

Industry Ecology

A newly emerging discipline called industrial ecology (IE), which uses the behav-ior of natural systems as its inspiration, provides some measure of hope for propo-nents of sustainability. The near perfect recycling of materials characteristic of nat-ural systems is being used as a model to modify industrial activities or *industrial metabolism* to not only greatly reduce industrial impacts on natural systems but also to reduce costs, increase productivity, and more efficiently utilize resources. The U.S. economy processes 10 tons of active mass per capita (on the order of 3 billion tons total) from U.S. territory annually, 75 percent of which is from nonre-newable resources and 25 percent from renewable resources. The final durable goods produced comprise just 6 percent of this mass, with the remaining 94 percent being waste. This waste does not simply disappear but ends up in the biosphere, frequently with negative consequences (Ayres 1989).

Connecting industrial processes in chains, such that the waste of one industrial activity is the input for another, is the cornerstone of IE. The industrial complex in Kalundborg, Denmark, is the most prominent example of an attempt at IE. This complex contains a power plant, an oil refinery, a chemical company, a wallboard company, and agricultural greenhouses. The waste heat from the power plant is used by the refinery, which in turn provides sulfur removed from petroleum to the chemical company and the wallboard manufacturer to displace the gypsum normally used in the manufacture of wallboard. Excess energy from the power plant in the form of steam both heats water and warms the air for the greenhouses. Each of these waste products is sold to the receiving user, providing an end use for resources normally wasted and reducing the costs for each company in the complex (Frosch 1995). IE concepts are not limited to the factory but can apply to all human activity, including mining, agriculture, construction, transportation, product use, and waste disposal (Graedel 1996).

Shifting industrial metabolism to behave more like natural systems will not solve all of the problems of emissions and waste prevalent in industrial activities. But it will definitely reduce their environmental impacts as well as begin the long, slow process of changing many of the wasteful resource practices of these extractive, energy- and material-intensive entities.

In addition to industry, viewing human economic behavior as metabolism can be applied to a wide range of individual activities, including agriculture, university campuses, government, and the built environment. Examining "construction metabolism" and its interconnection to other human-centered metabolisms could provide useful insights into better practices for the entire life cycle of the materials and other resources of the built environment.

Increasing Resource Efficiency and Reducing Waste

One of the key questions that must be answered in the short term is the role of technology in increasing resource efficiency. In general, recovery of resources is falling far short of the actual thermodynamic potential (see Table 2.7). Many authors have suggested that current and near-future technologies can dramatically increase resource efficiency (von Weiszäcker et al. 1997; Ausubel 1996). The commonly mentioned increase in resource efficiency to achieve worldwide sustainability is a factor of four to ten, depending on the source of the information and the resource involved. Taking into consideration that the doubling time of population in the United States is about sixty years and the historical doubling of economic activity per capita is thirty years, a factor of twelve increase in resource consumption and emissions would occur by 2100 (Ausubel 1996).

Table 2.7. Theoretical versus actual recovery rates for metals in industrial hazardous waste streams

Metal	% Theoretically Recoverable	% Actually Recycled (1986)
Sb	74–87	32
As	98–99	3
Ba	95–98	4
Be	54–84	31
Cd	82–97	7
Cr	68–89	8
Cu	85–92	10
Pb	84–95	56
Ag	99–100	1

Source: Allen and Behmanesh 1993.

Efficiency of Materials Use

Humans are now responsible for more materials movement than geological and weather forces combined. While there has been obvious concern over the introduction of small quantities of very toxic substances into the biosphere by human activities, what has remained largely unnoticed is the *ecological rucksack* of materials extraction as described by Friedrich Schmidt-Bleek, formerly of the Wuppertal Institute in Germany. The megatons of material movement must be examined in addition to the microgram quantities of especially harmful substances. The production of a simple ring containing 10 grams of gold requires the processing of 3 metric tons of materials extracted by mining operations. Material intensity per service (MIPS) is one measure of the efficiency of materials use, with the ratio for the ring being 1:300,000. Schmidt-Bleek estimates that a factor of ten improvement in MIPS in OECD countries must be achieved to reduce the consequences of the ecological rucksack and create a sustainable flow of materials (von Weiszäcker et al. 1997). This is achievable only through extensive reuse and recycling of materials and other measures that minimize the dissipation of materials. Approaches to the waste problem, such as incineration, that result in dissipation of the materials are not solutions. Recycling is still a much underutilized means of recovering previously used resources for other applications and results in significant energy savings. The amount of energy saved in recycling all types of metals and most other materials compared to extraction from virgin resources is substantial (see Table 2.8).

Significant progress has been made and continues to be made in the dematerialization of industrial economies. Today's automobiles are far lighter, fiberoptics transmit vast quantities of information at a fraction of the weight of copper wiring, computers are smaller and lighter, and the use of aluminum and plastics has significantly reduced the mass of packaging and of many common products (Ausubel

Table 2.8. Energy requirements for processing virgin and recycled materials

Material	Energy Needed to Process		
	Virgin Ore (Btu/lb)	Recycled Material (Btu/lb)	Energy Saved Recycling (%)
Steel	8,300	7,500 (40% scrap)	10
		4,400 (100% scrap)	47
Aluminum	134,700	5,000	96
Aluminum ingot	108,000	2,200–3,400	97
Copper	25,900	1,400–2,900	88–95
Glass containers	7,800	7,200	8
Plastics	49,500	1,350	97
Newsprint	11,400	8,800	23

Source: Hays 1978.

1996). However, these reductions in MIPS due to technology are more than offset by increasing consumption and population and, as a result, aggregate materials consumption continues to rise.

Energy Efficiency and Renewable Energy

Overall energy efficiency of industrial economies is about 5 percent, due largely to the number of stages of production (resource extraction to delivery of end service) and the relative inefficiency of each stage. Ultimate overall efficiencies could approach 50 percent if the number of stages were reduced and the stage efficiencies were greatly increased, both of which are feasible to accomplish (Ausubel 1996). Significant progress has been made in reducing energy use. Although energy use in the United States remained relatively flat between 1973 and 1986, economic production expanded by 40 percent. Similar developments occurred in Japan, the United Kingdom, France, and Germany (Sagoff 1995).

The fundamental problem with the widespread incorporation of energy-efficient strategies in the United States has been the availability of cheap energy and a general resistance on the part of the public and government to shift taxes from income and productivity onto carbon-based fuels. This latter strategy, a relatively common approach in other OECD countries, produces innovation, spurs the use of public transportation, and positions economies for a future less dependent on fossil fuels and their inherent environmental and political baggage. The reliance on a nonrenewable finite resource will undoubtedly prove to be shortsighted. A recent compilation on global energy supplies and production concludes that world crude oil production will begin to decline in the next decade and that the estimates of oil reserves by oil companies and some countries are unrealistically optimistic. Signif-

Table 2.9. Renewables versus conventional energy resources: energy generation and R&D investment in the United States, 1991 and 1992

Energy Source	Quads per Annum, 1991	R&D Investment ($million), 1992
Oil	34	
Coal	19	804.3
Natural gas	18.5	
Nuclear	5.6	1,769.0
Hydroelectric	2.8	1.0
Biomass	3.2	21.4
Low head hydro	2.9	
Landfill methane	1.0	
Geothermal	0.36	27.2
Solar thermal	0.10	29.0
Wind	0.03	21.0
Solar photovoltaic	0.01	60.0
Ocean thermal	<0.01	

Note: 1 Quad = 1 quadrillion Btus
Source: Rejeski 1997.

icant rises in oil prices caused by huge demand and diminished supplies are the wave of the future (Campbell and Laherre 1998).

Clearly, true sustainability requires primary dependence on solar income and, therefore, renewable energy sources. Unfortunately, in the United States, as is the case with virtually every other country, the sources of energy are primarily nonrenewable (see Table 2.9). Additionally, note that the fraction of R&D investment in renewable energy sources and systems is a small fraction of research into large-scale, conventional power systems.

A truly sustainable and safe energy system would be dependent only on the sun, which provides more than adequate power to the earth's surface for all of humankind's needs. At present, renewable energy provides a very small fraction of the power generated worldwide. Major shifts in technology investments to renewable energy would benefit humankind far more than the continued drain on limited resources benefiting fossil fuel power and discredited nuclear systems.

The Human Side of the Sustainability Equation

Although resource depletion and the destruction of natural systems are key issues in the sustainability discussion, human factors cannot be ignored because they are an integral part of sustainability. In the United States there has been a continual separation of the upper, middle, and lower income classes. The truly dramatic increases in productivity for which the United States is well known are not translating into increased wages for the working class. At present, the top 1 percent of the families have about the same amount of wealth as the bottom 95 percent. Workers lost about 16 percent of their inflation-adjusted weekly earnings between 1973 and 1993. While members of Congress provided themselves with ten pay increases since 1982 to keep well ahead of inflation, they have steadfastly held the line on increasing the minimum wage. In 1974, CEOs made 35 times the average worker's salary, and today this multiple is 150 times. Meanwhile, American companies are racing to hire top-level talent in China and India for a fraction of what U.S. workers and technical people earn. This is nothing more than a race to the bottom in wages. Like the destruction of the environment, this shift from democracy to oligarchy is unsustainable and must be examined both overall and especially within the construction industry.

Applying Sustainability to the Built Environment

If sustainability principles are to apply to industry, government, and the economy, it is clear they must also apply to construction, an industry whose end products consume a significant proportion of all materials and electricity in their creation, operation, and deconstruction. In the United States, the construction and operation of the built environment consumes in excess of 30 percent of all energy and 40 percent of the materials produced by the economy. Compared to other commercial activity, construction may be the one least able to respond to a shift toward sustainability, due largely to the nature of its creation. Buildings are assembled from a combination of manufactured goods (windows, doors, air handlers, transformers), products tailored for the building on site (lumber, gypsum board, roofing, electrical wiring, conduit, ductwork), special liquids with low mass (paint, glues, mastics, sealants), and items comprised largely of raw materials moved in bulk to the construction site (fill materials, aggregate, concrete). Each building is assembled on site with little thought to its final disposal and, for the most part, each building is unique. Much effort has been invested in reducing the operating costs of buildings and technology has been developed to reduce energy and water consumption. However, little or no investment has been directed toward creating a systematic and standardized method of DFE for buildings. Environmentally sustainable design and green building efforts have focused on energy and water consumption, indoor environmental quality, and some methods of reducing building impacts on the local environment during construction and operation. But again, there has been virtually no effort devoted to designing all components and the entire structure for ultimate disassembly for component reuse or recycling. For sustainable construction to evolve, the built environment must be rethought using the ideas emerging from IE and DFE. The result, in addition to the significant progress resulting from ESD, sustainable construction, and green building movements, would be structures that are designed with total reuse or recycling of all materials as a front-end goal. This thinking must be instilled at three levels of design. First, all materials in buildings must be recyclable or the components they comprise must be reusable. Second, all manufactured products must be able to be easily disassembled for recycling, implying a standard or universal labeling system that identifies the materials in each component. Third, the building itself must be designed for ready, future disassembly. In light of the ideas of IE, all activities involved in producing the building must provide for the recycling of waste created during the construction process. Where there are repetitive construction activities, for example in large housing developments, shifting to on-site manufacturing plants designed to minimize and recycle waste could help achieve this end.

Building Design

Building design itself must be transformed for sustainability to be adequately addressed. Changing the energy consumption profiles of buildings is crucial for reducing their resource and environmental impacts. Creating buildings that derive most of their energy from the sun via rooftop or curtain wall photovoltaics is an emerging strategy that can help achieve sustainability in the built environment (see Figure 2.1). Widespread incorporation of graywater, rainwater harvesting, and

Figure 2.1. Skylight-integrated photovoltaics in the Thoreau Sustainability Center, The Presidio, San Francisco, California.

reclaimed water systems in buildings will help reduce the tremendous burden on limited potable water supplies. Low-flow fixtures are now mandatory in all U.S. construction, and emerging technologies will drive the use of water even lower.

The fundamental principle that must be kept in the forefront is that the best protection that can be afforded natural systems is to use the minimum amount of resources—that is, as little material, energy, water, and land as possible. Minimizing resource consumption is the maxim that designers must follow to cause this to occur. The ingredients for success include (1) excellence in planning; (2) design of adaptable, durable, structures; (3) extensive application of passive energy design; (4) incorporation of high-efficiency energy-consuming systems; and (5) the use of renewable energy systems.

Long-life, durable, adaptable structures provide by far the best means of minimizing materials consumption. High-quality design provides buildings with an inherent character that society will value, prolonging the desire to preserve their use for the long term.

Roles of Planning in the Sustainable Built Environment

Well thought out planning that provides for stable activity in specified zones for the distant future ensures that buildings will maintain their purpose for long time frames without the need for their removal. Proximity to multimodal transportation comprised of mass transit and bicycle routes is one of the crucial steps to reducing reliance on automobiles for transit. Mixed-use communities are also a necessity and transit-oriented and new urbanist developments are planning measures being adopted in the United States to emphasize bicycle and pedestrian transit over automobile use.

Sustainable Construction Programs in the United States

In the United States, significant progress is being made in diverting construction onto a path of sustainability. The Austin (Texas) Greenbuilder Program, initiated by the municipal government in the early 1990s, is a program that has had considerable success in bringing both attention and practical solutions to the challenges of sustainability in construction. The National Park Service has also been a leader in the field of sustainability in the built environment and intends to ensure that the facilities they design, build, and operate throughout the National Park System are in keeping with the environmental values they are seeking to protect. They have issued a guidebook spelling out design, materials, and other aspects of their future buildings.

Sustainability in the built environment is also a prime concern of the U.S. federal government. Several prominent greening projects have been undertaken, including the greening of the White House and the Pentagon. The Federal Energy Management Program has an extensive array of initiatives in place, including one that provides information to federal facility managers on how to green their facilities in the course of maintenance, retrofits, and renovations. The sum total of these activities is raising the level of consciousness throughout the government and is creating a large demand for products and services that fit the mold of reduced environmental impacts.

Greening Construction Materials and Eliminating Waste

Because of its remoteness from the actual construction process, resource extraction for the production of construction materials and systems sometimes receives scant attention. Changing the entire chain of production of products to one that is more in sync with nature requires feedback loops from the end users to the industrial production system. The feedback has to demand new products that make more efficient use of resources by focusing on materials and products that can be reused and recycled in cyclic loops. Consequently, recyclable materials or renewable resources need to be the primary constituent of building materials. It is also intuitive that ease of disassembly of both the structure and building components is a necessary quality of green building materials. Shifting to construction products that can be considered environmentally responsible or "green" is hampered by a lack of definition of what comprises these materials. In the case of wood products, the Forestry Stewardship Council is working diligently to ensure that lumber and other forest resources originate from properly managed forests. The U.S. arm of this effort, the SmartWood Program, has made good progress in convincing product producers, forest owners, specifiers, and end users that forestry certification is in their best interests. The desired result is that buyers will create a demand for certified wood products, thus forcing the industry to respond with better care of the nation's forest resources, by far the largest potential source of renewable materials for construction industry.

Beyond wood products there are virtually no standards for green certification of construction products in the United States. End users are totally dependent on the claims of manufacturers about the relative environmental impacts of their products. One fundamental step that could help solve this dilemma would be for green products to carry a label specifying their constituents and recycled content from various sources (postindustrial, postconsumer, and postagricultural). The notion is that the choice of what makes a material or product green varies greatly from user to user and in the end it may have to be left to the judgment of the buyer as to the relative environmental merits of individual products. The very fact of carrying a truth-in-contents label provides the user at least the minimal indication that a manufacturer is striving to provide some of the basic information needed to judge their products.

Energy Efficiency in the Built Environment

Energy efficiency continues to be at the forefront of the sustainable construction agenda because of the continued reliance on fossil fuels with their contributions to particulate emissions, greenhouse warming gases, and acidification gases. Buildings in the United States have a fairly dismal energy consumption record, with typical consumption being on the order of 30.0 kWh/square meter annually. The simple addition of bioclimatic or "passive" design strategies has been demonstrated to cut energy consumption in half, to about 15.0 kWh/square meter annually. Implementing other well-documented strategies, such as energy-efficient lighting, conditioning systems, transformers, and motors, can reduce energy consumption by another 50 percent to about 7.5 kWh per square meter per year.

The U.S. Environmental Protection Agency (USEPA) has had remarkable success in pushing its agenda of energy efficiency in the built environment. The USEPA's Energy Star Program has been the primary factor in this success, prescribing performance 30 percent better than model and state energy codes for buildings. The program also covers a host of related systems and products, including lighting, transformers, and office machines (computers, fax machines, and copiers). Working in tandem with both producers and buyers, the result has been a tremendous buy-in to the importance of reducing energy consumption, even in an era of relatively cheap energy prices.

High-Performance Green Buildings

A new class of buildings began to emerge in the late 1980s that reflects the broad range of design, construction, operation, resource efficiency, and environmental protection imperatives of the sustainable construction movement. These high-performance buildings excel in a number of ways that set them apart from their predecessors. They are often designed and built to connect the occupant to nature, to be human in scale, to provide excellent interior environmental quality, to use minimal resources, and to stand the test of time. The environmental impacts of all components are taken into account, and these buildings generally include provisions for advanced construction waste management and site protection in their actual creation.

The ING Bank Building in Amsterdam, erected in 1987, is perhaps the most famous building in the Netherlands (see Figure 2.2). It is an organic building with integrated art, natural materials, natural lighting, interior gardens with small waterfalls, high energy efficiency systems, and low noise. Containing 2,400 employees and 50,000 square meters of interior space, the footprint is an irregular S-curve with gardens and courtyards on top of the parking structure and service areas. The footprint is narrow to allow sunlight to penetrate to all working spaces. The precast concrete structure is used to store heat from the sun and from internal heat gains. It is not air-conditioned and uses natural ventilation through operable windows with some mechanical ventilation to cool the spaces when necessary. An absorption chiller powered by waste heat from a cogeneration system is used as backup and provides dehumidification. Other banks designed and built in the same time frame consume five times as much energy. Artistry is part of the building fabric, with colored metal strategically located in the tops of the atria towers,

Figure 2.2. Atrium in the ING Bank building in Amsterdam.

reflecting colored light into the interior. Cisterns capture rainwater for use in the fountains and landscaping and flow form sculptures that serve as handrails, the water flowing past the building occupants as they transit the stairs. The wonderful working environment contributes to exceptionally low absenteeism. The cost, $1,500 per square meter, is comparable to or cheaper than similar bank buildings.

The Queen's Building at the New School of Manufacturing and Engineering at De Montfort University, Leicester, U.K. (see Figure 2.3) is the largest naturally ventilated building in the United Kingdom. Most of the shell area is operable so that the occupants can open and close windows to adjust their comfort conditions. Air flows through the building via chimney effect. Heating is accomplished via passive solar design and internal heat gain from the occupants and equipment. Actually a collection of smaller domestic scale buildings, the massive masonry structure has beautiful polychromatic brickwork by local masons and provides the thermal mass for the structure. Carefully calculated overhangs and a narrow footprint allow sunlight in during the cooler months and block it during the heat of summer. The classrooms in this superior building have natural daylighting and require virtually no powered lighting.

The Gerling Insurance Company Building in Nurnberg, Germany (see Figures 2.4 and 2.5) utilizes a passive solar heating and cooling approach that ground-

Figure 2.3. The Queen's Building
at the New School of Manufacturing and
Engineering at De Montfort University,
Leicester, U.K.

couples the building to the natural water table and uses natural forces to move air
through the structure. The architect, Seegy and Bisch, employed the services of a
computational fluid dynamics specialist, Dr. Majid Majidi of the Univesity of
Stuttgart, to perform a finite element analysis of air flow around the building, of the
groundwater coupled heating and cooling system, and of the natural air flows
around the building. This unconventional approach to designing the heating, ventilating, and cooling (HVAC) systems resulted in a facility with extremely low
energy consumption, about 40 percent of conventional office buildings in Germany. Seegy and Bisch also carefully designed the structural elements to eliminate
the need for dropped ceilings and incorporated innovative power and communications conduits of biodegradable materials into the floor slabs. The result is that
not only can the building materials be readily recycled at the end of the structure's
useful life, but the building was constructed at a cost 20 percent lower than similar
buildings in Bavaria. Another innovation was to eliminate the use of composite
materials in all building elements, to include built-in cabinetry, and to promote end
of useful life reuse and recycling. The approach taken in the Gerling Insurance
Company building is being further advanced by Seegy and Bisch in the Neue
Mainzer Strasse Gerling Insurance Company building currently under construction in Frankfurt.

Figure 2.4. Front view of the Gerling Insurance Company building in Nurnberg.

Figure 2.5. View of the atrium in the Gerling Insurance Building in Nurnberg.

Summary and Conclusions

Sustainability may in fact be a grand illusion. The present rates of resource depletion, biodiversity degradation, and increasing pollution caused by population growth and consumption make sustainability an extraordinarily difficult proposition. Some would say that we have already surpassed the earth's limits to support today's mass of humanity and that we in the industrialized countries simply have not as yet been able to clearly see the evidence of catastrophic breakdowns. Humans are indeed a clever and adaptable species with a history of finding or inventing substitutes for depleted resources; cracking genetic codes and reengineering life to our liking; splitting and fusing atoms; and infiltrating the most microscopic and cosmic of spaces. At the same time we have shown an uncanny ability to destroy ourselves by pollution, disease, strife, and our own inventions. In the slightly more than 200 years since the Industrial Revolution we have caused untold alteration and destruction of complex natural systems. Respecting and protecting natural systems is perhaps where the future lies for our physical, economic, and social survival, and even more significantly, fulfilling our spiritual aspirations. Although often confronted by the destructive power of nature, we seem to be unable to learn the lesson of how utterly helpless we truly are relative to the forces it can muster. The creation of the built environment must therefore be consistent with these values by respecting nature and responding to the imperative that we are utterly dependent on the earth's systems for survival. Perhaps the path lies in mimicking ecosystems, behaving organically rather than mechanistically, and learning from the billions of years of design effort that have produced elegant, complex, and efficient solar-powered systems. Clearly, the built environment of the past several decades has strayed far from these ideals and it remains to be seen whether the design and construction of new buildings, communities, and infrastructure can make the long journey to an inspired future derived from nature.

REFERENCES

Abramovitz, J.N. 1998. "Putting a Value on Nature's 'Free' Services." *World Watch* (January–February) 11:10–19.

Allen, D.T., and N. Behamenesh. 1994. "Wastes as Industrial Materials." In *The Greening of Industrial Ecosystems* (B.R. Allenby and D.J. Richards, eds.). Washington, DC: National Academy Press.

Ausubel, J.H. 1996. "Can Technology Spare the Earth?" *American Scientist* 84:166–178.

Ayres, R.U. 1989. "Industrial Metabolism." In *Technology and the Environment* (J.H. Ausubel and H.E. Sladovich, eds.). Washington, DC: National Academy Press.

Ayres, R.U. 1993. "Cowboys, Cornucopians and Long-Run Sustainability." *Ecological Economics* 8:189–207.

Bates, A.K. 1990. *Climate in Crisis*. Sydney: The Book Publishing Company.

Brown, L.R., and E.C. Wolf. 1984. *Soil Erosion: Quiet Crisis in the World Economy*, World Watch Paper 60, Washington, DC: The World Watch Institute.

Brown, L.R., C. Flavin, and H. Kane. 1996. *Vital Signs 1996*. New York: W.W. Norton & Company.

Campbell, C.J., and J.H. Laherrere. 1998. "The End of Cheap Oil." *Scientific American* (March) 278:78–83.

Costanza R., et al. 1997. "The Value of the World's Ecosystem Services and Natural Capital." *Nature* 387:253–260.

Daily, G.C., and P.R. Ehrlich. 1992. "Population, Sustainability, and Earth's Carrying Capacity." *BioScience* 42:761–771.

Daly, H.E. 1991. *Steady, State Economics,* 2nd ed. Washington, DC: Island Press.

Daly, H.E., and J.B. Cobb, Jr. 1989. *For the Common Good.* Boston: Beacon Press.

Frosch, R.A. 1995. "The Industrial Ecology of the 21st Century." *Scientific American* 273:78–181.

Frosch, R.A., and N.E. Gallopoulos. 1989. "Strategies for Manufacturing." *Scientific American* 261(3):144–152.

Georgescu-Roegen, N. 1971. *The Entropy Law and the Economic Process.* Cambridge, MA: Harvard University Press.

Graedel, T.E. 1996. "On the Concept of Industrial Ecology." *Annual Reviews of Energy and the Environment* 21:69–98.

Hardin, G. 1968. "The Tragedy of the Commons." *Science* 162:1243–1248.

Hart, S.L. 1997. "Strategies for a Sustainable World." *Harvard Business Review* 75:67–76.

Hays, D. 1978. *Repair, Reuse, Recycling: The Steps to a Sustainable Society.* Worldwatch Paper 23. Washington, DC: The World Watch Institute.

Lovelock, J. 1988. *The Ages of Gaia: A Biography of Our Living Earth.* New York: W.W. Norton & Company.

Myers, N. 1993. "The Question of Linkages in Environment and Development." *BioScience* 43:306.

Postel, S.L., G.C. Daily, and P.R. Ehrlich. 1996. "Human Appropriation of Renewable Fresh Water." *Science* 271:785–788.

Rejeski, D. 1997. "Metrics, Systems, and Technological Choices." In *The Industrial Greening Game* (D.J. Richards, ed.). Washington, DC: National Academy Press.

Robèrt, K.-H. 1995. *The Natural Step: A Framework for Achieving Sustainability in Our Organizations.* Cambridge, MA: Pegasus Communications.

Sagoff, M. 1995. "Carrying Capacity and Ecological Economics." *Bioscience* 45:610–620.

Vitousek, P.M., P.R. Ehrlich, A.H. Ehrlich, and P.A. Marson. 1986. "Human Appropriation of the Products of Photosynthesis." *Bioscience* 36:368–373.

von Weiszäcker, E., A. Lovins, and H. Lovins. 1997. *Factor Four: Doubling Wealth, Halving Resource Use.* London: Earthscan Publications Ltd.

Wilson, E.O. 1989. *Biodiversity.* Washington, DC: National Academy Press.

Wilson, E.O. 1992. *The Diversity of Life.* Cambridge, MA: The Belknap Press of Harvard University Press.

Chapter 3

Ecological Challenge, Human Values of Nature, and Sustainability in the Built Environment

Stephen R. Kellert

Profound changes in our institutions and lifestyles will be necessary to resolve the current ecological crisis. These will inevitably include major shifts in our concepts and constructions in the built environment. They will not be easy changes or simple engineering or technical adjustments. They will require a far greater understanding of how humans depend on and derive value from healthy interactions with natural process and diversity, including not just physical and material rewards but also a host of critical intellectual and emotional benefits as well.

Developing more sustainable energy production and waste processing systems, for example, will not be enough to achieve the desired and necessary outcomes. We need to achieve a more complex and comprehensive understanding of how humans connect with natural process and diversity to attain lives of mental as well as physical well-being. The promise and success of sustainable design is to move beyond strategies of guilt and alarm that are largely dependent on motivating people by exhorting them not to cause environmental harm or injury because regulatory requirements encourage us to behave in certain ways. The ultimate success of green development and construction depends more on a positive elucidation of how, by adequately relating to natural process and diversity in the built environment, we may achieve lives of meaning and satisfaction.

This chapter amplifies these perspectives. I first note some of the critical environmental challenges of our time, arguing that the most damaging consequence of these impacts is a diminished capacity to engage natural processes in ways that adequately meet a range of basic human physical, emotional, and intellectual needs. I then describe nine values of nature that, I believe, require effective expression as a foundation for optimal personal and social development. Finally, I contend that the eventual success of sustainable design depends on adequately connecting people on all these valuational levels with natural process and diversity.

Unfortunately, these valuational levels rarely occur. Extraordinary progress has certainly been achieved in sustainable design and construction. Remarkable advances have occurred in energy efficiency, waste disposal, material use and recycling, landscape architecture and ecology, and in providing increased access to natural process and diversity. Yet, I believe much of this progress has unduly relied on a largely negative emphasis on avoiding environmental harm and injury, a stress on physical and material benefits, and changes more at the level of building systems than at the experience of individuals and groups. By contrast, I believe sustainable design has insufficiently considered how people derive a host of intellectual and emotional, as well as physical and material, benefits from connections with natural process and diversity. I conclude by suggesting green development will not achieve its full promise and potential until it more positively motivates individuals, developers, and planners by capturing in the built environment the widest range of physical, emotional, and intellectual values of nature.

Ecological Challenges

Let me start by briefly noting some of the critical ecological challenges of our time. Many variations on this theme can be offered, but I am inclined to separate our current environmental crisis into two broad categories—first, a broad range of contamination and pollution problems, primarily involving adverse human health affects; and, second, extensive ecological depletion, disruption, and degradation difficulties. Environmental pollution and contamination can be further divided into toxic impacts on varying food and energy chains (primarily expressed through the media of air, water, and soils) and problems of atmospheric perturbation, such as global climate change (e.g., mainly caused by increased human-produced heat-trapping gases such as carbon dioxide and methane) and depletion of upper stratospheric ozone. Ecological disruption and degradation can also be divided into two major threats: resource depletion (mainly stemming from unsustainable exploitation of minerals, forests, fisheries, terrestrial wildlife, grasslands, and other resources) and large-scale loss of biological diversity at the species, genetic, and ecosystem levels.

These problems are associated with varying human health and ecological consequences, including the extirpation and extinction of tens of thousands of species. However, many, including much of the general public, have questioned whether these constitute sufficiently serious threats to human welfare, especially if the long-term costs are seemingly offset by the short-term benefits of extensive reductions in poverty, disease, and an unprecedented improvement in material and economic well-being. Even from the perspective of human self-interest, however, impoverishing and degrading natural systems is ultimately self-defeating at the level of individual and community experience and well-being. Nature has been, and I believe continues to be, an essential medium for human physical, intellectual, emotional, and spiritual health and welfare (Kellert 1997). During the long course of our species' evolution, we have come to depend on a range of benefits derived from adequate contact and associated with natural process and diversity. The realization of these values has conferred distinctive advantages in the human struggle to persist, adapt, and thrive as a species. Moreover, the inclination to affiliate with nature remains a fundamental basis for healthy physical and mental development.

Edward O. Wilson and I have invoked the concept of "biophilia" to describe a complex of weak biological tendencies to affiliate with natural, especially living, process and diversity (Kellert and Wilson 1993; Wilson 1984). I associate the idea of biophilia with nine human values of nature, dependent, more or less, on adequate experience, learning, and social support to become fully and functionally manifest (Kellert 1996, 1997). The biophilia hypothesis suggests that when we impoverish and degrade environmental health and integrity, we inevitably diminish our material, emotional, and intellectual potential and capacity. Each value reflects a host of physical and mental rewards derived from nurturing connection with natural systems and processes. Collectively, these values suggest that effective human–nature relations function as an anvil on which human fitness continues to be forged. The inclination to impute worth to the natural world reflects how we remain creatures of our biological heritage and capable of exercising free will in developing particular social constructions of nature, which either nourish or frustrate the complex human need to affiliate with natural process and diversity.

The eventual success of achieving sustainability in the built environment depends on adequately addressing these varying valuational dependencies on the natural world. Before considering to what extent this has occurred and might be achieved, I will briefly review nine values of biophilia, which offer a template of broad design objectives for sustainable design and development.

Human Values of Nature

Utilitarian

The natural world has long functioned as an indispensable source of human sustenance and security. Despite this material importance, modern society often prides itself on domesticating the wild and, in the process, achieving food surpluses, material affluence, and physical health largely by eliminating wild competitors and by converting natural landscapes into cultivated and artificial landscapes. This belief in our material independence from nature is, however, an illusion. Modern society continues to rely extensively on natural diversity as an indispensable source of basic food stocks, medicines, scientific discoveries, building and decorative supplies, and other areas of commodity production (Myers 1983; Pimentel et al. 1997; Wilson 1992). Healthy ecosystem functioning also sustains a variety of basic life-support processes on which people and all species depend, including decomposition, oxygen and water production, pollination, and others (Bormann and Likens 1979; Groombridge 1992).

Even employing a narrow economic calculus, biophysical process and variability has been found to yield more than $300 billion in returns to the American economy each year and nearly $3 trillion, or 11 percent, to the total annual world economy (Pimentel et al. 1997; Prescott-Allen and Prescott-Allen 1986). Moreover, this utilitarian dependence on natural process and diversity will greatly expand in the future. For example, only an estimated 15 percent of the world's species have been identified, and rapid developments in taxonomy and scientific exploration, biochemical prospecting, and bioengineering will likely result in a revolution of new product development from exploiting a nearly limitless array of species solutions to survival fashioned over millions of years of adaptational trial and error.

For the individual and community, the recognition and experience of our utilitarian dependence on nature remains a wellspring of physical and mental well-being. We derive satisfaction and confidence from nurturing our material dependence on nature. People remain biologically inclined to respond to natural process and diversity with an abiding interest in discovering and exploiting its practical utility (Hartig 1993; Leopold 1966; Ulrich 1993). Modern people often participate in using nature, even in the absence of necessity, because these pursuits nourish their passion for extracting with skill a portion of their material needs and well-being from the land. Beyond the obvious practical gains, they also harvest physical fitness, emotional connection, critical thinking, and problem-solving capacities. Despite the technological marvels of the modern world, by engaging their utilitarian dependence on nature, people affirm their ability to persevere and sustain themselves with craft and skill.

Aesthetics

Few experiences in life exert as powerful an impact on people as the aesthetic appeal of certain features of natural process and diversity (Appleton 1975; Heerwagen and Orians 1993; Kaplan and Kaplan 1989). This tendency exists because it has fostered a range of adaptive benefits linked to the consistency and intensity of the aesthetic response. Beauty in nature, for example, can engender recognition of harmony, balance, and grace. People discern unity and order in certain natural features, and these aesthetic expressions inspire and instruct. Natural beauty and symmetry can function as a quasi-design model where, through understanding the prototype, people can capture analogous possibilities for human excellence and refinement. The ideal provides a template for action—a means where, through mimicry and ingenuity, people discern clues to a more rewarding and satisfying human existence.

The aesthetic preference for certain natural features can also be linked to the increased likelihood of achieving safety, sustenance, and security (Orians and Heerwagen 1992; Ulrich 1993). People aesthetically favor landscapes with water, which enhance sight and mobility, provide a greater chance for perceiving danger and locating shelter, and have bright flowering colors—all features that, over evolutionary time, have enhanced the probability of human survival.

Aesthetic preference for natural diversity also fosters interest and curiosity. These, in turn, encourage wonder and mystery, which enrich our capacities for exploration, creativity, and discovery. Finally, aesthetic quality in nature can be linked to physical and mental healing. When distressed, people seek the restorative power of beautiful flowers, gardens, seashores, mountains, and other aesthetically pleasing features of the natural world.

Scientific

As a species we possess the need to know and understand our world with authority—a tendency, independent of culture and history, where intellectual capacity can be nurtured and developed through study and observation of natural process and diversity (Bloom 1956; Shepard 1996). The natural world offers a nearly limitless stage for sharpening critical thinking skills, problem-solving abilities, and analytical capacities. Observing and examining natural process provides people with an array of challenging opportunities for acquiring knowledge, developing understanding, and honing evaluative aptitudes. These cognitive capacities can be advanced in other learning contexts, but natural diversity provides an especially accessible and stimulating context for pursuing intellectual competence, especially for the young and inquiring mind.

Moreover, the knowledge and understanding obtained from these intellectual pursuits can produce tangible benefits. Exploring the mysteries of even a fraction of the natural world expands the realization of how much we can learn from the extraordinary ingenuity of the biological enterprise. Moreover, the more we learn and benefit from studying natural process, the more we tend to recognize the virtue of its healthy perpetuation.

Symbolic

The natural world also offers an invaluable source for developing human capacities for communication and thought (Lawrence 1993; Shepard 1978). We employ natural diversity as a kind of raw material for expediting the exchange of information and understanding among and between our kind. We accomplish this through metaphor, analogy, and abstraction, and by using the media of language, story, myth, fantasy, and other communicative means.

Nature as symbol is especially instrumental in language acquisition. Language relies on the capacity for sorting objects into ever more refined categories and distinctions. Where does the young and inquiring mind encounter numerous, readily available, emotionally salient, and especially distinguishable objects for learning and practicing the act of classification? Natural process and diversity, particularly charismatic creatures, provide this powerful source of imagery and distinction.

Symbolizing and fantasizing nature also assists in confronting basic issues of human identity and selfhood. Symbolizing nature enables people and cultures to address universal dilemmas, such as authority and independence, order and chaos, good and evil, love and sexuality, in a tolerable yet instructive manner. This occurs in children's stories and fairy tales, in legends and myths, in totems and taboos, in fantasy and dream. These images allow us to encounter ourselves through a glass, darkly rendering more tolerable the enigmatic issues of conflict, need, and desire.

Finally, symbolizing nature assists in everyday communication. People employ natural imagery in the language of the street, in the metaphors of the marketplace, in oratory and debate. This imagery can be trivial, but sometimes eloquent and inspiring. Its occurrence in all cultures and historical epochs suggests a universal and indispensable role. Natural process and diversity provide a substrate for symbolic creation analogous to the way genetic variability offers a biochemical template for laboratory discovery. Each use represents the exploitation of nature's clay from which people mold and fabricate solutions to life's varied challenges.

Naturalistic

Natural process and diversity also fosters curiosity, imagination, and discovery through direct experience and immersion in its many rhythms and details (Driver et al. 1987; Ewert 1989; Kaplan and Kaplan 1989; Nabhan and Trimble 1994; Pyle 1993). People mine physical, intellectual, and emotional ore from personal exploration of the rich tapestry of nature's many shapes and forms, above all its conspicuous plants, animals, and landscapes. In doing so, people can achieve physical fitness and mental acuity as well as expanded capacities for adventure, curiosity, and imagination. Moreover, the more people explore the intricacies of natural process and diversity, the more wonder and discovery they typically extract.

Advantages further accrue in direct encounters in nature that enhance the ability to react quickly, resolve new and challenging situations, overcome difficulties, and consume with efficiency. Immersion in nature provides people with opportunities for focused attention and seemingly more authentic experience in the process, fostering feelings of calm, a clearer sense of priorities, and enhanced strength and resolve.

Humanistic

Nature further represents a powerful source for emotional bonding and attachment, especially through companionship with other creatures, although occasionally by strongly identifying with certain plants and landscapes (Katcher and Beck; 1983; Katcher and Wilkins 1993; Serpell 1986). The natural world constitutes, in this respect, a subject of deep affection, even at times a means for expressing love and friendship. These feelings of relationship and connection provide intimacy, a way of expressing trust, and a sense of kinship. By contrast, isolation and aloneness constitute heavy burdens for a largely social creature like the human animal. With rare exceptions, we crave the affection and companionship of others. By affiliating with other species, even landscapes, we can achieve a valued source of relationship and a means of expressing and sometimes receiving affection.

Bonding and affiliation remain critical pathways for developing the capacities for cooperation and sociability, evolutionarily important for a species like ours lacking particular strength or physical prowess. Humans covet relationships and responsibility for others and, in return, gratefully receive their affection and allegiance. Caring and sometimes being cared for by other creatures and, more generally, nature offers a means for expressing affection, companionship, and association. These benefits accrue under normal circumstances but become especially pronounced during moments of crisis and disorder. The nurturing response of others can be mentally and physically restorative.

Dominionistic

Despite these elements of kinship and affection, people also hone their physical and mental fitness through subduing and mastering the natural world (Ewert 1989; Ortega and Gasset 1986; Shepard 1973). People seek opportunities for outcompeting and outwitting others, as well as overcoming challenge and adversity. Natural process and diversity provides a valued context for developing these more competitive traits in the human animal. People may no longer rely on besting prey or eluding menacing predators or surviving in the wild, but the strength and prowess obtained from challenging nature remains an important pathway for developing physical and mental competence and well-being.

People also foster feelings of self-confidence and capacity by testing themselves in nature. By demonstrating the ability to function under challenging circumstances, they emerge surer and more certain of themselves. An inquisitive and creative capacity is encouraged by confronting and mastering natural process and diversity. By besting a formidable opponent, people enhance their ability to adapt under unfamiliar and difficult circumstances. Through contesting nature, they cultivate the willingness to take risks, face adversity, and master the unknown.

Moralistic

Nature's extraordinary diversity is reflected, for example, by the 1.7 million scientifically classified species, the estimated 10–100 million unclassified species, and the extinction of 99 percent of all species that ever existed. One is awed by the capacity of living matter to attain a unique adaptive foothold on the ladder of existence. Despite this incredible variability, an equally astonishing similarity seemingly unites much of life on earth. Most of the planet's species share common molecular and genetic structures, analogous circulatory and reproductive features, and parallel body parts. A remarkable web of relationships appear to connect a beetle on the forest floor, a fish in the ocean, an elephant on the savanna, even a human in the modern metropolis.

This unity and connection provides people with a sense of underlying meaning and order and a cornerstone for spiritual and religious belief (Kohak 1984; Leopold 1966; Nelson 1993; Rolston 1986). Perceiving universal pattern in creation offers a foundation for morality, which gives definition and shape to human existence. Through the shared conviction in life's underlying meaning, people achieve a sense of cohesion and mutual commitment. These sentiments encourage the belief that at the core of human existence resides a fundamental logic, even harmony, and goodness. Humans derive, in this way, faith and confidence through discerning a unity that transcends their individual aloneness and separation.

These convictions can also foster the inclination to conserve natural process and diversity. The willingness to protect nature derives as much from moral and ethical principle as from any calculated materialism or regulatory mandate. When people divine spiritual and moral connection with creation, they temper their inclination to harm and destroy its constituent parts. They see in their relation to nature the possibility for harmony and meaning. Environmental respect and care emerges as an element of a perceived link between human wholeness, natural process, and spiritual well-being.

Negativistic

Finally, the natural world also constitutes a powerful carrier of human fears and anxieties (Öhman 1985; Ulrich 1993). Avoidance and aversion of nature can provoke irrational and highly destructive tendencies, but more typically this inclination reflects a beneficial and functional aspect of the human or any other species' experience. The disposition to respond negatively to certain creatures and landscapes can avert harm, injury, and death. When rationally manifest, advantages accrue from isolating and occasionally eliminating threatening natural elements. Human well-being depends on skills and emotions that foster a healthy distancing from potentially injurious elements in the natural environment. Lacking such awareness, people often behave naively, constructing structures where they do not belong, or ignoring their inevitable vulnerability before an intrinsically uncertain and powerful natural world.

We also should not presume such anxieties and fears always breed contempt or destructive tendencies. Deference and respect for nature can arise as much from recognizing its ability to defeat and destroy us as from feelings of kinship and affection (Leopold 1966; Shepard 1996). A sense of awe combines reverence, wonder, and fear. Nature stripped of its power and strength can become an object of condescension and superficial amusement. Species and habitats utterly subdued and mastered provoke little admiration, humility, or respect.

The Challenge of Nature's Value in the Built Environment

Nine human values of nature have been described, and summary definitions of each are provided in Table 3.1. All these affinities and associated benefits stemming from human relationships to nature have suffered as a consequence of the current scale of global environmental degradation and destruction. Diminished human experience of healthy natural process and diversity has been especially evident in the built environment, particularly in the modern city and suburb. People consequently find themselves in an increasing cycle of disaffection and disconnection from the natural environment, where the more they are isolated from healthy natural process and diversity, the more they typically fail to recognize its critical role in their mental and physical well-being, and the more they tend to allow these destructive forces to continue.

The ultimate challenge of sustainable design is to restore in the built environment all our tattered valuational connections with healthy natural process and diversity. The complexity of this task is exacerbated by the need to foster this occurrence in at least three areas of the built environment: at the level of building systems (e.g., energy, production, waste); at the level of individual and group experience within and in relation to buildings and facilities; and in the various ways the built environment connects with both proximate and distant ecological processes.

Significant progress has, without question, occurred, particularly in the areas of energy efficiency, life-cycle design, waste processing, natural lighting, improved ventilation, and landscape planning (Graedel and Allenby 1995; Lyle 1994; Todd and Todd 1994; Van der Ryn and Cowan 1996; Wilson et al. 1998). The recently published book, *Green Development* (Wilson et al. 1998), for example, offers an impressive accounting of varying efforts at integrating ecology into the design and development of the built environment.

Yet, as suggested earlier, I believe most of these improvements have partially and often superficially addressed the previously described human needs for physical, emotional, and intellectual connection with natural process and diversity. While important accomplishments have occurred—particularly at the level of building

Table 3.1. A typology of values of biophilia

Aesthetic: physical attraction and appeal of nature
Dominionistic: mastery and control of nature
Humanistic: emotional bonding with nature
Naturalistic: exploration and discovery of nature
Moralistic: moral and spiritual relation to nature
Negativistic: fear and aversion of nature
Scientific: knowledge and understanding of nature
Symbolic: nature as a source of language and imagination
Utilitarian: nature as a source of material and physical reward

systems—the impression remains of sustainable design often lacking imaginative breadth and frequently relying more on negatively motivating people by urging them to avoid harmful and damaging environmental practices than positively revealing how sustainable development can foster a richer and more satisfying experience of self and community. I believe part of the problem stems from the lack of a template of understanding of how people attach meaning and derive value from nature and the use of this framework as a broad set of design objectives in the built environment. From this perspective, sustainability in the built environment means the avoidance of practices—whether at the systems, personal experience, or landscape levels—that diminish or impair any of the described basic values of nature.

An illustration might help elucidate my frustration with what I believe is the prevailing paradigm of sustainable design. In this regard, I will briefly discuss the acclaimed effort, *Audubon House,* headquarters of the National Audubon Society, in a retrofitted building in New York City (National Audubon Society and Croxton Collaborative 1994). This building's restoration is unquestionably a significant achievement, having transformed an old building into a much higher standard of environmental efficiency and performance. Its accomplishments include improved energy use, pollution avoidance, solid waste control, resource conservation, and enhanced ventilation and lighting.

Despite these significant and often technologically challenging achievements, I believe the paradigm of sustainable design represented by Audubon House falls short of the full promise and potential of sustainable architecture. My primary criticisms occur in three related areas: an over-reliance on "systems" benefits, an inordinate emphasis on material rewards, and an inadequate consideration of all basic values of nature. Let me briefly elaborate on each.

The focus at Audubon House, as with much sustainable design, is improved systems performance. The primary criteria of success typically focus on processing energy, waste, and other resources, and associated impacts on air, water, and occasionally lighting quality. These systems' functions are certainly critical and greatly affect a range of significant environmental problems, including pollution, resource depletion, and biodiversity loss. Yet, these benefits are largely abstract and depersonalized. The average person or group living, working, recreating, or being educated in the built environment remains, for the most part, aloof and apart from these rewards, the gains residing mainly in the realm of institutional improvements. Moreover, the motivational emphasis of this design approach largely stresses the avoidance of environmental harm or injury rather than the enrichment or enhancement of personal, group, or community experience.

This leads to a second concern with this design paradigm—an overemphasis on material benefits. Ameliorating the environmental crisis will certainly require more efficient and effective consumption and production systems. Yet, technology and physical rewards represent the means, not the ends, to achieving lives of meaning and satisfaction. People crave emotional and intellectual well-being reflected in the experience of meaning, beauty, companionship, creativity, imagination, inspiration, spiritual wholeness, and more. As I attempted to describe, adequate connection with natural process and diversity has and will remain integral to the experience of these critical mental as well as physical values and benefits.

Unfortunately, most of these emotional and intellectual rewards derived from association with the natural environment have been omitted from explicit consideration by Audubon House and most sustainable design. Audubon House commendably addresses what it terms "humanistic" issues of improved lighting, operable windows, enhanced views, and the use of natural materials. These efforts represent, however, only a very partial consideration of the complex and multifaceted ways people depend on sustained experience and connection with natural process and diversity. Audubon House accomplishes much in the way of more sustainable building systems but little in the way of providing a fundamentally different work environment at the level of individual and group experience. Consequently, when we visually examine the rooms, offices, hallways, and other areas of human experience and interaction at Audubon House, we fail to observe much difference from more conventional office design, with the possible exception of improved natural lighting and ventilation. Moreover, although I have focused on Audubon House, we encounter analogous deficiencies in many sustainable design efforts (Crosbie 1994; Slessor 1997; Wilson et al. 1998).

Beyond diagnosing these deficiencies, can I offer any practical alternatives? I must confess that, at this point, I can only recommend some general design goals, again relying on the typology of values previously described. Yet, I believe these values offer a useful, albeit broad, template of design objectives focusing our attention on the various ways individuals and groups could experience natural process and diversity in the built environment. I will, therefore, conclude with a speculative consideration of how these values might find expression as broad design goals.

Let me start by considering *utilitarian* and *negativistic* values, because most design efforts address these fundamental human–nature relationships. Audubon House, for example, largely emphasizes a range of utilitarian benefits stemming from more sustainable utilization of energy, water, air, and other natural resources.

The negativistic value as a sustainable design objective focuses on the allied goals of protecting humans from various threatening and aversive elements in nature (e.g., cold, heat, wind, earthquakes), while minimizing the infliction of harm and injury on natural process and diversity. Sustainable design can strive to accomplish this basic protective task without insulating people from their need for ongoing contact with nature, or unduly supporting the conquest or repression of natural systems. Our structures should express the human need for comfort and security from natural elements, yet foster a deep respect and deference for environmental forces greater than ourselves. In this way, we are less likely to build in ecologically sensitive areas, such as flood plains or earthquake zones; discharge pollutants and contaminants into the environment; or erect structures that suggest a naïve indifference or disrespect for the forces of nature (e.g., too much glass, exposure).

We should also include in our sustainable design efforts, when pragmatically possible, an interest in *naturalistic, scientific,* and *dominionistic* values of nature. As previously described, these values can foster many adaptive benefits, including creativity, intellectual capacity, self-esteem, problem-solving, and critical thinking. Developing these qualities is especially important for young people and, thus, should represent important design considerations in constructing homes, schools, recreational facilities, parks, and open spaces. But, adults also benefit from these types of environmental experience, and this may creatively occur even in the urban work place. The design of Audubon House, for example, includes, "a rooftop deck where . . . a . . . garden [would] be added . . . offering employees respite from the office routine" (National Audubon Society 1994:54). I would suggest that this represents the proverbial "tip of the iceberg" of what can be accomplished through more imaginative design seeking to facilitate opportunities for direct contact with nature, not just for rest and relaxation purposes, but also to enhance creativity, critical thinking, and, ultimately, productivity.

Aesthetic and *symbolic* values of nature can also be deliberate design objectives in the built environment. One of the glaring deficiencies of the contemporary city, and much sustainable design, is the relative absence of inspiring aesthetic and symbolic celebrations of the natural world. I believe this tendency reflects a modern bias toward environmental aesthetics as unimportant and, thus, dispensable, and a related failure to recognize the instrumental physical and psychological significance of the human attraction and metaphorical relation to nature. The importance of this relationship is suggested by studies revealing that people working in windowless environments often seek, through such means as potted plants and pictures, to restore their severed connections with the natural world (Heerwagen and Orians 1993). When we also examine many, if not most, corporate logos, we discern a tendency to infuse in these organizational images representations of the natural world. Unfortunately, these efforts largely represent futile attempts at connecting largely artificial and oppressive work environments with the real and authentic in nature. Yet, we can capture inspiring aesthetic and symbolic expressions of the natural world in the built environment by more creative and imaginative design. The result could be not only enhanced morale but also greater inventiveness, stimulation, and productivity.

Finally, pushing the edge of the attempt to include all values of nature in the built environment, I would argue for the virtue, when feasible, of designing for *humanistic* and *moralistic* values. The potential benefits that might result are suggested by an intriguing finding from a hospital setting. A study by Roger Ulrich and his colleagues reported, "Exposure to unthreatening nature promotes recovery from mild and even acute stress" (1993:106). Comparing postoperative recovery rates of patients experiencing similar surgical procedures—

but differing in having window views of trees and a lake, no window views, or exposure to a brick wall—the researchers found the window view patients recovered significantly faster, required substantially less pharmaceutical assistance, and had fewer postoperative complications. I would argue, by analogy, that enhanced opportunities for emotionally bonding with nature—whether in homes, outdoor recreational facilities, or even office buildings—promotes feelings of calm, confidence, and personal well-being. Architecturally achieving this effect will require considerable creativity and experimentation. Yet, one can imagine how this could occur through increased exposure to natural settings, park and atrium creation, and inserting living organisms into the work place (e.g., vegetation, aquariums).

Finally, we confront the matter of the human spirit. Modern society typically places the secular over the sacred, often for good reason. Yet, when thinking about the built environment, we recognize that few structures inspire us more than certain churches, cathedrals, and temples. These buildings often derive their impact from simulating natural design—the concentrated use of materials like stone and glass, arches and columns insinuating ancient forests, domes and spires rising into the sky like natural prominences. Our finest structures, those that inspire and seemingly connect us to a reality greater than ourselves, often convey the impression of a fundamental order and harmony in nature. Perhaps, the ultimate objective of sustainable design is to bring, through our enhanced connection to natural process and diversity, the divine back into our lives.

Incorporating all these values of nature into the built environment constitutes an enormously creative and technological challenge. The extent and appropriateness of this effort will vary greatly depending on the opportunity and context. Yet, I believe this achievement could move us closer to the full promise and potential of sustainable design as a means of helping humanity experience increased meaning and satisfaction through celebrating our multifaceted connections with the natural world.

REFERENCES

Appleton, J. 1975. *The Experience of Landscape.* London and New York: John Wiley.

Bloom, B., ed. 1956. *Taxonomy of Educational Objectives, Handbook 1: Cognitive Domain.* New York: David McKay.

Bormann, F.H., and G. Likens. 1979. *Patterns and Process in a Forested Ecosystem.* New York: Springer-Verlag.

Crosbie, M. 1994. *Green Architecture: A Guide to Sustainable Design.* Rockport, MA: Rockport Publishers.

Driver, B. et al. 1987. "Wilderness Benefits: A State-of-the-Knowledge Review." In *Proceedings of the National Wilderness Research Conference* (R.C. Lucas, ed.). Ft. Collins, CO: USDA Forest Service.

Ewert, A. 1989. *Outdoor Adventure Pursuits: Foundations, Models and Theories.* Scottsdale, AZ: Publishing Horizons.

Graedel, T., and B. Allenby. 1995. *Industrial Ecology.* Englewood Cliffs, NJ: Prentice-Hall.

Groombridge, B. ed. 1992. *Global Biodiversity: Status of the Earth's Living Resources.* London: Chapman & Hall.

Hartig, T. 1993. "Nature Experience in Transactional Perspective." *Landscape and Urban Planning* 25:17–36.

Heerwagen, J., and G. Orians. 1993. "Humans, Habitats, and Aesthetics." In *The Biophilia Hypothesis* (S.R. Kellert and E.O. Wilson, eds.). Washington, DC: Island Press.

Kaplan, S., and R. Kaplan. 1989. *The Experience of Nature.* New York: Cambridge University Press.

Katcher, A., and A. Beck. 1983. *New Perspectives on Our Lives with Companion Animals.* Philadelphia: University of Pennsylvania Press.

Katcher, A., and G. Wilkins. 1993. "Dialogue with Animals: Its Nature and Culture." In *The Biophilia Hypothesis* (S.R. Kellert and E.O. Wilson, eds.). Washington, DC: Island Press.

Kellert, S.R. 1996. *The Value of Life: Biological Diversity and Human Society.* Washington, DC: Island Press.

Kellert, S.R. 1997. *Kinship to Mastery: Biophilia in Human Evolution and Development.* Washington, DC: Island Press.

Kellert, S.R. and E.O. Wilson, eds. 1993. *The Biophilia Hypothesis.* Washington, DC: Island Press.

Kohak, E. 1984. *The Embers and the Stars: A Philosophical Inquiry into the Moral Sense of Nature.* Chicago: University of Chicago Press.

Lawrence, E. 1993."The Scared Bee, the Filthy Pig, and the Bat Out of Hell: Animal Symbolism as Cognitive Biophilia." In *The Biophilia Hypothesis* (S.R. Kellert and E.O. Wilson, eds.). Washington, DC: Island Press.

Leopold, A. 1966. *A Sand County Almanac.* New York: Oxford University Press.

Lyle, J. 1994. *Regenerative Design for Sustainable Development.* New York: John Wiley.

Myers, N. 1983 *A Wealth of Wild Species: Storehouse for Human Welfare.* Boulder, CO: Westview Press.

Nabhan, G.P., and S. Trimble. 1994. *The Geography of Childhood.* Boston: Beacon Press.

National Audubon Society and Croxton Collaborative. 1994. *Audubon House.* New York: John Wiley.

Nelson, R. 1993 "Searching for the Lost Arrow." In *The Biophilia Hypothesis* (S.R. Kellert and E.O. Wilson, eds.). Washington, DC: Island Press.

Öhman, A. 1985. "Face the Beast and Fear the Face: Animal and Social Fears of

Prototypes for Evolutionary Analyses of Emotion." *Psychophysiology* 23:123–145

Orians, G., and J. Heerwagen. 1992. "Evolved Responses to Landscapes." In *The Adapted Mind: Evolutionary Psychology and the Generation of Culture* (J. Barlow et al., eds.). New York: Oxford University Press.

Ortega and Gasset, J. 1986. *Meditations on Hunting.* New York: Macmillan.

Pimentel, D. et al. 1997. "Economic and Environmental Benefits of Biodiversity." *BioScience* 47 (1997):747–757.

Prescott-Allen, C., and R. Prescott-Allen. 1986. *The First Resource.* New Haven, CT: Yale University Press.

Pyle, R. 1993. *The Thunder Tree: Lessons from an Urban Wildland.* Boston: Houghton Mifflin.

Rolston, H. III. 1986. *Philosophy Gone Wild: Essays in Environmental Ethics.* Buffalo: Prometheus Books.

Serpell, J. 1986. *In the Company of Animals.* Oxford: Basil Blackwell.

Shepard, P. 1973. *The Tender Carnivore and the Sacred Game.* New York: Scribner's.

Shepard, P. 1978. *Thinking Animals: Animals and the Development of Human Intelligence.* New York: Viking Press.

Shepard, P. 1996. *The Others: How Animals Made Us Human.* Washington, DC: Island Press.

Slessor, C. 1997. *Sustainable Architecture and High Technology.* New York: Thames and Hudson.

Todd, N., and J. Todd. 1994. *From Eco-Cities to Living Machines: Principles of Ecological Design.* Berkeley, CA: North Atlantic Books.

Ulrich, R. 1993 "Biophilia, Biophobia, and Natural Landscapes." In *The Biophilia Hypothesis* (S.R. Kellert and E.O. Wilson, eds.). Washington, DC: Island Press.

Van der Ryn, S., and S. Cowan. 1996. *Ecological Design.* Washington, DC: Island Press.

Wilson, A., J. Uncapher, L. McManigal, L.H. Lovins, M. Cureton, and W. Browning. 1998. *Green Development: Integrating Ecology and Real Estate.* New York: John Wiley.

Wilson, E.O. 1984. *Biophilia.* Cambridge, MA: Harvard University Press.

Wilson, E.O. 1992. *The Diversity of Life.* Cambridge, MA: Harvard University Press.

Chapter 4

Environmental Ethics

Sarah van Gelder

Many of us believe that the systems, institutions, and values of industrial society are in a deep crisis. Every natural system is in decline. Every institution of society is in transition or upheaval. It is becoming increasingly clear that a few changes around the edges will not be sufficient to overcome the challenges we face.

Fortunately, there are a great many people who recognize the inadequacies of either the whole system and its underlying world view or some aspects of it. And with this recognition comes the development of new value systems, new experiments with more sustainable approaches, and new understandings of the ways in which these tie together. In particular, people all over the world are experimenting with ways to emulate natural systems in the design of industrial processes and the built environment, exploring the meaning of sustainable economics, seeking the means to bring about greater equity, and living a less consumptive lifestyle.

One way to see this transition from the old world view to the new is to consider the main thrust of the environmental movement. In the 1960s and 1970s, most people believed that environmental problems could be solved without making any fundamental changes to the foundations of industrial society. For example, one of the big campaigns of the time, "Keep America Beautiful," was primarily aimed at litter prevention.

This sort of effort was an important step in raising awareness about the human impact on the environment, especially in regard to nonbiodegradable waste. In some cases, this translated into law, as in the Oregon bottle bill, which required a five-cent deposit on bottles and cans. In Oregon instead of tossing cans on the side of the road, people would keep and return them to get back their deposits. I remember driving behind a pick-up truck when I lived in Oregon and seeing it abruptly pull over to the side of the road so someone could retrieve a beer can that had not quite made it into the back of the truck. Thus, with a simple nickel deposit, an environmental goal became mainstream.

Reducing litter was not the only environmental issue in people's awareness, of course. Rachel Carson's book, *Silent Spring,* alerted people to the effects of pesticides on bird and human populations, and the famous incident in which the Cuyahoga River in Ohio caught fire alerted people to water pollution. Air pollution was obvious simply by looking around.

However, these were relatively straightforward, confined issues. The problem for the birds could be solved by banning DDT. The rivers could be cleaned by identifying the big industrial polluters and compelling them to treat their effluents or move elsewhere. Except for the looming issue of overpopulation, most people felt that environmental issues could be dealt with locally without real changes to the basic processes of industrialism and without real changes in our way of life.

Environmentalism in the New Era

Much has changed in the time since Earth Day 1970. We are now up against environmental challenges that cannot be solved by the level of thinking that created them, to paraphrase Albert Einstein. We are facing challenges that extend well beyond "Don't be a litterbug," well beyond banning a chemical here or there that is found to be harmful, well beyond treating industrial effluent before it is released into the biosphere. This is not to say that those were not important steps—they were, perhaps for no other reason than they got people in the modern, industrial world thinking of themselves as having some responsibility for the health of the environment. In that respect, the widespread practice of recycling bottles, cans, and newspapers may have been most important because it got so many people to perform a daily practice of being conscious of resource use and waste.

The level of challenge that we face now is at another scale, however. In a warning signed by 1,600 scientists worldwide, including 102 Nobel Prize winners, the Union of Concerned Scientists said, the continuation of human activity may "so alter the living world that it will be unable to sustain life in the manner we know."

Hardin Tibbs, who specializes in developing scenarios of the future, describes some of the possible sources of disruption of modern civilization, any one of which could have a major impact: global climate disruption, food and water shortages and the waves of refugees that would result, the use of weapons of mass destruction, genetic depletion and damage, antibiotic-resistant epidemics, social inequity and injustice, energy shortfalls, economic depression, chemical pollution, or ecosystem failure (Tibbs 1998).

This is not the first time humans have faced ecological collapse; however, in the past such collapses were localized. There is evidence that prehistoric humans wiped out the mammoth through over-hunting (Ward 1997). Some believe that the Mayan civilization in Central America declined as its cities grew too large to be supported by the surrounding jungle ecosystem: jungle soil can be rapidly depleted once trees are cleared.

Other groups lived in harmony for thousands of years within ecosystems as diverse as the Arctic and the tropical rain forest. The reason each one of us is here today is because of the success of these people of ancient times.

So humans have a history of enormous success in living within ecosystems (which is how we came to be dispersed so widely across the planet). We also have a history of *localized* collapses. But now, thanks to the successes of the industrial age, we have, for the first time in human history, the opportunity to have a world-wide collapse. That opportunity is one given to us by the industrial era, which, in terms of the time span of human history, evolved in the blink of an eye. Since 1940, Americans alone have used up as large a share of the earth's mineral resources as all previous generations put together (Durning 1992). Americans have cut 90 percent of the nation's old-growth forests. Fifty percent of the wetlands are gone, as are 99 percent of prairie lands (World Resources Institute 1993). The hole in the ozone layer, global climate change, and the ubiquity of various persistent, bioaccumulating chemicals are evidence that the environmental limits we are reaching first may be those involving sinks for the wastes of industrial society, even before we reach the limits of some critical resources, such as fresh water and soil.

Paul Hawken says we should hold a banquet celebrating the many accomplishments of industrialism, give it a gold watch, and applaud as it retires (Hawken 1993, 1997a). Industrialism has given us much to applaud. It has provided ways of doing a lot of work with far less human effort, and the prospect—for the most part unrealized—of having our needs met with far less time spent working. It has provided the technology to understand our universe, the nature of life, and ourselves, and it has allowed us to communicate across the globe instantaneously. And it has given us a lot of toys for adults and kids—more than any previous generation has had at its disposal—and many sources of distraction.

It has also given us something no previous humans have ever had—the opportunity to compromise the global ecosystem to the point where it can no longer sustain life. The very success of the industrial era has now brought us to the point of reaching the limits of the natural systems that support it.

An Opportunity and a Challenge

Our capacity to destroy the natural systems of the earth or to choose to save them, and ourselves, makes us a very special generation. We are the first to have the capacity to do global experiments with the life-support capacity of the entire planet, to cause one of the largest die-outs of species in the history of our planet, and to have the awareness that allows us to choose what we do.

• We have the capacity to put holes in the ozone layer of the upper reaches of the atmosphere—and we have the capacity to make the choice to stop that destruction.

- We have the capacity to dump chemicals into the biosphere that later turn up in the breast milk of people living in the most remote corners of the earth, like the Inuit people who live in the northern reaches of Canada (Colborn et al. 1996). And we have the capacity to stop creating and dumping those chemicals.
- We have the capacity to so alter the composition of the atmosphere that weather patterns worldwide are disrupted. Many believe the frequency and strength of the El Niño weather disruptions during the winter of 1997–1998 are related to what is generally called "global warming" but would more accurately be called "global climate disruptions" (Rysavy 1997/1998).

We are throwing the dice on whether there will be a habitable planet for our children and their children, whether our planet will continue to have the capacity (unique in our solar system and perhaps in the universe) to provide each of us with breathable air, drinkable water, and soil that can grow the food we need to sustain us.

Leadership for Change

Where is the leadership to address these issues? Who can instigate serious debate about the level of change needed to assure our children of a viable future? What can we expect from leaders in government? business leaders? the big environmental groups? local officials?

As an editor of a journal that focuses on these questions, I have many opportunities to talk to people all over the United States and in many other parts of the world who are taking leadership roles in addressing the need for change. These people are taking matters into their own hands, experimenting with various approaches to creating a more sustainable future, advocating changes in policy, starting green businesses, practicing low-impact ways of living, protecting watersheds, building new approaches to engaging people in making choices for their community. The flip side of the cynicism about the capacity of government to accomplish anything is the growing belief that everyone plays a role in creating the crises that humankind is facing, and that everyone has the capacity to be part of the solution. Realizing that the big institutions of government and corporations cannot or will not make the changes needed—at least not right away—these people are making needed changes now:

1. Industrial ecologists, business leaders, and consultants are redesigning production processes in ways that mimic natural systems and vastly increase efficiency, reduce material and energy throughput, dematerialize, provide services rather than produce products, and turn waste into usable material

(Friend 1998). Likewise, architects, planners, home builders, and home owners are looking for and in some cases designing communities, infrastructure, homes, transportation, and businesses in ways that sustain and even restore natural systems.

2. Ecological economists, community development experts, and visionary business leaders are looking for ways to restructure our economy so that consumers get the right market signals, business leaders get feedback on the impacts of their decisions, and communities have some say over their future (Esters 1996; Henderson 1996; Roddick 1998).

3. Nonprofit organizations, UN agencies, and religious leaders are challenging the worldwide trend toward the concentration of wealth. There is a growing realization that greater equity is the only way, short of mass starvation and social chaos or tyranny, of substantially reducing population growth and achieving sustainability (Tibbs 1998).

4. People in all walks of life are coming to see that in many respects we are also changing ourselves, our sense of what is important and what lifestyles we strive for, and what we believe has status and meaning. Some are calling this phenomenon "downshifting," others voluntary simplicity. In either case, there is evidence that thousands of Americans are choosing to live less consumptive lives.

New Values, New World

For the remainder of this chapter, I'll focus on the indications that people are actually going about building sustainability by emulating natural systems in the design of industrial processes and the built environment, exploring the meaning of sustainable economics, seeking the means to bring about greater equity, and living less consumptive lifestyles. And I'll discuss the new world view emerging that underlies these new experiments.

Natural Design

During the height of the industrial era, we thought we had transcended biology—that all our intelligence and technology somehow made us immune to the need for clean water, soil for food, oxygen in the air, and that any illness could be cured. We are beginning to see that we are as subject to biology as we are to physics. Race your car into a brick wall and there will be repercussions. Run into an ecological wall and plants, animals, and humans die.

We are coming to understand that we are part of an ecosystem. The world functions, in many respects, like a large living thing. Early bacteria that produced oxygen made the next more complex life forms possible. Our lives depend on many forms of simpler life in a complex chain of interdependence that we only partially understand. But we are discovering now that we can alter the basic life-support systems and life-protection systems, such as the ozone layer and the populations of plankton, which are not only at the foundation of the ocean's food chain but also produce the bulk of the oxygen in the atmosphere. And we are learning that we must follow the rules or we will suffer the same consequences as other species that are unable to live within the support capacities of their ecosystem.

This new understanding of natural systems brings not only an awareness of the danger of neglecting the biological foundations of life; it also brings with it a gift— the design principles found in nature. As industrial ecologist Gil Friend points out, "Nature's ecosystems have 3.5 billion years experience in evolving efficient, complex, adaptive, resilient systems. Why should companies reinvent the wheel, when the R&D has already been done?" (Friend 1998).

This does not mean that we go back to preindustrial times. We could not do that if we wanted. It means that we need to build on the engineering savvy and scientific understanding of the industrial era using design principles based on natural systems.

Architect Bill McDonough has laid down some simple but powerful principles, here explained by author Paul Hawken:

1. Waste equals food. This principle encourages the elimination of the concept of waste in industrial design. We need to design every process so that the products themselves, as well as leftover chemicals, materials, and effluents, can become "food" for other processes.

2. Rely on current solar income. This principle has two benefits: First, it diminishes, and may eventually eliminate, our reliance on hydrocarbon fuels. Second, it means designing systems that sip energy instead of gulping it down.

3. Respect diversity. We need to evaluate every design for its impact on plant, animal, and human life. For a building, this means, literally, what will the birds think of it? For a product, it means where will it go and what will it do when it gets there? For a system, it means weighing immediate and long-term effects and deciding whether it enhances people's identity, independence, and integrity (Hawken 1997b).

Natural Design in Action

On a global scale, we have found that we can galvanize action to protect the earth's natural systems. The agreement to phase out the use of ozone-depleting CFCs was a precedent-setting agreement of global responsibility. This is even more the case with the Kyoto agreement on global warming, in which we implicitly acknowledged that burning fossil fuels must be phased out. This is a remarkable shift on a planetary scale, inadequate in timing to the level of cuts needed, but nonetheless remarkable (Gilding 1998).

Within these global contexts, the work of bringing human systems into harmony with natural systems is actually local—in households and communities and businesses.

In households, one of many examples of the action being taken can be found in the Global Action Plan in which small groups of households join together to form eco-teams—groups of neighbors, co-workers, or friends who work together on reducing their consumption and waste. It's a six-month project that results in a typical household saving 600 gallons of gasoline, 73,000 gallons of water, 10 trees, 10 tons of carbon dioxide emissions, 3,000 pounds of garbage, and 100 cubic feet of landfill space.

In business, Interface Carpets' CEO Ray Anderson has set a goal for sustainability that is talked about worldwide. Interface, with annual sales of $1 billion, makes 40 percent of the world's carpet tile. Anderson challenged his employees to invent factories that have "no smokestacks and no sewer pipes." Anderson has taken the idea of eliminating waste even further.

Typically, after a carpet has spent six to ten years on the floor of a home or office, it goes to a landfill, where it will remain for the next 25,000 years, slowly emitting various chemicals into the biosphere.

At a recent conference, Anderson said: "Our company's technology is plundering the earth. Society considers me a captain of industry, but I stand convicted by myself alone as a plunderer and legal thief. . . . Maybe the 'new industrial revolution' can keep my kind out of jail. Renewable, cyclical, benign, emulating nature, where there is no waste, we can begin to reinvent civilization in a quest to become sustainable, then restorative" (Friend 1997).

How will he do that? Anderson plans to lease the services of these carpets to his customers—when they're worn, he'll take them back, take them apart and remanufacture them. This quantity of the biosphere's resources sequestered for carpet remains as carpet. Anderson does not have to go back to the natural world for more resources, and he can minimize his contribution of chemical soup to the biosphere.

Anderson is very much influenced by McDonough's principles—anything we produce should be literally consumed, it should turn into dirt, or it belongs to the maker indefinitely. Interface is taking the latter approach.

How can this company afford to do this? Anderson's employees found $70 million worth of possible savings in disposal costs in just one of his twenty-six factories—$20 million of which they have captured so far. So there are real bottom-line advantages. But perhaps more important, this design challenge energizes employees far more than looking for ways to return a few extra dollars to the stock holders. For companies looking for the creative edge that will keep them competitive in today's world, the motivation and enthusiasm of employees can make the critical difference.

There is also evidence that consumers want the option of buying greener products. A market research firm, the Hartman Group, has identified four market segments made up of people who are interested in buying based on environmental criteria. While the group they call the "True Natural"—those deeply committed to environmental values—total only 7 percent, an additional 45 percent are interested in environmentally friendly products "under the right circumstances" (Green Markets 1996/1997).

That's the good news. The bad news is that these examples are still a drop in the bucket. The vast majority of industrial production, construction of the built environment, and consumption is carried out using industrial-era practices with little or no thought to sustainability.

A New Economy

If consumers want sustainable products, engineers and designers can design them, and the fate of the planet depends on them, why isn't the standard of manufacturing and construction changing?

Sir James Goldsmith once said, "What an astonishing thing it is to watch a civilization destroy itself because it is unable to re-examine the validity, under totally new circumstances, of an economic ideology" (Goldsmith 1994).

The pro-growth, pro-globalization economic ideology has taken on the characteristics of a state religion—one that cannot be questioned. Growth is always good. Nature can supply an infinite quantity of resources for industrial production and sinks for waste. Growth benefits the poor and positions us to take better care of the environment. There is a technical solution for every problem. The bigger the business and the bigger the production scale, the better.

Interestingly, this ideology of global capitalism has an awful lot in common with the Marxist economy as practiced in the former Soviet Union. Author David Korten (1996) points out that while there are important differences, in both cases:

1. There is a concentration of economic power in unaccountable and abusive centralized institutions (state or transnational corporations).
2. There is a destruction of ecosystems in the name of progress.
3. There is an erosion of social capital by dependence on disempowering mega-institutions.
4. There is a narrow view of human needs by which community values and spiritual connection to the earth are eroded.

Korten goes further: "a modern economic system based on the ideology of free market capitalism is destined to self-destruct for many of the same reasons that the

Marxist economy collapsed in Eastern Europe and the former Soviet Union" (Korten 1996).

The kind of growth we've been experiencing is actually leading to a reduction in the things that we really care about—like natural ecosystems, community, democracy, and even our productive capacity.

Getting the Correct Information

So how do we measure progress? If growth isn't always a benefit, how can we tell when we're moving ahead?

At the community level, cities like Seattle are developing new indicators to measure whether they are moving toward or away from sustainability. Some indicators may be consistent across communities—drinking water quality or high school drop out rates. But other indicators are unique to a place—in Seattle we measure salmon returns and the number of days Mt. Rainier is visible, for example.

Ted Halstead, Jonathon Rowe, and their colleagues at Redefining Progress are developing tools to measure which growth actually increases well-being and which simply increases "Illth." In an *Atlantic Monthly* article entitled, "If the Economy is Up, Why is America Down?" (Rowe et al. 1995), the authors describe an alternative measurement to the gross domestic product (GDP), the measure used worldwide to measure the progress of the economy. The alternative, the genuine progress indicator (GPI), measures progress in terms of education, quality of life, health, standard of living, environmental quality, as well as the flow of cash. The GPI shows an aggregate increase in well-being until the mid-to-late 1970s, when it begins to decline, even as the GDP—which forms the foundation of policy decisions—continues to increase.

So one important first step to halting this sapping of natural and societal capital is simply to know what is happening. The genuine progress indicators that Jon Rowe and others are working on are one way to aggregate that.

Businesses can also measure their own efforts through environmental and social audits. The Body Shop is one company that now does both; independent contractors assess the company's impact on the environment and on all stakeholder groups: employees, franchise owners, trading partners around the world, and communities where The Body Shop does business. The results of the audit show company management areas in which they are living up to their goals and areas in which they are not. Because the management, employees, franchisers, customers, and the general public all have access to the results of the audits, both the tools and the motivation to improve are present (Roddick 1998).

Sending the Right Market Signals

Investors, too, are choosing to use their influence to widen business's definition of the bottom line to include environmental, social, and ethical criteria. One out of every ten dollars of investment is now screened using an ethical, environmental, or social criteria. This $1 trillion total is an 85 percent increase in screened investing in just two years (Feigenbaum 1998).

And government has a role in restructuring the economy so that growth really does lead to greater environmental and social well-being. There is a trend away from command-and-control regulation toward incentives that internalize costs, thereby including in price the real environmental and social costs of doing business.

In the past, we had subsidized carbon fuels—taxpayer money supported roads and bridges and employers and stores provide "free" parking. We spent and still spend enormous amounts on the military to protect our access to oil. Everyone pays these prices in taxes and higher costs of all goods, even if we don't drive. When the market signal is correct, those who choose to burn carbon will pay more. Those who choose to ride a bike or take a bus won't be subsidizing those who drive. As the price begins to include the real cost we will do some things very differently.

So a critical role of government is to help ensure that the market signal is right, that the environmental and social costs of producing and distributing a product are included in the price we pay at the cash register, that these costs are not externalized, forcing someone else, now or in the future, to pay.

The Kyoto agreement on global climate change is potentially especially important because it begins to *internalize* the costs of carbon. If the agreement is ratified and implemented, consumers will pay more for harming the earth and less for preserving it, with important implications for gas mileage, solar energy, wind, conservation, and changes in transportation.

Getting Local

A third part of developing a sustainable economy involves stemming the move toward a globalized economy. This involves rooting capital in place, where those who make the decisions—consumers, owners, employees—are also there to experience the impact. The defeat of Fast Track trade legislation—despite the support of the president, the Republican congressional leadership, virtually all the major newspapers, and the big Fortune 500 companies—indicates that there are serious doubts among Americans about the direction and pace of globalization. Family farmers and owners of small and medium-sized business joined with labor groups, environmentalists, and civil rights groups to defeat the Fast Track trade bill (Korten 1998).

People in both the industrialized and the poorer countries of the world are beginning to question who benefits when large corporations can locate and relocate anywhere in the world to look for the cheapest labor, the lowest environmental standards, and the biggest tax breaks. In effect, these corporations are able to pit each community against all the others as they seek ways to externalize costs and gain subsidies.

The alternative to economic globalization is rooting production in community. This is a clear and direct way of providing the feedback loops that let people better understand the effects of their actions. If you sully your own nest, you see, drink, and breathe the pollution. If your community no longer has a tax base, you experience the decay. When business is owned locally, jobs can be more secure—you can keep money flowing locally, rather than seeing profits transferred daily to corporate headquarters. Because of the need for corporations to compete globally for investment money, they may have to close a factory, even if it is profitable, because it would be more profitable to open it somewhere else. A locally owned business (whether a business owned by a local resident, a worker cooperative, or a municipally owned company like the Green Bay Packers) can stay in town as long as its able to make *enough* profit to stay in operation. This is a way to build stable communities.

The Mondragon cooperatives are an excellent example of the effects of keeping ownership local. Started over forty years ago by a Catholic priest who was concerned about unemployment and poverty in the Basque region of Spain, the businesses began as small, worker-owned cooperatives. However, with the support of the local community, they grew. Over time, the cooperatives started a bank, which supported the start of promising ventures, helping in all ways possible to make them successful.

Mondragon now includes a network of 170 worker-owned and operated cooperatives, and it has created over 21,000 secure and well-paid jobs. Instead of laying off workers during economic recessions, the Mondragon approach is to send surplus workers to get additional training so that the cooperative's long-term productive capacity is constantly being built and their communities are stable, not subject to the ups and downs of the global economy (Morrison 1991).

Equity

Between 1960 and 1990, the richest 20 percent of the world's population increased its share of world income from thirty times greater than the poorest 20 percent to sixty times greater, according to the UN Human Development Report. In the United States and in countries throughout the world, the rich are getting substantially richer and the poor are getting substantially poorer (see Figure 4.1).

What does inequity have to do with sustainability?

First, the wealthy use energy, resources, and other services of nature at a far greater rate. Americans are just 5 percent of the world's population, yet Americans use 20 percent of the world's resources. It would not be possible for the whole world to live at the level of consumption of the United States. According to William Rees, one of the authors of *Ecological Footprints,* if everyone were to live at the standard of living of the United States, it would take the equivalent of three planet Earths' worth of resources (Rees 1996).

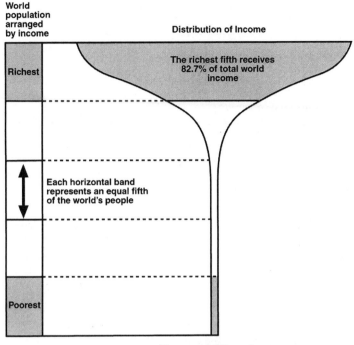

Figure 4.1. Between 1960 and 1990 the richest 20 percent of the world's population increased its share of world income from thirty times greater to sixty times greater. *Source:* UNDEP Human Development Report 1992.

Second, impoverishment is destabilizing. People desperately seeking a livelihood leave rural communities and more sustainable practices and move to crowded shanty towns, where they try to find scarce employment, and to remote areas as yet unfarmed, where they attempt to eke out a living by plowing steep slopes or clearing forests.

Third, it is now widely understood that when women have access to family planning methods, and when they feel some control over their future, they tend to have fewer children. More people were added to the world in the 1990s than lived in the entire world in 1750. The world population has doubled over the last forty years, and if current rates continue, it will double again in the next forty to fifty years (Tibbs 1998).

For this reason, one of the little-known facts about the Grameen Bank is one of the most important of its outcomes: women who are borrowers from the Grameen Bank use birth control at twice the rate of other women in Bangladesh. The Grameen Bank was started by Professor Muhammed Yunus to provide the poorest

Table 4.1. Comparison of quality-of-life data for
Kerala, India, and Europe

	Kerala	India	Europe
Total fertility rate	1.7	3.4	1.5
Infant moratlity rate	13	74	11
Female-to-male ratio	103/100	93/100	107/100
Life expectancy	72	60	73
Literacy rate	95%	52%	95%
Purchasing power parity	$1,250	$1,250	$11,870
Population (millions)	30	930	729

Source: UNDEP Human Development Report, 1992.

women of Bangladesh with access to credit with which they then launch micro-enterprises, such as small handicraft businesses. There are now 36 million people in fifty-two countries who have access to micro-credit based on the Grameen model. In the case of Grameen, the borrowers own 90 percent of the bank, so interest paid into the bank keeps circulating within the country. Repayment rates are 94 percent—higher than most commercial banks who lend only to those who already have some assets. The Grameen owner/borrowers have developed a set of principles for living, among which is the goal of having smaller families (Yunus 1997).

Kerala, in southern India, is a province that has achieved virtually zero population growth. Kerala has the same per capita GDP as the rest of India, but it has achieved a quality of life comparable with Europe, as measured by literacy, life expectancy, gender equity, and infant mortality (see Table 4.1). And the birth rate is half that of the rest of India—just slightly higher than Europe's. Kerala also has a much weaker caste system than is present in other parts of India, and it has a history of land reform that ensures a greater level of economic equity (Alexander 1996).

If we are to achieve a sustainable world, the wealthy will have to consume less and the poor will need greater security and more access to basic resources. There will be a far better chance of meeting everyone's needs within a stable social context when our system of production and distribution is not so completely focused on meeting the material desires of the wealthiest to the neglect of those lacking the money to have their needs met. This greater equity will also result in a lower birth rate.

Meaning

So far, we've considered three aspects of this new more sustainable world view: a new understanding of how to produce and build using natural design principles, a different view on how to do business, and the critical role of equity in sustainability. But what does sustainability mean to us as individuals? One of the ironies of modern life is that going from a state of poverty and deprivation to having enough to meet basic needs really does increase happiness. But achieving greater wealth beyond sufficiency doesn't result in a greater sense of well-being. About 5 percent of Americans who earn under $15,000 report that they feel they have achieved the American dream. That number goes up insignificantly to 6 percent among those earning more than $50,000 (Harper's Index 1988).

A study commissioned by the Merck Family Fund shows that the deepest aspirations of most Americans are not material (see Figure 4.2). Time with friends and family, less stress, and making a difference for one's community were considered most important by more than twice as many Americans as those who put priority on having a nicer car or a bigger house or apartment (Yearning for Balance 1996).

Spending more on consuming means more time must be spent earning, shopping, and caring for possessions. This leaves less time for family, community, and reflection. Spending all our time working, buying, and watching TV cannibalizes the uncounted economies of family and community, which many people find is the real source of meaning, connection, and joy, in favor of growth and consumption (see Figure 4.3). Advertisers tell us we can fill the emptiness that results with stuff, but this cycle of buying, debt, and long work hours impoverishes time—time des-

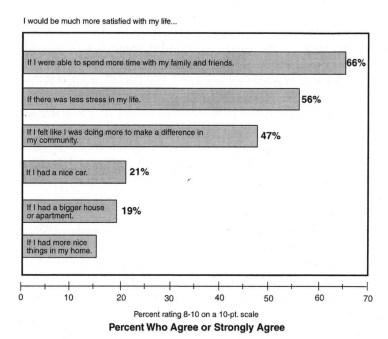

Figure 4.2. Results of Merck Commission survey on human aspirations in the United States.

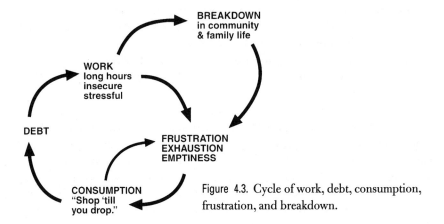

Figure 4.3. Cycle of work, debt, consumption, frustration, and breakdown.

perately needed by kids and time necessary to build real friendships and real communities.

This behavior is also impoverishing the prospects of future generations and the poorer people of the world, as modern consumption addiction drains the world's natural resources and creates effluents that saturate the biosphere with waste products.

The consumption cycle is also impoverishing our view of who we are as human beings. Enormous amounts are spent on keeping us unsatisfied with ourselves and demanding various products that we think will make us more attractive to romantic partners and more prestigious to our peers. There is little support in this world of consumption for a deeper sense of self.

There is a growing number of people who are turning away from this addictive cycle, finding ways to live a simpler lifestyle. Specific steps for cutting spending, increasing savings, and becoming less and less dependent on a job are outlined in *Your Money or Your Life,* by Vicki Robin and Joe Dominguez (Dominguez and Robin 1992). In a world where jobs are so unreliable, their book has a powerful message.

The idea of a simpler way of life is gaining ground not only because people are seeking greater independence from an undependable job market; they are also seeking more meaningful ways to live. They are tired of cluttering their homes with unneeded stuff and tired of cluttering their minds and hearts with trivia. An old tradition is being rediscovered. Thoreau, the Quakers, the utopian communities of the early days of the United States, and most of the world's religions have taught simplicity as a spiritual practice. Buddhist teacher Thich Nhat Hanh says the most valuable gift you give someone is your time spent with them being totally "present" (Hanh 1996).

"Voluntary simplicity" is one term that has been attached to this philosophy of living (Elgin 1993). It's a philosophy that in some parts of the country is growing into a movement of people who are consciously creating a way of living deliberately. By moving out of the consumption-debt-work cycle, people in this movement are finding they have the freedom to work less and to choose the kind of work they do. They have more control over their time and their integrity.

They are also finding security in watching out for each other instead of retreating into homogenous gated communities. In the co-housing community where I live, we throw parties and talent shows that involve kids and adults; we take care of each other when needs arise; we watch each others homes and provide no-cost security. We share tools, meals, and expertise. Reductions in consumption coupled with this cashless community economy, where people voluntarily help one another, can regain ground taken over by the cash economy.

This movement has a third spin-off. It allows people to be respectful members of a world community in which resources are shared and conserved for coming generations.

Voluntary simplicity is about *becoming* much more than is possible if we live lives of addiction. It creates the space in which it is possible to discover who we are and what we have to contribute—not only what is valued by the cash economy.

New Values, New Ways of Life

There is evidence that a growing number of people are adopting a value system, and in many cases a way of life, that supports the four areas previously discussed: emulating natural systems, sustainable economics, greater equity, and a less consumptive lifestyle. Paul Ray, a market researcher, has identified a subculture of Americans that didn't exist just one generation ago. After World War II, there were essentially two main subcultures: the modernists—who advocated technological progress, economic growth, rapid use of natural resources to fuel the economic engine, mobility, and scientific rationalism; and traditionalists— who were more rooted in rural cultures, were uneasy about change, and did not necessarily think bigger was better. Over the course of one generation, another subculture has arisen, which Ray has named cultural creatives. This subculture is made up of people who value at least some of the qualities of sustainability, community, spiritual or humanistic development, the role of women and qualities associated with the feminine, and cultural diversity. There are, according to Ray's research, some 44 million cultural creatives in the United States today. However, because they are so poorly represented in the media, most are unaware of their numbers. The emerging awareness of the scope and potential clout of this group could bring about what Ray describes as a cultural revitalization movement (Ray 1996).

It's Up to Us

Historian Arnold Toynbee says that civilizations are particularly vulnerable after they have achieved great success. This success can lead to inflexibility, a denial of the changes needed, and a tendency to redouble efforts to maintain the status quo. Civilizational development requires "perpetual flexibility and spontaneity" (Toynbee 1947).

These qualities are within us. We have the capability of changing our systems, our values, our behavior to respond to the challenges that are unique to our times. The big institutions are not going to do it for us—flexibility and change are not among their strong suits. It will take many people who consistently question the viability and appropriateness of the industrial-era world view and industrial-era institutions, and many more who start building the new, not waiting for permission, not waiting for a blueprint.

This change is already beginning. People are choosing to make a difference through voluntary simplicity, recycling, buying green, and through investing in businesses with strong labor and environmental records. They're creating new processes to enrich democratic participation, advocating for change in multilateral organizations, and writing and speaking about new ways of doing things. Systems and institutions must eventually change as well, but the culture of big institutions is often the last to change. Once the changes get going, however, things could happen quickly. Just a short time ago, people thought the totalitarian systems of the Soviet Union and South Africa would be with us for a long time. But the legitimacy of both systems had been eroding over the course of decades, and when they went, they went quickly. The legitimacy of industrial era values and institutions is eroding as well, as it is unable to deliver sustainable livelihoods, equity, or meaningful lives. We must develop the alternatives now.

A collapse of our civilization due to ecological overshoot, social rifts caused by untenable levels of social inequity, all-out war, or any of a number of other causes could reduce or eliminate many forms of life on the planet today. The earth has recovered from previous massive extinctions resulting in vast losses of biodiversity, although it took 25–150 million years to recover comparable levels of diversity. But the tragedy extends beyond these biological losses. As far as we know, we are the only species to develop the capacity to reflect on ourselves, our place in the larger universe, and the use of our unprecedented power. We have such capabilities! The question facing us now is this: Will we choose wisely what to do with these gifts?

REFERENCES

Alexander, Will. 1996. "The Kerala Phenomenon: Throughput, Information, and Life Quality Lifestyle Choices for the 21st Century." Unpublished paper prepared for the International System Dynamics Society meeting, July 22–26.
Colborn, Theo, Dianne Dumanoski, and John Peterson Myers. 1996. *Our Stolen*

Future: Are We Threatening Our Fertility, Intelligence, and Survival? A Scientific Detective Story. New York: Penguin Books.

Dominguez, Joe, and Vicki Robin. 1992. *Your Money or Your Life: Transforming Your Relationship with Money and Achieving Financial Independence.* New York: Viking/Penguin.

Durning, Alan Thein. 1992. *How Much Is Enough? The Consumer Society and the Future of the Earth.* New York: W.W. Norton & Co.

Elgin, Duane. 1993. *Voluntary Simplicity: Toward a Way of Life That Is Outwardly Simple, Inwardly Rich.* New York: Morrow.

Esters, Ralph. 1996. *Tyranny of the Bottom Line: Why Corporations Make Good People Do Bad Things.* San Francisco: Berrett-Koehler Publishers.

Feigenbaum, Cliff. 1998. "Responsible Investing," *YES! A Journal of Positive Futures* (Spring) 5:10.

Friend, Gil. 1997. "Strategic Sustainability: Facing the Facts at Interface." *The New Bottom Line: Strategic Perspectives on Business and Environment* (September 25) vol. 6, no. 20. Web site: http://www.eco-ops.com/eco-ops/nb.

Friend, Gil. 1998. "A Simple Business Model. A Profound Business Challenge." *The New Bottom Line: Strategic Perspectives on Business and Environment* (January 2) vol. 7, no. 2. Web site: http://www.eco-ops.com/eco-ops/nb.

Gilding, Paul. 1998. "Kyoto: A New Era?" *YES! A Journal of Positive Futures* (Spring) 5:6.

Goldsmith, Sir James. 1994. *London Times,* March 5, 1994, as cited in Elisabet Sahtouris, *The Biology of Globalization,* 1997. Web site: http://www.ratical.org/LifeWeb/index.html

"Green Markets." 1996/1997. *YES! A Journal of Positive Futures* (Winter) 1:8.

Hanh, Thich Nhat. 1996. Conversation with youth attending the 1996 State of the World Forum, San Francisco, California.

"Harper's Index." 1988. *Harper's Magazine,* October 1988, as cited in New Road Map Foundation pamphlet, *All-Consuming Passion: Waking Up from the American Dream,* Seattle: New Road Map Foundation, 1993.

Hawken, Paul. 1993. *The Ecology of Commerce.* New York: HarperBusiness.

Hawken, Paul. 1997a. From a speech delivered in Seattle, Washington. October.

Hawken, Paul. 1997b. "Natural Capitalism." *Mother Jones* (March/April) 22:50.

Henderson, Hazel. 1996. *Building a Win-Win World: Life Beyond Global Economic Warfare.* San Francisco: Berrett-Koehler Publishers.

Korten, David. 1996. "The Mythic Victory of Market Capitalism." In *The Case Against the Global Economy and For a Return to the Local* (J. Mander and E. Goldsmith, eds.) San Francisco: Sierra Books.

Korten, Fran. 1998. "Fast Track-Dead End," *YES! A Journal of Positive Futures* (Spring) 5:56.

Morrison, Roy. 1991. *We Build the Road As We Travel.* Philadelphia: New Society Publishers.

Ray, Paul. 1996. "The Great Divide: Prospects for an Integral Culture." *YES! A Journal of Positive Futures* (Fall) 2:55.

Rees, William. 1996. "Ecological Footprints." *YES! A Journal of Positive Futures* (Spring) 1:26.

Roddick, Anita. 1998. "Business and Compassion." *YES! A Journal of Positive Futures* (Spring) 5:50.

Rowe, Jonathan, Ted Halstead, and Clifford Cobb. 1995. "If the GDP is Up, Why is America Down?" *Atlantic Monthly* (October) 276: 59–78.

Rysavy, Tracy. 1997/1998. "Ocean Warming." *YES! A Journal of Positive Futures* (Winter) 4:8–9.

Tibbs, Hardin. 1998 "Millennium Scenarios." *YES! A Journal of Positive Futures* (Spring) 5:24.

Toynbee, Arnold. 1947. *A Study of History,* abridgment of vols. I–VI, abridged by D.C. Somervell. New York: Oxford University Press, p. 278.

Ward, Peter. 1997. *The Call of Distant Mammoths: Why Ice Age Mammals Disappeared.* New York: Springer-Verlag.

World Resources Institute. 1993. *The 1993 Information Please Environmental Almanac.* Boston: Houghton Mifflin.

"Yearning for Balance." 1996. A report on a survey conducted for the Merck Family Fund by the Harwood Group, *YES! A Journal of Positive Futures* (Spring) 1:16.

Yunus, Muhammad. 1997. "Beyond Poverty." *YES! A Journal of Positive Futures* (Winter) 1:42.

Chapter 5

Uneconomic Growth
and the Built Environment:
In Theory and in Fact

Herman E. Daly

That which seems to be wealth may in verity be only the gilded
index of far-reaching ruin . . .

—John Ruskin, *Unto this Last* (1860)

Uneconomic growth is growth that, at the margin, increases environmental
and social costs by more than it increases production benefits. It is theoretically
possible, yet appears anomalous within the neoclassical paradigm. Nevertheless,
it is empirically likely that some northern countries have already entered a phase
of uneconomic growth. Why does the dominant neoclassical paradigm make
uneconomic growth seem anomalous, if not impossible? Why, by contrast,
does uneconomic growth appear as an obvious possibility in the alternative paradigm of ecological economics? Although the neoclassical paradigm permits growth
forever, it does not mandate it. Historically, the mandate came because growth was
the answer given to the major problems raised by Malthus, Marx, and Keynes. But
when growth becomes uneconomic we must find new answers to the problems of
overpopulation (Malthus), unjust distribution (Marx), and unemployment
(Keynes). However, national policies required to deal with these three problems
are undercut by "globalization"—the current ideological commitment to global
economic integration via free trade and free capital mobility. The consequent era-
sure of national boundaries for economic purposes simultaneously erases the ability of nations independently to enforce policies for solving their own problems of
overpopulation, unjust distribution, and unemployment. Many relatively tractable
national problems are converted into one intractable global problem, in the name
of "free trade," and in the interests of transnational capital.

Uneconomic Growth in Theory

Growth in GNP, which may be thought of as the "built environment" broadly conceived, is so favored by economists that they call it "economic" growth, thus ruling out by terminological baptism the very possibility of "uneconomic" growth in GNP. But can growth in GNP in fact be uneconomic? Before answering this macroeconomic question let us consider the same question in the perspective of microeconomics—can growth in a microeconomic activity (firm production or household consumption) be uneconomic? Of course it can. Indeed, all of microeconomics is simply a variation on the theme of seeking the optimal scale or extent of each micro-activity—the point where increasing marginal cost equals declining marginal benefit, and beyond which further growth in the activity would be uneconomic because it would increase costs more than benefits.

But when we move to macroeconomics we no longer hear anything about optimal scale, nor about marginal costs and benefits. Instead of separate accounts of costs and benefits compared at the margin we have just one account, GNP, that conflates cost and benefits into the single category of "economic activity." The faith is that activity overwhelmingly reflects benefits. There is no macroeconomic analog of costs of activity to balance against and hold in check the growth of "activity," identified with benefits, and measured by GNP. Unique among economic magnitudes, GNP is supposed to grow forever. Although macroeconomists see no limits on the size of GNP, they have recognized a limit on its rate of growth in the form of inflation that results as the economy approaches full employment. This is seen more as an institutional limit than a biophysical one. Of course there really are costs incurred by GNP growth, even if not usually measured. There are costs of depletion, pollution, disruption of ecological life-support services, sacrifice of leisure time, disutility of some kinds of labor, destruction of community in the interests of capital mobility, takeover of habitat of other species, and running down a critical part of the inheritance of future generations. We not only fail to measure these costs, but frequently we implicitly count them as benefits. This occurs when we include the costs of cleaning up pollution as a part of GNP, and when we fail to deduct for depreciation of renewable natural capital (productive capacity) and liquidation of nonrenewable natural capital (inventories).

There is no *a priori* reason why at the margin the costs of growth in GNP could not be greater than the benefits. In fact, economic theory would lead us to expect that to eventually happen. The law of diminishing marginal utility of income tells us that we satisfy our most pressing wants first, and that each additional unit of income is dedicated to the satisfaction of a less pressing want. So the marginal benefit of growth declines. Similarly, the law of increasing marginal costs tells us that we first make use of the most productive and accessible factors of production—the most fertile land, the most concentrated and available mineral deposits, the best workers—and only use the less productive factors as growth makes it necessary. Consequently, marginal costs of growth increase. When rising marginal costs equal falling marginal benefits, then we are at the optimal level of GNP, and further growth would be uneconomic—would increase costs more than it increased benefits. Why is this simple extension of the basic logic of microeconomics treated as inconceivable in the domain of macroeconomics? Mainly because microeconomics deals with the part, and expansion of a part is limited by the opportunity cost inflicted on the rest of the whole by the growth of the part under study. Macroeconomics deals with the whole, and the growth of the whole does not inflict an opportunity cost, because there is no "rest of the whole" to suffer the cost. Ecological economists have pointed out that the macroeconomy is not the relevant whole but is itself a subsystem, a part of the ecosystem, the larger economy of nature.

These ideas are represented in Figures 5.1 through 5.3. These figures show the preanalytic vision of ecological economics—the economy as a subsystem of a larger ecosystem that is finite, nongrowing, and materially closed. The ecosystem is open with respect to a flow of solar energy, but that flow is itself finite and nongrowing. There is an "empty-world" (Figure 5.1) and a "full-world" (Figure 5.2) version of this basic vision, reflecting the fact that people who share the same paradigm can have differing senses of urgency based on different interpretations of "the facts." Both will agree, however, that the goal is an optimal scale of the economy relative to the ecosystem. The optimal scale is that for which welfare is greatest.

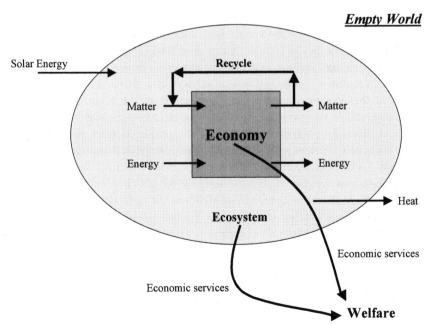

Figure 5.1. The "empty world" preanalytic vision.

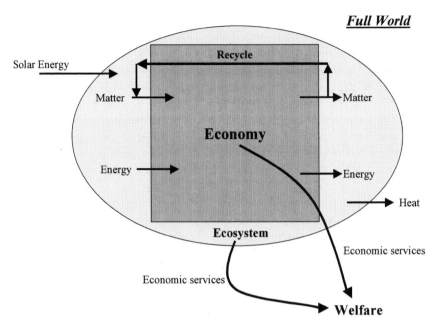

Figure 5.2. The "full world" preanalytic vision.

We have two general sources of welfare: services of human-made capital and services of natural capital, as represented by the thick lines in Figures 5.1 and 5.2. As
the economy grows, natural capital is transformed into human-made capital. More
human-made capital results in a greater flow of services from that source. Reduced
natural capital results in a smaller flow of services from that source. Moreover, as
growth of the economy continues, the services from the economy grow at a
decreasing rate. As rational beings we satisfy our most pressing wants first—hence
the law of diminishing marginal utility. As the economy encroaches more and more
on the ecosystem we must give up some ecosystem services. As rational beings we
presumably will sequence our encroachments so that we sacrifice the least important ecosystem services first. This is the best case, the goal. In actuality we fall short
of it because we do not understand very well how the ecosystem works and have
only recently begun to think of it as scarce. But the consequence of such rational
sequencing is a version of the law of increasing marginal cost—for each further unit
of economic expansion we must give up a more important ecosystem service. Costs
increase at an increasing rate.

This first step in analysis of the preanalytic vision can be expressed graphically
in a diagram (see Figure 5.3) whose basic logic goes back to William Stanley Jevons
and his analysis of labor supply in terms of balancing the marginal utility (MU) of
wages with the marginal disutility (MDU) of labor. The MU curve reflects the

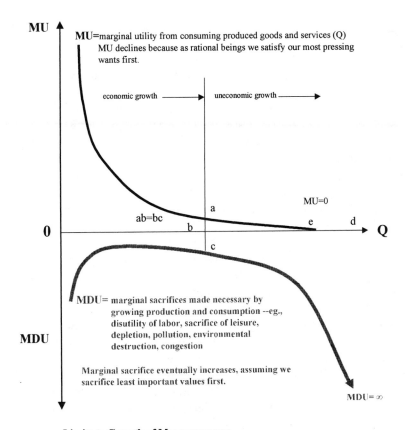

Figure 5.3. Marginal utility (MU) and marginal disutility or sacrifice (MDU) versus quantity of produced goods and services (Q).

diminishing marginal utility of additions to the stock of human-made capital. The MDU curve reflects the increasing marginal cost of growth (sacrificed natural capital services, disutility of labor, disruption of community), as more natural capital is transformed into human-made capital. The optimal scale of the macroeconomy (economic limit to growth) is at point *d*, where MU = MDU, or where *ab* = *bc*, and net positive utility is a maximum.

Two further limits are noted: point *e*, where MU = 0 and further growth is futile even with zero cost; and point *d*, where an ecological catastrophe is provoked, driving MDU to infinity. These "outer limits" need not occur in the order depicted.

The diagram shows that growth out to point *b* is literally economic growth (benefiting us more than it costs), while growth beyond point *b* is literally uneconomic growth (costing us more than it benefits). Beyond point *b*, GNP, "that which seems to be wealth," does indeed become "a gilded index of far-reaching ruin," to recall the introductory quote from John Ruskin.

The concepts of optimal scale and uneconomic growth have a universal logic—they apply to the macroeconomy just as much as to microeconomic units. How did we come to forget this in macroeconomics? How did we come to ignore the existence of the MDU curve and the issue of optimal scale of the macroeconomy? I will suggest two possibilities: one is the "empty-world vision" that recognizes the logical coherence of the concept of uneconomic growth but claims that we are not yet at that point—MU is still very large, and MDU is still negligible. Here we can discuss the factual evidence, as will be done in the next section.

The other possibility for explaining the total neglect of the costs of growth is a paradigm difference: the economy is simply not seen as a subsystem of the ecosystem, but rather the reverse—the ecosystem is a subsystem of the economy (see Figure 5.4). The ecosystem is merely the extractive and waste disposal sector of the economy. Even if these services become scarce, growth can continue forever since technology allows us to "grow around" the ecosystem sector by substitution of human-made capital for natural capital, following the dictates of market prices—if and when prices of natural capital rise. Nature is really nothing but a supplier of indestructible building blocks that are substitutable and superabundant. The only limit to growth is technology, and there is, supposedly, no limit to technology, ergo no limit to economic growth. Therefore, the very notion of "uneconomic growth"

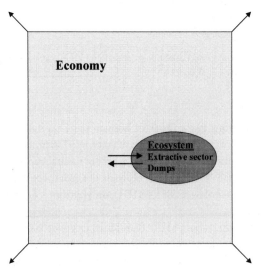

Figure 5.4. The "ecosystem as subsystem of the economy" paradigm.

makes no sense in that paradigm. Since the economy is the whole, the growth of the economy is not at the expense of anything else—there is no opportunity cost to growth. On the contrary, growth enlarges the total to be shared by the different sectors or subsystems. Growth does not increase the scarcity of anything, rather it diminishes the scarcity of everything! How can one possibly oppose growth? Growth forever, or a steady state at optimal scale? Each is logical within its own preanalytic vision and absurd from the viewpoint of the other. We will return later to the paradigm issue, but first let us consider some evidence in favor of the full-world version of the preanalytic vision of ecological economics.

Uneconomic Growth in Fact

As noted above, one might accept the theoretical possibility of uneconomic growth but argue that it is irrelevant for practical purposes since, it could be alleged, we are nowhere near the optimal scale. We are thought to be far to the left of point b in Figure 5.3—where the benefits of growth are still enormous and the costs still trivial at the margin. Economists all agree that GNP was not designed to be a measure of welfare, only of activity. Nevertheless, they assume that welfare is positively correlated with activity, so that increasing GNP will increase welfare, even if not on a one-for-one basis. This is equivalent to believing that the marginal benefit of GNP growth is greater than the marginal cost. This belief can be put to an empirical test. The results turn out not to support the belief.

Evidence for doubting the positive correlation between GNP and welfare in the United States is taken from two sources.

First Nordhaus and Tobin asked, "Is Growth Obsolete?" as a measure of welfare, hence as a proper guiding objective of policy (Nordhaus and Tobin 1972). To answer their question they developed a direct index of welfare, called measured economic welfare (MEW) and tested its correlation with GNP over the period 1929–1965. They found that, for the period as a whole, GNP and MEW were indeed positively correlated—for every six units of increase in GNP there was, on average, a four-unit increase in MEW. Economists breathed a sigh of relief, forgot about MEW, and concentrated again on GNP. Although GNP was not designed as a measure of welfare, it was and still is thought to be sufficiently well correlated with welfare to serve as a practical guide for policy.

Some twenty years later John Cobb, Clifford Cobb, and I revisited the issue and began development of our index of sustainable economic welfare (ISEW) with a review of the Nordhaus and Tobin MEW (Cobb and Cobb et al. 1994; Daly and Cobb 1989). We discovered that if one takes only the latter half of their time series (i.e., the eighteen years from 1947–1965), the positive correlation between GNP and MEW falls dramatically. In this most recent period—surely the more relevant for projections into the future—a six-unit increase in GNP yielded on average only a one-unit increase in MEW. This suggests that GNP growth at this stage of U.S.

history may be a quite inefficient way of improving economic welfare—certainly less efficient than in the past.

The ISEW was then developed to replace MEW, since the latter omitted any correction for environmental costs, did not correct for distributional changes, and included leisure, which both dominated the MEW and introduced many arbitrary valuation decisions. The ISEW, like the MEW, though less so, was positively correlated with GNP up to a point (around 1980) beyond which the correlation turned slightly negative. Neither the MEW nor ISEW considered the effect of individual country GNP growth on the global environment and consequently on welfare of citizens of other countries. Neither was there any deduction for legal harmful products, such as tobacco or alcohol, nor illegal harmful products such as drugs. No deduction was made for diminishing marginal utility of income resulting from growth over time (although there was a distributional correction for the higher marginal utility of income to the poor). Such considerations would further push the correlation between GNP and welfare toward the negative. Also, GNP, MEW, and ISEW all begin with personal consumption. Since all three measures have in common their largest single category, there is a significant autocorrelation bias, which makes the poor correlations between GNP and the two welfare measures all the more impressive.

Measures of welfare are difficult and subject to many arbitrary judgments, so sweeping conclusions should be resisted. However, it seems fair to say that for the United States since 1947, the empirical evidence that GNP growth has increased welfare is weak, and since 1980 probably nonexistent. Consequently, any impact on welfare via policies that increase GNP growth would also be weak or nonexistent. In other words, the great benefit for which we are urged to sacrifice the environment, community standards, and industrial peace appears, on closer inspection, likely not even to exist.

Uneconomic Growth in Two Paradigms

Within the standard neoclassical paradigm, uneconomic growth sounds like an oxymoron, or at least an anomalous category. You will not find the concept in any macroeconomics textbook. But within the paradigm of ecological economics it is an obvious possibility. Let us consider why in each case.

Neoclassical Paradigm

The paradigm or preanalytic vision of standard neoclassical economics, as noted earlier and depicted in Figure 5.4, is that the economy is the total system, and that nature, to the extent that it is considered at all, is a sector of the economy—for example, the extractive sector (mines, wells, forests, fisheries, agriculture, including dumps). Nature is not seen as an envelope containing, provisioning, and sustaining the economy but as one sector of the economy similar to other sectors. If the products or services of the extractive sector should become scarce, the economy will "grow around" that particular scarcity by substituting the products of other sectors. If the substitution is difficult, new technologies, in this view, will be invented to make it easy.

The unimportance of nature is evidenced, in this view, by the falling relative prices of extractive products, generally, and by the declining share of the extractive sector in total GNP. Beyond the initial provision of indestructible building blocks, nature is simply not important to the economy in the view of neoclassical economics.

That the above is a fair description of the neoclassical paradigm is attested to by the elementary "principles of economics" textbooks, all of which present the shared preanalytic vision in their initial pages. This, of course, is the famous circular flow diagram, depicting the economy as consisting of a circular flow of exchange value between firms and households—as an isolated system in which nothing enters from outside nor exits to the outside. There is no "outside," no environment. The economic animal has neither mouth nor anus—only a closed-loop circular gut—the biological version of a perpetual motion machine! Further confirmation is found by searching the indexes of macroeconomics textbooks for any entries such as "environment," "nature," "depletion," or "pollution." The absence of such entries is nearly complete. As if to reaffirm the unimportance of nature, the advanced textbook chapters on growth theory are based on a neoclassical production function in which production is represented as a function of labor and capital only, with resources totally ignored!

A personal experience confirmed to me even more forcefully just how deeply ingrained this preanalytic vision really is. I think it is worth taking the time to recount this experience, which had to do with the evolution of the World Bank's 1992 *World Development Report, Development and the Environment* (WDR92) (World Bank 1992).

An early draft of the WDR92 had a diagram entitled "The relationship between the economy and the environment." It consisted of a square labeled "economy," with an arrow coming in labeled "inputs" and an arrow going out labeled "outputs"—nothing more. I worked in the Environment Department of the World Bank at that time and was asked to review and comment on the draft. I suggested that the picture was a good idea, but that it failed to show the environment, and that it would help to have a larger box containing the one depicted, and that the large box (or circle, perhaps) would represent the environment. Then the relation between the environment and the economy would be clear—specifically that the economy is a subsystem of the environment and depends on the environment both as a source of raw material inputs and as a sink for waste outputs. The text accompanying the diagram should explain that the environment physically contains and sustains the economy by regenerating the low-entropy inputs that it requires, and by absorbing the high-entropy wastes that it cannot avoid generating, as well as by supplying other systemic ecological services. Environmentally sustainable development could then be defined as development that does not destroy these natural support functions.

The second draft had the same diagram, but with an unlabeled box drawn around the economy, like a picture frame, with no change in the text. I commented that, while this was a step forward, the larger box really had to be labeled "environment" or else it was merely decorative, and that the text had to explain that the economy was related to the environment in the ways just described.

The third draft omitted the diagram altogether. There was no further effort to draw a picture of the relation of the economy and the environment. Why was it so hard to draw such a simple picture?

By coincidence a few months later the chief economist of the World Bank, under whom the WDR92 was being written, happened to be on a review panel at the Smithsonian Institution. In the book under review there was a diagram showing the relation of the economy to the ecosystem as subsystem to total system, identical to what I had suggested (and to Figures 5.1 and 5.2). In the question-and-answer time I asked the chief economist if, looking at that diagram, he felt that the issue of the physical size of the economic subsystem relative to the total ecosystem was important, and if he thought economists should be asking the question, "What is the optimal scale of the macro economy relative to the environment that supports it?" His reply was short and definite, "That's not the right way to look at it," he said.

Reflecting on these two experiences has strengthened my belief that the difference truly lies in our "preanalytic vision"—the way we look at it. My preanalytic vision of the economy as subsystem leads immediately to the questions: How big is the subsystem relative to the total system? How big can it be without disrupting the functioning of the total system? How big should it be, what is its optimal scale, beyond which further growth in scale would be uneconomic? The chief economist had no intention of being sucked into these subversive questions—that is not the right way to look at it, and any questions arising from that way of looking at it are simply not the right questions.

That attitude sounds rather unreasonable and peremptory, but in a way that had also been my response to the diagram in the first draft of *Development and the Environment* showing the economy receiving raw material inputs from nowhere and exporting waste outputs to nowhere. "That is not the right way to look at it," I said, and any questions arising from that picture, say, how to make the economy grow faster by speeding up throughput from an infinite source to an infinite sink, were not the right questions. Unless one has in mind the preanalytic vision of the economy as subsystem, the whole idea of sustainable development—of an economic subsystem being sustained by a larger ecosystem whose carrying capacity it must respect—makes no sense whatsoever. It was not surprising therefore that the WDR92 was incoherent on the subject of sustainable development, placing it in solitary confinement in a half-page box where it was implicitly defined as nothing other than "good development policy." It is the preanalytic vision of the economy as a box floating in infinite space that allows people to speak of "sustainable growth" (quantitative expansion) as opposed to "sustainable development" (qualitative improvement). The former term is self-contradictory to those who see the economy as a subsystem of a finite and nongrowing ecosystem. The difference could not be more fundamental, more elementary, or more irreconcilable.

Ecological Economics Paradigm

This story of course leads to a consideration of the alternative paradigm, that of ecological economics within which uneconomic growth is an obvious concept. The big difference is to see the economy as a subsystem of the natural ecosystem.

The neoclassical "evidence" for the unimportance of nature (falling relative price of many natural resources and small share of the extractive sector in GNP) is seen quite differently in the ecological economics paradigm. In an era of rapid extraction of resources, their short-run supply will of course be high and their market price consequently will be low. Low resources prices are not evidence of nonscarcity and unimportance but rather evidence of rapid drawdown and increasing technological dependence on a large throughput of cheap resources. As for the neoclassical claim that the small percentage of GNP arising from the extractive sector indicates its unimportance, one might as well claim that a building's foundation is unimportant because it represents only 5 percent of the height of the skyscraper erected above it. GNP is the sum of value added by labor and capital. But added to what? Resources are that to which value is added—the base or foundation on which the skyscraper of added value is resting. A foundation's importance does not diminish with the growth of the structure that it supports! Nevertheless, economists habitually argue the contrary. For example, some maintain that we need not worry about global warming because the only climate-sensitive sector of the economy is agriculture, and agriculture accounts for only 3 percent of GNP.

If GNP growth resulted only from increments in value added to a nongrowing resource throughput, then it would likely remain economic growth for much longer. Such a process of qualitative improvement without quantitative increase beyond environmental capacity is what I have elsewhere termed "development without growth," and suggested as a definition of "sustainable development" (Daly 1996). But that is not yet what happens in today's world. According to the World Resources Institute et al., per capita resource requirement increased, albeit slowly, over the period 1975–1993 in Germany, Japan, and The Netherlands (World Resources Institute et al. 1997). It also increased in the United States if one does not count reductions in erosion. Population growth in these countries is low, but not zero, giving a further boost to total throughput growth. Since current levels of resource use in these countries range from 45 to 85 thousand kilograms per person per year, a level already causing severe environmental degradation, it seems a bit premature to herald the advent of the "dematerialized economy."

What happens, according to ecological economics, is that the economy grows by transforming its environment (natural capital) into itself (human-made capital). The optimal extent of this physical transformation (optimal scale of the economy) occurs, as previously shown, when the marginal cost of natural capital reduction is equal to the marginal benefit of human-made capital increase. This process of transformation takes place within a total environment that is finite, nongrowing, and materially closed. There is a throughput of solar energy that powers biogeo-chemical cycles, but that energy throughput is also finite and nongrowing. As the economic subsystem grows it becomes a larger part of the total system, and there-fore must conform itself more to the limits of the total system—finitude, non-growth, and entropy. Its growth is ultimately limited by the size of the total system of which it is a part, even under neoclassical assumptions of easy substitution of human-made capital for natural capital.

But if human-made and natural capital are complements rather than substitutes, as ecological economics claims, then expansion of the economic subsystem would be much more stringently limited. There would be no point in expanding human-made capital beyond the capacity of remaining natural capital to complement it. The fish catch used to be limited by number of fishing boats (human-made capi-tal) but is now limited by the remaining populations of fish in the sea (natural cap-ital). What good are more fishing boats when the fish population has become the limiting factor?

When factors are complements, the one in short supply is limiting. If factors are substitutes, then there cannot be a limiting factor. Economic logic says that we should focus attention on the limiting factor by (1) in the short run maximizing its productivity, and (2) in the long run investing in its increase. This is a major impli-cation for economic policy—economize on and invest in natural capital. Economic logic stays the same, but the identity of the limiting factor has gradually changed from human-made capital to natural capital—for example, from fishing boats to remaining fish in the sea, from saw mills to remaining forests, from irrigation sys-tems to aquifers or rivers, from oil well drilling rigs to pools of petroleum in the ground, and from engines that burn fossil fuel to the atmosphere's capacity to absorb CO_2.

Viewed from the perspective of ecological economics, even the usual neoclassi-cal assumption of easy substitution of human-made capital for natural capital (and consequent neglect of limiting factor phenomena) provides no argument for growth—at least not when growth is viewed as the transformation of natural capi-tal into human-made capital. If human-made capital substitutes for natural capital, then natural capital substitutes for human-made capital. Substitution is reversible. If our original endowment of natural capital was a good substitute for human-made capital, then why, historically, did we go to the trouble of transforming so much natural capital into human-made capital? Neoclassical believers in easy substitution have no good answer. Nor do they have a very good answer to the question: How can you make more capital without using more resources? The problem does not arise for ecological economists because they affirm from the beginning that natural capital and human-made capital are basically complements and only marginally substitutes.

The smaller the optimal scale of the economy, the greater is (1) the degree of complementarity between natural capital and human-made capital, (2) our desire for direct experience of nature, and (3) our estimate of both the intrinsic and instrumental value of other species. The smaller the optimal scale of the economy, the sooner its physical growth becomes uneconomic.

From Permitting Growth, to Mandating Growth, to Limiting Growth

The neoclassical paradigm permits growth forever but does not mandate it. Historically, what pushed the growth-forever ideology was the answer given to the problems raised by Malthus, Marx, and Keynes. Growth was the common answer to all three problems. Overpopulation, unjust distribution, and involuntary unemployment would all be solved by growth. Overpopulation would be cured by the demographic transition initiated by growth. Unjust distribution of wealth between classes would be rendered tolerable by growth, the rising tide that lifts all boats. Unemployment would yield to increasing aggregate demand, which merely required that investment be stimulated, which of course implies growth. Continuing this time-honored tradition, the World Bank's WDR92 argued that more growth was also the automatic solution to the environmental problem. But of course the assumption in all cases was that growth was economic, that it was making us richer rather than poorer. But now growth is becoming uneconomic. Uneconomic growth will not sustain the demographic transition and cure overpopulation. Neither will it help redress unjust distribution, nor cure unemployment. Nor will it provide extra wealth to be devoted to environmental repair and clean-up. Indirect growth-based solutions to the big problems no longer work.

We now need more direct and radical solutions to the problems of Malthus, Marx, and Keynes: population control to deal with overpopulation; redistribution to deal with excessive inequality; and direct measures, such as ecological tax reform or auctioned depletion quotas, to raise resource productivity and employment. These must be national policies. It is utopian (or dystopian) to think of them being carried out by a world authority. Many nations have made progress in controlling their population growth, in limiting domestic income inequality, and in reducing unemployment. They have also improved resource productivity by internalizing environmental and social costs into prices. But nations' efforts in this regard are undercut by the ideology of globalization—a boundary-erasing last gasp attempt to reestablish the conditions of the empty-world economy by growing into the economic and ecological space of other countries and into the remaining global commons.

REFERENCES

Cobb, Clifford W., John B. Cobb, Jr., et al. 1994. *The Green National Product.* New York: University Press of America.

Daly, H. 1996. *Beyond Growth: The Economics of Sustainable Development.* Boston: Beacon Press.

Daly, H., and J. Cobb. 1989. *For the Common Good.* Boston: Beacon Press.

Nordhaus, William, and James Tobin. 1972. "Is Growth Obsolete?" In *Economic Growth,* National Bureau of Economic Research, New York: Columbia University Press.

Ruskin, John. 1860. "Unto This Last," republished in *Four Essays on the First Principles of Political Economy* (Lloyd J. Hubenka, ed.). Lincoln: University of Nebraska Press.

World Bank. 1992. *World Development Report, Development and the Environment.* New York: Oxford University Press.

World Resources Institute, et al. 1997. *Natural Resource Flows: The Material Basis of Industrial Economies.* Washington, DC: World Resources Institute.

Part II

Content

Chapter 6

Introduction to Renewable Energy Technologies

Stephen J. Strong

Policymakers have typically viewed renewable energy as a niche resource, at best. However, when taken in a historic context, and in light of progress over the past twenty years, many energy planners are now viewing it as a critical part of the integrated energy mix on which we must build our future.

Until the advent of cheap fossil fuels in the middle to late 1800s, people typically relied on, or took into account, natural lighting and solar thermal gain in the design and orientation of their homes and commercial buildings; they relied on hydropower, wind, biomass, human, or animal power for mechanical energy; and they relied on biomass, animal fat, or plant oils for cooking, heating, and light. The cave dwellings of the Anasazi in the American Southwest are a perfect example of designing with renewable and sustainable technologies in mind. They took maximum advantage of the limited winter sun for light and heat, and they built under substantial rock overhangs to keep out the summer sun. These are design principles that have been used for thousands of years by cultures around the world.

Now, with the growing awareness of the finite nature of fossil fuels, their unstable cost in many markets, and improvements in the technologies to take better advantage of renewables, the commercial resource base is gradually diversifying to again include renewables. In some cases, it is even being dominated by them. In all cases, though, common sense would dictate that energy efficiency be considered and incorporated before generating options are designed.

Hydropower

The renewable resource with the greatest global impact is hydropower, generating 24 percent of the world's electricity (see Figure 6.1). From the first hydroelectric power plant, built in Appleton, Wisconsin, in 1882, worldwide hydro today constitutes an installed capacity of 675,000 megawatts (MW), generating 2.3 trillion

Figure 6.1. The Hungry Horse Dam, in Montana, is part of the network of Bonneville Power Administration hydroelectric generating facilities. *Source:* Union of Concerned Scientists/U.S. Department of Energy.

kilowatt-hours (kWh) of inexpensive baseload electricity and supplying power for more than a billion people (National Renewable Energy Laboratory 1996). However, while hydropower will likely grow 50 percent in the next twenty-five years, its environmental impacts and the fact that most of the primary hydro sites are already utilized will hinder the installation of additional large-scale projects. A highly visible example is the Three Gorges Dam in China—a projected twenty-year project begun in 1994—which is designed with a generating capacity of 18,000 MW but which will submerge 60,700 ha (150,000 acres) and displace 1.3 million people. The real potential for growth lies in retrofitting the existing network of dams that are not currently fitted for hydroelectric generation. In the United States alone, there are more than 80,000 dams, with only 2,400 used for hydroelectric power.

Biomass

Biomass energy—stored in plants and organic matter (Figure 6.2)—provides thermal energy, liquid and gaseous fuels, and electricity around the world, ranking fourth as an energy source and providing 13 percent of the world's energy needs. In developing countries, biomass accounts for approximately 36 percent of the energy used, and it is the only available and affordable energy source for 2.5 billion residents in remote, rural areas (45 percent of the world's population) (Flavin and Senssen 1994).

Figure 6.2. Fast-growing trees—here poplar—as well as herbaceous crops like switch-grass may be produced exclusively for energy production.

Among its benefits, the use of biomass rather than fossil fuels reduces sulfur emissions and recycles carbon dioxide, while reducing the amount of waste sent to landfills. Obstacles to the growth of this technology include the relatively high cost of some of the products and the competition that organized biomass fuel sources might present for cropland and water.

At more than 10,000 MW (7,000 MW from forest products and agricultural residues; 2,500 MW from municipal solid waste; and 500 MW from other sources, such as landfill gas), biomass is the second largest renewable source of electrical generation in the United States, after hydropower. And, like hydropower, biomass resources can be used in baseload generation. More than 350 facilities produce electricity through the direct combustion of waste and by-products from wood and paper facilities as well as from waste gases. Biomass generators are drawing methane from diverse sources, taking advantage of a resource that is available and otherwise would, at best, go to waste or, at worst, enter the atmosphere as a greenhouse gas. While these generators are becoming more common in countries with significant agricultural resources and the appropriate demand, a common application in the United States is tapping into the methane generated in landfills.

In addition to electricity, biomass is used as a feed source for liquid fuels for transportation, including ethanol, methanol, biodiesel, and reformulated gasoline components. With many countries importing substantial quantities of oil (the United States imports more than half of its demand), and with vehicle emissions accounting for as much as 65 percent of urban air pollution, biofuels hold the promise of a secure, clean, domestic resource.

Geothermal

Geothermal energy, accessed by tapping into the earth's thermal resources, has provided people with residential and commercial heating, as well as medicinal relief, for thousands of years. There are five basic forms of geothermal energy, of which only two are commercial today: hydrothermal reservoirs and earth energy. The other three—geopressured brines, hot dry rock, and magma—will require advanced technologies before they are commercially viable. The two commercial technologies, though, provide an environmentally benign resource that is providing reliable electrical power around the world (7,000 MW world-wide, with an additional 2,000 MW expected by the year 2000, mostly in Asia), in addition to driving district heating systems and geothermal heat pumps in diverse communities.

Wind

Wind power has been used for centuries to pump water and grind grain; today, wind farms are springing up like wild flowers in areas with good wind profiles, generating electricity at US$0.05 to US$0.10 per kilowatt-hour—commensurate with traditional grid power. Many utilities are now offering their customers green power, allowing them to purchase part or all of their power from renewable sources—mostly wind farms—while paying a small premium for the privilege.

The market for wind power is generally viewed in two distinct groups: small-scale distributed systems and utility-scale systems. Both have the advantages of being environmentally benign, requiring little or no scheduled maintenance, and allowing for a dual use of the land at the generation site. Less positive aspects include the fact that wind is an intermittent resource (a 30–50 percent capacity factor) and that generators are visually unappealing to some.

The small-scale systems typically range in size from 0.25–20 kW and are most cost-effective in off-grid or facility-specific applications. At an installed cost of US$2,500–8,000 per kilowatt of installed capacity, these systems generate power in the cost range of US$0.12 to US$0.70 per kilowatt-hour. These systems are used cost-effectively for remote residential power, pumping water, and remote cathodic protection, though the noise level is sometimes a concern in residential systems.

For utility-scale systems—often 100–1,000 machines clustered in an area with a substantial wind resource—the wind turbines typically range from 100 kW to 500 kW each, though individual machines can range to a megawatt or more. The world's installed capacity is dominated by the United States, with more than 1,700 MW (90 percent installed at Altamont Pass, Tehachapi, and Palm Springs), followed by Europe with more than 1,000 MW installed (see Figure 6.3). The world capacity, though, is growing rapidly, with between 4,000 MW and 10,000 MW of

Figure 6.3. Field of wind turbines at Tehachapi Pass, California. *Source:* Union of Concerned Scientists.

new capacity either planned or currently under construction. Of concern in the development of utility-scale systems, though, beyond those issues mentioned above, are the impact on avian mortality and the fact that these systems are substantially distant from their point of use, requiring transmission and distribution systems like those of conventional central station generators.

Solar Thermal

The United States alone uses more than 71 trillion Btus of solar energy (equivalent to 2,900,000 metric tons [6.39 billion pounds] of coal, or 2.4 billion liters [568 million gallons] of gasoline) divided among the residential, commercial, industrial, and utility sectors (National Renewable Energy Laboratory 1996).

Solar thermal energy is used in several ways, including passive heating of buildings, heating of domestic and commercial process water supplies, and generating electricity. In addition, solar energy is used to condition buildings through the use of daylighting and passive cooling through the appropriate use of convection and local wind resources. Among their benefits, solar thermal technologies in the built environment can be designed into structures, displacing conventional envelope materials; they present no negative environmental impacts or emissions; and they use a free and renewable source of fuel. Impediments to market penetration have included their high up-front costs, the lack of a maintenance infrastructure, and the fact that early systems presented aesthetic concerns to designers and users alike.

In one of its largest and most distributed incarnations, more than 1 million solar hot water systems have been installed in the United States for use in homes, commercial businesses and offices, factories, and swimming pools, with life-cycle costs as much as 80 percent lower than conventional water-heating methods.

Solar thermal power systems have been around for more than 100 years, first providing mechanical work to pump water and, more recently, using similar processes (dish, parabolic, and central receiver systems) to generate electricity. In these technologies, sunlight is reflected and concentrated onto a receiver, which converts the light into heat. This heat is used to convert a working fluid to steam, which powers a generator or engine, thus generating electricity. Current research includes both small-scale (7-kW to 25-kW dish systems) and large-scale (10–80 MW parabolic and central receiver systems). These technologies are used today to provide more than 390 MW of electrical capacity (354 MW in the United States), with projections of a 130 percent increase by the year 2000.

The small-scale dish systems use a parabolic array of mirrors (stretched membrane or flat mirror) to focus and concentrate light onto a receiver located at the focal point (see Figure 6.4). The systems with the most current activity are

Figure 6.4. Dish Stirling solar thermal-to-electric concentrator systems. *Source:* Science Applications International Corp.

designed with a Stirling engine at the focus, generating 7 kW to 25 kW of electricity per unit. The units can be used individually or linked together to create a larger generating field.

Of the larger system technologies, the one with a commercial presence is the parabolic trough (see Figure 6.5). This technology uses parabolic mirrors to focus sunlight on a tube that runs the length of the trough, carrying the working fluid. The majority of the world's installed capacity (354 MW) was constructed by Luz International in Southern California, in a series of systems ranging from 14 MW to 80 MW. As they are designed, they are hybridized up to 25 percent with natural gas to provide a dispatchable power source.

The final large technology is known as a power tower, which is currently under research evaluation at the 10-MW Solar Two facility in Barstow, California (see Figure 6.6). In this technology, a large, near-circular array of heliostats (tracking mirrors) focuses light onto a central receiver on the top of a central tower. The first version of this facility, Solar One, used water/steam as the working fluid in the central receiver. Solar Two is a retrofit of this facility, demonstrating a molten salt receiver and thermal storage system. This new technology gives the power tower a dispatchable power capacity at load factors of up to 65 percent. The Solar Two research phase began in 1996, with a plan to run for three years. Based on the results of this work, the potential exists for commercial systems in the range of 30 MW to 200 MW.

Figure 6.5. One of the nine Luz solar electric generating systems (SEGS), all of which sell power to Southern California Edison. *Source:* Union of Concerned Scientists.

Figure 6.6. A power tower central receiver solar thermal-to-electricity concentrator system. Pictured is Solar One, the predecessor to the currently operating Solar Two, in Barstow, California. *Source:* Solar Energy Industries Association.

Photovoltaics

Photovoltaics (PV) is the newest of the commercial renewable technologies, and it is poised to make a significant contribution to the world energy market. While it has been the dominant power resource for spacecraft, remote telecommunications systems, and many cathodic protection systems for decades, it has had little direct impact on people's personal power needs until recently. Today, PV supplies basic electricity to hundreds of thousands of people in scores of countries around the world—mostly in developing economies—with more than 700 MW of power modules installed worldwide. The available technologies include flat-plate (divided among crystalline and thin-film) and concentrator systems. The general applications categories include consumer products (watches, calculators, etc.); remote, stand-alone (telecommunications, monitoring, lighting, residential); grid-tied (residential and commercial); and, grid-support (central station flat-plate and concentrator).

Now, after several early efforts, PV is making inroads in the grid-serviced markets of the developed economies. In addition to several existing and proposed central-station power systems, designers are now incorporating PV into the exterior skin of buildings, taking advantage of the existing surface area, and reducing the installed cost of the PV systems by the cost of the glass or other building materials they replace. This is a potentially massive market and one in which the demand matches the power production curve very well, as commercial buildings typically have the highest loads at the time of day when PV is producing the most power.

Photovoltaics in the Built Environment

The last two decades have brought significant changes to the building design profession. Economic, environmental, and aesthetic pressures have converged to point up the critical role design professionals play in the development of the physical infrastructure and its ultimate impacts on the global environment, national security, local health and safety, and the corporate bottom line. By designing buildings to minimize waste and generate power rather than just consume it, architects are moving beyond the goal of simply creating buildings that are aesthetically pleasing, toward an ethic of environmentally and socially responsible design (see Figure 6.7). These buildings, rather than merely using less conventional fuel and creating less pollution, will rely on renewable resources to produce some and, ultimately, all of their own energy without creating any pollution. And, the primary technology for this capability will be PV.

There are several factors driving the integration of PV with commercial buildings. One is the available surface area of the buildings with the proper orientation, much of which could receive PV materials, either in new construction or in retrofit. Another factor is the coincidence of the building power loads with the peak production of PV. Another is financial, in that part of the cost of the PV module components will be offset by the cost of the materials they replace, whether roofing materials, facade materials, or shading elements. Commercial building developers and owners often consider the value of an architectural element as much as

Figure 6.7. The Georgetown Intercultural Center.

its cost—otherwise, why would a building be finished in granite or marble? And, initial experience shows that building-integrated PV (BIPV) provides an image that appeals to potential tenants, providing a marketing advantage in leasing the building space.

Photovoltaic Technologies

Ultimately, modular PV systems can be expanded over time without losing the investment in earlier installations, and they can be physically distributed over a wide geographical area and fielded on both new and existing structures, minimizing their installation impact and cost of land and power transmission and distribution systems.

Photovoltaic technologies used in building-envelope applications include both crystalline and thin-film technologies. Crystalline PV has the advantage of higher conversion efficiencies of light energy to electricity, with the drawback that it is rigid and not always architecturally appropriate. Thin-film PV has advantages such as deposition on a variety of materials, including flexible or unusually shaped materials, and selective deposition that allows varied transmission of light—looking much like architecturally tinted glazings—making it an ideal replacement for conventional building glazings. A drawback of thin-film PV, particularly amorphous silicon, is that its conversion efficiencies are much lower than those of crystalline PV materials. However, in building-integrated systems, where the PV materials are replacing conventional materials on a large structure, establishing a credit against the cost of the PV system equal to the cost of the conventional materials displaced, this may not necessarily be a disadvantage.

Another technical iteration of PV involves harvesting the associated thermal resource, along with the electric component, in hybrid PV/thermal systems. Because PV systems—particularly crystalline silicon-based systems—operate more efficiently when cooled, it is important to design systems that ventilate the modules to minimize heat buildup. As design professionals have worked with this issue, it has become increasingly obvious that what was previously considered "waste heat" could be captured for use on site, increasing the overall system energy conversion efficiency. In an effort to capitalize on the efficient use of this otherwise wasted system asset, significant research is underway to characterize the various components of the thermal portion of the hybrid systems and the impacts of external factors (wind, illumination, thermal gradients).

As for BIPV technologies, companies in the United States, Japan, and Europe are actively pursuing module designs that lend themselves to easy installation and provide an aesthetically pleasing substitute for traditional building materials. These can vary from single-crystal modules, with opaque backings, to semi-transparent thin-film-on-glass modules, with a range of alternatives in between, with sizes ranging up to 2 square meters. Or, they might be designed into shingle or tile elements. The Japanese company Sanyo, the German companies Pilkington and Laumans, and the Swiss companies Alpha Real and the Atlantis Group are marketing roofing tiles. Sanyo and the U.S. company USSC have developed amorphous silicon thin-film roofing shingle modules, and USSC has developed a standing-seam metal roof–based module.

History of Photovoltaics

Following on the heels of the major energy cost and supply disruptions of the 1970s, designers, engineers, and policymakers began looking seriously at renewable energy and conservation as solutions to problems of cost and security. These same concerns helped to mobilize the general public. Then, as conventional energy supplies stabilized and prices dropped, public and political support to pursue these solutions waned, and the anticipated market penetration for these technologies slowed. However, in the late 1980s and early 1990s, public and political concerns over pollution and global climate change produced a renewed interest in these technologies. Groups associated with utility power production and commercial and residential building energy use took particular interest.

Early projects integrating PV into residential and commercial buildings involved mostly government-financed or supported opportunities to field test and demonstrate the technology. In the United States, projects included the Carlisle House (7.5 peak kilowatts, or kWp), the Georgetown University Intercultural Center (337 kWp), and three regional Residential Experimental Stations, which served as test beds for numerous technologies and innovative designs. On a more ambitious scale, electric utilities have followed with several projects, such as the 100 kW of distributed PV systems on existing homes and commercial buildings in Gardner, Massachusetts (1985; see Figure 6.8), the Sacramento Municipal Utility Dis-

Figure 6.8. A PV neighborhood in Gardner, Massachusetts. *Source:* New England Electric/Solar Design Associates.

trict's (SMUD's) "Solar Pioneers" program, and the projects of other utilities, including Delmarva Power and Light, the New York Power Authority, Southern California Edison, and the city of Austin (Texas) municipal electric utility. In a broader effort, the electric utility industry, in September 1992, created the Utility PhotoVoltaic Group (UPVG), with support from the U.S. Department of Energy (DOE), to provide a common forum for utilities active or interested in PV to support commercial and demonstration projects and to educate the utility industry and other audiences. Today, the UPVG has eighty-eight members representing seven nations.

Residential Solar Electric Buildings

The first solar electric building market envisioned for PV was on residential roof tops. In the United States in the 1970s, there was a rush to install solar domestic hot water systems, encouraged by tax credits, and many assumed that the PV market would follow suit. In the late 1970s and early 1980s, much research and commercial development effort focused on this market. The DOE sponsored the development of three regional Residential Experimental Stations—in Massachusetts, New Mexico, and Florida—to test prototype systems in varied climates. Based on results from these research stations, DOE and the Massachusetts Institute of Technology (MIT) commissioned Solar Design Associates to design the first utility-interactive, building-integrated, PV-powered residence—the Carlisle House. However, in the early 1980s, government and corporate support for this market waned with the loss of the tax credits. Interest has only recently reemerged in the United States, as designers and architects, often supported by forward-thinking utilities or philosophically inclined private clients, have begun to take advantage of advances in technology. Examples of systems of this type include the PV Pioneer program, in Sacramento, California, and the Lord residence, on the coast of Maine (see Figure 6.9). Another indication of support from conventional quarters is the townhome demonstration project by the National Association of Home Builders (NAHB), where the PV system replaced a conventional metal roofing system (see Figure 6.10).

The Critical Nature of Utility Connections and Metering Options

Besides the technology itself, other areas of importance to the commercialization of distributed PV systems include the work with utilities and federal authorities to establish uniform utility interconnection standards and "net metering" policies. Net metering is a system in which the utility credits a user, on a one-to-one cost basis, for the power produced versus the power consumed. Any power produced in excess of the amount consumed is typically repurchased by the utility at the lower "avoided cost" rate, while any power consumed beyond the level of the

Figure 6.9. A SMUD "PV Pioneer" home in Sacramento, California. *Source:* Sacramento Municipal Utility District.

Figure 6.10. PV standing-seam roof on an NAHB test home. *Source:* United Solar Systems Corp.

power produced is sold to the customer at the utility's standard rate. This system is a win-win proposition, with the utility offsetting its peak loads with customer-supplied power, while the PV system owner benefits by using the utility as a backup, avoiding the cost of a battery storage system. Currently, Japan, Switzerland, and more than fifteen states in the United States mandate net metering. Equally important is the need for national uniform interconnection standards. In countries without a national utility (Switzerland, alone, has more than 1,000 individual utility companies), the requirement of commercial designers and vendors to meet the connection requirements of many different utilities could provide a strong disincentive to the successful market penetration of BIPV.

International Focus

In 1990, a working group was created within the International Energy Agency (IEA) to assess, research, and encourage international PV activities. This group, termed "Task XVI: Photovoltaics in Buildings," involved experts from some fifteen nations. The group worked to assess techniques for maximizing the benefits of PV in buildings and optimizing the economics of these systems. Task XVI work includes information on residential and commercial buildings, including both grid-connected and stand-alone systems. The results of this work are evident in many of the examples discussed here.

Having completed its charter in 1996, the Task XVI efforts were documented in the book *Photovoltaics in Buildings: A Design Handbook for Architects and Engineers,* published by James & James (London) for the IEA. The technology and its applications continue to evolve, though, and work on solar electric buildings continues in the IEA under Task VII—PV in the Built Environment—in effect since January 1997. The goals of Task VII are to enhance the architectural quality, the technical quality, and the economic viability of PV systems in the built environment and to assess and remove nontechnical barriers for their introduction as a significant energy option (Schoen et al. 1997).

Architects and engineers in Europe and Japan have, with the convergence of strong public interest and significant government support, become very creative in the integration of PV elements into commercial building facades. Other building applications include using PV as sun shades, skylights, semi-transparent windows, spandrel glass, and sloped glazings or roofing materials. Each element can use either single-crystal or thin-film PV, depending on the needs of the architect and the client. More recently, architects in the United States have begun to field some exceptional examples of BIPV systems.

Photovoltaics in the Built Environment: World Overview

The following sections review the progress of implementing photovoltaics into the built environment in countries throughout the world.

United States

In the United States, in 1992, DOE launched a five-year cost-shared program, called "Building Opportunities in the U.S. for Photovoltaics (PV:Bonus One)," to encourage the development of building-integrated PV systems. Under PV:Bonus One, Solarex, of Frederick, Maryland, developed a line of building-integrated components for commercial building facades and sloped glazing applications in conjunction with architectural curtain wall giant Kawneer of Atlanta. Other projects under subcontracts of PV:Bonus One include the work of ECD on the USSC roofing shingles and standing-seam roofs; the work of Fully Independent Residential Solar Technologies, Inc. (FIRST) to develop factory-built homes with PV modules integrated into the roofs; a project by Delmarva Power and Light Company, of Wilmington, Delaware, to develop PV/battery systems to study dispatchable peak-shaving on the utility grid; and the effort of the American Institute of Architects and the Associated Collegiate Schools of Architecture Research Corporation to develop a course for architecture schools on incorporating PV into building designs.

On April 2, 1997, following PV:Bonus One, DOE issued Phase 1 of the three-phase, five-year PV:Bonus Two to develop technologies and foster business arrangements that integrate PV or hybrid products into buildings in a cost-effective way. Under Phase 1, some 17 companies received awards for Concept Development and Business Planning. Successful bidders under Phase 2, a 50/50 cost-share, will proceed with product and business development. And in Phase 3 the companies will focus on product demonstration and marketing. The goal of this project is the expansion and improvement of building-integrated PV products.

To support and encourage the development of PV, the U.S. government, on June 26, 1997, announced the Million Solar Roofs Initiative, with a goal of 1 million solar energy systems on buildings by the year 2010. This project is designed to accelerate the commercialization of PV and solar hot water technologies. At the federal level, the program will organize and streamline available federal financial and technical support and improve the delivery of services and support to communities and individual purchasers (Rannels 1997). This initiative has already encouraged several states and utilities to commit to substantial PV installation programs. Just as he did when directing the work of SMUD, S. David Freeman has committed his current organization, the Los Angeles Department of Water and Power, to 100,000 solar roof systems by the year 2010. This builds on the success of the pioneering systems already installed. The following examples include a broad cross section of technologies, applications types, and geographic locations.

- The SMUD PV program has installed more than 5.7 MW of PV through early 1998, including more than 400 residential rooftop systems, 20 commercial and church rooftop systems, and a utility substation. Its plan is to obtain at least half of its energy from energy-efficiency measures and renewables by the end of the decade. The near-term plan is to add an additional 10 MW between 1998 and 2002. SMUD's residential PV Pioneers receive SMUD-installed and owned PV systems on their roofs and pay a monthly premium for participating in the program. There is a long waiting list of customers who wish to participate in the SMUD program, even though they receive no direct benefit from the electricity generated, because the connection is made on the utility side of the meter.

• The systems at the 1996 Olympic Natatorium, on the campus of the Georgia Institute of Technology in Atlanta, include a 340-kWp roof-top Solarex array on the main structure and a 4.3-kWp custom-arched semi-transparent PV canopy of Solarex modules designed for the entrance to the complex (see Figure 6.11).

• The grid-tied 15-kWp building-integrated sunshade system and 5-kWp system designed as a landscape element at the Center for Environmental Sciences and Technology Management at the State University of New York at Albany uses custom Solarex alternating current modules (see Figure 6.12).

• The retrofit, roof-integrated 22.4-kWp PowerLight PV system for the library

Figure 6.11. The 340-kW roof-top system on the 1996 Olympic Natatorium, *Source:* Solar Design Associates.

Figure 6.12. AC PV module sun shades on the State University of New York at Albany. *Source:* Solar Design Associates.

and community center for the village of Tuckahoe, New York, was developed in partnership with the New York Power Authority. They installed a 167-square-meter system that functions as both a roof paver and a solar electric power plant (see Figure 6.13).

- A 1.5-kWp stand-alone USSC amorphous silicon roofing shingle system was installed at the University of Denver's Astronomical Observatory on Mt. Evans, Colorado, at 4,305 m (14,125 ft) (see Figure 6.14).
- A 10-kWp grid-tied USSC amorphous silicon, standing-seam metal roof system has been designed as a shading roof structure for a parking facility.
- The New York Department of Sanitation's 40-kWp roof-integrated PV system on its recycling center on Rikers Island, near LaGuardia Airport, incorporates 216 translucent Atlantis Energy PV modules, each rated at 0.186-kWp, to dis-

Figure 6.13. Tuckahoe Library.

Figure 6.14. Mt. Evans PV roofing shingles.

place the building's conventional metal sheet roofing to provide clean electricity and daylighting to the work area below.
- There is a 1.25-kWp Atlantis Energy crystalline silicon skylight glazing system on the Thoreau Center at the Presidio National Park in San Francisco.
- Grid-tied, large-area, amorphous silicon awning, skylight, and facade systems, totaling 8.4 kWp, were integrated into the Advanced Photovoltaic Systems facility (now the BP Solar facility) in Fairfield, California.

Canada

Interest in PV has increased in Canada, even though conventional energy resources are plentiful and inexpensive, and the northern climate leads one to believe that PV would not be an obvious choice for most applications. Activities within the Canadian R&D program focus on improved system design and performance modeling. Projects include software development for system optimization and simulation, including modeling of battery storage characteristics. More than a dozen PV systems are being monitored, codes and standards for PV systems are being developed, and PV-powered buildings are being fielded. Some Canadian examples include:
- The 30-kWp PV array atop the Canadian Department of Energy, Mines and Resources (CANMET) research laboratory, near Montreal. This system works as a building peak shaver, while providing PV power to support research efforts in power conditioning development and system simulation modeling.
- The 75-kWp roof-top PV system at the McMillian Rehabilitation Center, developed by Ontario Hydro, in collaboration with the Canadian Energy Diversification Research Laboratory (EDRL), and fielded as a demand-side-management measure to help shave the hospital's summer air conditioning peak.
- The 13.4-kWp PowerLight building-integrated PowerGuard roofing system on the EPCOR corporate headquarters in Edmonton, Alberta.
- The Innova House, which, with its 2.7-kWp system, was the first grid-connected residence in Canada and was chosen as Canada's low-energy demonstration house for the IEA Task XVI.

European Highlights

In Europe, a program called THERMIE began in January 1995 and is scheduled to end in December 1998. The program was instituted to promote greater use of European PV technologies and increase the competitive nature of the European PV industry in international markets. It supports the application of these energy technologies and provides for the enhanced dissemination of information to encourage their wider use. In concert with this, the JOULE program was developed to deal with research and development in the field of innovative energy technologies.

Throughout Europe, governments support the installation of residential PV systems, and the European Community has considered proposing a European 500,000-roofs program and a total installed capacity of 1,300 MW by 2010. This proposal is largely based on the success of the installation programs that started in the early 1990s. In Germany, the government implemented its "1,000 Roofs" program, subsidizing 70 percent of the cost of residential PV systems of between 1 and 5 kWp. The program, begun in 1990, expanded to a final count of more than 2,000 installations, totaling approximately 5.3 MW. Even before Germany instituted the 1,000 Roofs program, Switzerland developed a privately funded program that resulted in 333 installations with 3-kWp grid-connected PV systems, using private, long-term financing with low interest rates and volume purchases. The Dutch government plans to field 250 MWp of PV by the year 2010, including an initial 1,000 homes by the year 2000. In Austria, the government modeled a plan after the German 1,000 Roofs program with the goal of subsidizing the installation of 200 kWp of PV. This program is nearly completed and discussions are now under way to expand it by an additional 100 kWp. In Finland, more than 20,000 vacation homes are currently powered by PV, and estimates indicate that there are approximately 200,000 vacation homes that are ideal candidates for using PV. Nearby, Sweden has more than 20,000 vacation homes powered by PV with more than 5,000 new installations each year, while Norway has more than 50,000 vacation homes powered by PV with more than 8,000 new installations annually.

European participants in the IEA's Task VII—PV in the Built Environment— include Austria, Belgium, Denmark, Finland, Great Britain, Italy, The Netherlands, Norway, Spain, Sweden, and Switzerland. The following examples of systems in these and other European countries show the commitment and creative approach that the European Community countries have taken in integrating PV into their physical infrastructure.

AUSTRIA. Interest in distributed PV applications has increased in recent years in Austria, along with the rest of Europe. The Austrian government has announced a comprehensive plan to reduce CO_2 emissions, and PV is seen as an important part of this effort. Examples of PV projects include:

- The 40-kWp utility-intertied sound barrier system along the A1 motorway (see Figure 6.15).
- The 3-kWp low-energy house completed in 1993, near Vienna. This system was installed with approximately one-half the capacity mounted on the roof and the remainder integrated into the south-facing facade. The house also incorporates solar thermal collectors for domestic water heating.
- The 13-kWp PV facade-integrated system on an office building in Innsbruck.

Figure 6.15. Austrian roadway sound barrier.

BELGIUM.

• The first grid-tied, roof-integrated system in Belgium, a 2.3-kW residential roof-tile replacement system in Flanders.
• A 2.3-kW grid-tied residential system in Flanders using semi-transparent AC modules in two subsystems: a shading system and a roof array.
• A 10-kWp system on the Kelag office building in Klagenfurt.

DENMARK. A 100-kWp system was integrated into a five-story apartment building during renovation of the Solgaarden building in Kolding. The system is divided into two subsystems, consisting of an 89.5-kW roof system and a 16.5-kWp system integrated into the glazing of the building's south-facing balconies.

FINLAND. Finland's 1993–1998 national energy research program, NEMO2, was set up for the evaluation, development, and promotion of new and renewable forms of energy. The main emphasis of the program is on wind and solar energy. The research program also promotes the construction of demonstration plants. A primary aim of solar energy studies is to develop cheaper and more efficient photovoltaic systems and their constituent parts and also to foster the development of local industry to manufacture solar cells.

Examples of BIPV development efforts in Finland include:

• The 30-kWp Pietarsaari Solar House pilot plant built in 1989 by Imatran Voima Oy, the national utility of Finland.
• A 2.3-kWp PV house built in 1994.
• Several demonstration facades.

GERMANY. Germany's strong commitment to distributed PV systems for buildings has spurred considerable activity in the development of PV modules, specifically for building-integrated applications. A sampling of the variety of systems includes:

- The 53.4-kWp building-integrated PV facade and sunshades on the headquarters of the Bavarian Environmental Ministry building installed in 1993.
- The 1-MW cantilevered roof system divided as subsystems among six halls of the Munich Trade Fair Centre installed in July and August 1997.
- The 1-MW of Pilkington Optisol modules at the Academy, in Herne, near Essen.
- The Expo2000 Region systems: a 77.7-kW facade on the ADAC (auto club) building in Laatzen; a 73-kW railway station roof-integrated system in Uelzen; and a 10-kW system on a boat station and kiosk on an artificial island.
- Three 10-kW PV sound barriers, from the PV Sound Barrier Competition, inaugurated June 13, 1997, along the A96 motorway in Bavaria. (One uses module-integrated inverters.)
- The 435-kWp system of ASE 300 modules, designed in five subarrays (four fixed, one tracking), on the Mercedes Benz factory in Bad Cannstatt, Stuttgart.
- The 3.76-kW BIPV facade in the Future House of the Saarbrücken Stadtwerke AG.

GREAT BRITAIN. The British government has funded a comprehensive evaluation of the potential of building integrated PV systems in the United Kingdom. The study, conducted by Professor Robert Hill and his colleagues at the Newcastle PV Applications Centre, was initially only to include the south-facing facades, but it was expanded to include all building surfaces regardless of orientation. The study concluded that there were 111 gigawatts (GW) of potential generating capacity available from distributed PV systems on buildings.

Recently, Greenpeace challenged the British government to support the development of 50,000 PV homes by 2010. In a project that is currently active, the Scolar Programme will install PV systems on 100 schools and colleges between 1997 and 2000. Examples of this activity include:

- In 1997, Greenpeace and the Peabody Trust installed 1.1-kWp PV systems on three houses in West Silvertown.
- The 39.5-kWp BIPV facade retrofit on The Northumberland Building, in Newcastle upon Tyne, operating since January 1995 (see Figure 6.16).
- A 96.2-kWp system (26 skylights @ 3.7 kWp each) on the Ford Motor Company plant in Bridgend, South Wales.
- A 70-kWp system on The Solar Office, Oxford International Business Park, in Sunderland, installed in April 1998.

GREECE. In June 1997, the Greek government announced its decision to begin the construction of the world's largest solar PV system on the island of Crete. The solar power station is part of a two-year campaign by Greenpeace to transform

Figure 6.16. Northumberland Building, U.K., window shades.

Crete into a solar-powered island. The announcement included the funding for the first 5 MW of a proposed 50-MW system on Crete with the U.S. company Enron Solar. Enron Solar's plan proposes building 9 MW a year subsequently to reach 50 MW by 2003, providing electricity for nearly 100,000 people—an eighth of Crete's population.

While Greece has fielded many remote, stand-alone PV systems in the past, it now has examples of several grid-tied systems.

- The 4.6-kWp roof-mounted system on a BP gas station, installed in October 1997.
- A 60-kWp system on the island of Sifnos.
- A 4.5-kWp system on the 5th High School, in Nikea, Athens.

ITALY. Italy's federal funding for PV has increased significantly in the 1990s, and interest in building-integrated PV applications is rising as a result of growing environmental concerns and the dependence of Italy on foreign oil. The most recently proposed national program is a five-year effort to install 10,000 roof-top systems, with a final capacity of 50 MW, between 1998 and 2002.

Currently, the Italian PV program has a number of building-integrated PV demonstrations, including:

- The 30-kW integrated PV roof for the Eurosolare factory of Nettuno near Rome, which combines PV with daylighting.

- The retrofitted 21-kWp large-area amorphous silicon PV facade system on a building of the Joint Research Facility of the EC, in Ispra.
- A 20-kW terrace at the German School of Rome.
- A 4-kW shading structure at the ENEL headquarters in Rome.
- A series of ten systems installed in 1995, with cost-sharing from the THERMIE Project. These include ENEL offices, training and information centers, and parking structures.
- Parking structure–integrated systems that include the 100-kWp parking structure system at the ENEA Casaccia research facility; an 85-kWp parking structure system in Leponori, Rome; a 94-kWp parking structure system in Reggio Emilia; and a 24-kWp parking structure system in Palermo, Sicily.

THE NETHERLANDS. The Dutch coordinated the first worldwide design competition on PV in buildings, sponsored by the IEA Task XVI and NOVEM. The competition was open to A&E professionals as well as students. One hundred entries from around the world were received, and awards were presented at the twelfth EC PV conference in Amsterdam in April 1994. A book of the most creative designs has been published and is available from NOVEM.

The Netherlands PV Programme (NOZ-PV) has a budget of 8.5 million ECU, growing to 15 million ECU from 1997–2000, with a goal of 10 MWp in 2000, 100 MWp in 2007, 250 MWp in 2010, and 1400 MWp in 2020. The program started in 1995 with a goal of 3,000 PV houses (2.5 kW average) by 2000, growing to 100,000 in 2010 and 500,000 in 2020.

Hundreds of PV systems have been integrated into the house boats that line the canals in and around Amsterdam, as well as the cargo barges. In the interest of further integrating PV solutions that utilize existing aperture area and available structural elements, the Dutch have also developed PV for highway sound barriers. Examples of BIPV systems activity include:

- Residential developments, including a ten-unit multifamily housing development in Heerhugowaard, a town 50 km north of Amsterdam, where a roof-integrated 25-kWp utility-interactive PV system was installed as a demonstration of building-integrated PV applications (see Figure 6.17); a 250-kWp system divided among seventy-one roofs and facades on homes and on an apartment building in Amsterdam.
- PV integrated into sound barriers, including an 80-kWp system installed in 1994; and a 52-kWp system, operating since spring 1995; twenty-two residential systems, integrated as shading elements, with 1 kW on each unit; and a 1-MW development, planned for installation in 1998, distributed among 501 residences in Amersfoort.
- A 7.96-kWp roof-integrated system on the National Environmental Education Centre De Kleine Aarde, in Boxtel, installed in September 1995.

Figure 6.17. Residential systems in The Netherlands.

NORWAY. Norway has long had a strong market for small distributed residential PV systems with the large number of vacation cottages located off the power grid. There are presently more than 60,000 PV-powered vacation homes in Norway with more than 8,000 new installations completed every year. As a result, Norway has increased its program involvement in this area and participates in the IEA PV in Buildings Tasks. The Norwegian Institute of Technology and SINTEF are representing Norway. An example of the distributed PV systems includes a 2.2-kWp roof-integrated, utility-interactive PV system on a demonstration low-energy row house with three apartments, in Hamar, built to provide housing for foreign journalists at the 1994 Winter Olympics.

SPAIN. While the potential market for remote PV applications in isolated areas of Spain is considered the most significant in the European Community, the country maintains a strong interest in grid-tied systems. For example,

• The Spanish Task XVI demonstration house, which is a four-plex incorporating four roof-integrated, utility-interactive PV arrays of 2.2 kWp each.
• The Toledo 1-MW ground-mounted system, operating since June 1994.
• The 53-kWp semi-transparent Mataró Public Library systems, operating since March 1996. These PV/thermal library systems are integrated into the facade and skylights (see Figure 6.18).
• A 54-kW integrated roof for a games court at the Nuevo Horizonte Assn. school in Las Rozas (Madrid).

Figure 6.18. View through the facade wall of the Mataró Library, Spain.

- A 68-kWp grid-tied PV system at the Jaén University campus as the first phase of a three-phase, 200-kWp system.

SWEDEN. In Sweden, as in Norway and Finland, PV is often employed to power remote vacation cottages. There are now more than 30,000 PV-powered cottages in Sweden, with the market increasing at more than 5,000 new installations every year. In addition, several hundred lighthouses along remote stretches of the Swedish coast are now powered with PV.

Sweden's activity in distributed PV has increased along with that of other European countries. Present program activities include both stand-alone and grid-connected distributed PV systems. Photovoltaics-related work includes the development and testing of DC–AC inverters and battery charge-control regulators. Examples of Swedish PV systems include:

- A 3.5-kWp grid-connected demonstration system that was completed in 1990 on a single residence in Linkoping, approximately 200 km south of Stockholm.
- A 10-kWp utility-interactive PV system that was installed on an existing apartment building in downtown Stockholm in 1993 by the Swedish utility, Stockholm Energi AB. This is Sweden's IEA Task 16 demonstration building.

SWITZERLAND. The immediate future for building-integrated PV in Switzerland looks very promising. With generous government incentives to underwrite the cost of introducing a new technology, Swiss architects and engineers have responded with very innovative concepts in the design of building-integrated PV. In 1997, the Swiss government began support of every on- and off-grid PV installation of 1 to 100 kWp, with approximately US$2,000/kW per system. The subsidy is about 25 percent of the on-grid market price. In addition, the Swiss government has considered a special tax to fund the further installation of building-integrated systems. Through 1996, Switzerland had installed more than 8.2 MW of PV. The following are examples of this activity:

- Twenty-six vocational colleges with PV systems totaling more than 200 kW.
- The SOFREL project installed 200 kWp of flat-roof-mounted systems through 1997.
- Three 10-kW PV sound barriers, from the PV Sound Barrier Competition, inaugurated late summer 1997.

JAPAN. In Japan, the Ministry of International Trade and Industry (MITI) began a seven-year program in the fall of 1993 to subsidize the price (up to 2.7 million yen [approximately US$27,000] in the first three years, dropping to zero after the seventh year) of residential PV systems up to 3 kWp per home. The goal is more than 70,000 home systems, and a total installed capacity of 4,600 MW by 2010.

Perhaps as significant as its installation support program is Japan's policy of country-wide policies regarding connections. These include net metering and uniform interconnection guidelines. The utilities are also encouraged to offer a 10 percent premium for renewables for the good of the country. Examples of PV systems in Japan include:

- The Rokko Island test site, with its 500 kWp of small, distributed PV systems under test. Most of these systems are 2 kWp. Some are mounted on test houses, while others are ground mounted and all are connected to the same distribution feeder through a complex of switchgear that allows simulation of any possible combination of events.
- The "Eco Energy House," built by the largest home builder in Japan, Misawa Homes (see Figure 6.19). The entire south-facing roof is fitted with crystalline PV modules manufactured by Solarex. The PV array is actually the weathering skin of the roof and consists of custom-sized PV modules, aluminum extrusions, and a network of rubber gaskets and splines to hold it all together. This factory-built home is the prototype for the more than 1,000 similar homes already sold, with an average array size of 3.28 kW.

AUSTRALIA. Most of Australia's installed PV capacity of approximately 13 MW is in remote, stand-alone systems—primarily to power telecommunications. There are only two BIPV systems currently on line. However, Australia plans to develop

Figure 6.19. Misawa "Eco Energy House."

the world's largest PV community by building more than 600 homes with 1-kW PV systems for the athletes village for the 2000 Summer Olympics in Sydney.

KOREA. As a response to concerns about the environment and energy security, researchers at Daebul University and Samsung Corporation designed and installed the first building-integrated PV system in Korea. This 100-kW system includes 40 kW of semi-transparent window shades and a 60-kW system divided into two roof-mounted arrays.

Conclusions

The potential market for solar electric building systems is enormous, and many companies are now beginning to work on the development and commercialization of specialized components and systems. Residential and commercial systems will likely be the nearest term large-scale markets for PV in the developed countries. Buildings provide substantial surface area, allowing systems designers and integrators to displace the cost of conventional materials with PV; building-integrated systems supply power at the point of use, avoiding the costs and losses inherent in power transmission and distribution; and PV-powered buildings send an important message to the world about their owners, which is becoming increasingly appreciated.

As PV has moved from the research laboratory, to full-scale demonstration systems, to commercial applications with participation of professional designers and architects, the technology has taken a progressively more sophisticated, elegant, and appropriate shape in the real world. BIPV components that displace conventional building materials become part of the form and aesthetic of the structure, as well as part of a more sustainable future.

REFERENCES

Flavin, C., and N. Senssen. 1994. *Power Surge: Guide to the Coming Energy Revolution.* New York: W.W. Norton and Company.

National Renewable Energy Laboratory. 1996. *Highlights: Hydroelectric Power, Turning Water's Mechanical Energy into Electricity.* Golden, CO: National Renewable Energy Laboratory.

National Renewable Energy Laboratory. 1997. *Photovoltaics in the Built Environment: A Design Guide for Architects and Engineers.* Golden, CO: National Renewable Energy Laboratory.

Rannels, J.E. 1997. "Market Impact of a Large-Scale PV Buildings Program." *Proceedings of the 26th Photovoltaics Specialists Conference.* Picataway, N.J.: Institute of Electronics Engineers, Inc.

Schoen, T., M. van Schalkwijk, D. Prassad, P. Toggweiler, and H. Sorensen. 1997. "Task VII of the IEA PV Power Systems Program: PV in the Built Environment—A Strategy," *Proceedings of the 14th European Solar Energy Conference.* Bedford, U.K.: H.S. Stephens and Associates.

Sick, F., and T. Erge, eds. 1996. *Photovoltaics in Buildings: A Design Handbook for Architects and Engineers.* London: James and James Science Publishers Ltd.

Strong, S. 1997. *The Solar Electric House.* Emmaus, PA: Rodale Press.

Chapter 7

Environmentally Responsible Building Materials Selection

Nadav Malin

Before getting into the topic of choosing and using building materials, we should ask the question "Why?" Why should we care about environmental issues when choosing building materials? Isn't it enough just to get the best materials for the job, at an affordable price?

My answer to that challenge is that getting the best material is indeed the goal, but we need to expand our vision of what makes for the "best" material or product. In conventional terms, material selection is just one component of good design. Many in this field of "sustainable design" have pointed out that a building isn't really a "good" building unless it is functional, comfortable, energy-efficient, healthy, and durable. All these are things that make a building more environmentally responsible as well.

But I believe that there is also a broader prerogative here. There is a statement attributed to Thoreau that gets to this issue: "What is the use of a house if you haven't got a tolerable planet to put it on?" This statement applies to any building, not just houses, and it raises a whole new set of questions: Is it enough if I as a designer or builder provide what my client asks for, without considering the impact the project is having on the environment as a whole? Who or what am I really serving if that is how I see my role? In rare cases we might be lucky enough to have a client who comes in with this broader vision of how his or her building affects, and is affected by, the global environment. The rest of the time, however, there is still much we can do both to educate the client and to bring our own environmental awareness into the project, even without the client's participation.

Buildings require an enormous amount of material. They sit on valuable land. Energy and water and other resources cycle through them every day. Those of us involved with the construction of buildings—more so than other citizens—have a responsibility to see that our buildings serve their function while causing a minimum of harm—perhaps even while doing good by restoring a damaged site, or making use of a waste resource. Keeping the broader environment in mind, we can provide our clients with better buildings *and* a better planet to put them on.

To address the issue of environmentally responsible material selection, there is a series of questions that one might ask while looking into the entire life cycle of a product or material.

Analyzing a Product's Whole Life Cycle

When looking at a building material, it just makes sense that one would want to consider the entire life cycle: cradle-to-cradle. How one divides those stages varies, but that is just a matter of how one chooses to organize the research. Between each of these stages materials are transported from one place to another, so there are also environmental impacts from transportation to be considered (see Figures 7.1 and 7.2)

While the life cycle assessments (LCAs) of many consumer products focus on the production and disposal issues, in the case of many building materials it is the *use* phase of the product that is most significant because of the relatively long life-time over which building materials are in use. Throughout the functional life of a material in a building it may have an impact on energy use, indoor air quality, and maintenance requirements. In this sense building materials have what is called a *use-dominated life cycle.*

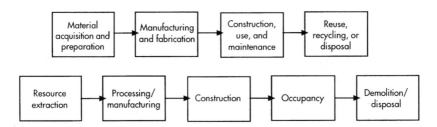

Figure 7.1. Life cycle stages. In the top row are the four stages as defined in the *Environmental Resource Guide* from the American Institute of Architects. Forintek Canada Corporation uses five stages for their sustainable materials project (bottom row).

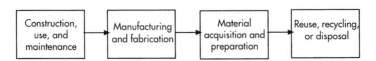

Figure 7.2. Hierarchy of stages. Arranging the life cycle stages in order of importance would lead to this configuration for many, but not all, building materials.

Other than the use phase, the manufacturing or production stage is usually the most important, especially for highly processed or manufactured materials that are becoming increasingly common. Many of these materials contain hazardous or toxic components, or they require a great deal of energy for processing. The raw materials extraction and preparation phase is typically next in importance.

Finally, the disposal stage can be important because of the shear volume of material that goes into making a building. It falls at the end of this list, however, because of the long useful life of most building materials and the recyclability of many of them. Additionally, much of a building's mass can be utilized as clean fill, so the potential impact on solid waste landfills is mitigated.

It is important to note that while this hierarchy is a useful guide, it is not meant to suggest that all materials will have their environmental burdens ranked in this order. For materials that are used in a natural or minimally processed state, such as wood or stone, the raw material extraction phase may be more significant than the use or production phases, while the most significant impacts of many synthetic materials may be found in the manufacturing stage. And a few products, such as preservative-treated wood, may be most problematic in the fourth stage, disposal.

The twelve key questions for analyzing a product's life cycle are listed in the following sections in the order of their typical priority because it makes sense to address the most important issues first. If a particular product doesn't perform well on a high-priority issue, it doesn't make sense to spend much time thinking about its performance in less critical areas.

Questions 1–3: Construction and Use Phase

The questions relating to construction and use are summarized graphically in Figure 7.3. Often the most significant environmental burdens from building materials are energy use in the building and possible impacts on occupant health. These impacts in the use phase depend not just on the material itself but also on how it is used. So, the first question we should ask is:

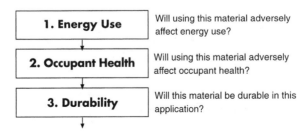

Figure 7.3. Construction and use phase issues.

Question 1: Will the material (in the relevant application) have a measurable impact on building energy use?

If it does, we should avoid options that do not minimize energy use and instead design the application to minimize energy use. Components for which this issue is particularly important include glazings, insulation, lighting, controls, and mechanical systems. For materials that can be used in an energy-efficient manner only with the addition of other components, the impact of including those additional components must be factored in. For example, in some circumstances glazing systems require exterior shading systems for efficiency, and light-gauge steel framing may require foam sheathing to prevent thermal bridging if it is used in an exterior wall.

Question 2: Might products in this application affect the health of building occupants?

If the products in question are interior furnishings, interior finishes, air distribution systems, or other components that are likely to affect indoor air quality, it's important to avoid those that are likely to adversely affect occupant health. One should also design systems to minimize any possible adverse effects when sources of indoor pollution cannot be avoided.

Question 3: Are products in this application likely to need replacement, special treatment, or repair multiple times during the life of the structure?

If durability is an issue, as it is for components such as roofing, coatings, sealants, and carpets, we should avoid products with short expected life spans (unless they are made from low-impact, renewable materials and are easily recycled) or products that require frequent, high-impact maintenance procedures. Another strategy to minimize the impact of replacing worn out or obsolete components is to design the structure for flexibility so that materials can be replaced with minimal disruption and cost.

Questions 4–6: Manufacturing Phase

Figure 7.4 summarizes the important questions regarding manufacture.

Question 4: Are significant toxic or hazardous intermediaries or by-products created during manufacture? If so, how significant is the risk of their release to the environment or risk of hazard to worker health?

Where toxic by-products are either generated in large quantities or in small but uncontrolled quantities (smelting of zinc, production of petrochemicals), the building material in question should be avoided if possible, or sourced from a company with strong environmental standards.

Some panel manufacturers are switching from urea-formaldehyde or phenol-

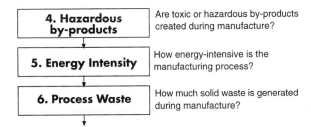

Figure 7.4. Manufacturing phase issues.

formaldehyde binders to a binder known as MDI, or methyl diisocyanate. This is an interesting case because it cuts both ways on the toxicity issue. It contains no formaldehyde and is very stable once it has cured, so it is preferred over phenol formaldehyde or urea formaldehyde in situations where formaldehyde emissions are a concern. But, before curing it is highly reactive and can be hazardous to anyone who handles or works with it.

So this raises an interesting dilemma, and to answer the question properly one would ideally like to have a sense of how responsible the manufacturer is in handling such chemicals. It's hard to get this information plant by plant, but sometimes one can get a sense of a company's overall corporate culture as it relates to worker safety just by looking at regulatory violations and the company's reaction to them.

Question 5: How energy-intensive is the manufacturing process?

The energy that goes into making products—their "embodied energy"—has been studied as a way to compare alternative materials. Embodied energy lends itself more readily to quantification than the other criteria here, so people naturally try to get real numbers to compare. Some materials, such as aluminum and plastics, are relatively energy-intensive to produce, so it makes sense to minimize their use.

When comparing the results from different embodied energy research around the world, one finds huge discrepancies for some materials, such as nickel, while others are relatively consistent. A typical example might be cement: European numbers from the 1980s are as low as 4.9 MJ/kg, while 1970s data from the United States is 9.4 MJ/kg. Although they appear quite discrepant, these numbers may actually both be accurate for their context. It makes sense that cement manufacture in Europe in the 1980s would be significantly more efficient than it was in the United States in the 1970s given the cost of fuels and overall higher efficiencies for processes in Europe.

This sort of discrepancy is just one of the many variables that make it hard to compare embodied energy data from different times and places. Some of the other tricky issues are:

- Which processes are included within the boundaries of the study and which are ancillary to it? Are we addressing direct energy only or also secondary uses?
- Some studies consider the "source energy" for electricity used, while others rely only on the "delivered energy" in the electricity. This can change the results for the electricity component by a factor of three.
- When using embodied energy data to compare materials, it's critical to have comparable "equivalent units" because just comparing the materials by weight or volume doesn't necessarily represent the amount of material needed for comparable performance. When comparing wood and steel for structural uses, for example, one should not compare pounds to pounds, but rather the material needed for comparable structural performance. For example, in Table 7.1 an "insulating unit" is defined as the amount of insulation needed to provide R-20 over an area of 1 square foot. The different insulation materials are then compared based on this unit to ensure comparable performance.

Table 7.1. Estimated embodied energy of insulation materials

Material	Embodied Energy in Btu/lb (MJ/kg)	Mass per Insulating Unit[a] in lb (kg)	Embodied Energy per Insulating Unit in Btu (MJ)
Cellulose[b]	750 (1.8)	0.90 (0.41)	676 (0.7)
Fiberglass[c]	12,000 (28)	0.38 (0.17)	4,550 (5)
Mineral wool[d]	6,500 (15)	0.76 (0.34)	4,950 (5)
EPS[e]	32,000 (75)	0.39 (0.18)	12,700 (13)
Polyiso[f]	30,000 (70)	0.48 (0.22)	14,3000 (15)

[a] "Insulating unit" refers to the mass of insulation required for R-20 for 1 square foot at standard density.

[b] Cellulose embodied energy data from personal communication with manufacturers. Assumes density of 2.0 lb/ft^3, R-value of 3.7/inch.

[c] Fiberglass embodied energy data from the final report: "Comparative Energy Evaluation of Plastic Products and Their Alternatives for the Building and Construction and Transportation Industries," 1991, Franklin Associates, Ltd., prepared for The Society of the Plastics Industry, Inc. Assumes density of 0.75 lb/ft^3, R-value of 3.3/inch.

[d] Mineral wool embodied energy data from Roxul, Inc. Assumes density of 1.66 lb/ft^3, R-value of 3.6/inch.

[e] EPS embodied energy data from the German report, *Lebenswegbilanz von EPS-Dämmstoff*, Interdisziplinäre Forschungsgemeinschaft (InFo), Kunstoff e.V. Includes caloric Btu value of EPS. Assumes density of 0.94 lb/ft^3, R-value of 4.0/inch.

[f] Polyisocyanurate embodied energy data from the final report cited above for fiberglass. Includes caloric Btu value of polyisocyanurate. Assumes density of 2.0 lb/ft^3, R-value of 7.0/inch.

Source: Used by permission of *Environmental Building News.*

Table 7.2. Carbon dioxide emissions by fuel type

Fuel type	CO_2 Produced per Unit of Energy	
	lb/million Btu	kg/GJ
Coal	210	90
Oil	190	82
Natural gas	118	51
Electricity from coal	694	299
Electricity from oil	628	270
Electricity from natural gas	388	167

Source: Consumer Guide to Home Energy Savings, by Alex Wilson and John Morrill, Washington, D.C., 1998, American Council for an Energy Efficient Economy. Used by permission.

Despite all of these mitigating factors, when comparing materials for a particular purpose, it makes sense to consider embodied energy. One reason for this is that, since we're working to minimize energy use in a building, it's worth asking if there is a danger of using so much energy to make the energy-efficient building that we're undermining the effort. Research architect Ray Cole at the University of British Columbia looked into that question, and he found that for typical houses operating energy exceeds embodied energy after just a few years. Only for superefficient houses does the embodied energy become significant in comparison to operating energy.

It is not the energy use itself that is of concern, however, but the pollution from its generation and use; industries using clean-burning or renewable energy sources have lower burdens than those relying on coal or petroleum. This adds yet another factor to consider: what fuel was used to provide the process energy? If the fuel is electricity from nuclear or hydroelectric plants, carbon dioxide emissions will be much lower, but there are other serious environmental concerns to be considered (see Table 7.2)

Question 6: How much solid waste is generated in the manufacturing process?
If significant amounts of solid waste are generated, and these are not readily usable for other purposes, it might be appropriate to seek an alternative product. Examples of materials that generate large amounts of waste are copper and other metals, which create huge tailings piles. In the case of copper, over 400 tons of waste and by-products are mined for each ton of copper produced.

If alternative materials are not suitable, it may be possible to source materials from a company with more progressive recycling and waste management programs.

Questions 7–9: Raw Materials Phase

A summary of questions for the raw materials phase is given in Figure 7.5.

Question 7: Are any of the component materials from rare or endangered resources?

Fortunately, environmental laws now forbid trade in many endangered species, and market forces make many rare materials exorbitantly expensive to use. Nevertheless, there are some materials that continue to be widely available in spite of their tenuous condition in nature. Mahogany, for example, is a species that is in limited supply, and its harvest causes damage to large areas of sensitive rain forest ecosystems. In 1997, the Convention on International Trade in Endangered Species (CITES) failed to restrict trade in mahogany for the third consecutive time.

Similarly, old-growth temperate forest woods, such as Douglas-fir, red cedar, and redwood, are becoming less available as old-growth forests are replaced with fast-growing plantation or second-growth forests. Unfortunately, it can be difficult to distinguish old-growth from second- and third-growth wood, except by tightness of grain and size of the timbers—the largest and mostly tightly grained logs are usually from virgin forests.

Some old-growth wood is available when salvaged from various sources, including old buildings that are being taken down, wine vats, and even bridges. In the South, logs that sank during river runs in the last century are now being dredged up and milled into lumber of exceptional quality. There are some questions about the possible impacts of this dredging on the river ecosystems, however, and the state of Florida has banned the practice.

Question 8: Are there significant ecological impacts from the process of mining or harvesting the raw materials?

Examples of adverse impacts from materials extraction include damage to rain forests from bauxite mining for aluminum and timber harvesting on steep slopes. with unstable soils. In the case of aluminum, one can assume that most virgin aluminum comes from bauxite mined in ecologically sensitive areas. When it's avail-

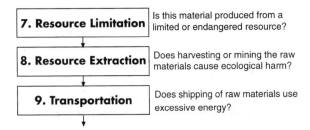

Figure 7.5. Raw materials phase issues.

able, recycled aluminum is highly preferable. In the case of timber harvesting, it is hard to determine exactly the forest conditions from which a particular shipment of lumber originates. The best way to ensure ecologically sound harvesting practices is to only use suppliers with credible third-party verification of responsible forest management.

The harvesting of sisal in Mexico's Yucatan Peninsula presents an interesting story because historically the production of sisal was so widespread that most of the region's forests were cleared to accommodate it. As a result, sisal production represented a significant negative regional environmental impact. Starting in the 1950s, however, demand for sisal dropped as synthetic polymers replaced natural fibers for ropes and fabric. Now, the limited sisal production that is being revived is considered both economically and environmentally advantageous because it is taking place on a limited scale and in a region where the income is desperately needed.

Question 9: Are the primary raw materials located a great distance from your site?
Italian marble, tropical timber, New Zealand wool—these are all examples of materials that must travel a long distance to reach building sites in North America. Even regionally sourced domestic products do not represent a guarantee of minimal transportation, though, as one environmentally inclined architect learned when he discovered that the local granite he specified for a building in the Upper Midwest was to be shipped to Italy for finishing, and then shipped back! Similarly, some plywood made with veneers of domestic hardwood is actually fabricated in Indonesia, where its luaun core is harvested. Apparently, the hand assembly process available in Indonesia can make use of thinner veneers than the mechanized process in the United States, which covers the cost of shipping the veneers all that way to be processed and then shipping the finished product back.

Examples of materials with minimal transportation impacts include walkways and patios made of local stone and structures made from lumber that is milled on-site using a portable band-saw mill.

Transportation is important largely because of the energy and pollution from the fuels used, so it's not just the distance but also the mode of transport that's important. Oceangoing vessels are the most efficient on a per-ton-mile basis. Large tractor-trailers are more efficient than small trucks, as long as they are carrying full or nearly full loads (see Table 7.3).

The Final Steps: Disposal or Reuse Phase

Questions relevant to disposal or reuse, as well as a final process review, are shown graphically in Figure 7.6.

Table 7.3. Energy efficiency by mode of transport

	Btu/ton-mile	*kJ/tonne-km*
Truck	2,946	2,128
Railroad	344	248
Barge	398	287
Ship	170	123

Sources: Truck, railroad, and barge data from *The Transportation Energy Data Book: Edition 15,* edited by Stacy Davis, Oak Ridge National Lab, Oak Ridge, Tennessee. Ship data (for oceangoing vessels) from the Total Emission Model for Integrated Systems by the Institute for Applied Ecology, Germany.

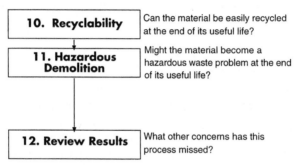

Figure 7.6. Disposal or reuse phase issues.

Question 10: Can the material be easily separated out for reuse or recycling after its useful life in the structure is over?

While most materials that are used in large quantities in building construction, such as steel and concrete, can be at least partially recycled, others are less recyclable and may become a disposal problem in the future. Examples of materials that are difficult to recycle include products that combine different materials, such as fiberglass composites, or those that undergo a fundamental chemical change during manufacture, including such thermoset plastics as polyurethane foams. Consider the future recyclability of products chosen.

Question 11: Might the material become a toxic or hazardous waste problem after the end of its useful life?

Any material that may need to be handled in the future as hazardous waste should be avoided, or at least its use should be minimized. Wood treated with chromated copper arsenate (CCA) preservative is one such material. While this pressure-treated wood is not technically considered hazardous waste, that is only because it was given a special congressional exemption. It does not reliably pass the standard toxics leaching test used to determine if a material is to be considered hazardous waste.

Fluorescent lamps contain mercury, a highly toxic heavy metal. At least one brand of lamp is available with greatly reduced levels of this toxin. This situation provides an example of a product choice in which specifying one brand over another can make a large difference in the amount of mercury that may escape into the environment.

The Squint Test

Question 12: What has been missed?
Go over any concerns that have been raised about the products under consideration, and look for other life-cycle impacts that might be specific to a particular material.

One example of a possible concern that is not mentioned in the list above is the matter of excessive waste generated at the construction site. Both drywall and spray-in open-cell polyurethane foam insulation are materials that, as typically installed, create a lot of on-site waste.

Recycled Content—A Hot-Button Issue

It might be surprising to some that recycled-content materials aren't mentioned as an item to look for on the list above. However, there is a good reason for this apparent omission. When one works from a life-cycle assessment perspective, one doesn't look for any particular solution but rather at the issues of concern for each stage. Use of recycled content is a specific solution that might be applied to address some of the concerns raised. For example, materials with high levels of recycled content have:

• Few manufacturing impacts, because they have already been (at least partially) manufactured.
• Less extraction of raw materials from sensitive areas.
• Reduced impact on landfills because materials are removed from the waste stream.

However, one also must be aware of the potentially hidden costs in recycling. Energy and transportation costs of collection of used materials for recycling may be significant. In fact, some researchers suggest that the energy expended to collect paper for recycling makes cellulose as energy-intensive to manufacture as fiberglass! Also, some remanufacturing processes may release large quantities of pollution.

The Complexity of the Question

Sometimes the choices and trade-offs one faces in trying to make the best environmental choice can become quite complex. For example, there has been an increase in the use of flyash from coal-fired power plants in concrete and other cementitious construction materials. This application is generally regarded as a good environmental choice, but the matter may not be so clear cut.

If one considers the fact that coal is the most polluting way we produce electricity, and that one of the economic constraints faced by coal-burning power plants is the disposal of the flyash they generate, one could decide that it's better not to make the use of coal more economically viable by providing an outlet for this waste. On the other hand, in many applications flyash is used as a replacement for cement, which is itself very energy-intensive and polluting to produce. To the extent that cement production can be reduced by making use of a waste resource that is readily available, the benefits of that choice will likely outweigh the drawbacks of inadvertently supporting the use of coal. In autoclaved aerated concrete, however, flyash is only used to replace some of the sand, not the cement. In this case, flyash may not be the best overall environmental choice.

Help with the Choices

To help make some of these choices more manageable, there are now independent organizations that specialize in verifying the environmental claims of manufacturers. This approach is called *third-party certification* because an outside party, aside from the vendor and the customer, is vouching for the product's environmental performance. This certification can take a number of forms. The two most common types are single-issue certification and standards-based certification.

With single-issue certification, the product manufacturer or materials supplier has a specific claim they want to promote, and they hire an outside party to vouch for the accuracy of that claim. Most often, this is a claim concerning the amount of recycled content the product contains. Scientific Certification Systems, Inc., based in Oakland, California, specializes in this approach.

The other common approach to certification is to set a standard based on a series of criteria that a product should meet in order to stake its claim as a "green" product. The process of determining what the standard should be can be long and arduous, but if it is done well, the result is a defensible distinction between conventional and green products in the marketplace. This standards approach has been led in the United States by the Washington, D.C.–based nonprofit organization Green Seal.

A specific version of standards-based certification for the forest products sector has been championed internationally by the Mexico-based Forest Stewardship Council. This group has managed to add value to the standards approach by coming up with a widely accepted common set of standards that can be used by many different certifiers of environmentally sound forest management practices. The Forest Stewardship Council accredits the certifying organizations that work according to its minimum standards, which revolve around three primary areas of concern: sustainable harvest, ecosystem health, and community health. Because the baseline standards are common to many different certifying organizations, the resulting certifications carry more weight and are recognized more widely. Scientific Certification Systems, mentioned above, also practices forest practice certification according to these principles.

Learning About Materials

Aside from relying on outside certifiers, the only effective way to assess the environmental performance of building materials is to learn as much as possible about their entire life cycles: what is in them, how they are made, how they perform in the building, and what happens to them afterward. This is a complex topic, but fortunately there are some good resources available to help.

The *Environmental Resource Guide,* produced by The American Institute of Architects, includes descriptive life cycle analyses in the form of technical reports. These are then summarized and compared for specific applications. The comparison matrices in these "application reports" provide a rough (non-numeric) rating of how the material performs across a range of environmental criteria.

An interesting aspect of this rating is that in some cases a range is provided rather than a single result. These ranges generally represent an area in which there may be several options concerning exactly which product is chosen or how the material is used. For example, glazings can have either a positive or negative net effect on building energy use, depending on which product is specified and how the building is designed. Thus, these ranges point out to the designer an issue for which his or her choice can affect the environmental performance of the product in the building.

A publication from the United Kingdom, the *Green Building Digest,* provides reports in a similar format to those of the *Environmental Resource Guide,* but these are less formal and lack the technical life cycle analysis reports to back them up. The industry trade publication *Environmental Building News* also provides overviews of the issues and performance of a range of products for a particular application. Several books also address these issues, and more are coming out each year.

Finding Specific Products

To help with the search for specific products that are more environmentally sound than their conventional alternatives, a number of directories and databases are available. These range from titles that provide contact information but no explanation of the products' benefits to those that offer considerable supplementary information. An example of the former is the *Resources for Environmental Design Index*.[1] Directories with more explanatory text include the *Environmental Building News Product Catalog*,[2] *Guide to Resource Efficient Building Elements*,[3] *The Harris Directory*,[4] and the *Good Wood Directory*.[5] Questions that should be asked regarding any of these listings include: "What criteria are they using for inclusion?" and "Do you trust their judgment on these issues?" With the ever increasing availability of tools and high-quality resources, it should be possible for designers to make environmental considerations a part of every material selection process. Doing so should help us make better buildings while also protecting the global environment.

NOTES

1. Available on the Internet at http://www.oikos.com/
2. Produced by *Environmental Building News* in Brattleboro, Vermont, and What's Working, Inc., in Boulder, Colorado.
3. Published by the Center for Resourceful Building Technology in Missoula, Montana.
4. Produced by B. J. Harris in Tucson, Arizona.
5. Produced by the Certified Forest Products Council in Beaverton, Oregon.

Chapter 8

Ecological Design, Living Machines, and the Purification of Waters

John Todd

H. T. Odum, in a small but milestone book entitled *Environment, Power and Society* published in 1971, transformed how I view the world. He redefined the meaning and breadth of the science of ecology. Odum argued that there were significant implications for humanity in this emerging discipline. In his view, ecology would extend far beyond the study of natural ecosystems and ultimately become the intellectual framework for the rethinking of technological foundations and the design of modern societies.

Odum had come to this point of view out of experience. For over a decade he had studied ecosystems under stress. He went on to create artificial microcosms of aquatic and terrestrial environments and had exposed these to high levels of stress, including nuclear irradiation. Through this work he came to appreciate the fundamental self-design and organizing power in nature. Living systems, both natural as well as artificially assembled ecological microcosms, had an overriding "intelligence" that is strikingly powerful. They have within themselves formidable organizing forces that he believed could be harnessed technologically.

In conjunction with his work on ecosystems, Odum began to develop models of human-based systems, including industrial agriculture and conventional waste treatment as well as energy, manufacturing, and transportation. These models were dynamic and they portrayed a picture of contemporary society that was unsettling. None of the infrastructure systems that modern cultures currently depend on for our long-term survival turned out to be sustainable over the long run. They all depend on external subsidies of materials and energy while negatively impacting both local and distant environments. In his models, industrial cultures were out of balance with the resource base that sustained them.

Odum's genius lay in the fact that he didn't just end with a critique. Instead, he turned to nature to search for models of systems that worked. He explored the ecology of mangroves, rain forests, coral reefs, and salt marshes in an attempt to decode the underlying mechanisms that organized most, if not all, ecosystems. This information, derived from nature, might well prove to be a template for the design of living technologies. He reasoned that these ecologically inspired technologies might one day serve humanity without ruining the earth's biological capital.

Design in nature, having evolved over 3 billion years, is far more powerful and complex than objects or engines that humans can design. Within ecosystems there are architectural forms and complexities, food webs, species combinations, and systems where materials, including gases and nutrients, are exchanged. Within all of this is a biological pattern language, a language that can be extracted and used by human designers to invent and ecologically engineer new technologies. H. T. Odum's message was that nature designs brilliantly and efficiently, and by learning its strategies, we might too.

The Emergence of Ecological Technologies and Living Machines

The same year that Odum's *Environment, Power and Society* was published I began to ecologically design greenhouse-sized living systems for food production, waste conversion, fuel generation, and climate regulation. All of these systems utilized sunlight for heating and photosynthesis. Out of the early work emerged the concept of the bioshelter, an architectural form designed to house many living systems. This exciting period of research and demonstration has been chronicled in several earlier volumes (Todd and Todd 1980, 1984, and 1994). More recently, we have begun work on bioshelters as key elements within ecological industrial parks (Todd 1997).

By the second half of the 1980s we had developed enough ecological design experience to begin to focus on the difficult task of treating wastes, including toxic substances. This enabled the purification of wastewater, including sewage, and the remediation of degraded aquatic environments. Experience assembling these ecologically engineered systems provided the impetus for the formulation of the theoretical foundations for the design of Living Machines™ (Todd and Josephson 1996).* The term *Living Machine* was coined to define a family of ecological technologies that, like most conventional machines, are designed to undertake directed work. We have designed and built Living Machines to generate fuels, grow foods, convert wastes, purify waters, restore degraded environments, and regulate and improve the quality of climate within buildings.

---

* Living Machine is a trademark of Ocean Arks International, 233 Hatchville Road, East Falmouth, MA 02536.

The differences between a Living Machine and a conventional machine are quite fundamental. They differ in four basic respects:

1. The vast majority of a Living Machine's working parts are live organisms, hundreds of species ranging from bacteria to higher plants and vertebrates such as fish and amphibians.
2. Living Machines have the ability to self-design. The engineer provides the containment vessels that enclose the Living Machine and then seeds them with diverse organisms from specific environments. Within the Living Machine the organisms self-design the internal ecology in relation to their prescribed tasks and the energy and nutrients streams to which they are exposed.
3. Living Machines have the ability to self-repair when damaged by a toxic shock or an interruption of an energy or nutrient source. The self-repair ability enables Living Machines to be quite robust and capable of dealing with unexpected and unpredictable events.
4. Living Machines have the ability to self-replicate through reproduction by the vast majority of organisms within the system. This means that, in theory at least, Living Machines can be designed to operate for centuries or even millennia. In Living Machines the intelligence of nature is reapplied to human ends. They are both garden and machine.

At the present time we have built, or have under construction, Living Machines in eight countries and fifteen states within the United States. These range in size from household-scale systems to the largest, in Brazil, which treats high-strength organic wastes equivalent to over a million gallons of sewage per day. Because of their cellular design, Living Machines are not limited to any size scale. Nevertheless, it is our hope that Living Machines will start a trend toward treating wastes, including sewage, close to their points of origin, and that the by-products and cleaned water will be used to support local economic, civic, and environmental functions.

The South Burlington (Vermont) Sewage Treatment Facility

This facility was built in 1995 and treats 80,000 gallons of municipal sewage per day in two parallel treatment trains. A third smaller treatment facility within the greenhouse is used for research purposes. It is housed within a 6,400-square-foot structure (see Figures 8.1 and 8.2). The South Burlington waste treatment plant has been part of a U.S. Environmental Protection Agency (USEPA) demonstration project to verify the performance of Living Machines in cold climates. It has proven to be a cost-competitive alternative treatment system that is aesthetically beautiful and compatible with a residential environment. Odors from the incoming sewer lines are controlled with soil-based and vegetatively planted biofilters mounted directly over the first tank in the treatment process.

A schematic of one of the two main treatment trains is shown in Figure 8.3. Each

Figure 8.1. Exterior view of the South Burlington, Vermont, sewage treatment facility.

Figure 8.2. Interior view of South Burlington, Vermont, sewage treatment facility.

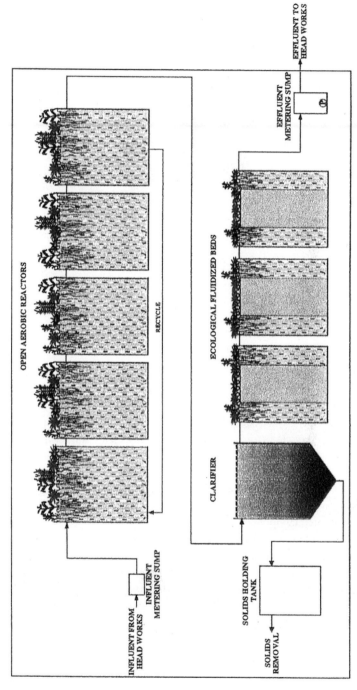

Figure 8.3. Living Machine main treatment train at the South Burlington, Vermont, sewage treatment facility.

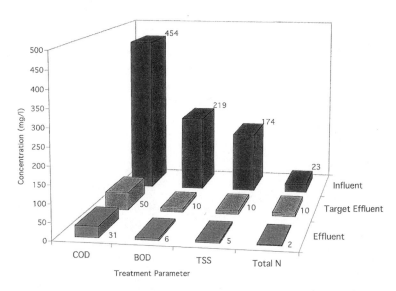

Figure 8.4. Performance of the South Burlington, Vermont, sewage treatment facility, July 1996 through July 1997.

train has five aerobic reactors planted with a wide variety of higher plants housed within racks mounted on the surface. The plant racks serve a secondary function of directing the flow of the aerated water. Biochemical oxygen demand (BOD) and total suspended solids (TSS) are reduced and ammonia is mostly nitrified in this stage of treatment. A clarifier follows the open aerobic reactors to settle and recycle solids.

Three ecological fluidized beds (EFB) follow the clarifier for final treatment. Two of the beds operate aerobically for BOD and chemical oxygen demand (COD) polishing, nitrification, and suspended solids digestion. Anoxic denitrification with organic carbon addition is carried out in the second EFB in each train. The EFBs are a patented component of the system.

The performance of the facility from July 1996 through July 1997 is shown in Figure 8.4. All of the effluent targets for the advanced wastewater facility have been met. In Figure 8.5, the stable total Kjeldahl nitrogen (TKN) output clearly illustrates excellent system performance, even when the input is highly variable. Also noteworthy is the fact that winter performance is comparable to performance during the warmer times of year.

The Corkscrew Swamp Living Machine—Naples, Florida

The Living Machine at the Corkscrew Swamp visitor's facility in Naples, Florida, was designed to protect an adjacent bald cypress swamp from sewage pollution

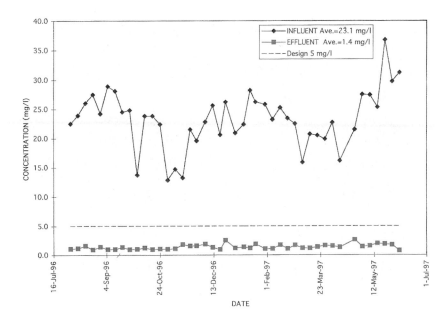

Figure 8.5. TKN performance of the South Burlington, Vermont, sewage treatment facility.

(see Figure 8.6). The National Audubon Society commissioned a Living Machine for this facility that would recycle purified wastewater back to the toilets after treatment and sterilization. It was designed to be close to a zero-discharge facility suitable for a fragile habitat. It has proven to be a low-cost treatment option that can handle wide fluctuations in flows from holiday crowds. A screen has been constructed around the Living Machine to house a diverse butterfly community.

The Corkscrew Swamp Living Machine treats up to 10,000 gallons per day. The sewage is treated in two anaerobic reactors (see Figure 8.7) Two trains within a screened enclosure contain five open aerobic tanks each, followed by a small clarifier. Final polishing is in a constructed wetland. A chlorination–dechlorination unit disinfects the effluent. Ninety percent of the treatment water is recycled and 10 percent is discharged to an absorption mound.

Performance of the Corkscrew Swamp Living Machine has proven to be excellent. BOD removal has exceeded 99 percent and TSS removal has exceeded 99.5 percent during the heavy traffic winter months. A similar Living Machine for a 4,300-visitors-per-day facility has been designed and built at a rest stop on Interstate 91 at Guilford, Vermont. The Guilford facility is housed within a greenhouse. This type of system is suitable for tour centers, rest areas, amusement parks, and other areas with high visitor counts and limited leach field capacity.

Figure 8.6. The Corkscrew Swamp Living Machine, Naples, Florida.

The Industrial Wastewater Treatment Living Machine at Ethel M. Chocolates in Henderson, Nevada

Ethel M. Chocolates, owned by the M & M Mars Corporation, was constrained by tightened discharge requirements and a need to expand their production of chocolates. They required advanced treatment of confectionery process wastewater. Their Living Machine was designed to be a zero-discharge facility with on-site treatment of the sludges in a composting reed bed. The purified water is used for on-site landscape irrigation and other nonpotable uses. The central part of the facility is shown in Figure 8.8.

This Living Machine treats up to 32,000 gallons of high strength confectionery wastewater per day. The zero-discharge facility eliminates discharge fees and conserves water in an arid climate. The on-site biosolids treatment reduces costs and risks associated with off-site sludge disposal. It is computer-controlled, uses no synthetic chemicals in the treatment process, and is relatively simple to operate.

The schematic diagram in Figure 8.9 illustrates the process. Wastewater is pumped from a grease trap into sealed aerobic reactors where microbial communities begin digesting the waste. A biofilter scrubs odors from the exhaust gases at this stage of treatment. In the planted aerobic tanks, vegetation hosts organisms that further digest the waste while minimizing sludge generation. EFBs polish organic material and suspended solids from the effluent. The effluent is stored in

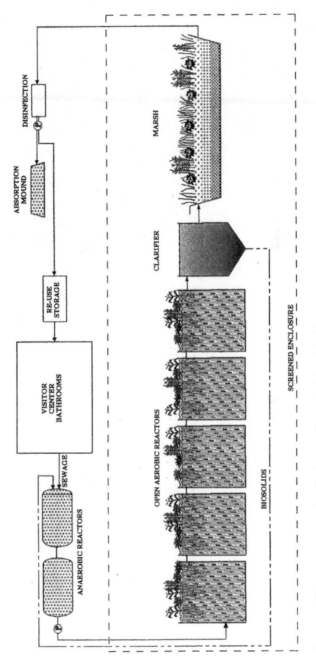

Figure 8.7. Treatment train at the Corkscrew Swamp Living Machine.

Figure 8.8. The Ethel M. Chocolates industrial wastewater treatment Living Machine.

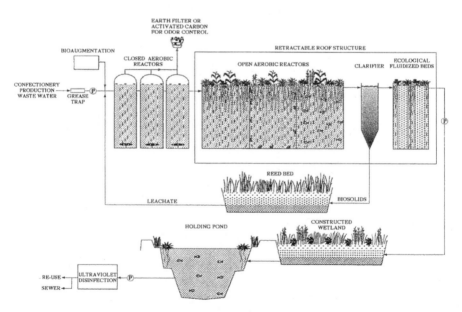

Figure 8.9. Schematic diagram for the Ethel M. Chocolates Living Machine.

Table 8.1. Performance of Ethel M. Chocolates Living Machine

Parameters	Influent	Design Effluent	Effluent
Biochemical oxygen demand (mg/l)	1,270	10	6
Total suspended solids (mg/l)	309	10	5
Fats, oils, and grease (mg/l)	200	5	1

an attractive pond and wetland. After ultraviolet disinfection, the effluent is used to irrigate a famous cactus garden.

The performance of the facility between September 1995 and July 1997 is shown in Table 8.1. BOD removal is 99.5 percent; TSS removal is greater than 98 percent; and fats, oils, and greases are 99.5 percent removed. Comparable facilities have been built for the food industry in other parts of the world.

Brewery Living Machine in Glenn Allen, California

The Sonoma Mountain Brewery was built in a vineyard without access to a community sewer system. On-site treatment and reuse was a requirement for the project. The Living Machine provided a cost-effective option that integrated well with the beautiful setting. The Living Machine is a central component of the brewery tour (see Figure 8.10).

The Living Machine was built to treat 7,800 gallons per day. The design can be expanded as the brewery grows. The wastewater from the brewery is treated and recycled for irrigation of adjacent vineyards and hop fields. Biosolids are composted and used as fertilizer. Sonoma Mountain Brewery is a zero-discharge facility. Figure 8.11 is a schematic diagram of the facility. The Living Machine has proved to work well treating brewery wastes. The effluent has a BOD and TSS of less than 10 mg/l.

Industrial Wastewater Treatment at Master Foods in Wyong, New South Wales, Australia

Master Foods makes over 350 shelf-stable food products in a single processing facility in Wyong. A Living Machine was designed and built to help the company reduce their high costs for sewage discharge, sludge disposal, and wastewater treatment chemicals (see Figure 8.12). The facility was built in 1995 and has proven to be cost-effective. The effluent is suitable for safe reuse for bin washing and for other nonpotable uses, as well as for irrigation of the natural environment sur-

Figure 8.10. The Sonoma Mountain Brewery Living Machine.

rounding the facility. Cost savings have been realized from decreased BOD and hydraulic sewer fees, reduction in sludge disposal costs, and elimination of costly polymers and coagulants used in the original dissolved air flotation (DAF) separation and treatment regime.

The Master Foods Living Machine treats approximately 50,000 gallons of production wastewater per day with wide fluctuations in flows and strength. The design employs an anaerobic phase and usable amounts of methane gas are captured and blended with natural gas for use within the factory. Figure 8.13 illustrates one of the two identical treatment lines. Following equalization in a balance tank, treatment continues with a DAF using no chemicals. A three-stage upflow anaerobic sludge blanket (UASB) reactor follows. The third stage of this reactor is designed for horizontal flow with a bioweb substrate. A closed aerobic reactor transitions to an aerobic ecosystem. Exhaust gases from this tank are scrubbed with an earth-based biofilter. Five planted aerobic reactors follow. The aerobic reactors are followed by a clarifier and a patented fixed-film reactor, an EFB. The Living Machine is located outdoors in a climate subject to frost.

Table 8.2 describes the performance of the Master Foods Living Machine between April 1996 and April 1997. BOD reduction averaged 99.7 percent, and levels of fats, oils, and grease (FOG) were reduced 96.5 percent.

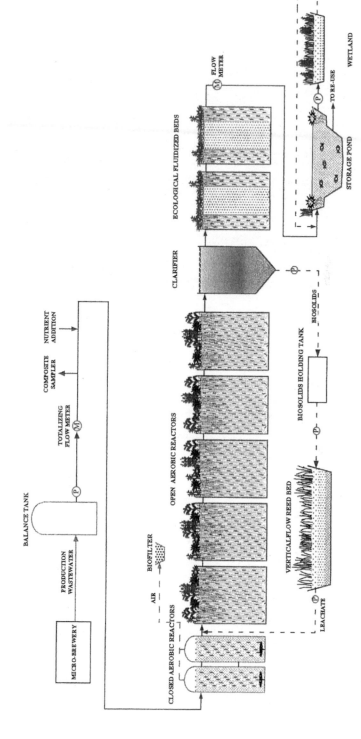

Figure 8.11. Schematic diagram of the Sonoma Mountain Brewery zero-discharge facility.

Figure 8.12. Industrial wastewater treatment plant at Master Foods, Wyong, New South Wales, Australia.

Table 8.2. Performance of the Master Foods Livings Machine (averages for the period April 1996–April 1997)

Parameters	Influent		Effluent	
	mg/l	*(kg/day)*	*(mg/l)*	*kg/day)*
Biochemical oxygen demand	2,334	341	7	1
Total suspended solids	1,100	161	26	2
Fats, oils, and grease	368	54	13	2

Integrating Living Machines into Architecture

There are four examples of Living Machines being integrated into the architecture and operations of buildings. The first was a single-family home that has operated successfully for over five years.

The second Living Machine to be linked to architecture was designed and built for the Body Shop, an international cosmetics firm with a factory and bottling facility in Toronto, Canada. This Living Machine was built to reclaim wastewater from restrooms for nonpotable reuse at the facility. It is housed within a greenhouse that provides supplemental heating for the building. The Living Machine is planted with many of the species that are used in the company's cosmetics in order to familiarize visitors and employees with the sources of materials for their products.

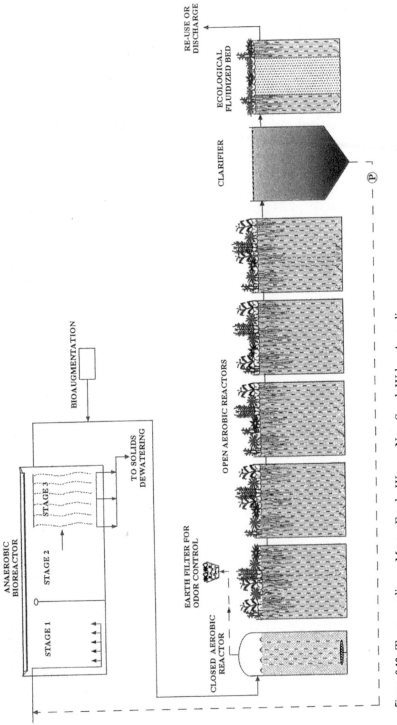

Figure 8.13. Treatment line at Master Foods, Wyong, New South Wales, Australia.

The Body Shop facility is shown in Figure 8.14. Wastewater flows to an underground septic tank. After anaerobic digestion the waste is pumped into closed aerobic reactors where microbial communities continue digesting the waste. Odorous compounds are eliminated and water flows to an open pond tank planted with a diverse group of aquatic species. Here plants interact with a wealth of microorganisms, snails, and fish to digest wastes and reduce sludge accumulation. After a short settling stage, the remaining suspended particles are polished in a beautiful subsurface flow wetland in the greenhouse. The final effluent is disinfected in an ultraviolet filter prior to storage and reuse.

The facility has performed well. BOD is reduced 99 percent to 3 mg/l in the effluent. TSS is reduced 99 percent and averages 3.2 mg/l. The facility requires very little maintenance—less than three hours per week of operator attention—and provides water that can be reused for nonpotable purposes. The treatment facility is a favorite retreat of visitors and employees. A schematic diagram of this facility is shown in Figure 18.15.

Figure 8.14. Living Machine integrated at the Body Shop factory in Toronto, Canada.

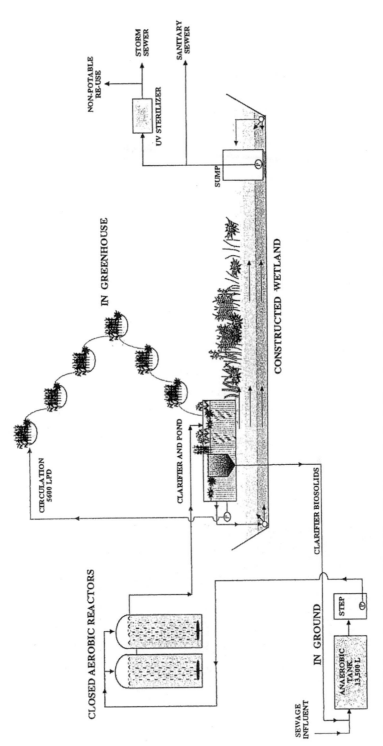

Figure 8.15. Schematic diagram of the Living Machine at the Body Shop factory in Toronto, Canada.

The third Living Machine incorporated into a building is at the Boyne River School Ecology Center operated by the Toronto Board of Education. The school was designed to be heated and cooled naturally and to derive its power from solar and wind systems. The south atrium houses a Living Machine in a visually accessible, but separated, environment. The Living Machine converts the sewage to sterilized water that is reused in the toilets. Excess liquid is diverted to an exterior leach field. The Living Machine is designed to display for students a range of ecological principles.

The fourth facility is currently under construction. It is at the Oberlin College Environmental Studies Center in Oberlin, Ohio. The 14,000-square-foot building, designed by William McDonough and Partners, employs ecological design throughout. It uses solar energy for electricity and for heating, cooling, and air circulation. A Living Machine will recycle the wastewater and provide an advanced teaching tool for students in environmental studies. The southeast view of the building is shown in the model (see Figure 8.16). The Living Machine is situated on the right-hand side of the photo. The northwest view of the building illustrates how the building is shaped and integrated into the landscape to reduce its climate control requirements (see Figure 8.17).

The Oberlin Environmental Studies Center is intended to be a model of ecological design, serving as a pedagogical tool that encourages mindfulness of materials selection, energy efficiency, water use, and wastewater recycling. It will be an example of whole-systems thinking applied to the built environment. We hope it will set a standard for the twenty-first century.

Figure 8.16. The Oberlin Environmental Studies Center with Living Machine.

Figure 8.17. Landscape integration of the Oberlin Environmental Studies Center.

Conclusions

The examples presented here represent the beginning of a marriage between the natural world and the built environment. Ecological design and ecological engineering bring together the intrinsic potential of natural systems and the human ability to design and fabricate new technologies. This represents the beginning of a new partnership with nature, a partnership that H. T. Odum insisted was necessary for long-term human survival. It is my belief that a civilization in harmony with and supporting the natural world is a realizable dream. I am aware of the incredible political, economic, and psychological forces that support the status quo. They are countered by the state of the world, a world in which many more people are living off a dwindling resource base. The challenge will be to create a new vision for our world and restore the ecological fabric that sustains us all.

DEDICATION

This chapter is dedicated to H. T. Odum, the founding father of ecological engineering. He has made the University of Florida at Gainesville a mecca for ecologists and engineers pioneering a practice of earth stewardship.

ACKNOWLEDGMENTS

I would like to thank the staff at Living Technologies Incorporated in Burlington, Vermont, for their assistance in gathering and presenting the information in this chapter.

REFERENCES

Odum, H. T. 1971. *Environment, Power and Society*. New York: Wiley Inter-science.

Todd, J. 1997. "The Intervale Ecological Park." *Annals of Earth Stewardship* 15:13.

Todd, J., and B. Josephson. 1996. "The Design of Living Technologies for Waste Treatment." *Ecological Engineering* 6:109–136.

Todd, J., and N. J. Todd. 1980. *Tomorrow is Our Permanent Address: The Search for an Ecological Science of Design*. New York: Harper and Row.

Todd, N.J., and J. Todd. 1984. *Bioshelters, Ocean Arks, City Farming: Ecology as the Basis for Design*. San Francisco: Sierra Club Books.

Todd, N. J., and J. Todd. 1994. *From Eco-Cities to Living Machines: Principles of Ecological Design*. Berkeley, CA: North Atlantic Books.

Chapter 9

Landscape: Source of Life or Liability

John Tillman Lyle

As all landscape architects know to their great distress, landscape is a most difficult subject to talk about. The meaning of the word is imprecise at best and it has different meanings for different people in different places. Just as any landscape conjures up varied memories and associations in any human mind, so the word itself evokes different implications. To see what I mean, consider two very different landscapes that exist just a few miles apart.

The first is a naturally evolved landscape, little changed by human presence (see Figure 9.1). It is a small stretch of coastal sage scrub that lies at the edge of a wash near the base of the San Gabriel Mountains in Southern California. To an easterner, this landscape might look rather sparse, certainly dry, perhaps uninviting. To me, because it is a typical landscape of the region where I live, it looks like home. Most of the plants are small because in this semi-arid zone there is not enough water to support large trees except in places where water concentrates, such as along stream courses. In their forms, the plants have adapted to the regional condition of little water and high levels of solar energy by their small size and by developing fine textured foliage and small leaves that are adequate for converting solar energy through photosynthesis but that present limited surfaces for losing water through transpiration. In many of the plants, the leaves stand perpendicular to the sun, which also helps to minimize solar radiation gain and thus minimize transpiration loss. Notice also that many of the plants have a gray-greenish color in contrast to the deep and bright greens typical of plants in more humid regions.

If you walked into this landscape, you would find dead and decaying leaves and branches scattered about, though not the thick duff layer typical of forest floors in humid zones. Microorganisms are at work nonetheless, breaking these dead leaves and branches and whole plants down, returning the nutrients that were embedded in them to the soil to be taken up again by growing plants. As in all landscapes, most of the biological activity is invisible—the unseen but absolutely essential work

Figure 9.1. Coastal sage scrub near the base of the San Gabriel Mountains in Southern California.

of bacteria, fungi, and other organisms too small to be seen, breaking down plant matter and preparing it for its role in the next cycle of growth.

You would also see rabbits and other small mammals scurrying about as well as birds on the ground and among the leaves of the plants, many of which produce small berries and seeds that feed the animals. The coastal sage scrub is habitat for numerous species, including several on the endangered list. Most famous of these is the California gnatcatcher, a small, nondescript song bird that lives only in the coastal sage and has caused the demise of a number of ambitious development proposals.

Although this is a dry landscape, it plays an important role in the flow of water. When it rains, most of the water is absorbed into the soil, either right away or through small pools and puddles that store the water for a while, giving the wildlife time to have a drink. Plant roots take up much of the water absorbed into the soil to supply the plants' needs. The rest slowly filters down through the layers of soil, gravel, and rock into groundwater storage.

Only a very small portion of the rainwater runs off the land into streams and rivers. On average in this landscape the runoff is less than 10 percent of rainfall, though the percentage is much less at the beginning of a period of rain and can be much greater after the ground is saturated.

The point I want to make here is that this landscape is the source of life for the community of creatures that inhabit it and in many ways for the people of the region as well. Through photosynthesis, it is the primary converter of the solar energy that supports all life in this landscape. Its roles in the flow and processing of water are part of the regional watershed system, and in producing oxygen and taking in carbon dioxide it also helps to create the air we all breathe.

Now let's consider a quite different landscape (see Figure 9.2) one that was designed and shaped by humans primarily for humans to look at. Although it is also located in Southern California, its forms have nothing to do with the natural environment or processes of the region; rather, they derive from the forms of the English landscape garden. It is not a community of plants all interacting within a shared environment but a collection of plants living more or less independently. Since there is no plant community, there is also no wildlife community. Most species native to the region can make no use of the plants in this landscape and so choose not to live within it. Walking through this landscape, one sees only the occasional squirrel or rat.

As for water, rainfall is not nearly enough to serve the needs of these plant species that evolved in more humid regions, so they require irrigation in large amounts. The turf grass is especially thirsty, requiring the equivalent of an additional 30 inches of rainfall every year. This means that every year each acre uses nearly 800,000 gallons of water brought from distant watersheds at least 233 miles away. Meanwhile, much of the water falling naturally on the site as rain is directed

Figure 9.2. Human designed and modified landscape in Southern California.

quickly into the storm drain system and rushed off through concrete channels to the ocean.

There is little internal cycling in this landscape. The grass is mowed as often as every two weeks and the trimmings are removed. Leaves falling from the trees are raked up and removed as well. Both are considered waste materials. Even if they were left on the ground to be broken down and returned to the soil, they could not supply the nutrient needs of these plant species from wetter regions rapidly enough. Chemical fertilizers, mostly derived from nonrenewable fossil fuels, are brought in to feed the plants. Some small portion of the fertilizer, generally less than half, is actually taken up by the plants while a major portion is left to be picked up by water and carried either into streams and rivers or into the groundwater.

These exotic plants, especially the turf grasses, are also subject to a range of pests and diseases in this alien environment. Thus, keeping them reasonably healthy requires application of various pesticides in sizable quantities. These also often find their way into the groundwater or surface water.

Thus, we can see that this landscape is not serving in the earth's larger pattern as a source of life but is itself kept alive by an external life-support system. This system includes the distant watershed from which water is taken, the concrete channels through which it flows to get here, and the pipes that deliver it to the site. It includes the gas wells from which material is taken for making the fertilizer, the factories where it is made, the trucks that transport it, the highways and roadways they travel on, the petroleum they burn, and the spill-prone oil tankers that transport it and the oil they burn. It also includes the trucks that haul the waste organic matter away from the site, the petroleum they burn, and the roads they travel on. The list could go on but the fundamental message seems clear at this point: through the prevailing practices of design and maintenance, humans have converted the landscape, which in nature is the source of life, into a net ecological and economic liability requiring a large and widespread infrastructure of life support, continuously and endlessly consuming nonrenewable resources and costing a great deal of money. Moreover, such an industrialized landscape does not renew itself with emerging life but instead dies a little at a time, eventually requiring reestablishment by human agency.

Linear Flows of the Industrial Era

This industrially based way of shaping the landscape is among the most visible expressions of the modern way of using natural resources, which has become almost universal. We have replaced the evolved processes of nature with an imposed infrastructure of petroleum, steel, concrete, and chemicals. This infrastructure forms a system of one-way linear flows by which we supply our cities, including their landscapes, with energy and materials, and it is at the very core of ecological dysfunction. We take energy and materials from source landscapes, transport them to our cities through the industrial infrastructure of steel and concrete, use them for short periods, and then discard them into waste sinks where they are concentrated in quantities that the environment cannot assimilate and that thus become pollution.

This imposed and artificial infrastructure has replaced the local and natural function of the landscape in providing for our basic needs, leaving the landscape with no essential functions in our lives. The local landscape in the urban environment no longer processes, treats, and stores water. It no longer grows our food; it no longer supports complete and diverse wildlife communities. It no longer reassimilates materials and prepares them for reuse. It no longer even renews itself. All that is left to the landscape of our cities is its role as social setting and its appearance. Often we shape landscapes as decorative features or as visual backdrops to enhance and set off our buildings, and this relegates them to a minor and peripheral place in our consciousness of the world we live in.

Sad as it is, we might be able to accept this state of affairs if it were not for one overwhelming and increasingly obvious factor: it is not sustainable. We are nearing the time when the chemicals and fossils fuels run short, the water is no longer available, the steel and concrete become too expensive to maintain and replace, the web of life begins to unravel, and pollution reaches levels that we can no longer tolerate.

Clearly, we need to change our ways of thinking about the way we view the world and how it works and our ways of reshaping it. Because it lies at the heart of the matter, rethinking landscape is a good place to start. We need to reestablish the landscape in our consciousness as the source of life, not an adjunct to roads and buildings but the essential living matrix within which roads, buildings, and the whole complex composition of urban life can achieve a sustainable state.

Regenerative Landscapes

Natural systems provide the best model. In nature there is no waste because, after use, materials are reassimilated into the landscape by the prodigious work of microorganisms. Instead of an industrial pattern of one-way flows from source to use to waste sink, natural systems are based on cyclical material flows from source to use back to source. And instead of relying on nonrenewable fossil fuels dug out of the earth, natural systems derive their energy from the sun, which infuses the earth with new supplies of energy every day. Thus nature's pattern is regenerative, or inherently self-renewing, in contrast to the degenerative industrial pattern, which is inherently self-destructive.

The next question is this: how can we design regenerative landscapes based on nature's model that also serve the physical needs, the aspirations, and the spiritual yearnings of humans? I think we begin by thinking about fundamental processes, including the conversion of energy, the processing of water, reassimilation of wastes, and support of biotic communities. Added together these are the most basic functions of ecosystems, whether natural or made by humans. By reincorporating them by design, we can return the landscape to its central place in our lives. Beyond that, we cannot only make the landscape itself sustainable but we can use the design of landscape as a pathway toward making the city as a whole both livable and sustainable. This requires us to reintegrate our ways of design.

Examples: Industrial and Regenerative Processes

Next, I want to contrast some examples of industrialized infrastructure performing highly specialized functions with some examples of regenerative landscapes that perform similar functions but in entirely different ways. We will consider the flow of water, production of food, and the processing and reassimilation of wastes.

Flow of Water in the Landscape

Figure 9.3 shows a concrete flood control channel designed to prevent flooding by rushing rainwater off the land as quickly as possible. This is a typical example of the kind of infrastructure that robs the landscape of its purpose. Moving the water away takes one of the sources of life away. By replacing the stream that was once here, the bare and sterile concrete replaces the fecundity of soil and plants. The concrete has just one purpose, ignoring the multiplicity of other purposes served by the landscape it replaced, which included delivering water to floodplain com-

Figure 9.3. Concrete flood control channel.

munities here and downstream, supporting the rich life of aquatic and riparian communities, and absorbing and filtering water as it recharges the underground aquifers.

Figure 9.4 shows a more regenerative means for managing potential flooding. This is a retention basin at the Center for Regenerative Studies at California State Polytechnic University in Pomona. The basin collects runoff from the surrounding area, stores it for some period of time, and allows it to slowly infiltrate to groundwater. The plants around the edges are native wetland species typical of the region. None of these was planted; all of them simply moved in, and naturally formed a wetland community. As the plants moved in, so did the wildlife. All of the wetland species of Southern California now spend some time around the edges of the retention basin. The diversity of both plants and wildlife is far greater than was the case when this landscape was still in its naturally evolved state.

The basin also provides some water treatment. While no agricultural chemicals are used in the area draining into it, all runoff water is to some degree polluted—primarily by nutrients washing out of the soil and the organic matter applied to it. Microorganisms occupying the roots of aquatic plants—including duckweed and water hyacinth—take up these nutrients from the water and use them in their own growth processes.

Thus, this simple retention basin fulfills the full range of functions of a natural wetland ecosystem, including that of flood control. The cost was far less than that

Figure 9.4. Natural regenerative flood control basin.

Figure 9.5. Natural flood control system at Earthworks Park near Kent, Washington.

of even the smallest concrete channel—merely the cost of digging a depression in the ground at the right place.

A second example is shown in Figure 9.5. This is a park called Earthworks Park on the edge of the town of Kent in the state of Washington. The park is a very subtlely shaped bowl that forms a large retention basin. During heavy rains a stream flowing into it from the side opposite the town fills it with water that otherwise would move into the town and cause flooding. After the water soaks into the ground, the bowl is a park again, featuring the picnic area and sports fields typically found in a city park. But it also contains an amphitheater, a bicycle path, a wetland for wildlife, and a duck pond and swimming hole that are always filled with water.

Soil and Food

Figure 9.6 shows a typical industrial farm. The characteristics are obvious: vast acres plowed barren and planted in a single crop. The soil supports the rows of seedlings, but their sustenance comes not from the soil but from chemical fertilizers. Chemical pesticides keep their predators at bay—if all goes well. The ground is plowed and the crops are both planted and harvested by machines fueled by petroleum. This is short-term agriculture. Besides polluting both groundwater and surface waters, the chemicals in time destroy the productive capacities of the soil. Even if the soil survives, the petroleum that powers the machines and from which the chemicals are derived will run short.

Figure 9.6. Single-crop industrial farming.

As industrial agriculture runs its course, we will learn to grow food in other ways, and at least some, if not most, of these will be based on nurturing of the soil, using its inherent productive capacities, and returning nutrients that are now treated as wastes to the production process. There is great potential for growing much of our food—especially fresh fruits and vegetables—near where we consume it and where the organic wastes produced by consumption are readily available for regeneration. Figures 9.7 and 9.8 show some of the fruit and vegetable growing areas at the Center for Regenerative Studies. Here, the processes of producing food and cycling nutrients are built into the daily lives of the residents and into the landscape where they live. Most of the plants that form the center's living environment produce food in some form and serve other purposes as well. Grapevines grow on trellises over the south-facing glass areas of the buildings, allowing the sun to shine in during the winter when they have no leaves but shading the glass during the summer. Deciduous fruit trees provide shading in other areas. Various herbs and vegetables grow just a few steps outside from the dining commons. Vegetables also grow in planter boxes on the flat roofs and around the buildings. As in any urban environment, the varied combinations of buildings and hard surfaces create endless variations in microclimate. By using these to good advantage, it is possible to grow a great diversity of food plants that require different conditions. For example, in an area between two buildings in front of a concrete retaining wall is the warmest microclimatic zone on the site. Here, several tropical

Figure 9.7. Fruit and vegetable growing areas at the Center for Regenerative Studies near Pomona, California.

Figure 9.8. Integration of food growing and built environment at the Center for Regenerative Studies.

fruit trees, including a banana, a loquat, and a papaya, are growing and producing fruit, though this region in general has cool periods that prohibit fruit production by these species.

Several of the food-growing areas are next to stands of native walnut trees that are the evolved tree cover of the site and that were retained when the center was built. These native trees are habitat for a number of wildlife species, including several pairs of nesting hawks and owls. Surprisingly, these birds chose to remain in their homes after the center's residents moved in, and now they prey to some extent on rodents and small birds that feed on the crops. Thus, in a sense, the center, with its great diversity of species, has expanded the food chain to the benefit of resident native species. The result is a landscape with an organic richness, fertility, and diversity far greater than existed here before humans came on the scene.

Waste and Reassimilation

Of the many forms of waste produced in our society, probably the most pervasive, and certainly among the most damaging, is sewage. Figure 9.9 shows a typical mechanical treatment plant—steel and concrete and often marginally effective. There are better, cheaper ways that more effectively follow nature's way— that is, that are more regenerative. Ironically, there is no better example than

Figure 9.9. Typical mechanical wastewater treatment plant.

the lowly and repugnant subject of sewage treatment for showing the potential for reassimilation and organic growth; sewage is among our great untapped resources.

Figure 9.10 shows an aquaculture/treatment pond at the Center for Regenerative Studies. The water used for both crop irrigation and aquaculture at the center is treated sewage effluent piped here from the City of Pomona Sewage Treatment Plant. This water is generally good in quality with one exception—its high ammonia content. Since ammonia is a nutrient, this is an asset for irrigation; but because ammonia is toxic for many fish, it presents a problem for aquaculture. The solution was to incorporate a simple natural treatment system in the first ponds in the series. This system uses aquatic plants, including water hyacinth and duckweed, floating on the pond's surface. Bacteria living on the roots of these plants take up the ammonia and use it in their own growth processes. To a somewhat lesser degree, the plants themselves do likewise. With this bountiful nutrient supply, the aquatic plants grow rapidly and are harvested frequently. They are then composted, often in mixture with animal manure, and the compost is used for soil enrichment. Thus, the nutrients go back into food and the cycle goes on in a kind of seamless continuity.

Figure 9.10. Wastewater treatment using aquaculture system at the Center for Regenerative Studies.

Figure 9.11. Wetlands wastewater treatment system, Denham, Louisiana.

This same principle can be used to treat much larger volumes of sewage from the primary stage of treatment through advanced stages. Figure 9.11 shows a treatment plant in Denham Springs, Louisiana, that uses a combination of ponds and wetlands with diverse species of aquatic and wetland plants removing nutrients, metals, toxins, and other materials from the town's sewage. At the end of the process, the water is pure enough to be discharged into a nearby bayou. The capital and operating costs for this natural treatment system are less than half that of a comparable mechanical plant. Moreover, it is odorless, looks like a water garden, and is always teeming with wildlife. At the center, urban organic wastes are used in the food-growing process in a number of different forms, including composted kitchen wastes and sewage sludge, animal manure, and greenwaste.

While the most important means for dealing with organic matter is reassimilation into the processes of organic growth, there is an endless range of ways of dealing with other levels of material usually considered as waste in the landscape. Important among these is direct reuse. Figure 9.12 shows broken concrete and worn out tires used to build retaining walls. These walls were built by students cheaply and quickly using no mortar and have held up very well through extremely heavy rains.

Figure 9.12. Direct reuse of waste concrete and tires in retaining wall system.

Visible Qualities of Regenerative Landscape

Through recent centuries, linear reductionist thought, breaking the wholeness of the environment into ever smaller pieces, has inured us with the illusion that we could quite reasonably break apart an object—or a building or a landscape—in our minds and consider its various properties, including its outward appearance, in isolation from one another. Immanuel Kant (1792) proposed the notion that the aesthetic quality (that quality which gives pleasure or displeasure upon seeing it) was a property that could be considered apart from the actual physical substance, and even apart from the qualities that stimulate thought or desire. Through the Industrial Era, we have come to accept this idea much too readily and to think of aesthetic and utilitarian characteristics as separate and not necessarily related. This has led to ever greater abstraction of aesthetic qualities and therefore to a pervasive sense of unreality in much of our environmental design (Thayer 1994). Typical of the results are such absurdities as the image of a nineteenth-century park imposed on the ecology of semi-arid Southern California. Increasingly through the Industrial Era, image and substance have parted ways. This parting has contributed greatly to our alienation from the natural world and probably to our environmental crises.

  The ecological approach to design does not allow such a separation of parts and qualities. A landscape, including its aesthetic quality, is an integrated whole and visible form is an expression of the merging of natural processes and culture, which are themselves inseparable. Any landscape is an integral part of a larger landscape that is its natural, cultural context.

The forms that emerge from this integrative way of thinking and design are necessarily somewhat different from the forms of landscapes that live on industrial life-support systems. Often, people assume that landscapes founded on nature's processes must look like natural landscapes. This is not necessarily the case. The visible forms of regenerative landscapes vary greatly because local circumstances and processes vary and human culture varies. However, I think we can identify certain qualities or characteristics, all quite different from the qualities of the industrial landscape, that reflect the processes of regeneration and therefore typify the regenerative landscape. There are four of these that I consider especially indicative of the processes of regeneration; these are locality, fecundity, diversity, and continuity.

Locality

A regenerative landscape grows out of the earth in a particular place. The combinations of climate, water flow, soil, landform, and the movement of the sun in a place is unique to that place, and that combination guides any design for that place. Culture—that is, real evolved and evolving culture, not media culture—is also unique to a particular place. Local human culture is an essential shaper of form not only because culture and landscape grow from the same soil but because the character of local culture is itself an important influence.

Fecundity

Fecundity is the expression of fertility, the ongoing reproduction and growth that characterizes natural environments and that is essential to the long-term survival of human environments as well. Thus, fecundity is at the heart of regeneration. The expression of fecundity, the richness of ongoing organic growth balanced by the equal richness of organic decay, makes nature's fundamental processes visible and is therefore an essential quality in the design of landscape.

Diversity

Diversity is a quality closely associated with stability and thus with sustainability. The exact nature of the relationship is not clear and remains a subject of discussion among scientists. Clearly there are exceptions; some highly diverse environments can be unstable, and vice versa. Cause-and-effect relationships are not well understood. However, it seems clear that to be effective in fostering stability, the quality of diversity should not reflect an arbitrary collection of elements but instead an ongoing interaction of elements. Such interactive stability, when made visible, becomes an expression of longevity, or long-term sustainability.

Continuity

In nature, landscapes are always changing—from day to day, season to season, year to year. Landscapes change in predictable patterns through continuing processes of succession and evolution. Such orderly mutability is a fundamental characteristic of landscape. Less orderly change in response to altered conditions and unpredictable circumstance are characteristic as well. In the regenerative landscape, change is accepted not only as inevitable but as a necessary characteristic of ongoing processes. Thus it is celebrated and expressed, not fought off.

Continuity in space is analogous to continuity in time. While the natural landscape is far from uniform in character, it is rarely fragmented. While the natural landscape varies greatly in form over large areas, the variations clearly relate to changes in topography, soil, microclimate, hydrology, and other physical factors. They are marked by more or less gradual transitions. Rarely is there a sense of fragmentation. In the industrialized landscape, by contrast, fragmentation is the rule rather than the exception, as pieces of landscape are designed independently of adjoining pieces. Often the lines between pieces are determined by property or political boundaries or by functional or land use differences, and rarely is there any serious attempt at transition from one to the other. In the regenerative landscape, the sense of continuity—indeed the reality of continuity—is important in achieving wholeness in the landscape.

ALL OF THESE QUALITIES can conflict with some of the more traditional qualities often sought in the design of landscapes. Modernist design of the Industrial Era sought universality of form usually supported by unlimited infusions of energy and often reflecting concentration of power, in preference to locality of form. It was not merely incidental that early modern (industrial) architecture was called the International Style. Fecundity can be messy and hard to predict in contrast to the neatness and sharpness of form often sought in industrialized landscapes. Designers of the late industrial period often prefer large areas of highly controllable paving to the use of living plants. Diversity can conflict with the sense of uniformity and the desire for expression of centralized control that often characterize industrial landscapes. The sense of continuity in regenerative landscapes, when it can be achieved, often stands in strong contrast to the fragments of landscape often produced by Industrial Era patterns of land use, ownership and political control.

Thus, we need to be aware that regenerative landscapes sometimes may be perceived as strange and different within the industrial context that still prevails. It is important to recognize these perceptions and the barriers they can present to the wider acceptance of regenerative landscapes. People do not readily accept new and unfamiliar forms, especially in their everyday environment.

Culture and Regeneration

Now matter how successful regenerative landscapes may be in integrating humans with natural processes and in achieving sustainability, they will not be effective on the larger scale—that is, they will not make a real difference in the world—until they become part of our culture. Three of my recent projects, located in three very different places, help to illustrate the strong influences of locality on form and also attempt to give expression to the qualities of fecundity, diversity, continuity, and mutability in ways that try to achieve a sense of cultural harmony and correspondence with their local and regional settings.

The first of these is the plan for the campus of the Appalachian Ministries Educational Resource Center (AMERC) in Berea, Kentucky. This small center is in some ways like the Center for Regenerative Studies. Its campus, however, is considerably larger—80 acres compared to 16—and the land is badly degraded. For this reason, in addition to regenerative systems similar to those of the Center for Regenerative Studies, the AMERC plan includes several land rehabilitation programs. The largest of these is a grazing rotation designed to restore the badly overworked cropland, degraded by years of tobacco farming, to native prairie. Also included are a forest rehabilitation program to restore the health of the native hardwood forest, a wetland enhancement program to increase habitat value, and a riparian zone protection program along the disturbed banks of the stream that flows through the site.

The buildings and the surrounding landscape, as shown in the site plan in Figure 9.13, are designed to fit harmoniously into the majestic Appalachian hardwood forest setting and to achieve a sense of continuity with the very strong cultural traditions of the regions (see Figures 9.14 and 9.15). In form and detail, the architec-

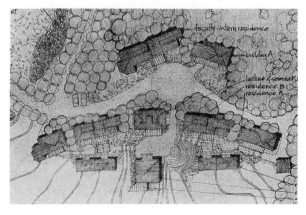

Figure 9.13. Plan view of the campus of the Appalachian Ministries Educational Resource Center (AMERC) in Berea, Kentucky.

Figure 9.14. Integration of buildings and landscape on the campus of the Appalachian Ministries Educational Resource Center.

Figure 9.15. The built environment at the Appalachian Ministries Educational Resource Center relies on passive solar design for heating and cooling.

ture draws on the traditional wood buildings of Appalachia while applying the principles of passive solar heating and natural cooling. The food-growing areas intermingle with the buildings, stepping down the hill in a series of terraces.

The next project is the Environmental Studies Center at Oberlin College in Ohio. This was very much a team project, guided by an advisory team composed of David Orr, Amory Lovins, William McDonough, and myself. The building was designed by William McDonough and Partners. Andropogon, Inc., worked with me on the design of the landscape.

As a learning environment, the landscape includes the basic life-support processes, all functioning in regenerative ways, in addition to a sample of the native hardwood forest that evolved on this site before it was altered by humans. Emphases here are on the locality as shaped by evolution and succession and on continuity over time. As shown in the plan (see Figure 9.16), the section of forest wraps around the north and east areas of the center and forms a transition from this complex to the larger campus. On the south side of the building, the Sun Plaza is an extension of the building's atrium, which is a collector of solar energy for heating. The plan of the Sun Plaza forms a gnomon with a vertical shaft casting shadows that mark the position of the sun at sunrise and sunset at key times during the year—especially solstice and equinox. In this effort to reconnect people with their

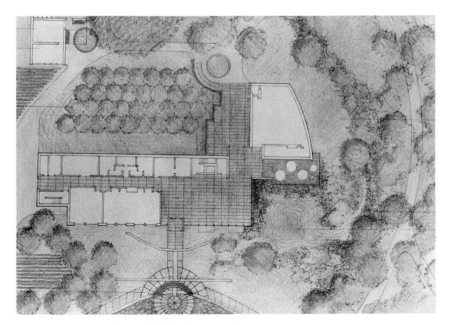

Figure 9.16. Plan view of the Sun Plaza at the Environmental Studies Center, Oberlin College, Ohio.

cosmic environment, the design draws on traditions that date back thousands of years in the Middle East and Meso America—monuments as solar time keepers. On the east side, between building and forest, is the landscape featuring the flow of water. This landscape is not connected to the campus storm sewer. Instead, the landscape is designed to absorb much of the rainwater where it falls and infiltrate it into groundwater storage. The portion that runs off flows across a small meadow, which filters out some particulates, and into a shallow swale that guides it through a wetland, where it is further treated, and into a basin, where it is stored for irrigating the food-growing areas. This pond–wetland system is adjacent to and visually continuous with the Living Machine that treats the building's sewage (Figure 9.17). Together, these will form a lush continuous indoor–outdoor landscape, emphasizing the rich fecundity of the aquatic environment.

Food-growing areas are on the western and northern portions of the site. These use various organic methods and include herb and vegetable growing and orchards of deciduous fruit trees. One orchard is on the berm that earth-shelters the north side of the building, stepping down from the building wall in a series of terraces.

The food-growing area centers on a small greenhouse–workshop structure with an attached composting area. The key position of composting is important here, giving this reassimilation process its rightful place at the very heart of the food cycle.

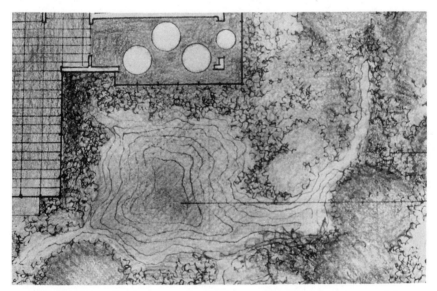

Figure 9.17. Pond–wetland system at the Environmental Studies Center, Oberlin College, Ohio.

The last project that I want to discuss is a biblical-meditation garden on the campus of the Claremont School of Theology (see Figure 9.18). The garden is fundamentally symbolic in character, reflecting the school's spiritual and theological foundation and tradition. However, it is also a regenerative landscape, reflecting the school's commitment to landscape and giving visible form to the school's long-standing commitment to care of the land as a moral commitment.

The Claremont School of Theology has long recognized and embraced a strong relationship between religious belief and environment. Several of its faculty members were among the pioneer environmental theologians. Housed on the campus is the Center for Process Studies, which is an internationally important institute for the study of the works of Alfred North Whitehead. Whitehead's emphasis (1928) on process in our relationship with the world has been an important influence on the development of ecological design (Lyle 1985).

The garden is conceived as a system of intersecting curving pathways, representing the ongoing, never straight and simple, process of life, following the contours of the site. The pathways are made of the natural decomposed granite of the site. Where they intersect are hard-edged geometric decision points with surfaces of recycled concrete (see Figure 9.19) mostly made from an old sidewalk that was on the site. Two of these have low seat-walls, also made from recycled concrete, looking onto rock and sculpture displays (see Figure 9.20).

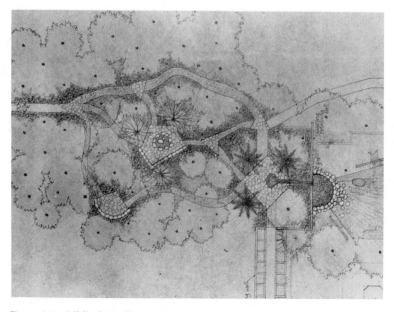

Figure 9.18. Biblical Meditation Garden at the Claremont School of Theology, California.

Figure 9.19. Pathways constructed of decomposed granite and recycled concrete at the Claremont School of Theology, California.

Figure 9.20. Recycled concrete seats in the Biblical Meditation Garden at the Claremont School of Theology, California.

Figure 9.21. Circular pools in the Biblical Meditation Garden of the Claremont School of Theology, California.

The plantings, to suggest both ancient theological connections and continuity, are species that grew in the biblical lands during biblical times. Since the climate and topography of these areas are very similar to Southern California, they fit very comfortably into this setting, using minimal water. A few California natives, including one species on the endangered list—the Engelmann Oak—are among them to establish both a sense of locality and a correspondence with a distant place. The plants are growing in a mix of native soil and composted sewage sludge, and the surface is covered with a mulch of chipped tree trimmings from the surrounding area.

In another part of the garden, representing the fusion of human thought and the natural processes of this particular place, water bubbles up from a circular pool (see Figure 9.21), spills over a low retaining wall, and washes over an inscription from the Bible on the surface of the wall (see Figure 9.22). At the base of the wall, the water drops into a pond with the food chain of a natural water body. And around the pond is a rock and driftwood garden meant to recall the broad wash that once covered this site (see Figure 9.23). Southern California washes commonly feature scatterings of boulders and driftwood that have tumbled down from the rugged mountains to the north. The composition here includes boulders of various sizes and pieces of wood in various states from freshly milled lumber to logs in an advanced state of decay (see Figure 9.22). These suggest the cycle of use,

Figure 9.22. Boulders and wood pieces near biblical inscription wall in the Biblical Meditation Garden of the Claremont School of Theology, California.

Figure 9.23. Rock and driftwood in the Biblical Meditation Garden of the Claremont School of Theology, California.

decomposition, reassimilation, regrowth, and reuse. As in other parts of the garden, the emphasis is on process rather than on objects for their own sake.

I believe these three examples, small though they are, adequately demonstrate that both the regenerative processes and the visible qualities of ecological design are entirely in harmony with our prevailing culture. Locality, fecundity, diversity, and continuity in the landscape are anything but strange and alien qualities. On the contrary, I believe that by making the landscape whole again, and by returning its fundamental role as the source of life, we can give substance and visible expression to qualities and meanings that have been lost since the time of disaggregation.

REFERENCES

Kant, Immanuel. 1792. *Critique of Aesthetic Judgment.* Translated by James Creed Meredith. Oxford: Clarendon Press.

Lyle, John Tillman. 1994. *Regenerative Design for Sustainable Development.* New York: John Wiley and Sons.

Lyle, John Tillman. 1999. *Design for Human Ecosystems: Landscape, Land Use and Natural Resources.* Washington, DC: Island Press.

Thayer, Robert L. Jr. 1994. *Gray World, Green Heart.* New York: John Wiley and Sons.

Van der Ryn, Sim, and Stuart Cowan. 1996. *Ecological Design.* Washington, DC: Island Press.

Whitehead, Alfred North. 1928. *Process and Reality: An Essay in Cosmology,* Corrected Edition (David Ray Griffin and Donald W. Sherburne, eds.). New York: Free Press.

Chapter 10

Construction and Demolition Waste: Innovative Assessment and Management

Peter Yost

In recent years, there has been growing interest at both the local level and the national level in the construction and demolition (C&D) waste stream. The types and amounts of materials represent both environmental challenges and opportunities. For the past four years, the National Association of Home Builders (NAHB) Research Center has been working with the U.S. Environmental Protection Agency in the exploration of innovative alternatives to C&D waste disposal. While the focus of the Research Center's work was residential C&D waste management in new construction, renovation, and demolition, much of the discussion is relevant to nonresidential C&D waste management.

C&D waste management follows a logical progression:

1. Characterization of the C&D waste stream
2. Regulations affecting C&D waste management
3. Steps to be taken in exploring C&D waste management alternatives
4. Methods for the management of specific C&D waste materials

The chapter discusses each of these parts of the progression and then closes with a look to what the future may hold in the development of alternatives to C&D waste disposal. Note that for easy reference, NAHB Research Center publications are referenced in the text by letters (A through J) and the complete titles are contained in the References section at the end of the chapter.

Characterization of the C&D Waste Stream

Before any assessment of a material stream can be made, a clear definition of the term must be established. Challenges begin here for this waste stream since no standard or federal regulatory definition of the construction and demolition waste stream has been offered. Regulatory definitions of the C&D waste stream are left to the states, leaving room for substantial variation. In the soon-to-be-released EPA publication *Characterization of Building-related Construction and Demolition Debris in the United States,* the following definition is used:

> Construction and Demolition (C&D) Debris is waste material that is produced in the process of construction, renovation, or demolition of structures. Structures include buildings of all types (both residential and nonresidential) as well as roads and bridges. Components of C&D debris typically include concrete, asphalt, wood, metals, gypsum wallboard, floor tile and roofing. Land clearing debris, such as stumps, rocks, and dirt, are also included.

It is important to note that the waste stream is not defined by its destination or its specific composition but rather the activities that result in its generation. This means that as the materials used in the activities vary, so will the types and amounts of waste materials associated with the activities. Table 10.1 provides a representative snapshot of the types of materials to be expected in the C&D waste stream.

Even more challenging than defining C&D waste is quantifying the waste stream. Assessments of other waste streams have often relied on a good relationship between the types and amounts of materials and the number of people in a given area—a technique commonly referred to as per capita multiplication. As Figure 10.1 demonstrates, this method is particularly unreliable for the C&D waste

Table 10.1. What's in construction waste and demolition debris?

Waste Type	Contents
Rubble	Dirt, bricks, cinder blocks, concrete
Asphalt	Roads, bridges, parking lots
Tar-based materials	Shingles, tar paper
Ferrous metal	Pipes, roofing, flashing, steel
Nonferrous metal	Aluminum, copper, brass, stainless steel
Harvested wood	Stumps, tops, limbs
Untreated wood	Framing, scraps
Treated wood	Plywood, pressure-treated, creosote-treated, laminates
Plaster	Sheetrock, gypsum, drywall
Glass	Windows, doors
Plastic	Vinyl siding, doors, windows
White goods	Appliances
Contaminants	Lead-based paint, asbestos, fiberglass, fuel tanks

Source: Donovan 1990.

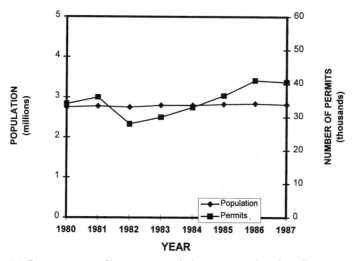

Figure 10.1. Boston metropolitan area population/construction demolition permits.

stream because the relationship between population and C&D waste generation can be highly variable.

A more representative technique relies on the relationship between the economic activities of building and building removal and waste generation. An innovative approach to assessing the C&D waste stream based on this relationship was first offered by the author in his graduate master's thesis and then recently employed in substantial part in the soon-to-be-released EPA publication *Characterization of Building-related Construction and Demolition Debris in the United States* conducted by Franklin Associates, Ltd. The basic premise is to use empirical data on the types and amounts of waste materials generated from representative C&D activities at job sites and then use available economic data from the Department of Commerce's Census Bureau to extrapolate waste generation to the local, regional, or national level. Representative empirical site data are given in Figures 10.2 and 10.3 and in Table 10.2, with the outcome of the technique as employed by Franklin Associates, Ltd., given in Table 10.3.

Note that the Franklin Associates totals for C&D waste generation do not include major contributing activities such as road, bridge, and land clearing debris. When representative empirical samples for these activities become available, the same method of assessment can be employed to bring these materials into the total characterization.

The most important results of this characterization are the following:

1. Standards for defining and assessing the C&D waste stream need to be established before meaningful attempts to characterize the waste stream can be conducted.

Site:	Anne Arrundel Cty. Winchester Homes Shipley's Choice
Date:	March 28, 1995

House Description: Production Standard 2 story- 2450 sq. ft., full basement, 2 car garage, brick facade, '4 bdrm., 2 1/2 bath

Waste Type	Description	Weight	Notes [Estimated volumes]
Wood	Dimensional Lumber	1220	[5.5 cy] 1/3 total pile used in shpg. & pkgng.
	Plywood	-------	none recovered
	Composite sheathings	1898	[5.3 cy] OSB(1/2"roof, 3/4" floor, 3/8" pkg.)
	Pressure-treated	144	[0.2 cy.] mostly preprimed ext. trim 1x
	Pallets (& other hardwood)	-------	[1.2 cy] (weight incl. with dimensional lumber)
	Other (trim)	57	[0.2 cy] Interior trim waste
Wood Subtotal		3319	[12.4 cy.]
Gypsum Products	Board -,standard content	2940	[11.4 cy] mostly 1/2" frag.; few half sheets
	Board - (MR,X, f-f,etc)	-------	
	Other		
Gypsum Subtotal		2940	[11.4 cy]
Corrugated Cardboard	Uncoated	478	[12.7 cy] Packaging; windows, cabinets,
	Coated		door frames, siding
Cardboard Subtotal		478	[12.7 cy]
Metals	Ferrous	220	[3.1 cy] Mostly banding; incidental duct work
	Non-Ferrous misc.	-------	mostly corner bead; incidental copper piping
	Alum. siding/molded trim	96	[.45 cy] All cutoff material
Metal Subtotal		316	[3.1 cy]
Plastics	Plumbing pipe/fittings	-------	Incidental PVC fittings
	Sheeting	67	[6.7 cy] Mostly carpet protection
	Other		
Plastics Subtotal		67	[6.7 cy]

Waste Type	Description	Weight	Notes [Estimated volumes]
Containers	Adhesives, Caulk Tubes	58	[0.3 cy] lg. and small tubes, few unused
	Plumbing Adhesives	-------	One empty can of PVC joint compound
	Paint Cans	0	No paint cans recovered
Containers Subtotal		58	[0.3 cy]
Miscellaneous Materials	Brick	1240	[0.6 cy] mostly cutoff waste some full pieces
	Sweepings/Electric wire	398	[1.7 cy] rubble, rigid foam, unstripped wire
	Carpet & Pad	51	[1.2 cy] small strips, short lengths
	Thermo-ply	25	incidental, very small pieces
	Asphalt Shingles	544	[3.3 cy] nothing recoverable
Miscellaneous subtotal		2258	[6.8 cy]
Total		9262	[53.4 cy]

Figure 10.2. New residential construction waste assessment.

Site:	Wheatley Kitchen/Sitting Addition & New Roof
Date:	May 3, 1997

Project Description:	400 SF kitchen addition (including a sitting area and eating area); 160 SF new exterior deck (small, existing deck removed); New roof for entire house (14 square), including double-layer tear-off.
Project Budget:	$50,000
Audit Logistics:	A 30 cubic yard & a 10 cubic yard dumpster were hauled to a nearby processing facility for sorting and weighing.

Waste Type	Description	Weight (pounds)	Volume Estimates & Notes [cubic yards]
Wood	Dimensional lumber, Plywood, OSB	1600	[6 cy] mostly cut-off - approx. 50% solid-sawn, 50% engineered wood
	Pressure-treated	1940	[6 cy] exterior deck removed
	Contaminated wood	892	[3 cy] mostly tear-out - painted cabinets, subfloor with glue, etc
Wood Subtotal		4,432	[15 cy]
Gypsum Products	Gypsum board, plaster	671	mostly cut-off; some tear-out
Gypsum Subtotal		671	[1.5 cy]
Corrugated Cardboard	Uncoated	297	mostly broken-down, slightly damp
	Coated	0	
Cardboard Subtotal		297	[4.5 cy]
Metals	Ferrous	62	piping, flashing, banding
	Aluminum	81	trim, flashing, gutters
	Copper	2	pipes
Metal Subtotal		145	[1.5 cy]
Plastics	Vinyl siding, soffit, and banding	95	mostly siding tear-off, some cut-off
	Sheeting	19	
	Other	25	Celotex (polyisocyan.) boards
Plastics Subtotal		139	[2.5 cy]

Figure 10.3. Residential remodeling waste assessment.

2. The C&D waste stream, once thought to total between 30 and 40 million tons of waste materials annually in the United States, is more likely to total over three times that amount.

3. For new construction, wood, drywall, and cardboard make up as much as 75 percent of the total waste stream by volume or weight.

4. For renovation, reusable building materials and specialty wastes, such as asphalt roofing and carpeting, represent significant recovery opportunities.

5. For building removal, significant recycling opportunities for concrete, wood, and metals can be augmented by equally significant opportunities for salvage/reuse of building materials.

Table 10.2. Residential demolition waste assessment

	Volume (cubic yards)	Weight (tons)
MATERIALS DIVERTED		
Reuse and resale		
Framing lumber/sheathing	49	8
Brick	12	17.9
Hardwood flooring	7	1.1
Stair units/treads	4	0.4
Windows	2	0.3
Reuse and donation		
Tubs/toilets/sinks	3	0.7
Doors	3	0.4
Shelves	0.5	0.1
Kitchen cabinets	1	0.2
Recycle		
Rubble	88	61.6
Metals	13	2.3
Asphalt shingles	10	3.5
Diversion subtotal	192.5	96.5
MATERIALS LANDFILLED		
Plaster	48	21.6
Painted wood (moldings, baseboard, etc.)	16	4.2
Rubble	7	4.9
Landfill subtotal	81	30.7
DIVERSION RATE[a]	70%	76%

[a] The diversion rates used here are based on common building material densities.

Table 10.3. Summary of estimated building-related C&D debris generation, 1996[a]

Source	Residential		Nonresidential		Totals	
	Thousand tons	Percentage	Thousand tons	Percentage	Thousand tons	Percentage
Construction	6,560	11	4,420	6	10,980	8
Renovation	31,900	55	28,000	36	59,900	44
Demolition[b]	19,700	34	45,100	58	64,800	48
Totals[c]	58,160	100	77,520	100	135,680	100
Percentage	43		56		100	

[a] Roadway, bridge, and land-clearing debris not included.

[b] Note that in some areas, demolition debris (particularly foundations and driveways) may be managed on site (quantities are unknown).

[c] Details may not add to totals due to rounding.

Source: Franklin Associated, Ltd.

Regulations Affecting C&D Management

Any firm involved in the generation, transport, processing, or final disposition of C&D waste materials in the United States should be aware of the following laws and regulations:

1. The Resource Conservation and Recovery Act (RCRA)
2. The Comprehensive Environmental Response, Compensation, and Liability Act (CERCLA)
3. Local and state solid waste regulations
4. EPA and OSHA regulations regarding the handling of asbestos-containing materials (ACM) and lead-based paint (LBP) materials

The Resource Conservation and Recovery Act (RCRA)

This federal legislation sets national standards for the management and disposal of municipal solid waste, present and future. Its scope includes C&D waste. Although the legislation and the language of the resulting rules do not explicitly deal with C&D waste, RCRA is important in the management of C&D waste for the following reasons:

1. *RCRA defines hazardous materials.* RCRA sets standards for the key characteristics of "hazardous" materials—ignitability, corrosivity, reactivity, and toxicity. Although the burden of identifying specific materials as hazardous falls completely on the generator, examples of potentially hazardous materials include the following: adhesives, coatings, sealers, antifreeze, paint stripper, shellac, paint/lacquer, solvents, resins/epoxies, caulking, waterproofing agents, and asphaltic materials. For more detailed information on RCRA, see NAHB's *The Regulation of Solid and Hazardous Waste: A Builder's Guide* (1993).

2. *Conditionally exempt small-quantity generators (CESQG).* A new rule implemented in July 1996 by the EPA for the first time sets some de facto standards for the operation of C&D landfills. Construction and demolition activities are considered CESQG if they generate less than 220 pounds per month of potentially hazardous materials. This rule addresses CESQG by requiring C&D landfills to either prohibit C&D material that contains CESQG materials from entering the landfill or continuing to accept this material given specific landfill design and operation requirements. The importance of this rule will vary from state to state—for states with existing regulations that meet or exceed the landfill requirements it will mean business as usual; for states, and there are many, with less restrictive requirements, landfills will have to make changes over the next several years that may have a significant impact on costs. For an excellent summary of the CESQG rule, see *C&D Debris Recycling* magazine, January/February 1997.

The Comprehensive Environmental Response, Compensation, and Liability Act (CERCLA)

More commonly called "Superfund," CERCLA involves the management of hazardous cleanup at designated contaminated sites. It is important to C&D management because of its far-reaching effects on generators or transporters of waste linked to sites identified under CERCLA. CERCLA provides an incentive for builders, demolition firms, and haulers to carefully track and document the handling of C&D wastes in their businesses. For a layman's presentation of CERCLA and its relevance to C&D waste management, see NAHB's *The Regulation of Solid and Hazardous Waste: A Builder's Guide* (1993).

Local and State Solid Waste Regulations

Local and state regulations can apply to the transport, the processing, and the final disposition of C&D waste materials. Their most significant impact on C&D waste management can be in their lack of recognition of or distinction between C&D waste materials and other wastes. Health and safety rules and regulations set up for management of putrescible municipal solid waste can, when inappropriately applied to C&D, place significant barriers to the establishment of alternative C&D management operations.

EPA and OSHA ACM and LBP Regulations

EPA regulations generally cover the final disposition of ACM and LBP materials, and OSHA covers the handling of the same materials. These regulations can be important in the development of C&D alternatives to disposal for two reasons:

1. *The lack of relationship between EPA and OSHA regulations.* For C&D waste management businesses that involve both the handling and disposition of C&D materials, this can create significant difficulties in compliance as alternatives to traditional landfilling are explored. Even at the basic level of definitions, EPA and OSHA regulations were not established with common terminology and categories of materials.

2. *The lack of recognition of alternatives to conventional disposal.* If EPA and OSHA rules assume that the only destination of C&D waste materials is the landfill, rules for the disposition and handling of the materials can inadvertently establish real obstacles to the exploration of alternatives to landfilling. Specific issues regarding ACM and LBP materials are discussed in greater detail later in this chapter as well as in the NAHB Research Center publication (D).

Steps to Be Taken in Exploring C&D Waste Management Alternatives

In each of the projects the Research Center conducted with EPA, the structure of the work was as follows: detailed assessments, workshops, pilot projects, and directories.

While the result of each of these investigations was at least one publication seeking to disseminate the most successful innovations from many areas of the country, the successful case studies are, by their nature, context-specific and locally derived. Communities looking to develop and encourage alternatives to C&D disposal will likely need to follow these same steps, using the offered publications as the seeds for local efforts.

1. *Conduct detailed waste assessments.* The quantities and types of waste materials generated at typical job sites will strongly influence the exploration and development of waste management alternatives to disposal. Individuals and businesses considering waste reduction and recovery opportunities will require accurate information on the waste materials and the manner in which they are generated. While the exact methods of waste assessment can depend largely on financial resources, a methodology developed by the Research Center is available. (See Tables 10.2 and 10.3 for representative results.) Key issues in assessment include categorization of waste materials, assessing both mass and volume (the compressibility of and captured air space in many C&D waste materials must be systematically addressed), and dealing with the highly variable moisture content of many materials.

2. *Conduct local workshops.* For any waste stream, there are a host of existing and potential key players who need to be involved in the development of alternatives to disposal. For example, in locally based workshops conducted by the Research Center for residential new construction waste management, the following entities participated: builders, landfill owners and operators, haulers, local and state solid waste officials, recyclers and processors, and building product manufacturers. Each comes to the table with their own perspective and expertise, both of which are important to the process of identifying and exploring obstacles and opportunities. The workshops almost always represent the only time that all these players have been brought together. The assessments, along with other available information on existing local outlets and local examples of successful strategies, can be used to drive the discussion of alternatives. The Research Center publication *A Manual for Conducting a Local Waste Management Forum* (available in the fall of 1998) can be used to develop and conduct the workshop. A hopeful outcome of the exploratory workshop is the establishment of a working group to move forward on steps 3 and 4 discussed below.

3. *Conduct pilot projects.* One of the typical outcomes of a C&D waste management forum or workshop is the identification of at least one strategy that players want to test. The combined resources of the working group can be used to determine how a new approach will work in the local context. Pilot projects are important to the process because learning curves for new approaches can be steep and the costs of testing an alternative are best borne

by a team of key players working together. The goal of pilot projects is, of course, to document a successful alternative to be used as an incentive for others to consider.

4. *Create recovery directories.* Another outcome of a local C&D waste management forum will be the discovery of existing resources in waste reduction and recovery. It's important that these resources be presented in a format that is available to all key players and that the resource base be kept current. The resource base should contain all the information needed to make use of the resource: location, hours of operation, point of contact, materials accepted, requirements on the condition of materials, and costs/premiums. The creation and maintenance of information resources such as directories often can be an extension of existing information services of local and state solid waste, recycling, or department of public works offices.

As alternatives to conventional C&D waste disposal are being considered, recognition of incentives is crucial. There are five primary incentives to exploring alternatives to disposal:

1. *Cost savings.* It's no surprise that every building, renovation, and demolition contractor would like to lower their total disposal costs. What can be surprising is the number of contractors who do not really know their total waste management costs or assign costs to recovery alternatives that are not considered in conventional disposal costs. For example, it is common for the "extra" handling costs of separation for recycling to be unfairly compared to conventional disposal costs that do not include any handling costs. As alternatives are being explored, careful attention must be paid to equivalent cost comparisons and to identifying which costs of a new approach may be reduced or eliminated as the new alternative becomes routine.

2. *Convenience.* Many building, renovation, and demolition contractors consider more reliable or more convenient service as important if not more important than cost savings. Because waste management is simply a necessary cost of doing business, which can represent a distraction from the contractor's ultimate goal of delivering a home or other building, a waste management strategy that increases convenience or decreases the amount of time and energy that a contractor must spend on waste management is all the incentive needed to make the move from conventional disposal.

3. *Liability.* The building and demolition industries understand the long-term advantage that reduced liability provides. If a waste management alternative can be shown to reduce a construction or demolition company's legal exposure for waste they generate, this can be a strong incentive for considering an alternative to traditional practice.

4. *Marketing.* Greater distinction in the marketplace and increased business can be a strong incentive to construction and demolition firms to embrace

new approaches to C&D waste management. The impact on business of targeted media attention, either for the best or the worst of business activities,
is lost on no firm.

5. *Social responsibility.* Although the construction and demolition industries
are rarely perceived or portrayed as the most progressive of businesses, it's
hard to find firms that prefer disposal to any alternative. It's not uncommon
on job sites to hear workers state that they would like to "do the right thing
for their kids' sakes." Waste reduction and recovery are often perceived and
portrayed as "the right thing to do" and, as an incentive for considering new
approaches, social or environmental responsibility can be a powerful force
for change.

Methods for Management of Specific C&D Waste Materials

Different waste management strategies seem to be suited to different waste streams.
This section of the chapter presents strategies for the following C&D activities:
(1) new construction, (2) general renovation, (3) light-frame building removal—
deconstruction. Carpet and asphalt roofing recycling are two special recovery
opportunities that could not be included in this discussion. For more information,
refer to NAHB Research Center publications (I) and (J).

New Construction

There are promising waste management strategies for both waste reduction and
recycling for new residential construction.

Waste Reduction

Two approaches to waste reduction show the most promise in new residential construction: supply–install–dispose contract language and efficient framing techniques. Supply–install–dispose contracts link responsibility for all stages of a subcontractor's activities on the job site. The more that the responsibility for the
supply and installation of building materials and the disposal of waste from the
installation can be confined to one business entity, the more inherent the incentive
to use materials cost-effectively and efficiently. For one general contractor documented in NAHB Research Center publication (A), waste reduction on the job site
reached 80 percent with contract language of this nature.

Efficient framing techniques have been available to residential builders for the
last twenty years. And with wood waste representing at least 25 percent of the total
waste from most job sites, efficient framing represents the most significant single
waste reduction opportunity. However, as shown in Table 10.4, the real cost savings that can result from efficient framing are in reduced material purchase.
Demonstrating to builders the substantial savings in material costs as well as waste
disposal has proven the most successful approach to waste reduction.

Table 10.4. Estimated savings of efficient framing techniques

Value-Engineering Technique	Savings	
	Argos/Deluca	*Eastbrooke/Erb*
In-line framing @ 24" O.C. (joists and floors)	$960	N/C[a]
Increased spacing of floor joists from 16" to 24"	$747	N/C
Increased spacing of floor joists from 16" to 19.2"	N/C	$450
Header sizes	$162	$45
Relocated openings (doors, windows, stairs)	$45	N/C
Roof design (24" module)	Negligible	Negligible
Excessive waste factors or take-off tools	N/C	$130
Corner framing details	$30	N/C
Ladder framing detail	$45	N/C

[a] N/C = Not Considered

Recycling

The overall success of job site recycling is dependent on the following factors: proximity to landfills and their tipping fees; availability of recycling outlets; hauler fee structure; building type and production level; commitment level of both office and field staff; and the availability of hauling or recovery options. Specific methods of recovery include the following:

- *Commingled processing.* Commingled recovery processes involve separation and recovery of the materials off the construction job site. The waste is generally contained and collected in the same roll-off containers used for construction waste disposal. Materials are recovered by mechanical or manual separation. If markets exist for cardboard, drywall, and all uncontaminated wood waste, then conceivably 70–80 percent recovery rates are obtainable. The advantage to this approach is that no change in operation is required of the builder—construction waste is handled in the same manner as for disposal. The disadvantage to this approach is that separation costs reduce the net value of the recovered materials, and contamination resulting from commingling (dirt, dust, spilled paint, etc.) can render some materials unrecoverable or not worth separation. Additionally, significant capital investment is required to initiate and operate such a facility.
- *Source separation.* Source separation involves individual containers on the construction job site with materials identified for recovery going into designated

containers. This approach involves the greatest change in waste management practices for builders and all of their subcontractors. Prior experience has shown that the general contractor must aggressively educate all job site workers, with requirements to separate the materials written into subcontracts. A commitment is required not only of upper management but of site supervisors as well to make the separation effort work. Prior experience has also shown that the educational and retraining efforts must be ongoing for up to a year before the system begins to be self-managing. The advantage to this approach is that easily separated materials are kept, so and contamination from commingling is eliminated.

- *Clean-up services.* Job site clean-up services take advantage of the fact that certain construction materials—wood, drywall, cardboard (to some extent), and siding materials—are generated during specific and discrete stages of construction. If job site service by the waste hauler can be coordinated with the construction cycle, waste materials can be passively separated over time. Advantages to this type of waste management include:

  1. Charges for the service are often determined up front on a square-foot basis and an employee (laborer to clean up job sites and place construction waste in the roll-off) may be eliminated from the general contractor payroll.
  2. Builders value the convenience of having a subcontractor assume complete responsibility for job site waste.
  3. Waste can be collected in simple fenced or designated areas to eliminate the problems associated with large roll-off containers, the most significant being the up to 30 percent of waste in roll-offs that is not construction waste.
  4. A waste management firm rather than the builder makes the decision as to which materials are recovered or discarded, based on ever-changing local factors, as presented above.

- *On-site techniques.* On-site recovery of wood, drywall, and possibly cardboard may be possible after the materials have been processed in a mobile grinder. At least one manufacturer markets a low-speed, low-noise, mobile grinder well suited for this method. While the environmental acceptability of this technique has been documented [see NAHB Research Center publication (A) cited previously], requirements for local approval are to be expected. The Research Center is currently working with a local home builders association and state recycling office to determine the overall feasibility of job application of wood and drywall waste at residential new construction sites.

General Renovation

General residential waste management opportunities are limited by two factors: the overall small scale of most residential remodeling jobs and the typical cogeneration of both C&D waste at each job. Interestingly, the best recovery opportunity—reuse or the recovery of material for its functional value—is the one often limited at new construction sites. Research Center pilot projects resulted in diversion for salvage of up to 10 to 15 percent of the total volume of job site waste. Building material reuse during renovation can include the following: cabinetry, doors, windows, plumbing fixtures, electrical fixtures, wood flooring, and large dimension framing.

Reuse can take the following forms:

1. *At the job site.* Used building materials can be redeployed in a new setting at the job site. Kitchen cabinets can be relocated to the garage, workroom, laundry room, or basement. Characteristic paneling or interior trim can often be carefully removed for current or future reuse at the job.

2. *At subsequent job sites.* Many, if not most, remodelers have a garage, barn, or other storage space filled with salvaged and surplus materials that they have "been meaning to get back to." The remodelers problem of unfailingly placing these materials into storage but rarely remembering to pull them out for the appropriate job can be overcome with a basic inventory system. The savings resulting from treating these materials as organized resources can be significant.

3. *Informal donation setup.* Some remodelers have established a "free tree," placing reusable materials in a publicized set location for the community to take and make use of. The remodeler reduces disposal costs and creates a positive public image for his business.

4. *Donation centers.* A growing number of nonprofit and for-profit used building material stores accept salvaged and surplus building materials. An incentive added to the avoided disposal costs is the tax-deductible donation associated with nonprofit retail centers or the payment for certain building materials offered by for-profit stores. A critical issue for this form of reuse is the timely scheduling and clearly designated responsibility for pick-up and transport from the job site to the retail location.

For more detailed information on remodeling waste management, refer to NAHB Research Center publication (B).

Light-Frame Building Removal

As tipping fees at landfills increase, so does the likelihood of "stripping" prior to building demolition. Stripping is the selective salvage of building materials and components and is practiced by many demolition firms on a variety of building types. *Deconstruction* is a new term to describe the primarily manual disassembly of one- and two-story light-framed buildings with the salvage of as much as 75 percent of the total building volume. Doors, windows, framing, flooring, and masonry can all be reused in a "cleaned" state or remanufactured into value-added products such as wood flooring and furniture stock. The basic premise is that the added costs of manual disassembly and material processing are offset by the avoided disposal costs and salvage value of the materials. This approach to building removal has received considerable attention recently because of the very large stock of existing public housing about to be completely retired (an estimated 150,000 buildings from urban public housing stock and closed military bases) and the nationwide "welfare to work" initiative.

Many issues are being addressed in current or planned pilot projects:

1. *Lead and asbestos management requirements.* Both EPA and OSHA have environmental and worker protection standards with relevance and applicability to manual disassembly not completely delineated or understood.

2. *Davis-Bacon wage requirements.* Federal prevailing wage requirements may need clarification as to their applicability to apprentice and worker training initiatives.

3. *Worker compensation rates.* The issue of how existing rules and standards apply to innovative approaches is further reflected by the placement of new worker activities into existing risk categories for worker compensation.

4. *Timing.* Deconstruction can require as much as two to ten times more time to achieve site clearance. Are there methods to reduce the time required for deconstruction or to increase the amount of time that public property is available for site clearance?

5. *Reuse markets.* Because the used building material industry has traditionally been an informal and niche industry, how can the reuse and remanufacturing of building materials be transformed into a national industry network?

6. *Economic rules-of-thumb and training standards.* Information on building inventory, worker training, flow of materials on the job site, and assessing overall cost-effectiveness of the deconstruction approach for each building are all vital information that the industry needs.

These issues and others are being addressed by pilot projects across the country. A compilation of the issues and useful references and case studies can be found in NAHB Research Center publication (D).

New Directions in C&D Management

Forward-looking, innovative builders, remodelers, and demolition contractors still need incentives to accept the challenge of breaking from the easy path of straight disposal to move toward developing new recovery opportunities. In many areas of the country, the market price of materials from virgin resources and the market price of landfill disposal make the straight economics of alternatives far less than competitive. Pioneers in C&D waste management are often the same contractors that are employing resource-efficiency techniques in areas other than waste management. An area of real promise is the development of resource-efficient or green builder programs that give these contractors distinction in the marketplace. If public and private building owners, all other things being equal, show a preference for contractors that feature resource-efficiency in many aspects of their business, then building, remodeling, and demolition contractors can begin to use these practices as a marketplace advantage. Programs of this nature—green building or green development programs—are just beginning to emerge in the marketplace. And the key to their success is education and informational marketing. The buying public will select for resource-efficiency if they know the right questions to ask and features to demand. The greatest promise for more innovative C&D waste management is in its integration into the larger context of resource-efficient construction and demolition practices and marketing.

REFERENCES

Donovan, Christine T. 1990. *Recycling Construction and Demolition Waste in Vermont: Final Report.* Submitted to Vermont Agency of Natural Resources, Department of Environmental Conservation, Solid Waste Management Division. Recycling and Resource Conservation Section, published by C. T. Donovan Associates, Inc., Burlington, VT.

All of the following references were published by the National Association of Home Builders Research Center in Upper Marlboro, Maryland. They are referred to throughout the chapter by the letters listed here.

(A) *Residential Construction Waste Management: A Builder's Field Guide, How to Save Money and Landfill Space.* 1997.

(B) *Waste Management: A Field Guide for Remodelers,* Summer 1998.

(C) *Residential Construction Waste Management: A Coordinator's Guide for Conducting Local Workshops,* 1998.

(D) *Deconstruction: Building Disassembly and Material Salvage: The Riverdale Case Study,* June 1997.

(E) *Deconstruction: How and When to Salvage Materials During Building Removal,* 1997.

(F) *How to Clean-Up in the Construction Waste Management Business: A Small Business Opportunity in Disposal and Recycling Services,* 1997.

(G) *Jobsite Recycling: A Builder's Blueprint: Putting a Lid on a Waste Removal Costs,* August 1997.

(H) *Construction Waste Management, A Guide for Municipalities,* August 1997.

(I) *From Roofs to Roads . . . Recycling Asphalt Roofing Shingles into Paving Materials,* 1998.

(J) *Carpet & Padding: Reuse & Recycling Opportunities,* 1998.

Part III

Process

Chapter 11

Building Values

Gail A. Lindsey

What is the faithful process of spirit and seed that touches empty ground and makes it rich again? It's the greater workings I cannot claim to understand. I only know that in its care, what has seemed dead is no longer, what has seemed lost, is no longer lost, that which some have claimed impossible, is made clearly possible, and what ground is fallow is only resting—resting and waiting for the blessed seed to arrive on the wind with all Godspeed. And it will.

—Clarissa Pinkola Estes, Ph.D.

This chapter is dedicated to five-year-old Katie McCarter, who, with her parents, provided me wonderful hospitality when I stayed in Gainesville, Florida, to give the presentation for the Rinker Lecture Series. Katie was passionate that she, her parents, and I go on an unspecified "adventure" during my stay. The two-day forecast called for turbulent, rainy, weather; but Katie remained adamantly focused. No ideas or suggestions satisfied her until a trip to a nature park sparked her interest. Upon arrival at the park, her transformation was magical—she abounded with energy and raced everywhere to explore. Her excitement was contagious!

Have we forgotten that childlike wonder of the world around us? Apparently. I have asked countless people during lectures I've given to think about and then choose one of three chairs listed below to "represent their life":

1. A sleek metal chair from overseas that was designed by a well-known artist and that could be purchased at the New York Museum of Modern Art. (It's stipulated that all proceeds go to Amnesty International.)
2. A plastic chair constructed from 100 percent recycled postconsumer waste that could be recycled again and again. This plastic chair was made and sold in their region.

3. A hand-crafted wood chair that was made locally and had been passed down many generations and could now be purchased in the local Goodwill store.

I direct the lecture participants to: "Take a minute to envision your life as one of these three chairs. Got it?"

I've found that almost everyone chooses the last chair to represent their life. This is all well and good, but no one has ever said, "Gail, I don't like your choices—I want to choose differently—I would like to have a smooth rock (or a place of green grass) be my chair and the representation of my life." I believe that many of us have shut down our creativity, our visions, our childlike questioning and wonder. These skills are exactly what is needed to envision, design, and manifest a "sustainable world"—a world where we live within the laws of nature and act as an interdependent species.

My first steps into a "sustainable world" began on camping trips with my Girl Scout leader of many years ago. She constantly repeated to us, almost as a mantra, "Leave a place better than when you arrived." That statement has had a major effect on my life and continues, I sometimes joke, to haunt me daily! As an architect, I'm in the business of "making things"; of bringing physical form to visions, needs, and desires. The more I've engaged in this practice, the more I have realized five steps in the process of human intention and "manifestation" that I would like to share. In fact, throughout this chapter, I'd like to look at the concept of "designing" a sustainable world within the context of these five steps. I find these five steps "simple yet elegant," for they are basic but contain complexity. They are: (1) focus, (2) plan, (3) act, (4) evaluate, and (5) begin anew.

Let's explore together the conscious "design" of our own lives and of a sustainable world first by "focusing." Remember, this process is cyclical, like most processes found in nature.

Focus

I first began to focus on my life and not "wasting it" after a brain aneurysm left me partially paralyzed and in and out of hospital rooms when I was young. Such an episode can give one plenty of time to "focus," which is a rare thing for most of us in our ever more frenetic culture. I had just begun my architectural studies, so as I lay in bed I began to focus on what I would want my life and world to be if I could "design" it. This is not a suggested way to get the message, but I was able to learn that focusing/visioning is the first critical step in manifesting what you really want.

Donella Meadows, Dennis Meadows, and Jorgen Randers stated it best in the following quote from their book, *Beyond the Limits:*

> Visioning means imagining, at first generally, and then with increasing specificity, what you really want. That is, what you really want, not what someone has taught you to want, and not what you have

learned to be willing to settle for. Visioning means taking off all constraints of assumed feasibility, of disbelief and past disappointments, and letting your mind dwell upon its most noble, uplifting, treasured dreams.

Some people, especially young people, engage in visioning with enthusiasm and ease. Some people find the exercise of visioning painful, because a glowing picture of what could be makes what is all the more intolerable. Some people would never admit their visions, for fear of being thought impractical or unrealistic. They would find this paragraph uncomfortable to read, if they were willing to read it at all. And some people have been so crushed by their experience of the world that they can only stand ready to explain why any vision is impossible. That's fine; they are needed too. Vision needs to be balanced with skepticism.

We should say immediately for the sake of the skeptics that we do not believe it is possible for the world to envision its way to a sustainable future. Vision without action is useless. But action without vision does not know where to go or why to go there. Vision is absolutely necessary to guide and motivate action. More than that, vision, when widely shared and firmly kept in sight, brings into being new systems.

We mean that literally. Within the physical limits of space, time, materials and energy, visionary human intentions can bring forth not only new information, new behavior, new knowledge, and new technology, but eventually, new social institutions, new physical structure, and new powers within human beings.

A sustainable world can never come into being if it cannot be envisioned. The vision must be built from the contributions of many people before it is complete and compelling . . .

I question, as we consider focusing, whether we truly are aware of what is around us, what our cultural values and priorities are, and what we really want: Do we truly want, and will our cultural mores allow, a sustainably designed world based on a common framework of "interdependence"? I share this story to raise the issue of this type of awareness.

A group of sociologists studied the differences between children of two cultures, American and a small island community. Children ages five to seven were asked to study a picture of blocks that formed a structure and then reproduce the structure with a set of similar blocks. The American children all asked three questions immediately after being given the task.

1. How much time do I have to do it?
2. What happens if I get it wrong?
3. Do I get a prize if I get it right?

The island children didn't ask any of these questions; they proceeded to try for a while, run outside and do other things, bring their friends in to try the blocks again with them, and ultimately "finished" the structure.

The sociologists had some new questions to explore: Why, at such an early age, did the American children focus so differently than the island children? They began to look at ever younger children. The compelling difference was the first praise given to children in each culture. The sociologists saw the first major praise for an American child—when the child began to walk all by himself; with no help from anyone or anything—the first "step" to total independence. Back in the island culture, the sociologists watched for a similar reaction to a child's first steps. They were surprised to find that no significance was given to such an occurrence. An elder of the community, when asked about this indifference, replied simply that "all children had to walk sometime." The first major, universal praise from the island culture came to a young child when it unselfishly helped another child and began to understand the concept of "community."

I believe there are no right or wrong approaches in life, just an awareness and honoring of our choices. Have we been aware of our strong cultural focus toward independence? Isn't it intriguing that our culture is based on the Declaration of Independence? Only in the last five years has a group of international architects focused on a "Declaration of Interdependence"(see Figure 11.1).

If we truly desire to design a world interconnected with nature and each other, we must first focus with awareness on the issue of visioning such a place *together* and placing value on *community*. The next step is to plan for it.

Plan

Most of us learn more quickly if there is an element of fun in our life lessons. David Brower, at eighty-some years young, has valuable insights to share about sustainability. From his book, *Let the Mountains Talk, Let the Rivers Run:*

> People want to be part of something fun. It's exciting to change the world. If you're in it simply out of worry or guilt, you won't last, and normal people won't join you. People want to love life, if love hasn't been crushed out of them when they were children. Learning to read the Earth and saving it is fascinating stuff. Put fun in the movement to conserve, preserve, and restore, and celebrate it, and people will run to sign up.

A plan for a sustainable world must include fun! Deprivation, poverty, and "going without" are not fun. However, being part of a plan to increase our incredible natural abundance and diversity is. The plan, then, should include diverse ideas, cultures, ecosystems. Additionally, folks of all ages should be engaged in

DECLARATION OF INTERDEPENDENCE FOR A SUSTAINABLE FUTURE

UIA/AIA WORLD CONGRESS OF ARCHITECTS

CHICAGO, 18-21 JUNE 1993

RECOGNISING THAT:

A sustainable society restores, preserves and enhances nature and culture for the benefit of all life, present and future; ■ a diverse and healthy environment is intrinsically valuable and essential to a healthy society; ■ today's society is seriously degrading the environment and is not sustainable.

We are ecologically interdependent with the whole natural environment; ■ we are socially, culturally and economically interdependent with all of humanity; ■ a sustainability, in the context of this interdependence, requires partnership, equity and balance among all parties.

Buildings and the built environment play a major role in the human impact on the natural environment and on the quality of life; ■ a sustainable design integrates consideration of resource and energy efficiency, healthy buildings and materials, ecologically and socially sensitive land-use, and an aesthetic sensitivity that inspires, affirms and ennobles; ■ a sustainable design can significantly reduce adverse human impacts on the natural environment while simultaneously improving quality of life and economic well being.

WE COMMIT OURSELVES,

as members of the word's architectural and building-design professions, individually and through our professional organisations, to

- place environmental and social sustainability at the core of our practices and professional responsibilities;
- develop and continually improve practices, procedures, products, curricula, services and standards that will enable the implementation of sustainable design;
- educate our fellow professionals, the building industry, clients, students and the general public about the critical importance and substantial opportunities of sustainable design;
- establish policies, regulations and practices in government and business that ensure sustainable design becomes normal practice; and
- bring all existing and future elements of the built environment - in their design, production, use and eventual reuse - up to sustainable design standards.

Olfemi Majekodunmi,
President,
International Union of Architects

Susan A Maxman,
President,
American Institute of Architects

Figure 11.1. Declaration of Interdependence.

developing sustainable plans to ensure the manifestation of the initial vision. In addition to "fun," the plan should be economically sound. No one has fun when there are financial problems. The plan should take an honest look at the true costs associated with the vision—does it value our natural resources, does it promote social equity, does it encourage natural biodiversity? The plan must also have a reasonable schedule.

The plans for sustainable architectural projects that I have engaged in during the last several years—the U.S. Headquarters for the Body Shop (see Figures 11.2–11.4), the Educational Center for the Burnet Park Zoo, the "Commons house" for a co-housing development, a residence on Dewees Island, an intentional environmental development—have addressed all the above, from fun to schedule, in the context of five critical elements of sustainable design: site, energy, materials, indoor environment, and waste. I have found that the earlier these elements are addressed in a sustainable vision and subsequent plan, the higher the rate of successful integration.

Let's take a look at these elements and remember that in a plan it is better to set reasonable short-, mid-, and long-term goals or "benchmarks" to successfully achieve a sustainable vision than to initially take on too much and fail to meet the first benchmark. My belief is that the following integrated elements are as essential to a successful sustainable plan as is a strong feedback loop.

Figure 11.2. The Body Shop
Headquarters, exterior view.
(Photo by Doug Van de Zande.)

Figure 11.3. The Body Shop Headquarters, front entry. (Photo by Doug Van de Zande.)

1. *Site.* This issue addresses site considerations from ecosystems to transportation. Any parcel of land and its amenities should be carefully documented and inventoried for ecosystems. As a resource, it should be assessed for its highest and best use.
2. *Energy.* This issue addresses renewable and nonrenewable energies in our lives. Aspects of solar income, such as the value of natural daylighting to our well-being, should be considered. Existing structures and materials should be documented as existing resources having valuable "embodied energy."
3. *Materials.* This issue addresses the highest and best use of all materials and resources. The production, manufacture, transportation, installation, maintenance, and ultimate reuse of materials should be integral to the dialogue of a sustainable world. Materials and resources should be documented for both environmental and health aspects.
4. *Indoor environment.* This issue addresses the health, welfare, and comfort of people within a building. Good indoor air and acoustical and visual quality are essential to high occupant productivity, which will allow more energized thinking and creativity to abound.
5. *Waste.* This issue addresses the essential value we place on the materials and resources of our world. There should be no waste. All materials, systems, and technologies should optimally perform multiple functions.

Figure 11.4. The Body Shop Headquarters, interior view. (Photo by Doug Van de Zande.)

Soon after establishing this framework in order to plan sustainable projects, I realized how interconnected and cyclical all these items are and how they seem to be held together tightly by the concept of community. As we become more aware of each element and the numerous choices connected to it that display our value system, we must plan as a team to integrate these elements early into our sustainable visions.

Overall, a plan to help us reach our sustainable visions should address environmental, economic, and social concerns in terms of schedule, budget, and quality. It should also be fun.

And, it should get us to "act."

Act

What motivates us to act? Our passionate desire to see our vision manifested and a reasonable plan to attain it. Through our collective personal actions, sustainable visions can be manifested.

One well-known leader in the sustainability movement was asked what project he was currently working on; he responded that he was working on a sustainable life—his own. He enumerated steps that he was taking personally to lessen his environmental impact on the world.

This reminded me of a quote from M. K. Gandhi: "I believe that it is perfectly possible for an individual to adopt the way of life of the future . . . without having to wait for others to do so. And if an individual can observe a certain rule of conduct, cannot a group of individuals do the same? Cannot whole groups of peoples—whole nations? No one need wait for anyone else to adopt a humane and enlightened course of action."

I have concluded that the most significant sustainable actions all of us can undertake are those that confront us in our daily choices. Several years ago, my husband and I encountered numerous daily choices as we built our own home (see Figure 11.5 and 11.6). We noticed, early in the process, the influence of cultural values on our actions and choices. Planning department officials offered to show us how we could make a lot of money developing our land quickly with multifamily housing. Several design professionals visiting the site pointed to the most beautiful and lush areas as the "best place" for us to build. Financial institutions reluctantly talked to us about financing a small home on our large lot—but eagerly sought to help us finance a house much too large for our needs.

Nonetheless, we made our plans, took action, and manifested our vision. We built our house on the least environmentally diverse parcel of our land; we built our

Figure 11.5. The Cox-Lindsey residence, southern elevation. (Photo by Michael W. Cox.)

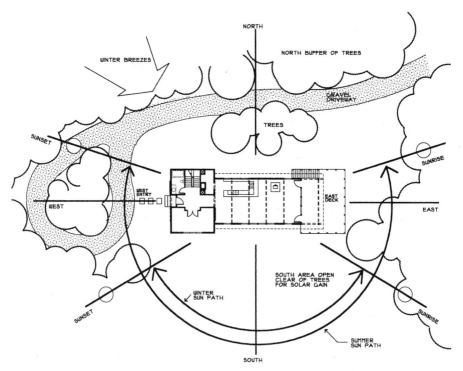

Figure 11.6. The Cox-Lindsey residence, site plan.

house to align with the compass directions that would provide us constantly with natural daylighting and free solar income. Where possible, we built out of salvaged, recycled content and local materials; we sought natural ventilation and the least toxic materials; and we built the house to last and be structurally flexible for reuse. In the process we learned firsthand about choices, about manifesting visions, about natural resources, about price versus cost, and about truly sustainable design.

You see, I discovered that on the lush, magical one-third of our land a Native American campsite had existed long ago at the site of an old spring; the site remains gorgeous and serene today. The adjoining third of our land was where the family before us lived. Remaining on this site are nine granite fieldstones in a 3 by 3 configuration within an eighteen-foot square. I'm told those were the foundation stones of their cabin; when they moved a bit further away they took down the cabin and reused the hewn lumber for their next house. The final third of our land was where we chose to build. It was the only portion of the property that had been clear-cut in the 1950s for pasture land, and it was populated mainly with a single variety of pine trees, unlike the rich variety of trees throughout the rest of the lot.

We acted, and now I often wonder how the next owners will evaluate our vision.

Throughout the design and construction of our house we incorporated and put into action the sustainable issues I felt were critical: site, energy, materials, indoor environment, and waste. At the same time, I was given a list of the five sustainable design principles created by the Royal Australian Institute of Architects, which seemed to dovetail nicely into our approach:

1. Maintain and, where it has been disturbed, restore biodiversity.
2. Minimize the consumption of resources, especially nonrenewable resources.
3. Minimize pollution of soil, air, and water.
4. Maximize the health, safety, and comfort of building users.
5. Increase awareness of environmental issues.

After completing our house, I became very intrigued with the economics of ecological design. I began to realize how closely connected ecology and economics are; how inseparable they are. Both are systems of value. It became quite clear to me, after consciously looking at what we as a culture value; we value, as evidenced in our everyday choices, convenience over durability.

I am reminded of two talks that I gave on succeeding days. On the first evening, I gave a talk to a group of elderly women who wanted to learn about "sustainability." They shared a potluck dinner where each person brought homemade dishes in reusable glass or ceramic containers. One woman brought the china, linens, and silverware; another a large container of homemade tea. What a lesson about sustainability I learned from them. The next night's lecture took place at a local women's college. This time, the dinner was brought in grocery bags by two girls: plastic bottles of Coke, crackers, "Cheese-whiz," and Oreos. A third girl brought the paper plates and plastic cutlery. The comparison was shocking.

In order to act responsibly and sustainably, we must start with our everyday choices. We must define what we need and what is "enough."

All of our plans are ineffectual unless we act on them. In turn, all of our actions will not ensure the manifestation of our sustainable vision unless we "course-correct" and "evaluate" them accordingly.

Evaluate

How do we evaluate our progress toward our sustainable vision? For starters, we should recheck our vision, review our plan and our benchmarks, scrutinize our actions, and determine our next steps.

Are we on track? Do we need to "course-correct"? Does our vision need to be revised? Has our plan been adequate? Does new information mean we should alter our plan? Have our actions brought us closer to our vision or further from it? Are we on schedule? Within our budget? Have our environmental benchmarks been met?

We learn as individuals and as a society by evaluating, measuring, observing, and noting the consequences of our actions over time—recording what works and what doesn't. Unfortunately, we have had few plans and benchmarks for our pursuits in the sustainable design world until recently. We are beginning to see such quantitative endeavors as the Building Research Establishment Environmental Assessment Method (BREEAM), the U.S. Green Building Council's Leadership in Energy and Environmental Design (LEED), and Ray Cole's and Nils Larsson's Green Building Challenge '98 (GBC '98). Each of these assessment tools is beginning to list, assess, and quantify what is a "green" or "sustainable" building. These sustainable building benchmarks are evolving and giving the world a starting point for evaluation.

Initial users of the LEED green building rating system are finding out how much harder it is to go back and address sustainable goals once a building is well underway than it is to "design to" those goals and benchmarks initially. As Lewis Carroll eloquently expressed: "If you don't know where you want to go, any road will take you there." Sustainable projects must begin with a clearly defined vision; they must document a plan of action with an initial starting point and subsequent benchmarks; and they must "take stock" along the way toward their vision.

We are all fumbling with sustainable visions, plans, actions, and evaluations. It's a new undertaking for all of us; in fact, many of the benchmarks for our visions are just being established, while most remain nonexistent. Consider the following from Paul Hawken:

> We do not know how many species live on the planet within a factor of ten. We do not know how many are being extirpated. We do not know what is contained in the biological library inherited from the Cenozoic age. We do not know how complex systems interact— how the transpiration of the giant lily, *Victoria amazonica,* of Brazil's rain forests affects European rainfall and agriculture, for example. . . . We do not know what happens to 20% of the CO_2 that is off-gassed every year (it disappears without a trace). We do not know how to calculate sustainable yields in fisheries and forest systems. We do not know why certain species, such as frogs, are dying out even in pristine habitats. We do not know the long-term effects of chlorinated hydrocarbons on human health, behavior, sexuality, and fertility. We do not know what a sustainable life is for existing inhabitants of the planet, and certainly not for future populations. (A Dutch study calculated that your fair share of air travel is one trip across the Atlantic in a lifetime.) We do not know how many people we can feed on a sustainable basis, or what our diet would look like. In short, we need to find out what's here, who has it, and what we can or can't do with it.

While the global picture is daunting, setting personal or communal sustainable visions and evaluating them is more feasible. We can begin to determine and define "where we are and where we want to be," on our own terms. Take for example, Ray Anderson, the CEO of Interface Corporation, who wrote less than five years ago *The Eco-Odyssey of a CEO*. Anderson is changing the face of industry, as one of the most forward-thinking industrialists who has set a sustainable vision, established a plan, engaged the actions of many toward this vision, and currently evaluates his company against the vision.

His company, Interface, published the first corporate "sustainability report" (as opposed to an annual corporate business report). In it is their clearly defined vision to become the first sustainable corporation in the world and then, ultimately, the first restorative company. This document graphically, depicts the company's plan, initial inventory or starting points, and short-, mid-, and long-term benchmarks for success.

As Anderson writes in this sustainability report, "We look forward to the day when our factories have no smokestacks and no effluents. If successful, we'll spend the rest of our days harvesting yesteryear's carpets, recycling old petro-chemicals into new materials, and converting sunlight into energy. There will be zero scrap going into landfills and zero emissions into the biosphere. Literally, our company will grow by cleaning up the world, not by polluting or degrading it. We'll be doing well by doing good. That's the vision. Is it a dream? Certainly, but it is a dream we share with our 6,300 associates, our vendors, and our customers. Everyone will have to dream this dream to make it a reality, but until then, we are committed to leading the way."

When we evaluate, we should begin to think of "next steps" and of focusing again. However, after evaluation and before focusing again, there must be a time for reflection, to "begin anew"

Begin Anew

When asked for the secret to his artistry, Leonard Bernstein replied, "it's not in the music, but in the pauses."

Energy efficiency is an underlying principle of a sustainable world. We must realize and value our own energy as a valuable resource to be conserved and used for the greatest effect. We must each determine what gives us energy and what takes it away—working smarter rather than harder.

There's a story of two men competing to chop the most wood in a single day. (Of course, all of the wood is from a sustainably harvested forest.) One man, determined to win, toils with unflagging energy throughout the day, never taking a break. He's heartened to see that his competitor doesn't share his stamina and thus takes frequent breaks. At the end of the day, the piles of chopped wood are measured, and to the astonishment of the steady worker, the other man is the clear winner. Crestfallen, the weary loser asks the winner how he did it. "Easy," he replies "during the breaks, I sharpened my ax." Many of us have been chopping away for a long time without stopping to sharpen our axes.

We've lived without question with the notion of humankind's dominion over nature. Shall we pause long enough to consider a new notion, co-creation with nature? The first step is to learn the ways of nature, as William McDonough has expressed:

1. *Waste equals food.* "Everything we have to work with is already here—the wood, the water, the air. All materials given to us by nature are constantly returned to the earth without even the concept of waste as we know it. Everything is recycled constantly with all waste equaling food for other living systems."

2. *Live off current solar income.* ". . . the one thing allowing nature to continually cycle itself through life is energy, and this energy comes from outside the system in the form of perpetual solar income. Not only does nature operate on current income, it does not mine or extract energy from the past, it does not use its capital reserves, it does not borrow from the future."

3. *Respect diversity.* "The characteristic that sustains this complex and efficient system of metabolism and creation is biodiversity. What prevents living systems from running down and veering into chaos is a miraculously intricate and symbiotic relationship between millions of organisms, no two of which are alike."

Learning from nature and beginning to co-create may open up a new level of manifestation of the world around us, leading to a dramatic and new level of design possibilities. When one begins to open up and collaborate with nature in the broadest sense, existing paradigms are transcended. As Donella Meadows brilliantly points out, "The highest level of all [for transcending existing paradigms] is to keep oneself unattached in the arena of paradigms, to realize that NO paradigm is "true," that even the one that sweetly shapes one's comfortable worldview is a tremendously limited understanding of an immense and amazing universe."

If we allow ourselves the time and opportunity to rethink and question the rarely questioned paradigms of this century, from our dominion over and independence from nature, to our standard, linear, logical approach to all phases of our lives, I believe that we'll be "sharpening our axes" and on our way to finding and creating (or co-creating) a more enriching world. Throughout life, I hope that we can all allow this quote from Walt Whitman to guide us as we constantly "begin anew": "Question all you have been told. Dismiss that which insults your soul." If each of us can find our own truth, our own sacred connection to nature, and share it honestly, I believe we will be well on our path to a sustainable future.

I will close with a wonderful quote from one who has done just that; it's by a Native American elder, Oriah Mountain Dreamer:

> It doesn't interest me what you do for a living. I want to know what you ache for, and if you dare to dream of meeting your heart's longing.
>
> It doesn't interest me how old you are. I want to know if you will risk looking like a fool for love, for your dreams, for the adventure of being alive. . . .
>
> I want to know if you can sit with pain, mine or your own, without moving to hide it or fade it or fix it.
>
> I want to know if you can be with joy, mine or your own, if you can dance with wildness and let the ecstasy fill you to the tips of your fingers and toes without cautioning us to be careful, be realistic, or to remember the limitations of being human.
>
> It doesn't interest me if the story you are telling me is true. I want to know if you can disappoint another to be true to yourself, if you can bear the accusation of betrayal and not betray your own soul. I want to know if you can be faithful and therefore be trustworthy.
>
> I want to know if you can see beauty even when it is not pretty every day, and if you can source your life from God's presence. I want to know if you can live with failure, yours and mine, and still stand on the edge of a lake and shout to the silver of the full moon, "Yes!"
>
> It doesn't interest me where you live or how much money you have. I want to know if you can get up after the night of grief and despair, weary and bruised to the bone, and do what needs to be done for the children.
>
> It doesn't interest me who you are, how you came to be here. I want to know if you will stand in the center of the fire with me and not shrink back.
>
> It doesn't interest me where or what or with whom you have studied. I want to know what sustains you from the inside when all else falls away. I want to know if you can be alone with yourself, and if you truly like the company you keep in the empty moments.

Bibliography

Anderson, Ray. 1995. *Eco-Odyssey of a CEO.* Atlanta: Interface Corporation.
Anderson, Ray. 1997. *Interface Sustainability Report.* Atlanta: Interface Corporation.
Brower, David. 1996. *Let the Mountains Talk, Let the Rivers Run.* Western Region: Ingram.

Demkin, J.A., ed., 1997. *Environmental Resource Guide.* New York: John Wiley & Sons.

Estes, Clarissa Pikola. 1995. *The Faithful Gardener.* San Francisco: Harper-Collins.

Hawken, Paul. 1993. "A Declaration of Sustainability." *Utne Reader* 59:54–61.

Hawken, Paul. 1993. *Ecology of Commerce: A Declaration of Sustainability.* New York: HarperCollins.

Lawson, Bill, and David Rudder. 1996. *Building Materials Energy and the Environment Towards Ecologically Sustainable Development.* Canberra, Australia: National Capital Printing.

Lopez Barnett, Dianna, and William D. Browning. 1995. *A Primer on Sustainable Building.* Snowmass, CO: The Rocky Mountain Institute.

Lyle, John Tillman. 1994. *Regenerative Design for Sustainable Development.* New York: John Wiley & Sons.

McDonough, William. 1995. *The William McDonough Collection of Environmentally Intelligent Textiles.* Charlottesville, VA: DesignTex.

Meadows, Donella. 1997. "Places to Intervene in a System." *Whole Earth* 91: 78–84.

Meadows, Donella, et al. 1992. *Beyond the Limits: Confronting Global Collapse and Envisioning a Sustainable Future.* Post Mills, VT: Chelsea Green.

Morrow, Rosemary. 1993. *Earth User's Guide to Permaculture.* Australia: Kangaroo Press.

Todd, Nancy Jack, and John Todd. 1994. *From Eco-Cities to Living Machines.* Berkeley, CA: North Atlantic Books.

Van der Ryn, Sim, and Stuart Cowan. 1996. *Ecological Design.* Washington, DC: Island Press.

Wilson, Alex, et al. 1998. *Green Development: Integrating Ecology and Real Estate.* New York: John Wiley & Sons.

Zeiher, Laura. 1996. *The Ecology of Architecture.* New York: Whitney Library of Design.

WEB SITES

1. E Build (http://www.ebuild.com). Includes back issues of *Environmental Building News.*
2. Green Clips (GreenClips@aol.com). Accessible, concise, frequently updated, real examples.
3. CREST (http://www.crest.org). A great starting point for finding other resources.
4. U.S. Green Building Council (http://www.usgbc.org). Information on the council, its activities, and its LEED rating system.
5. U.S. Department of Energy (http://www.eren.doe.gov/buildings/). Referral to more than 100 tools on energy efficiency and other information.

6. REDI Database (http://www.oikos.com). A searchable database with up-to-date information on products and materials.

7. E Design Online (http://edesign.state.fl.us/). Essays and articles on green building topics, most reprinted from other sources.

8. G.E.O. Green Building Resource Center (http://www.geonetwork.org/gbrc/). Great resources and referral to other Internet sites, books, professionals, etc.

9. U.S. Environmental Protection Agency (http://www.epa.gov/iaq). Includes EPA programs, publications, and software related to indoor air quality, as well as access to other EPA web sites on environmental regulations, research results, etc.

10. Sustainable Sources (http://www.greenbuilder.com/general/BuildingSources. html). Includes materials from the Austin, Texas, Green Builder Program and other resources.

Chapter 12

Architecture as Pedagogy

David Orr

The worst thing we can do to our children is to convince them that
ugliness is normal.
—Rene Dubos

As commonly practiced, education has little to do with its specific setting or locality. The typical campus is regarded mostly as a place where learning occurs but is,
itself, believed to be the source of no useful learning. It is intended, rather, to be
convenient, efficient, or aesthetically pleasing, but not instructional. It neither
requires nor facilitates competence or mindfulness. By that standard, the same
education could happen as well in California or in Kazakhstan, or on Mars, for that
matter. The same could be said of the buildings and landscape that make up a college campus (Orr 1993). The design of buildings and landscape is thought to have
little or nothing to do with the process of learning or the quality of scholarship that
occurs in a particular place. In fact, buildings and landscape reflect a hidden curriculum that powerfully influences the learning process.

The curriculum embedded in any building instructs as fully and as powerfully
as any course taught in it. Most of my classes, for example, are taught in a building
that I think Descartes would have liked. It is a building with lots of squareness and
straight lines. There is nothing whatsoever that reflects its locality in northeast
Ohio in what had once been a vast forested wetland (Sherman 1996). How it is
cooled, heated, and lighted and at what true cost to the world is a mystery to its
occupants. It offers no clue about the origins of the materials used to build it. It
tells no story. With only minor modifications it could be converted to use as a factory or prison. When classes are over, students seldom linger for long. The building resonates with no part of our biology, evolutionary experience, or aesthetic sen-
sibilities. It reflects no understanding of ecology or ecological processes. It is
intended to be functional, efficient, minimally offensive, and little more. What else
does it do?

First, it tells its users that locality, knowing where they are, is unimportant. To be sure, this is not said in so many words anywhere in this or any other building. Rather, it is said tacitly throughout the entire building. Second, because it uses energy wastefully, the building tells its users that energy is cheap and abundant and can be squandered with no thought for the morrow. Third, nowhere in the building do students learn about the materials used in its construction or who was downwind or downstream from the wells, mines, forests, and manufacturing facilities where those materials originated or where they eventually will be discarded. And the lesson learned is mindlessness, which is to say it teaches that disconnectedness is normal. And try as one might to teach that we are implicated in the larger enterprise of life, standard architectural design mostly conveys other lessons. There is often a miscalibration between what is taught in classes and the way buildings actually work. Buildings are provisioned with energy, materials, and water, and they dispose of their waste in ways that say to students that the world is linear and that we are no part of the larger web of life. Finally, there is no apparent connection in this or any other building on campus to the larger set of issues having to do with climatic change, biotic impoverishment, and the unraveling of the fabric of life on earth. Students begin to suspect, I think, that those issues are unreal or that they are unsolvable in any practical way, or that they occur somewhere else.

Through the design of buildings and entire campuses is it possible to teach our students that our ecological problems are solvable and that we are connected to the larger community of life (Lyle 1994)? I think so. For the past three years (1995–1998) I have worked with a team of students, faculty, and designers to design such a building. As a first step, we hired two graduates from the class of 1993 to help coordinate the design of the project and to engage students, faculty, and the wider community in the design process. We also engaged landscape architect John Lyle to help conduct the major design charettes or planning sessions that began in the fall of 1995. Some 250 students, faculty, and community members participated in the thirteen charettes that set the goals for the 14,000-square-foot building. The final program called for a building:

- Discharging no wastewater (i.e., drinking water in, drinking water out);
- Generating more electricity than it used;
- Using no materials known to be carcinogenic or mutagenic or to be endocrine disrupters;
- Maximizing energy and materials efficiency;
- Made from products and materials grown or manufactured sustainably;
- Landscaped to promote biological diversity;
- Promoting analytical skill such as least-cost end-use analysis and life-cycle costing as well as practical competence in horticulture, gardening, ecological engineering, landscape management, restoration ecology, and solar technologies; and
- Meeting rigorous requirements for full-cost accounting.

We intended, in other words, a building that did not impair human or ecological health somewhere else or at some later time and one that instructed passively through its design and actively through routine operations.

From twenty-six architectural firms that applied for the job, we selected William McDonough & Partners in Charlottesville, Virginia. Part of their task was to coordinate a larger design team that would meet throughout the process. To fulfill the requirement that the building generate more electricity than it used, we engaged Amory Lovins and Bill Browning from the Rocky Mountain Institute as well as scientists from NASA's Lewis Space Center. In order to meet the standard of zero discharge we hired John Todd and Michael Shaw, the leading figures in the field of ecological engineering. For landscaping we brought in John Lyle and the firm of Andropogon, Inc., from Philadelphia. To this team we added structural and mechanical engineers (Lev Zetlin, Inc., New York City), and a contractor. In all, some eighteen experts representing a dozen or more fields participated in the design phase. During programming and schematic design this team and representatives from the college met by conference call weekly and in regular working sessions.

The team approach to architectural design was new to the college. Typically, architects design a building, hire engineers to heat and cool it, and bring in landscapers to make it look pretty. By engaging the full design team from the beginning we intended to improve the integration of building systems and technologies and the relationship between the building and its landscape. Early on, we decided that the standard for technology in the building was to be state-of-the-shelf, but within state-of-the-art design. In other words, we did not want the risk of untried technologies, but we did want the entire building to be at the frontier of what is now possible with ecologically smart design.

The building program called for major changes not only in the design process but also in the selection of materials, relationship to manufacturers, and in the way we counted the costs of the project. We intended to use materials that did not compromise human or ecological health somewhere else or at some later time. We also wanted to use materials that had as little embodied fossil energy as possible, hence giving preference to those locally manufactured or grown. In the process we discovered how little is known about the ecological and human effects of the materials used in construction. Not surprisingly, we also discovered that the present system of building codes does little to encourage innovation that leads to greater resource efficiency and environmental quality.

Typical buildings give a kind of snapshot of the state of technology about one year before they open, which means that they are obsolete the day they open. But we intended for this building to remain technologically dynamic over a long period of time by making it possible to adapt easily to changing technology. The use of raised flooring, for example, will permit quick changes of wiring and air-handling systems. Similarly, we intend to lease a photovoltaic array from a manufacturer so that the system can be upgraded as technology improves.

The same strategy is being applied to some materials as well. Buildings represent a union of two different metabolisms, one technical and one ecological (McDonough and Braungart 1998). Materials that might eventually decompose into soil are part of an ecological metabolism. Otherwise they are "technical nutrients" to be leased from the manufacturer and eventually returned as a feedstock to be remanufactured into new product. Carpet in the building, accordingly, will be leased from Interface Corporation as a "product of service." When worn out or changed, it will be returned to Interface to be made into new carpet, not sent to a landfill. This means that Interface designs carpet that it wants back and that landfills do not fill up with a bulky material impervious to decay for thousands of years.

The costs of new buildings are typically calculated narrowly to include only those of design and construction, excluding life-cycle operating costs and costs to the environment and human health. The result is a gross underestimate of what buildings actually cost their owners over their useful lifetime and what price they exact from society. In contrast, we will assess life-cycle costs of this building, including the amount of carbon dioxide released in the construction phase.

From computer simulation (DOE-2) we anticipate that the total electrical budget to heat, ventilate, air-condition, and light the building will be ~63,000 kwh/yr, or 16,499 Btus/ft^2/yr. This is approximately 22 percent of the average for comparable new construction in northern Ohio, as shown below.

Energy costs to heat, ventilate, light,
and cool measured in Btus/ft^2/yr
_____

The Lewis Center: 16,500
Federal standards: 50,000
Average for new construction: ~75,000
_____

The electrical system for the center will consist of a 3,700-square-foot photovoltaic array that will eventually be combined with a fuel cell. In a cloudy climate, the technological problem is to level out energy production from sunlight and actual energy use. With help from NASA scientists and others, our plan is to do so as shown in Figure 12.1.

ADAM JOSEPH LEWIS CENTER ENERGY SYSTEM
PHOTONS →ELECTRONS→ HYDROGEN→ELECTRONS+HEAT→H$_2$O
SUNLIGHT→PHOTO VOLTAICS→ELECTROLYSIS→FUEL CELL

Figure 12.1. Strategy for converting solar energy into electrical energy for the Lewis Center.

The building is designed to purify wastewater on site using a Living Machine developed by John Todd. It will minimize or eliminate the use of toxic materials. It will be instrumented to display energy and significant ecological data in the atrium. The story of the building will be prominently displayed throughout the structure.

The landscape will include a restored wetland and forest as well as gardens, orchards, and greenhouse, all maintained by students. The south entry is a plaza, named in honor of its designer, John Lyle, featuring a sundial marking winter and summer solstices. The landscape will be used as much as classrooms to teach horticulture, gardening, landscape management, and ecological design.

Groundbreaking on the Adam Joseph Lewis Center for Environmental Studies occurred in September 1998, with a scheduled completion in late fall 1999. As important as the building and its landscape are, the more important effects of the project have been the impacts on those who participated. Many of the students, who learned ecological design by working with some of the best practitioners in the world, now describe the center as their "legacy" to the college. Faculty who participated perhaps are less pessimistic about the possibilities for institutional change. And the president, Nancy Dye, who initially authorized the project, has shown other administrators that risks for the right purposes can pay off.

The real test, however, lies ahead. It will be tempting for some, no doubt, to regard this as an interesting but isolated experiment having no relation to other buildings now in the planning stage or for campus landscaping or resource management. The pedagogically challenged will see no further possibilities for rethinking the process, substance, and goals of education. If so, the center will exist as an island on a campus that mirrors the larger culture. On the other hand, the project offers a model that might inform:

- Architectural standards for all new construction and renovation;
- Landscape management;
- Financial criteria for payback times and full-cost accounting;
- Courses and projects organized around real problems;
- How we involve the wider community; and
- Campus-wide planning.

Colleges like many other organizations are often risk averse, slow to innovate, administratively fragmented, and focused on the short term. To succeed, however, this project required a willingness to risk failure, the capacity to make timely decisions, integrated planning, and a long-term planning horizon. New wine should not be put in old wineskins. We set out to change the ecology of a single building only to discover that to do so it was necessary to change the ecology of the planning process.

By some estimates, humankind is preparing to build more in the next half century than it has built throughout all of recorded history. If we do this inefficiently and carelessly, we will cast a long ecological shadow on the human future. If we fail to pay the full environmental costs of development, the resulting ecological and human damage will be irreparable. To the extent that we do not aim for efficiency and the use of renewable energy sources, the energy and maintenance costs will unnecessarily divert capital from other and far better purposes. The dream of sustainability, however defined, would then prove to be only a fantasy. Ideas and ideals need to be rendered into models and examples that make them visible, comprehensible, and compelling. Who will do this?

More than any other institution in modern society, colleges and universities have a moral stake in the health, beauty, and integrity of the world our students will inherit. We have an obligation to provide our students with tangible models that calibrate our values and capabilities, models that they can see, touch, and experience. We have an obligation to create grounds for hope in our students who sometimes define themselves as the "X generation." But hope is different than wishful thinking, so we have a corollary obligation to equip our students with the analytical skills and practical competence necessary to act on high expectations. When the pedagogical abstractions, words, and whole courses do not fit the way the buildings and landscape constituting the academic campus in fact work, they learn that hope is just wishful thinking or worse, rank hypocrisy. In short, we have an obligation to equip our students to do the hard work ahead:

• Learning to power civilization by current sunlight;
• Reducing the amount of materials, water, and land use per capita;
• Growing their food and fiber sustainably;
• Disinventing the concept of waste;
• Preserving biological diversity;
• Restoring ecologies ruined in the past century;
• Rethinking the political basis of modern society;
• Developing economies that can be sustained within the limits of nature; and
• Distributing wealth fairly within and between generations.

No generation ever faced a more daunting agenda. True. But none ever faced more exciting possibilities either. Do we now have or could we acquire the know-how to power civilization by current sunlight or to reduce the size of the "human footprint" (Wackernagel and Rees 1996) or grow our food sustainably or prevent pollution or preserve biological diversity or restore degraded ecologies? In each case I believe that the answer is "yes." Whether we possess the political will and moral energy to do so remains to be seen.

Finally, the potential for ecologically smarter design in all of its manifestations in architecture, landscape design, community design, the management of agricultural and forest lands, manufacturing, and technology does not amount to a fix for all that ails us. Reducing the amount of damage we do to the world per capita will only buy us a few decades, perhaps a century if we are lucky. If we squander that reprieve, we will have succeeded only in delaying the eventual collision between unfettered human desires and the limits of the earth. The default setting of our civilization needs to be reset to ensure that we build a sustainable world that is also humanly sustaining. This is not a battle between left and right or haves and have-nots as it is often described. At a deeper level the issue has to do with art and beauty. In the largest sense, what we must do to ensure human tenure on the earth is to cultivate a new standard that defines beauty as that which causes no ugliness somewhere else or at some later time.

REFERENCES

Lyle, John. 1994. *Regenerative Design for Sustainable Development*. New York: John Wiley & Sons.

McDonough, William, and Michael Braungart. 1998. "The Next Industrial Revolution." *The Atlantic Monthly* 282:82–92.

Orr, D. 1993. "Architecture as Pedagogy." *Conservation Biology* 11:597–600.

Sherman, T. 1996. *A Place on the Glacial Till*. New York: Oxford University Press.

Wackernagel, M., and W. Rees. 1996. *Our Ecological Footprint*. Philadelphia: New Society Publishers.

Wilson, Alex, et al. 1998. *Green Development*. New York: John Wiley & Sons.

Chapter 13

Biourbanism and
Sustainable Urban Planning

Daniel Williams

The future of urban planning may well lie in the pursuit of sustainability. The term *sustainability*, in this context, is understood to mean "continuing" through the use of applied learning and adapting. A conceptual basis for achieving the goal of sustainable planning is the application of the knowledge of natural systems to the plan. Many urban services normally provided by human-made infrastructure can in fact be provided by natural processes for free. Integrating this natural "infrastructure" into the neighborhood plan is essential to the development of a sustainable urban plan. Biourbanism applies regional learning to urban planning. Site selection, orientation, building methods and materials, and resource use is learned from the regional systems (see Figure 13.1).

The advantage of using natural systems knowledge and renewable energies to replace the work of human-made infrastructure is that they are sustainable and free. Infrastructure tasks required for community functioning and well-being include important functions such as the storage and purification of water and the cooling and heating of cities and homes. These tasks can be accomplished without using nonrenewable energy and technology merely by incorporating the "free work" offered by natural systems into the design and planning of regions and urban communities.

Sustainability, when applied to urban planning, involves the application of regionally based information and the use of available renewable resources. This type of planning requires that infrastructure design consider natural and physical laws and maximize the use of "free work." Natural systems, specifically biology and the flows of energies and the materials within biological systems, provide an excellent model for any system adapting over time. Natural systems accomplishing this work within cities, towns, and neighborhoods can be called "green infrastructure."

Applying biological and natural systems knowledge to urban planning is essential in creating sustainable communities. The challenge is to apply natural systems

Figure 13.1. Building near needed resources such as water was essential. Building too close to water was learned.

thinking to urban form while creating more livable, efficient, and sustainable urban communities. Much of the current thinking in urban planning focuses on the "form" of communities and neighborhoods. In this pursuit many important objectives are stressed—walkable neighborhoods, small-scale streets, good edge definition, design and location of town and neighborhood centers and community gathering places, and transportation. Long-term sustainability, however, is achievable within communities only if they connect to its renewable resources. Any long-term scenario of a biological community including humans ties its long-term development to sustainable resources—those renewable energies and resources that helped create it and are needed to maintain it.

Present-day urban and community design and town planning re-create a comfort zone within the "form" discussion and are community "place-based" but provide little else for long-term sustainability. The world is full of quaint ghost towns and urban history has shown that renewable resources sustain towns and communities and that creating a sustainable neighborhood form is a function of understanding, connecting, and adapting to these renewable resources.

History

Up until the middle of the nineteenth century, the design and planning of urban communities had its basis in protecting, housing, and feeding their inhabitants while supplying essential resources. Natural resources and renewable energies have provided the foundation for urban settlements for over 5,000 years. The sun, a sustainable energy source, is converted to food energy that is consumed by the population. At present the loop from the population back to the energy-fixing food supply is missing in planning. Biourbanism reconnects this loop by locating and designing the connections.

Maximum commuting distances were based on the distance a farmer could travel with his produce before it spoiled. Community edges were based on walking distances, horse distances, and later, on bicycle distances.

The availability and use of fossil fuel has changed the criteria for the scale and distribution of urban communities. The present urban planning approach and consequently the urban policies and the resulting community form are the result of relying on nonrenewable energy. Because this energy supply is underpriced, it rewards sprawl and brings with its use pollution and congestion. The new travel distance is global rather than local and today's urban plans and travel distances are not sustainable.

Associated with fossil fuel usage are many indirect costs. The forecasted loss of coastal property due to rising sea level, a hypothesized consequence of global warming, is connected to fossil fuel use. The indirect losses of land are even more consequential to life. The water supply, for example, is tied to groundwater storage. When the sea level rises, salt water intrudes into the groundwater and there is a permanent and exponential loss of the storage capability in coastal communities. The regional impacts will include loss of habitat, reduction in potable water storage, loss of real estate, reduction in total arable land base, loss of the beginning coastal ecological food chains (increasing the total number of endangered species), and loss of human heritage (see Figures 13.2 and 13.3).

Figure 13.2. Biscayne Bay normal water level.

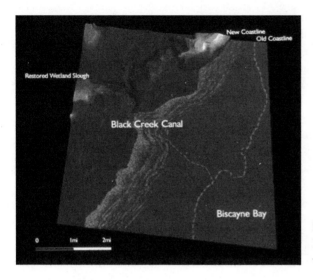

Figure 13.3. Biscayne Bay water level in global warming scenario.

Bioregionalism

To create urban planning that is once again sustainable, the approach must incorporate, as the primary ingredients, the sustainable energies and resources within the region. The community plans and designs must mimic the cycling of regional biological systems.

Bioregionalism is the overview of all biological and natural system sciences within a region. The study and understanding of biology and the resident natural systems within a region provide excellent examples of using the principles that have sustained human life for thousands of years.

Bioregionalism, when applied to planning and design, beneficially connects the historic working patterns of the regions' natural systems with those of urban planning principles. These natural systems include solar pathways, water, soil, geology, and climate. These systems generate and regenerate within the region at no cost—they are "free." Any process or work that is accomplished with this resident renewable energy is free. Bioregionalism maximizes the use of the "free work" of nature, increasing efficiency in urban and agricultural functioning while creating designs that provide for a higher quality of life. Designing and planning for the inclusion of these multisystem connections is an essential element of sustainable urban planning (see Figures 13.4 and 13.5).

The location and availability of renewable resources is critical to sustainable planning and design. Renewable resources such as sunlight, soil, and water are plentiful when viewed within the larger global picture; however, when looked at within the urban growth corridors where they are being used, the demand on these basic resources far exceeds the regional renewable supply.

Figure 13.4. Energy and form. Discovering and applying how energy creates form may provide helpful direction in urban design for hurricane protection as well as spatial requirements for water and food to sustain communities.

Figure 13.5. Mykanos, Greece. The form of the community allows residents to walk safely during gales because the urban pattern mitigates the wind.

Bioregionalism starts by inventorying all regional natural systems, enabling planning and design to be based on the incorporation of these local energies and processes. For example, applying the knowledge of the local climate to the orientation of buildings and streets can reduce consumption of nonrenewable energy by 40 percent. Regional and local parks can be located to reduce flooding and recharge the water supply system. These hydric parks provide open space while storing, cleaning, and redistributing gray and black water. This beautiful system can be applied to regional treatment plants and neighborhood park design (see Figure 13.6).

By the year 2020, the design of urban systems will rely on a mixture of 50 percent renewable and 50 percent nonrenewable energies. Globally, no urban systems work in this proportion today. To be ready for this retrofit in urban functioning, designers and planners must be able to apply the knowledge of sustainable energy principles to their plans and designs. Natural systems–based regional design, the design and planning of the entire region, is an important new responsibility for the urban planning and design profession.

Understanding and connecting to the "free work" of nature is fundamental to bioregionalism and sustainable design. Systems can be studied by looking at their components—nature, agriculture, and urban areas. Establishing positive connec-

Figure 13.6. Urban stormwater stored within neighborhood parks and regional greenways/blueways creates amenities while providing for flood protection and providing sustainable water supply. Civil engineering and plumbing tax dollars would be invested into "parks not pipes."

tions between resources and waste creates planning based on sustainable bioregional functioning. Phosphate pollution from farmland can flow into wetlands and be stored for biological cleanup. It can then be recharged into the soil for irrigation or be reused in agriculture itself. Designing these types of "fits" in the regional land use plan can control other agricultural pollutants such as sediment, heavy metals, and pesticides. When these connections are made, nature provides the "free work" of filtration and storage and the bioregion can work more efficiently.

Sewage in a concentrated form is poisonous, but much of it acts as a fertilizer when uniformly distributed. Regional sanitary treatment "parks" would integrate wetlands systems and the free work they provide. In contemporary society, wetlands have been used for secondary and tertiary treatment of sewage and for stormwater reclamation for over fifty years. The location of these treatment parks near agriculture would connect the agricultural need for water and nutrients with the nutrient-laden water of the urban system. Nutrients used on horticultural crops and feed crops re-create productive sustainable cycles, establishing a proper "fit" between land use and water.

Case Study: South Dade County, Florida, Watershed Project

Water is an essential renewable resource that is in constant danger of overuse. The following is a synopsis of a planning project completed for the South Florida Water Management District.

The objective of the South Dade Watershed Project was to analyze the relationship between water and land use and to establish regional planning criteria that would assure a sustainable water supply for southern Dade County, Florida. These criteria were used to create a vision of South Dade.

The following are the principles of watershed planning and sustainability that were used in the South Dade project:

- The total rainfall within the region is that region's water budget—supplies from outside the region are "borrowed or leased" and cannot be counted on during drought or after build-out. The aquifer "storages" allow us to average the variations in rainfall and should not be used to calculate the allocation of water for public use.
- Each land use must spatially contribute its share to the region's water budget— the postdevelopment hydrologic condition must equal the predevelopment hydrologic condition (i.e., the loss of recharge that is associated with "typical" development must be restored and protected).
- Stormwater, graywater, and wastewater must be recycled and recharged at a rate commensurate with use—the storage and recharge of these types of water must be achieved at the regional, community, and neighborhood scale.
- The location of surface water and groundwater storage areas for water resource

sustainability must be integrated in urban and community design—the development of "hydric parks" and the preservation of open space will create and reinforce strong edges for communities and create a sense of "place." Restoring recharge areas—lost to increased urban impervious surfaces—will simultaneously provide water for the future while supplying additional open space.

There are limits to all resources. Linear technological solutions often cause problems greater than those they were intended to solve. Biourbanism understands this and reduces the use of nonrenewable resources.

The impacts of nonrenewables, primarily fossil fuels, have been revealed in significant ways: inflation, higher taxes, energy and fuel shortages, water scarcity, and, even more significantly, in the breakdown of entire biological systems

To achieve an interactive network of humanity and nature—a landscape that has a "place" for both the needs of humans and the functions of nature—requires that planning and design be reoriented from using more resources to a view that there are resource limits. It then becomes the combined mission of science, planning, and design to discover these limits and work within them—to put "form" to a common vision and develop incremental strategies on how to get from here to there.

For the South Dade Watershed project, several key questions had to be answered. What are the critical elements in the South Florida landscape that must be taken into account to avoid calamity? What must be repaired and protected to prevent the continued decline in environmental quality and community quality of life? Once the requisite information is gathered, it can be applied to determine how development and environment can be incorporated into one system—what must be undone and what must be added. Bioregionalism applies the science of the region to the design within the limits imposed by both the natural environment and economics.

Historic development pattern images illustrate how the land and water interact naturally in South Dade (see Figure 13.7). The darker areas represent the areas located along the coastal ridge that are at elevations above the 100-year floodplain. These areas are more suitable for development and will remain out of harm's way and unaffected by rising sea levels. Stormwater flows off the coastal ridge from areas of higher land elevation to areas of lower land elevation. This water eventually flows to the drainage canals and ultimately to Biscayne Bay. Areas located on either side of the coastal ridge are open pervious or porous areas that provide critical water recharge to the Biscayne Aquifer. The lighter areas, representing the "lower" poorly drained soils of the Everglades, the transverse glades, and coastal marsh, tend to flood and are consequently not suitable for development. Of equal importance is the area's ability to store water for future use and to reduce impacts from drought.

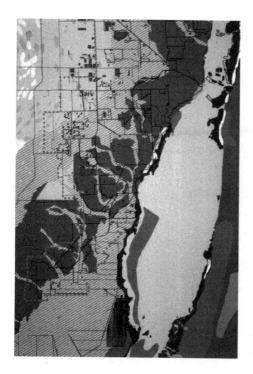

Figure 13.7. Historic development patterns image shows how land and water interact in South Dade.

Figures 13.8 and 13.9 overlay the 100-year floodplain on the existing development grid. Much of the recent development in South Dade has actually occurred in areas that are less suitable for development. The development of these areas for urban uses changes the flooding patterns. Groundwater levels decrease due to a loss of pervious recharge surfaces that are replaced by impervious roads and buildings. The result is a reduction in regional water storage. The replacement of recharge area by impervious surfaces degrades the water quality and seals off any recharge to the groundwater system (see Figure 13.10). Conventional engineering practices eventually lead to contaminated and concentrated toxic storage underground. Continued development within these areas, which is the present-day pattern, will cause more local flooding, eliminate critical aquifer recharge areas, and destroy valuable natural resources—all leading to the reduction of "green infrastructure."

Given that the limited land area suitable for development is in conflict with the water resource limits of South Dade, how can these sustainable principles be applied to urban and regional form? This bioregional/biourban approach is designed to use the "green infrastructure" to efficiently collect, store, clean up, and distribute water for all users—urban, agricultural, and natural systems.

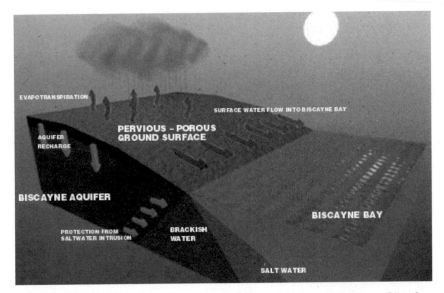

Figure 13.8. Historically, rainfall filtered through the vegetation and geology of South Dade in a period measured in weeks.

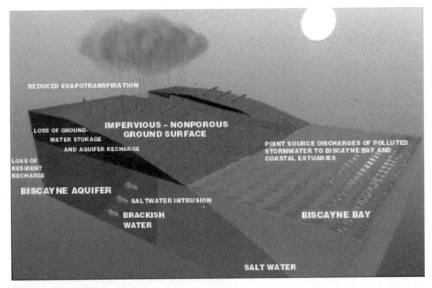

Figure 13.9. Rainfall now leaves the South Dade system within twenty-four hours and this recharge is lost to the bay. Irrigation must then be used to keep urban vegetation alive.

Figure 13.10. Streets and urban landscapes replace recharge areas with impervious surfaces.

Making Bioregional Connections

Figure 13.11 shows the drainage canals replaced by broad wetland systems similar to what was historically "the transverse glades." These topographic low points are an integral part of the region's natural flood protection. The north–south canal, separating the developed part of Dade County from the Everglades, is expanded to provide valuable storage and cleansing of water. This will improve the quality of water while preserving a sustainable water supply for future users. The coastal canals become "spreader" canals to enhance the distribution, timing, quantity, and quality of the water that flows to Biscayne Bay, while also protecting the biological food chain and supporting sport fishing and ecotourism.

The light squares in West Dade represent subregional wastewater treatment plants that will provide for 100 percent reuse of the waste effluent. This requires enhanced water quality treatment provided by technology supplemented with natural cleansing of the water in the newly created wetland areas. By reintroducing this water into the aquifer, much of the water that is consumed every day will be replenished within its cycle of use.

In this plan, open pervious land uses that provide valuable recharge to the aquifer are preserved. This will also provide for the preservation of the agriculture

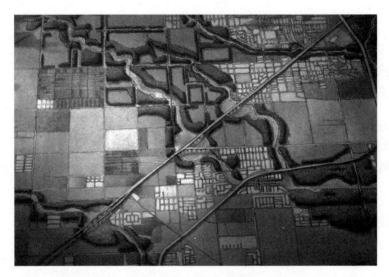

Figure 13.11. Drainage canals replaced by wetland systems.

and quality of life that exists in South Dade today. To support this objective, future development must be directed to the higher ground along the coastal ridge. Mass transit and community based transit centers within the developed areas must be established. These centers will encourage the development of closely knit communities with strong regional connections. This will create more livable urban planning while reinforcing the opportunity to provide for future water needs by leaving large open recharge areas (see Figure 13.12).

Figure 13.12. Water feature in South Dade.

Conclusion

Changes in the process of planning and design can have the largest impact on environmental protection. Incorporating the understanding and information embodied within natural systems into urban and regional planning practices ensures a true incorporation of historic and past lessons learned. The key concepts covered in this overview of sustainable planning at regional scale are:

1. *Bioregionalism* through research and understanding of the system at a scale larger than the project scale.
2. *Applying* this knowledge to the interaction of the urban components: infrastructure, utilities, and neighborhood patterns.
3. *Incorporating* the "free work" of natural systems—ecology, biology, physics, climate, hydrology, and soils—by using natural processes rather than technology for water storage and cleaning, microclimatic control and resource use, reuse and recycling.
4. *Designing the connections* to make use of this "free work"—*biourbanism*.

Chapter 14

Creating Greener Communities Through Conservation Subdivision Design

Randall Arendt

This chapter describes what is one of the most effective land-use planning techniques for protecting community-wide greenways and open space networks. Its simplicity, ease of use, and cost-free nature auger well for its expanding role as a very effective tool available to developers, conservationists, and planners for achieving their separate but complementary objectives of earning money, conserving land, and managing change in their communities.

The techniques addressed here provide a practical way in which a wide range of land-use professionals (including planners, landscape architects, civil engineers, and surveyors) can help communities shape their emerging development patterns more effectively so that features that are noteworthy or significant at the local or neighborhood level—but which are rarely protected under current codes—will become the central organizing elements around which each development is designed. With farsighted planning, local officials can help to ensure that most of the open spaces thus protected will ultimately form an interconnected network of conservation lands running throughout their communities.

This planning approach has already conserved more than 500 acres of prime farmland in one Pennsylvania township (Lower Makefield, Bucks County) in just five years, and that figure continues to increase as new conservation subdivisions are proposed and approved. At an average land value of $7,000 per acre, new land-use regulations have permanently protected $3.5 million worth of land without any cost to taxpayers, without any equity loss for property owners, and without requiring any controversial down-zoning of preexisting density allowances. A similar per-acre value can be attached to the 650 acres protected through conservation subdivision design in Hamburg Township, Livingston County, Michigan since 1992, and to the 2,000 acres saved in Calvert County, Maryland, during the first two years of new regulations having taken effect. The combined value of those lands is approximately $15 million, making this technique possibly one of most cost-effective conservation planning tools available to growing communities on the metro edge.

This approach can also be described as "the ultimate in property rights," which permits the "wise use" of land by landowners who no longer have to sell (and forfeit use of) their entire parcel to developers to receive its full development value. Through conservation design, such property owners may retain ownership and use of half or more of their land as "noncommon" open space, with all of the new development located on a fraction of the whole parcel.

As a first step, most local Comprehensive Plans need to be augmented with more detailed resource inventories and with practical policies describing new land conservation techniques that are both innovative and effective. To help implement such policies, zoning and subdivision ordinances must be revised to set higher standards governing the quantity, quality, and configuration of the open space that developers are required to conserve as a basic condition of approval. This chapter addresses the interrelated issues of conservation planning, conservation zoning, and conservation subdivision design.

Along these lines, an approach that has recently been devised in Pennsylvania is to establish a framework directly linking municipal Comprehensive Plans with new provisions for local zoning and subdivision ordinances that emphasize the conservation of natural lands and cultural features to form an interconnected network of protected open space weaving through each community.

This new "operating system" of municipal plans and ordinances is coordinated to conserve significant portions of individual tracts as they are proposed for residential subdivision. In this system, these potential conservation areas are identified prior to development and are permanently protected as individual "building blocks" in a community-wide open space network.

The principal problem faced by most communities in almost every metropolitan area is the suburban development density for which they are typically zoned. These densities, typically ranging from 0.5 to 2.0 acres per dwelling, severely limit the potential effectiveness of two oft-touted planning techniques—the "purchase of development rights" (PDR) and the "transfer of development rights"—that have been designed to minimize adverse economic impacts that zoning density reductions would have on landowners in these areas. These landowners generally look at their properties as investments on which they may depend to pay retirement expenses, college tuition, and medical bills.

In both cases, typical suburban zoning densities thwart these two alternative approaches by permitting a large number of homes to be built on the remaining vacant lands. Such zoning generally drives up land values beyond the point where PDR is economically viable on a broad scale and thus typically limits this technique to a small handful of selected parcels in any single community. Similarly, suburban zoning densities usually permit far more development rights on individual properties than can be feasibly lifted up and transferred to more suitable areas in other parts of the community without igniting political firestorms.

As long as significant "down-zoning" (reducing legal building density) remains politically unachievable, local governments must find other ways to control the *pattern* of new development so that it does not needlessly fragment and consume resource lands important for agriculture, forestry, wildlife habitat, and so on. This chapter describes Pennsylvania's new Growing Greener program, which integrates conservation planning with new model conservation provisions for local zoning and subdivision ordinances. Special features of this program are an expanded "menu" of up to five zoning density options for landowners (keyed to various levels of open space protection) and a logical "four-step" approach to designing subdivisions around the central organizing principle of land conservation.

Attributes of Successful Conservation Communities

To help communities determine whether they have taken the steps necessary to ensure that conservation values are adequately weighed against development needs, the Natural Lands Trust has prepared the following list of self-diagnostic questions. For many people, looking at the issues in this way helps them understand what their communities need to do to increase the effectiveness of their land-use planning and conservation efforts. These "measures of success" have been suggested by Michael Clarke, former Trust president.

1. *The community resource inventory.* Has the community adequately inventoried its resources, and does the public have a sufficient understanding and appreciation of them?

2. *The "community audit."* Is the community monitoring and assessing its likely future under its current growth management practices, and is it taking steps to change what it does not like?

3. *Policies for conservation and development.* Has the community established appropriate and realistic policies for land conservation and development in its Comprehensive Plan or Open Space Plan, and do these policies produce a clear vision of lands to be conserved?

4. *The regulatory framework.* Are the community's zoning and subdivision regulations specifically structured to help implement its policies for land conservation?

5. *Designing conservation subdivisions.* Do local officials have experience in working cooperatively and effectively with subdivision applicants so that each new subdivision contributes to the overall network of conservation lands?

6. *Landowner outreach and stewardship.* Has the community leadership cultivated good working relationships with its major local landowners so that

they are aware of all their options for conserving land or blending conservation principles with new development?

7. *Stewardship of conservation lands.* Does the community have in place the arrangements required for successfully owning, managing, and using lands set aside for conservation purposes?

8. *Ongoing education and communications.* How are local officials and the general public maintaining their knowledge of the state-of-the-art in managing growth to conserve land?

Simply asking these questions is likely to stimulate productive thought about subjects that are typically not in the forefront of issues on the minds of many local officials. These questions can therefore help people see gaps in their community's current approach and can help them propose mid-course corrections to the direction they are presently heading. It is my observation that many communities with moderate to high growth rates are essentially drifting toward a future of haphazard suburbanization produced by implementing conventional zoning and subdivision codes that are inherently visionless.

Relating Open Space Planning to Updated Zoning and Subdivision Ordinances

Even though most local governments in developing areas have not yet created an overall land-use planning framework into which "conservation zoning" would fit, some are beginning to do so and all should follow their leads. The potential for creating a network of open spaces still exists in many municipalities, however, and this concept lies at the core of the Growing Greener program. Through this statewide effort in conservation planning education, local officials are learning about the need for integrating their land-use plans and ordinances, from conservation elements of Comprehensive Plans, to conservation zoning provisions, to conservation development design standards in local subdivision ordinances.

Conservation lands that communities are able to protect through this approach typically encompass a wide variety of resources, including wildlife travel corridors and breeding/feeding grounds, mature woodlands, stream valleys, and prime farmland. One of the program's principal goals is to encourage the more progressive municipalities in each growth-impacted county to become "Conservation Leadership Communities," to demonstrate the effectiveness and practicality of these techniques. When these techniques have been in place for a number of years, with landowners being permitted to develop their land at limited, moderate, or full densities, in a manner respecting both resource values and property values according to an overall community-wide "green plan," an interconnected network of resource lands can be protected in which farmers, wildlife, naturalists, and hikers may comfortably coexist.

Recommended Sequence of Four Work Stages

In working with municipalities, the following sequence of work stages is generally recommended:

1. *Performing a community "audit."* This tool can take any of three forms. Two involve projecting trends to show what the community is likely to become or what it is likely to look like if current land-use policies continue to be implemented. These projections can be purely numerical (such as estimates of the ultimate population when all vacant, buildable land is developed) or pictorial (such as "build-out maps" showing the spread of suburban house lots and streets throughout the remaining undeveloped portions of the municipality). A third approach to the "audit" involves examining existing zoning and subdivision ordinances and preparing a constructive critique of their weaknesses and how those deficiencies could be corrected. This last approach is the one most frequently employed in the Growing Greener program.

2. *Supplementing the Comprehensive Plan* to include a community-wide Map of Potential Conservation Lands, including both "primary conservation areas" (wetlands, floodplains, and slopes exceeding 25 percent) and "secondary conservation areas" (otherwise buildable woodlands, farmland, riparian corridors, cultural landscapes and scenic viewsheds, and other noteworthy features that help define the municipality's special character). The revised plan should also include a description of specific zoning and subdivision ordinance language needed to ensure that this "greener vision" map illustrating the community's future open space network will be implemented as each undeveloped parcel is proposed for development.

3. *Updating the subdivision ordinance* to include several critical new requirements for all subdivisions such as a detailed Existing Resources/Site Analysis Plan, a Sketch Plan, *or* a Two-Stage Preliminary Plan (conceptual and detailed), plus a conceptually innovative design process requiring that conservation areas be identified first, followed by house site locations, and then streets and lot lines may be drawn in.

4. *Amending the zoning ordinance* to include a variety of mechanisms, as described later in this chapter.

This sequence is recommended because it is very important, at the outset, that the community have a clear understanding of what it will grow to become if it does not chart a mid-course correction in the way that its development patterns are proceeding. It is equally necessary that local officials and residents work together to produce a shared vision for the direction in which they would like their ordinances to take the community, before beginning the process of code revision.

After completing the "audit," securing agreement on community goals for open space conservation and development in the Comprehensive Plan, and deciding on the principal subdivision design methodologies involved in achieving those goals, municipalities are generally better equipped to deal with the more detailed work involved in their zoning revisions. Apart from the logic that this progression offers, another advantage is that the dimensional details of zoning will be seen, in a broader perspective, as the fairly minor items that they really are. When viewed in the context of a community-wide open space network of conservation lands, the relative insignificance of such details often becomes apparent. When municipal officials deal with zoning provisions in the abstract, they tend to place more emphasis on these details than is warranted, and they often spend extended periods debating the merits of this number or of that dimension. By working from the "big picture" of potential conservation lands to the intermediate level of the methodology involved in analyzing and laying out development proposals, before getting into the minutiae of zoning, local officials and residents are often more productive and better satisfied with the ultimate results.

Four Interrelated "Toolboxes" for Creating Greener Communities

Within the work stages described above, the Growing Greener program utilizes four "toolboxes" of complementary techniques to help municipalities implement their conservation goals. The techniques in each of the toolboxes should be integrated so that the location of the open space laid out pursuant to the conservation subdivision regulations (Toolbox C) is controlled by overall standards contained in the conservation zoning provisions (Toolbox D), which in turn should relate back to the community-wide Map of Potential Conservation Lands in the Comprehensive Plan (Toolbox B) and the community "audit" (Toolbox A). Some communities and park agencies are also discovering the value of this technique as a way of requiring developers to buffer their subdivisions from abutting parkland or active farmland in an "adjoining lands strategy," wherein at least part of the conservation areas is required to be located along the park or resource boundary.

Toolbox A. The Community "Audit": Envisioning the Future

The "community audit" visioning process helps local officials and residents see the ultimate result of continuing to implement current land-use policies. Most local ordinances allow or encourage standardized subdivision layouts consisting of nothing more than house lots and streets. This is because these codes ask little, if anything, with respect to conserving unconstrained land as open space or providing neighborhood amenities. Over a period of decades this process produces a broader pattern of "wall-to-wall subdivisions" (see Figure 14.1). Few communities

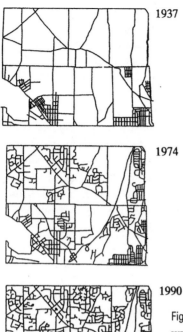

1937

1974

1990

Figure 14.1. The pattern of "wall-to-wall subdivisions" that evolves over time with zoning and subdivision ordinances that require developers to create nothing more than house lots and streets.

consciously plan to become bland suburbs without open space. However, most zoning codes program exactly that outcome, aided and abetted by conventional subdivision ordinances whose design standards typically encompass only streets, drains, and lot lines.

Municipalities perform audits to see the future before it happens, to help them judge whether a mid-course correction is needed. A community audit can entail any or all of the following three elements:

1. A *numerical analysis of development trends* to estimate the number of dwelling units and the number of acres that will probably be converted into house lots and streets under present codes.

2. A *"build-out" map* that realistically plots future development patterns on a map of the entire municipality or focuses only on selected areas in the municipality where development is of the greatest immediate concern.

3. *Regulatory evaluation* to assess the community's current land-use regulations, identifying their strengths and weaknesses, and offering constructive

recommendations about how they can incorporate the conservation techniques described in this chapter.

Toolbox B. Comprehensive Plan Revisions: Map of Potential Conservation Lands

Although local Comprehensive Plans range widely in their completeness, these documents generally include resource inventory maps that can form the core material for preparing a community-wide Map of Potential Conservation Lands, thereby establishing an overall direction for municipal growth that the ordinances can be carefully updated to implement.

On this composite Map of Potential Conservation Lands, a variety of resources is typically rendered in various shades of green or other related colors and is divided into the following three categories:

1. *Primary conservation areas* that include lands with severe environmental constraints rendering them unfit for development—such as wetlands, floodplains, and slopes exceeding 25 percent.

2. *Secondary conservation areas* encompassing lands with locally significant or noteworthy features constituting much of the community's resource base and contributing to its special character—such as stream valleys, moderately steep slopes, mature woodlands, wildlife habitats and travel corridors, fields and pastures with soils rated prime or of statewide importance or situated within the public viewshed as seen from existing public roads, historic structures and archaeological sites (including ruins and cellarholes), stone walls, noteworthy rock formations, and established trails. Usually these resource areas are totally unprotected and are simply zoned for one kind of development or another.

3. *Existing protected areas* consisting of eased land, public parks, conservancy properties, and so on.

The process for creating the community-wide Map of Potential Conservation Lands is as follows:

1. A base map is prepared showing all existing streets, roads, parcel boundaries, protected lands, and primary conservation areas.

2. Clear acetate sheets showing each kind of secondary conservation area are then placed on top of the base map in an order reflecting the community's preservation priorities (as determined through public discussion).

3. This overlay process reveals certain situations ("co-occurrences") where two or more conservation features appear together (such as woodlands and wildlife habitats, or farmland and scenic viewsheds). It will also reveal gaps where no features appear.

Although this exercise is not an exact science, it frequently helps local officials and residents visualize how various kinds of resource areas are related to one another, and it enables them to tentatively identify both broad swaths and narrow corridors of resource land that could be connected and protected in a variety of ways. Figure 14.2 shows a portion of a map prepared for one Pennsylvania township that has followed this approach. West Manchester's map gives clear guidance to landowners and developers as to where the new development is encouraged on their properties. Township officials engaged a consultant to draw, on the official tax parcel maps, the boundaries of the new conservation lands network as it crossed various properties, showing how areas required to be preserved in each new development could be located so they would ultimately connect with one another. In this formerly agricultural municipality, woodland remnants and the riparian buffer along the creek were identified as core elements of the conservation network.

The importance of this kind of map is that it can form the framework around which new development is either encouraged or required to be designed. This approach ensures that the municipality's evolving conservation network will be interconnected and that it will encompass a substantial amount of land that would otherwise be subdivided, cleared, graded, and developed. Such maps therefore provide the unifying vision defining the community's future pattern of conservation and development in a rational and orderly manner.

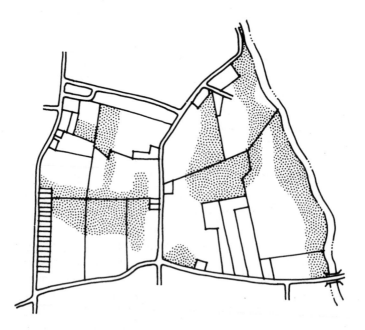

Figure 14.2. Part of a map of potential conservation lands for West Manchester Township, York County, Pennsylvania.

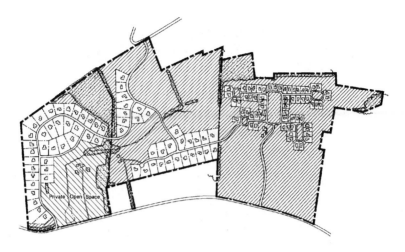

Figure 14.3. The conservation lands (shown in gray) were deliberately laid out to form part of an interconnected network of open spaces in these three adjoining parcels.

Figure 14.3 shows how certain resource areas in three adjoining subdivisions have been designed to connect, and it illustrates the way in which the Map of Potential Conservation Lands can become a reality.

Figure 14.4 provides a bird's-eye view of a landscape in which an interconnected network of conservation lands has been gradually protected through the steady application of conservation zoning techniques and conservation subdivision design standards.

Even though this process may produce a map on which all or most of the land within certain individual parcels is colored over, indicating that nearly every part of the property contains one type of resource area or another, there is a firm commitment under the Growing Greener approach that each property owner may exercise his or her right to develop to the full density allowed under the community's zoning ordinance. In other words, no reduction in lot yield is required, and thus there is less chance of a "takings" occurring.

Landowners wishing to develop their properties would either be encouraged or required to utilize flexible "conservation design" techniques to keep house lots away from those special areas, locating new homes, lawns, and streets within those parts of their properties containing the least significant resource areas.

This approach allows habitats that are currently fragmented into multiple ownerships to remain more intact after development, and it allows blocks of farmland or special woodlands to remain more whole. It is also a powerful tool for greenway planning, enabling continuous ribbons of open space to be created along streams, for example, as each riparian parcel is subdivided. To be effective, such maps

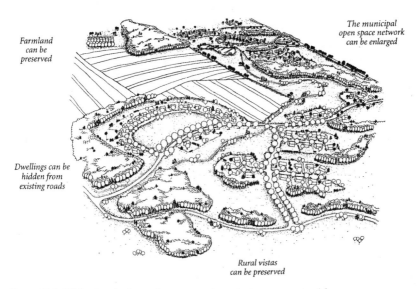

Figure 14.4. This sketch shows how to apply techniques to set aside open space, which preserves the rural character, expands community parkland, and creates privacy for residences. *Source:* Montgomery County Planning Commission, Morristown, Pennsylvania.

should be referenced in zoning regulations and treated as a "rebuttable presumption" that developers must deal with seriously (which includes an opportunity for them to suggest adjustments to the "potential conservation areas" identified on this map, respecting the spirit of the community's open space network goals).

Another very important aspect of updating Comprehensive Plans is the expansion of their "implementation" chapters to include a brief description of the specific zoning and subdivision ordinance techniques necessary to ensure that the plan's ultimate goal of protecting conservation networks becomes a reality. These techniques are detailed in Toolboxes C and D below.

Toolbox C. Subdivision Ordinance Revisions

Upon completing the "greener visions" map, the next step entails drafting revisions to the subdivision ordinance under which most of the critical layout decisions are made. This toolbox involves the specific *procedures* for analyzing each new subdivision site and also details the methodology for preparing a conservation-based development plan wherein the resource areas will be related to the community-wide Map of Potential Conservation Lands. Designing subdivisions around the central organizing principle of land conservation is not difficult. However, it is essential that ordinances contain clear standards to guide the development design process so applicants will understand the community's conservation priorities.

The highlights of this toolbox include the following elements:

1. *Existing Resources/Site Analysis Plan:* Sensitive subdivision design necessarily begins with preparing a comprehensive Existing Resources/Site Analysis Plan (see Figures 14.6 and 14.7 later in this chapter). This critical element identifies all the special characteristics of the subject property, from unbuildable areas such as wetlands, floodplains, and steep slopes, to other land types that are developable but contain certain noteworthy features. Such features might include mature or healthy and diverse woodlands, wildlife habitats critical for breeding or feeding, woodlands and hedgerows, prime or highly productive farmland, scenic views into and out of the site, and historic buildings in their context.

   This plan is typically prepared by a landscape architect, sometimes with input from conservation biologists, agricultural specialists, and historic preservationists. It tells reviewers virtually everything they need to know about the property in terms of the elements listed above in the Map of Potential Conservation Lands. Whereas that map is drawn at a scale appropriate for a community-wide document, the Existing Resources/Site Analysis Plan is typically drawn to a scale of 1 inch to 100 or 200 feet. It reflects a thorough understanding of the site by those who have walked it extensively, so that even the location of large trees or unusual geological formations can be identified. This is arguably the most important document in the subdivision application process because it is the factual foundation on which all design decisions are based.

2. *On-site visit:* With the above site analysis map in hand, local officials walk the property and offer suggestions about which natural or cultural features should be designed around and conserved. Without the benefit of experiencing the property firsthand, in a three-dimensional way (as opposed to viewing a two-dimensional plan in a meeting room), it is extremely difficult to judge the appropriateness of proposed layouts.

3. *Sketch Plan:* The Sketch Plan is the next most important document in the subdivision process. In this step the overall concept is outlined and can even take the form of a simple "bubble map" showing areas of proposed development and areas of proposed conservation. Sketch Plans may be quite simple and can be prepared on white tracing paper as an overlay sheet to be placed on top of the Existing Resources/Site Analysis Map so that everyone can see how well (or poorly) the proposed layout avoids potential conservation lands having resources ranked high on the priority list in the subdivision regulations. Ideally the proposed development "footprint" on the Sketch Plan should dovetail with the most significant or noteworthy resources documented on the Existing Resources/Site Analysis Plan. This section of the ordinance should also provide more evaluation criteria for local officials to

follow, so that everyone knows the parameters for approving or disapproving the Sketch Plan.

It is essential that this stage occur before applicants spend large sums on preparing the almost fully engineered drawings that typically constitute so-called "Preliminary Plans." Once a layout has been substantially engineered, developers are understandably reluctant to modify their drawings in any significant way. After agreement is reached on the Sketch Plan, the applicant moves to the Preliminary Plan.

Even in states where the planning legislation does not specifically authorize Sketch Plans (as is the case in Pennsylvania), municipalities might wish to consider this approach anyway. In Chester County, Pennsylvania, for example, many townships require Sketch Plans and find that developers are willing to submit them. Although the state enabling legislation does not grant municipalities the authority to require such a "third step" (in addition to preliminary and final plans), developers have not been inclined to press this point legally, probably because most of them recognize that Sketch Plans can represent time very well spent, as these sketches enable the larger issues to be resolved in broad, outline form before tens of thousands of dollars are spent engineering so-called "Preliminary Plans." In order for the Sketch Plan to become an accepted part of the process in these kinds of situations, it should be kept very simple and inexpensive to prepare—such as the "bubble map" on a tracing-paper overlay sheet mentioned earlier.

4. *Preliminary Plan as two phases—conceptual and detailed:* In states where municipalities are not specifically authorized to require Sketch Plans, and in communities where local officials are hesitant to include Sketch Plan requirements in their codes for this or other reasons, such submissions must remain entirely voluntary. When applicants in such situations decline the opportunity to submit a Sketch Plan, it might be legally possible to divide the normal Preliminary Plan process into two phases. The first phase, taking perhaps one-third of the total time allowed for Preliminary Plan reviews, would consist of an unengineered "Conceptual Preliminary Plan," in which the overall layout of conservation areas, streets, and house lots is shown to scale, as an overlay to the Existing Resources/Site Analysis Plan. This approach would enable local officials to examine the relationship between the elements shown on the Conceptual Preliminary Plan and the location of features depicted on the initial site analysis plan. Once the Conceptual Preliminary Plan has been approved, applicants move to the second phase, that of preparing a "Detailed Preliminary Plan," containing all the data normally required on so-called "Preliminary Plans."

5. *Simplifying the Preliminary Plan stage:* If a municipality is reluctant either to require simple sketch plans or to create a two-phase preliminary plan process, a third alternative exists. This alternative greatly simplifies the so-

called "Preliminary Plan" and makes it a truly preliminary document, like a fairly elaborate—but only lightly engineered—Sketch Plan. This approach returns to the original intent of many state legislatures when they first enacted their enabling legislation creating the "Preliminary Plan" stage, an intent that has become clouded over the years as municipalities have added more requirements to this initial presentation.

Four-Step Design Approach

Production of the Existing Resource/Site Analysis Plan sets the stage for a four-step design process that helps site designers lay out full-density developments around the most significant natural and cultural features. Simply stated, the four steps consist of:

1. identifying potential *conservation lands,* both primary and secondary;
2. locating *house sites,* at a respectful distance from resource lands;
3. *aligning streets and footpaths;* and
4. setting in the *lot lines.*

These four steps are more fully described below, with illustrations of a site zoned for twenty-one new house lots.

STEP ONE: IDENTIFYING CONSERVATION AREAS. The first step, identifying open space worthy of preservation, involves two kinds of resource areas relating back to the community-wide Map of Potential Conservation Lands in the Comprehensive Plan. They are *primary conservation areas* (see Figure 14.5) limited to regulatory wetlands, floodplains, and steep slopes, and *secondary conservation areas* (see Figure 14.6) including those unprotected elements of the natural and cultural landscape that deserve to be spared from clearing, grading, and development. On the site illustrated here, these features include mature woodland habitat, "serpentine barrens" rock outcroppings with their associated semi-rare wildflowers, the four-acre corner meadow and views across it into the property from existing roads, and several hedgerows bordering the old fields. The special features of secondary conservation areas are typically unprotected under local codes, yet they are a significant asset to the property value and neighborhood character. The secondary conservation areas are the most vulnerable to change but can easily be retained by following this simple four-step process.

The act of delineating conservation areas also defines *potential development areas,* which occupy the balance of the site (see Figure 14.7). This completes the first step and ensures that the site's fundamental integrity will be protected, regardless of the actual configuration of house lots and streets that follows. In other words, once the "big picture" of conservation has been brought into focus, the rest of the design process essentially involves only lesser details. Those details, of crit-

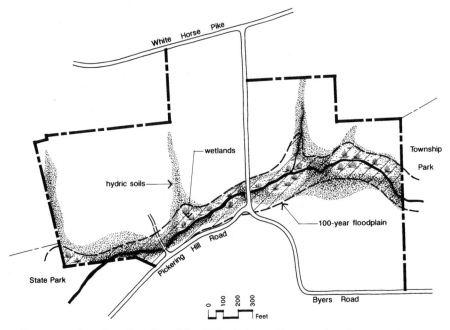

Figure 14.5. Step One, Part One: Identifying Primary Conservation Areas.

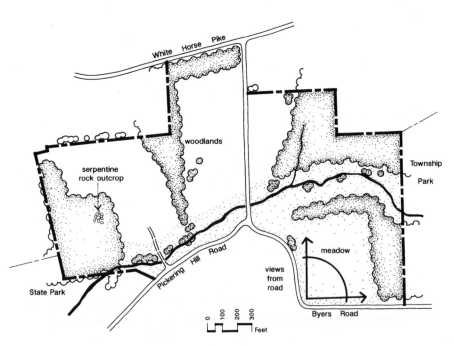

Figure 14.6. Step One, Part Two: Identifying Secondary Conservation Areas.

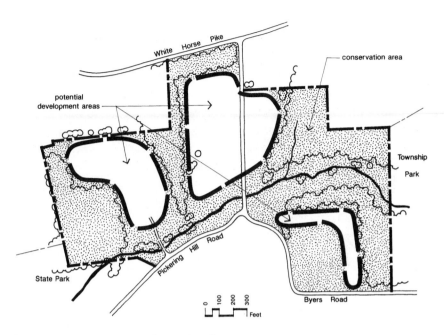

Figure 14.7. Step One, Part Three: Identifying Potential Development Areas for Options 1, 2, and 5.

ical importance to developers, realtors, and future residents, are addressed during the last three steps.

STEP TWO: LOCATING HOUSE SITES. The second step involves locating the approximate sites of individual houses, which for marketing and quality-of-life reasons should be placed at a respectful proximity to the conservation areas, with homes backing up to woodlands for privacy or enjoying long views across open fields or wildflower meadows (see Figure 14.8). In a full-density conservation plan the number of house sites would be the same as that shown on the "Yield Plan" illustrated in Figure 14.11 (twenty-one lots in this example), but the integrity of the site would not be lost and residents' views would not necessarily be of their neighbors' garage doors across the street.

STEP THREE: ALIGNING STREETS AND TRAILS. The third step consists of tracing a logical alignment for local streets accessing the twenty-one homes and for informal footpaths connecting various parts of the neighborhood, making it easier for residents to walk through the open space, observing seasonal changes in the landscape and meeting others living at the opposite end of their development (see Figure 14.9).

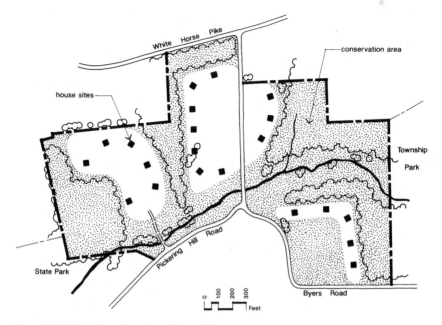

Figure 14.8. Step Two: Locating House Sites.

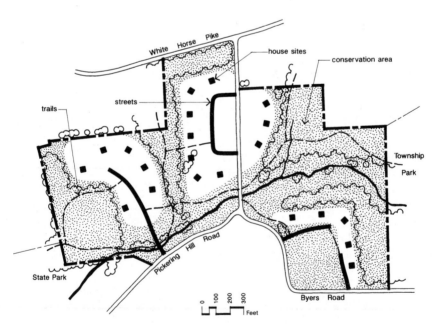

Figure 14.9. Step Three: Aligning Streets and Trails.

The opportunity for a streamside greenway as part of a larger community-wide network of open space is also obvious.

STEP FOUR: DRAWING IN THE LOT LINES. The final and least significant step involves drawing in the lot lines (see Figure 14.10). Successful developers of conservation subdivisions know that most buyers prefer homes in attractive parklike settings and that views of protected open space enable them to sell lots or houses faster and at premium prices. Such homes also tend to appreciate more in value, compared with those on lots in standard "cookie-cutter" developments offering no views or nearby open space.

This approach reverses the sequence of steps in laying out conventional subdivisions where the street system is the first thing to be identified, followed by lot lines fanning out to encompass every square foot of ground into house lots (see Figure 14.11). When municipalities require nothing more than "house lots and streets," that is all they generally receive. However, when the subdivision design process begins with the determination of natural and cultural resource areas as the first step, and when the ordinance also requires that a significant proportion of the unconstrained land be designated as open space as a precondition for achieving full density, officials can effectively encourage conservation subdivision design. The protected land in each new subdivision then becomes building blocks adding new acreage to community-wide networks of interconnected open space each time

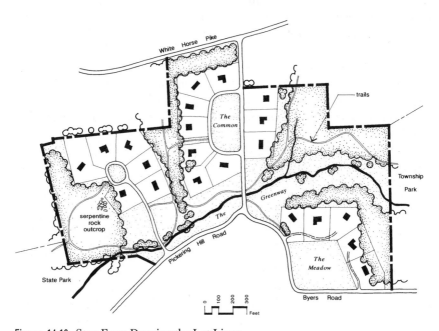

Figure 14.10. Step Four: Drawing the Lot Lines.

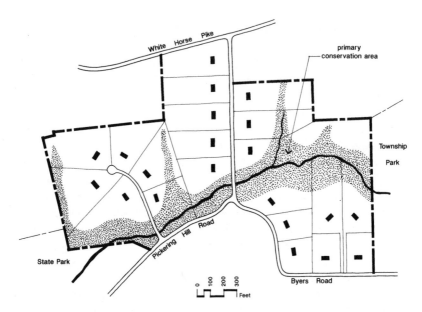

Figure 14.11. Yield Plan.

a property is developed. When following this four-step approach, it is nearly impossible to produce a truly inferior plan. In fact, to the extent that the property contains elements of the community-wide network of conservation lands, the plan is likely to be at least fairly good.

The kind of subdivision most frequently created is the type that blankets the development parcel with house lots, and which pays little if any attention to designing around the special features of the property. In this example, house placement avoids the primary conservation areas but disregards the secondary conservation areas. However, such a sketch can provide a useful estimate of a site's capacity to accommodate new houses at the base density allowed under zoning and is therefore known as a "Yield Plan" (see Figure 14.11).

Toolbox D. Zoning Ordinance Revisions

The conservation planning concepts typically recommended for zoning ordinances in the Growing Greener program include:

1. A "menu of choices" providing a greater variety of options for landowners, all of which would confer distinct advantages to the municipality.
2. Density *dis*incentives to actively discourage development without open space.
3. *Requiring* conservation design within certain overlay districts where the municipality feels that open space preservation (for active or passive purposes) is essential.

4. Possible density incentives to encourage public access to conservation lands and to encourage the endowment of maintenance funds.
5. Requiring management plans for conservation lands.
6. Replacing blanket zoning density with strong new "net-out" provisions related to actual environmental constraints on the development site.

These zoning approaches are described in the following sections.

A "Menu" of Choices Through "Multi-Optioned Zoning"

Much could be gained by permitting landowners to enjoy a wider range of alternative options for conservation and development of their properties than standard "Euclidean" zoning typically allows. Under the conventional approach, a "one-size-fits-all" provision applies to all properties within a residential zoning district, effectively preventing many creative solutions. Because each property, each landowner, and each housing market is different, zoning should allow a variation of responses, provided they all would benefit the municipality in one way or another.

Communities wishing to break the cycle of "wall-to-wall house lots" need to consider modifying their zoning in two ways: First, to actively encourage subdivisions that set aside 50 percent or more of the unconstrained land as permanently protected conservation areas; and second, to incorporate substantial density *dis*incentives actively discouraging developers from producing more "cookie-cutter" layouts with little or no functional open space.

In determining density, in using the Growing Greener program, applicants choose between two approaches for determining their site's base density or lot yield:

• *Formulaic approach.* The applicant calculates the acreage in various categories subject to various physical constraints, applies special "environmental weighting factors" to those acreages, and determines the number of "net buildable acres" on which density is to be based. This approach is further described later in this chapter under the heading "Net-Out" Provisions and "Performance Zoning" Criteria.
• *"Yield Plan" approach.* A very simple conventional lot layout concept plan is produced in a realistic manner, reflecting site constraints such as steep slopes, wetlands, floodplains, and (in unsewered areas) soils suitable for septic disposal (see Figure 14.11). In unsewered areas, officials should require a 10 percent sample of the most questionable lots—which they would select—to be tested for septic suitability. Any failing lots would be deducted and the applicant would have to perform a second or third 10 percent sample, until all the lots in a given sample pass.

This "menu" approach expands the choices open to landowners and developers compared with the more limited options available under typical zoning ordi-

Table 14.1. Yields, open space, and lot sizes on a sixty-three-acre tract with forty acres adjusted tract acreage[a]

	Option				
	1	*2*	*3*	*4*	*5*
Yield (lots)	21	28	10	5	42
% Open Space	50%	60%	—	—	70%
Max. Lot Size	40,000 sq. ft	24,000 sq. ft	—	—	12,000 sq. ft
Min. Lot Size	20,000 sq. ft	12,000 sq. ft	4 acres	10 acres	6,000 sq. ft

[a] The above numbers are based on rural zoning requirements of 82,000 sq. ft of land per dwelling, adjusted tract acreage (excluding unbuildable portions). Readers should note that multiple-density options can be offered at many different levels of base density. For example, the *Growing Greener* workbook contains a detailed table showing lot sizes and open space percentages for all or most of these five options where the original "base density" is as high as two, three, or four dwellings per acre.

nances. The principal characteristics of these options (in terms of lot yield, minimum percentage of open space, and lot size minima and maxima) are summarized in Table 14.1.

The basic option, "Option 1" (Density-Neutral with Preexisting Zoning), allows landowners full density provided that a conservation subdivision design is proposed, with substantial (often 50 percent) undivided open space, based on net buildable land area (i.e., in addition to unbuildable lands such as wetlands, floodplains, and slopes greater than 25 percent) (see Figure 14.12).

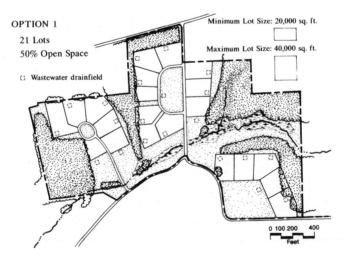

Figure 14.12. Option 1: Density Neutral with Preexisting Zoning (eighteen lots ranging from 20,000 to 40,000 square feet; 50 percent undivided open space).

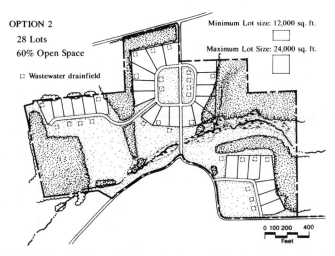

Figure 14.13. Option 2: Enhanced Conservation and Density (twenty-four lots ranging from 12,000 to 24,000 square feet; 60 percent undivided open space).

"Option 2" (Enhanced Conservation and Density) offers a small density incentive for layouts providing higher proportions of protected open space (at least 60 percent) (see Figure 14.13).

"Option 3" (Estate Lots) satisfies any demand for extra-large house lots with no undivided open space (except for possibly a greenway corridor connection along a stream valley or other natural feature). However, this option is subject to a density reduction with fewer house lots than the district's base density (see Figure 14.14).

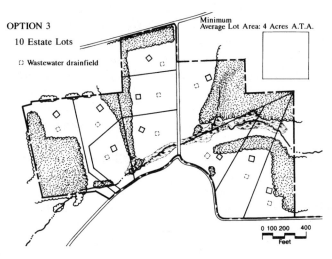

Figure 14.14. Option 3: Estate Lots (50 percent density reduction; nine lots, typically 160,000 square feet, or 4 acres).

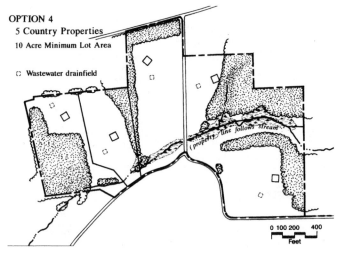

Figure 14.15. Option 4: Country Properties (five lots, with maximum density of 10 acres per principal dwelling; 70 percent density reduction).

"Option 4" (Country Properties) is designed to encourage lower-density development wherein country properties of at least 10 acres would be made more attractive by offering such incentives as relaxing street construction standards (to permit low-volume "country lanes" with gravel surfaces essentially functioning as shared driveways). Another incentive might allow one or two accessory dwelling units per country property, subject to certain design standards pertaining to maximum floorspace and architectural form. Further subdivision is prevented through conservation easements, which also protect the integrity of the conservation lands outside the individual "building envelopes" (see Figure 14.15).

"Option 5" (Hamlets and Villages), allows a significantly larger density than offered under Option 2, provided that an even greater percentage of open space is set aside permanently. In this "neo-traditional" design option, the four-step approach is modified so that the layout of streets and squares precedes house site location, as streetscapes and formal open spaces assume a higher degree of importance in such neighborhoods. A set of illustrated design standards for "villages and hamlets" appears in the *Growing Greener* workbook appendix, providing a clear understanding of street layout patterns, civic open space provision, and building siting reflecting the principal physical characteristics of small nineteenth-century settlements (see Figure 14.16).

It is also possible to combine two or more of these options. As shown in Figure 14.17, "country properties" can be successfully combined with village/hamlet design, enabling applicants to locate much of their open space within large private parcels as "noncommon" land. This design solution provides multiple advantages,

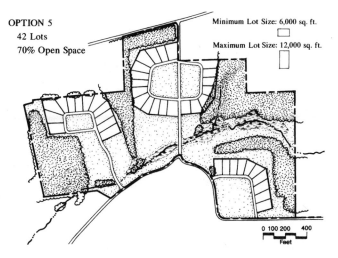

OPTION 5
42 Lots
70% Open Space

Minimum Lot Size: 6,000 sq. ft.

Maximum Lot Size: 12,000 sq. ft.

0 100 200 400
Feet

Figure 14.16. Option 5: Hamlet or Village (thirty-six lots ranging from 6,000 to 12,000 square feet; 70 percent undivided open space).

among them conserving roadside vistas, allowing the small-lot community to be situated in a less visible position, and enabling the developer to maximize his return on the majority of the conservation land while still providing active and passive open space for the village residents.

Absent from this "menu" of options is the "cookie-cutter" subdivision with no designated open space at the normal base density. It is a central tenet of the Growing Greener program that the principal problem with conventional "Euclidean" zoning is that it allows developers full density, by right, for unimaginative layouts converting every acre of land into lawns and cul-de-sacs. That type of approach, cutting all woodlands, fields, pastures, wetlands, and floodplains into a simplistic checkerboard of house lots and streets, should never be rewarded with full density. Rather it should be allowed only with a density reduction sufficiently large to discourage most developers from continuing that highly land-consumptive practice, which is frequently very destructive of the community's resource base.

Density Disincentives

As noted above, the land-consuming "Options 3 and 4" alternatives involve a density penalty because they convert all land into house lots and streets. By failing to designate any undivided open space (except perhaps for narrow "greenway corridors"), these kinds of layout effectively prevent any kind of coordinated management for the woodlands or meadows within the larger house lots (which are typically cleared or modified in ways that reduce their value for habitat and which suburbanize the formerly rural landscape). Developers who wish to pursue the

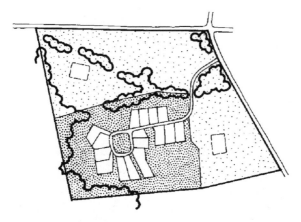

Figure 14.17. An Option 5 village surrounded by its own open space and buffered from existing roads by two "country properties" (Option 4).

large-lot option may continue to do so, with lots that would be larger than they would otherwise have created. Although the municipality would not see its open space network grow in a formal manner, it would benefit in other ways, such as by the reduction in traffic and schoolchildren that fewer homes would generate and by providing some opportunities to accommodate the highest end of the housing market, which values extreme privacy and seclusion.

Requiring Conservation Design

Certain areas, such as land along stream valleys and ridgelines, might be subject to special overlay zoning provisions limiting the alternatives to Options 1 and 2, with standards for locating the required open space in certain parts of the property. These would typically be areas where the municipality would not like to risk receiving proposals to subdivide the land under Options 3 or 4 with no effectively protected, undivided open space. Other examples in which such a requirement would be appropriate are for parcels abutting any public parklands, wildlife refuges, or conservancy preserves, or any active, productive farmland where new suburban neighbors would predictably object to agricultural operations.

Limited Density Incentives

To encourage certain desirable results where the legislative authority to require them is absent or subject to debate, communities should consider adding provisions offering density incentives. Examples of uses for such incentives include the creation of endowment funds to finance perpetual maintenance of the conservation areas when they are gifted to land trusts, public access to trail corridors that may traverse a proposed subdivision, and donation of subdivision open space to the municipality for public recreation purposes.

Management Plans for Conservation Lands

The land that is not divided into house lots should be managed comprehensively (usually by a homeowners' association) to maintain or enhance the ecological health of the habitat. The Natural Lands Trust has prepared model management guidelines for open space in new conservation subdivisions, with strategies for dealing with twelve different types of open space areas based on their vegetation characteristics and proposed uses. However, experience shows that maintenance difficulties are built into developments where the "open space" consists of parts of large individual backyards subject to conservation easements. Such is the case in Option 3 and 4 subdivisions, which is why they should generally be discouraged. In Option 1, 2, and 5 subdivisions with undivided open space, homeowners associations have the responsibility for maintenance (as well as for taxes and liability).

"Net-Out" Provisions and "Performance Zoning" Criteria

Communities should consider modifying their rules for calculating density in new subdivisions. Rather than dividing gross acreage by a certain density factor (such as one gross acre per dwelling), they could require that the acreage used for density calculation purposes be the *net* land area appropriate for home construction. Courts in Pennsylvania have praised municipalities that have adopted performance-related zoning that assigns very low "density factors" to lands that are severely constrained, moderately low density factors to lands that are moderately constrained, and full density (base density) on unconstrained lands.

Briefly stated, the acreage of land in each category is measured by the applicant's surveyor or engineer, and that acreage figure is then multiplied by the appropriate "environmental weighting factor" (EWF). The product of that exercise is then multiplied by the base density allowed in the zoning district. In other words, 12 acres of floodplain would produce a value of 6.0 (12 acres times the EWF of 0.5), meaning that only 6 of the 12 floodprone acres could be counted toward density. In a zoning district where the base density is 2 acres per dwelling, the applicant would qualify for three houses, provided that they are all located outside the floodplain.

Conclusions

Because of its low costs and inherent adaptability, the basic "building block" for creating Open Space Networks, as envisioned in a community's Comprehensive Plan and enabled in its zoning ordinance, is the "conservation subdivision." When local officials and residents are sensitized to the kind of "wall-to-wall" development that their existing conventional land-use codes will ultimately produce, they often become much more amenable to revising those codes to *require* that basic conservation principles be followed in the design of new subdivisions and that the open space thus protected be laid out so as to create an interconnected network of conservation lands. All this can be achieved without involving any "taking" because the undivided conservation land typically remains under private ownership (usually by a homeowners association or a local land trust). When the municipality desires all or part of the land for public park purposes, and the developer is agreeable, conservation land may be donated or sold at a negotiated price to the community. (Another alternative is for municipalities to offer density bonuses in exchange for public dedication of the conservation acreage, or for greenway trail easements through it).

BIBLIOGRAPHY

Arendt, Randall. 1992. "Open Space Zoning: What It Is and Why It Works." *Planning Commissioners' Journal* (July–August) 5:4–8.

Arendt, Randall. 1995. *Conservation Subdivision Design: A Four-Step Process,* Media, PA: Natural Lands Trust, 8 pp. (This article may be accessed on the Internet, on the Home Page of the *Planning Commissioners' Journal,* http://www.webcom/pcj/arendt/con1.html.)

Arendt, Randall. 1996. *Conservation Design for Subdivisions: A Practical Guide to Creating Open Space Networks.* Washington, DC: Island Press.

Arendt, Randall. 1997. *Growing Greener: A Conservation Planning Workbook for Municipal Officials in Pennsylvania.* Harrisburg: Pennsylvania Department of Natural Resources. (In-state copies available through the Natural Lands Trust, Media, PA. Out-of-state copies available directly from the author at Natural Lands Trust, 1031 Palmers Mill Road, Media, PA 19063.)

Arendt, Randall, et al. 1994. *Rural by Design: Maintaining Small Town Character.* Chicago: Planners Press.

Clarke, Michael G. 1992. "Community Land Stewardship: A Future Direction for Land Trusts." *Land Trust Exchange* 11:1–9.

McHarg, Ian. 1991. *Design with Nature.* New York: John Wiley & Sons.

Steiner, Frederick. 1991. *The Living Landscape: An Ecological Approach to Landscape Planning.* New York: McGraw-Hill, Inc.

Urban Land Institute. 1993. *Farmview,* Project Reference File Series, vol. 23, no. 7, April–June.

Urban Land Institute. 1994. *Hawksnest,* Project Reference File Series, vol. 24, no. 10, April–June.

Whyte, William H. 1964. *Cluster Development.* New York: American Conservation Foundation.

Whyte, William H. 1994. "Garnet Oaks." *Land Development,* Fall 1994.

Chapter 15

Environmentally Superior Buildings from Birth to Death

Thomas E. Graedel

A central theme of industrial ecology, the "science of sustainability," is the assessment of the environmental attributes of products throughout their entire life cycle, from conception to manufacture to use to end-of-life. Creating environmentally superior products is a difficult enough challenge when the product is manufactured on an assembly line, used by a single owner throughout its entire life, and then discarded as a unit. In the case of a building, added considerations abound: the need to consider the site being developed, the prospect of multiple owners and tenants during building life, the probability of renovations, the possibility of new uses, and the discarding of structural elements at many different times rather than all at once, to name a few. I will present life-cycle assessment (LCA) concepts that address these concerns and discuss their appropriateness for structures of different types, ages, locations, and uses.

Goals of Facility Assessment

Just as products and processes can be made in environmentally responsible ways, so too can facilities be designed, built, operated, renovated, and recycled in an environmentally responsible manner. However, buildings have characteristics sufficiently different from products and processes that facility assessment must be approached from a somewhat different framework. Among the obvious differences are that (1) the geographical location of a building has a strong influence on its design and construction (climate influences the degree to which heating and air conditioning are incorporated, for example); (2) it is common for the use of a building to change several times during its life span; (3) the end-of-life stage for a building is typically generations into the future, making it difficult to predict what materials recovery facilities may be desirable and what activities may be possible;

and (4) very often, the use phase is predominant (e.g., fifty years of energy consumption is the controlling stressor).

Other factors affecting building life cycles are reminiscent of product assessments but still present significant complications in the assessment process. For example, materials are used in different ways, some uses being more environmentally responsible than others (e.g., steel reinforcing bars in concrete present different problems for eventual recovery and recycling than do open steel beams over a manufacturing floor). Uses of a particular material may differ within a building as well, as in different window glazing on building exteriors directly exposed to sunlight. Finally, no matter what exemplary steps are taken in constructing the building, its overall environmental impact may be dominated by the way in which the facility is used, not by its structural features.

A number of architects, builders, and planners have approached the "green design" concept in recent years and have established some recommended actions to guide thinking in the greening of facilities (e.g., Lippiatt and Norris 1995; Seiter and Doxsey 1995):

• Avoid building new roads or widening existing roads at the site.
• Minimize the "footprint" of construction operations.
• Minimize the use of heavy construction equipment.
• To the extent possible, preserve and/or restore local ecosystems.
• Reduce the quantity of materials used in construction.
• Select building materials that themselves have low environmental impacts.
• Design and operate energy-efficient facilities (i.e., efficient heating, cooling, lighting, machinery).
• Locate with complementary facilities that can utilize by-products.
• Reduce the use of water in the operation of buildings and grounds.
• Maximize the longevity and reuse of buildings.
• Recycle existing buildings and sites rather than developing undeveloped sites.
• Minimize materials waste during demolition and construction activities.

Designating a building as "green" generally involves evaluating the characteristics of the building's design and construction, especially materials selection, its infrastructure (lighting, heating, and so forth), and its eventual conversion to other uses or "deconstruction" and associated materials recycling.

All of these aspects of a building's relationship to the wider world are important, but the list is incomplete without the inclusion of the impacts of the activities carried on within the building during its useful life. For an industrial facility, for example, one needs to evaluate not only the structure itself but also the products that are manufactured within it, the processes that are used in that manufacture, and the ways in which other activities within the building are performed. Clearly, a building cannot be truly green if the products, processes, and related operations associated with it are not.

Life Stages of Industrial Facilities

Any assessment approach should ideally be applicable to all varieties of facilities. It is useful, therefore, to briefly review how facilities of various types can be approached from the life cycle framework described in previous chapters. Table 15.1 lists a number of types of facilities and identifies their typical products and processes.

The first group of facilities are those that manufacture products for industrial or commercial customers. These are generally classical "industrial" facilities and have the processing of materials, or the production of components, subassemblies, or industrial infrastructure items such as machine tools, as their focus. Assessments of this type of facility are reasonably straightforward.

The second group of facilities are those that exist for the purpose of offering tangible products directly to individual consumers. The simplest are those that perform the minimal level of processing: unpacking and shelving. Hardware stores, clothing stores, and small appliance stores are examples of this type. Grocery stores are similar but typically perform some degree of food processing as well, such as meat cutting and packaging. Some facilities of this type have a more major involvement in processing, as with the agricultural activities of a typical garden center. Perhaps most like the industrial model is the restaurant, where materials (food) are transformed into products (meals) by specific processes (food preparation techniques).

Given the life-cycle perspective, the assessment of the environmental responsibility of a facility can be defined to include five stages or activities as shown in Fig-

Table 15.1. Product and process characteristics of typical commercial and industrial facilities

Facility	Product	Process
FACILITIES OFFERING PRODUCTS TO COMMERCIAL CUSTOMERS		
Ore smelter	Metal ingots	Smelting and refining of ores
Chemical works	Chemicals	Processing of chemical foodstocks
Appliance manufacturer	Washing machines	Assemble products from components
Recycler	Components, materials	Disassemble/reprocess obsolete goods
FACILITIES OFFERING PRODUCTS TO INDIVIDUAL CONSUMERS		
Hardware store	Tools, supplies	Unpacking, shelving
Grocery store	Food, related items	Unpacking, shelving, food processing
Garden center	Plants, related items	Agricultural activities
Restaurant	Meals	Food preparation

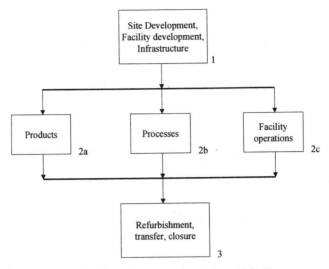

Figure 15.1. The life-cycle stages of an industrial facility.

ure 15.1. Environmentally responsible facility (ERF) assessment need not and should not be applied only to manufacturing facilities, but rather to any facility dealing with any type of products or services—oil refineries, fast-food restaurants, residential structures, and so forth. The assessment will obviously be more complex in some cases than in others, but managers of facilities, no matter what the facility's function, should strive to attain environmentally responsible status.

Stage 1: Site Development, Facility Development, and Infrastructure

A significant factor in the degree of environmental responsibility of a facility is the site that is selected and the way in which that site is developed. If the facility is an extractive or materials processing operation (oil refining, ore smelting, and so on), the facility's geographical location will generally be constrained by the need to be near the resource. A manufacturing facility usually requires access to good transportation and a suitable work force, but it may be otherwise unconstrained. Many other types of buildings can be located virtually anywhere.

Manufacturing plants have traditionally been in or near urban areas. Such locations often have suitable buildings available and have the advantages of drawing on a geographically concentrated work force and of using existing transportation and utility infrastructures. It may also be possible to add new operations to existing facilities, thereby avoiding many of the regulatory intricacies of establishing a wholly new plant site. A promising recent development is the trend toward cooperative agreements between governments and industries for the reuse of these "brownfield" sites.

For facilities of any kind built on land previously undeveloped as industrial or commercial sites, ecological impacts on regional biodiversity may result, and we can anticipate added air emissions from new transportation and utility infrastructures. These effects can be minimized by working with existing infrastructures and developing the site with the maximum area left in natural form. Nonetheless, given the ready availability of commercial buildings and facilities in many cities and countries, such "greenfield" choices are hard to justify from an environmental perspective.

The construction of new facilities or the rehabilitation of existing facilities offers great opportunities for environmentally responsible action. The selection of materials, the methods of construction, and the handling of debris are all areas for attention. A substantial thrust is the use in new building construction of a variety of recycled materials, including wallboard of compressed paper, tiles from mining aggregate and ground glass, carpet pads of shredded tire rubber, and roof flashing of reclaimed copper and aluminum. In some instances, the value of wood that could be reclaimed from old buildings and reused can make it economical to take the buildings apart rather than raze them and discard the rubble.

An activity that generally receives little attention is the disposal of construction debris. It has been estimated that as much as 25 percent by weight of all material brought to a building construction site is eventually consigned to the landfill, and approximately 20 percent of the waste flow to landfills is construction debris. It is probably difficult to avoid generating some of this debris—broken or defective materials, for example—but much of it could be reduced by an enhanced focus on manufacturing and building to standard dimensions, minimizing packaging, and promoting material reuse on site.

Stage 2a: Principal Business Activity—Products

Tangible products are items manufactured within the facility for sale to customers. The assessment of the environmental characteristics of products is relatively well developed and is described elsewhere (Graedel et al. 1995).

Stage 2b: Principal Business Activity—Processes

Processes are the techniques, materials, and equipment used in the creation of products. Process assessment has been presented and discussed by Callahan (1994) and Graedel (1998).

Stage 2c: Facility Operations

The impact of any facility on the environment during its active life is often heavily weighted by transportation issues. As with many other aspects of industrial activities, trade-offs are involved. For example, just-in-time delivery of components and modules has been hailed as a cost-effective and efficient boon for manufacturing. Nonetheless, it has been estimated that the largest contribution to the emissions that generate Tokyo smog comes from trucks making just-in-time deliveries (Tonooka 1992). The corporations delivering and those receiving these components and modules should bear some degree of responsibility for those emissions. It is sometimes possible to reduce transport demands by improved scheduling and coordination, perhaps in concert with nearby industrial partners or by siting facilities near principal suppliers. Options may also exist for encouraging ride sharing, telecommuting, and other activities that reduce overall emissions from employee vehicles.

Material entering or leaving a facility also offers opportunities for useful action. To the extent that the material is related to products, it is captured by product LCAs. Facilities receive and disperse much nonproduct material, however: food for employee cafeterias, office supplies, restroom supplies, and maintenance items such as lubricants, fertilizer, and road salt, to name just a few. An environmentally responsible facility should have a structured program to evaluate each incoming and outgoing materials stream and to tailor it, as well as its packaging, in environmentally responsible directions. Obviously, the most environmentally preferable products should be chosen in performing each function.

Facility energy use also requires careful scrutiny, as opportunities for improvement are always present. An example is industrial lighting systems, which are estimated to be responsible for between 5 and 10 percent of air pollution emissions overall. Another major energy consumer is the heating, ventilating, and air-conditioning systems. Office machines and computers in office buildings can also use significant amounts of energy. The environmental impacts chargeable to energy use generally occur elsewhere—emission of carbon dioxide from fossil fuel power plants, for example—but are no less real for not happening right at the facility.

As with many environmentally related business expenditures, energy costs for specific uses are often lumped in with "overhead" and not precisely known, yet the use of modern technology often has the potential to decrease energy expenditures by 50 percent or more, especially if energy use is charged to specific operations within the building and the managers of those operations are directed to monitor usage.

Stage 3: Facility Refurbishment, Transfer, and Closure

Just as environmentally responsible products are increasingly being designed for "product life extension," so too should environmentally responsible facilities. Buildings and other structures contain substantial amounts of material with significant levels of embodied energy, and the (especially local) environmental disruption involved in the construction of new buildings and their related infrastructure is substantial. Clearly an environmentally responsible facility must be designed to be easily refurbished for new uses, to be transferred to new owners and operators with a minimum of alteration, and, if it must be closed, to permit recovery of materials, fixtures, and other components for reuse or recycling.

Life Stages of Office and Residential Facilities

The life cycle approach outlined for industrial facilities needs to be modified for office or residential facilities, for which the concepts of "products" and "processes" are less applicable. Instead, the activities of the construction stage and the facility operation stage can be studied in greater detail. The result is five life stages defined in the following sections.

Stage 1a: Site and Infrastructure Development

This stage treats all aspects of the development of the site: ecological disturbance, provisioning of infrastructure, slope and drainage modifications, and the like.

Stage 1b: Facility Development

This stage treats all aspects of the construction of the building itself, including the choice of materials, their delivery to the site, techniques and equipment used in construction, and site cleanup.

Stage 2a: Facility Operations—Indoors

This stage includes activities taking place within the facility. It focuses on the use of energy and water; the choice and use of office and food supplies; choice and operation of heating, ventilation, and air-conditioning equipment; and recycling or disposal of paper, food waste, and other debris.

Stage 2b: Facility Operations—Outdoors

This stage treats activities taking place outside the facility. It focuses on the use of energy and water, the approach to the maintenance of vegetation and plantings, snow plowing and salting, and other activities having a potential ecological impact.

Stage 3: Facility Refurbishment, Transfer, and Closure

This stage is identical to Stage 3 for industrial facilities. The resulting life-stage diagram is shown in Figure 15.2.

Assessment Approaches for Facilities

Systematic valuation techniques for facilities are in the early stages of development. In one effort, a committee of the U.S. Green Buildings Council has produced an evaluation sheet that awards credits for the use of environmentally preferable building materials, ecologically sensitive landscaping and maintenance, energy efficiency, and water conservation, among other topics (U.S. Green Buildings Coun-

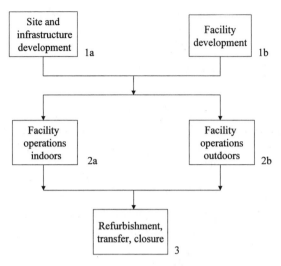

Figure 15.2. The life-cycle stages of an office or residential facility.

cil 1995). A somewhat more elaborate scheme has been developed by the Swedish Waste Research Council (Erlandsson et al. 1994), where attempts are made to assess global, local, and indoor issues. The most ambitious project is by the U.S. National Institute of Standards and Technology, which has under development a comprehensive LCA tool for buildings (Lippiatt and Norris 1995).

While there are obvious benefits to be realized from the assessment tool development attempts mentioned above, there are some obvious inadequacies as well. The most significant is that certain life cycle stages are emphasized, others ignored; in particular, facility closure has not generally been addressed. In addition, most assessment tool development has been for residential housing and is not easily adapted to commercial or industrial buildings. Finally, the emphasis tends to be on new construction, with little guidance available for the building rehabilitation activities that are potentially of great environmental advantage.

A suitable assessment system for environmentally responsible facilities should have the following characteristics: It should lend itself to direct comparisons among rated facilities, be usable and consistent across different assessment teams, encompass all stages of facility life cycles and all relevant environmental stressors, and be simple enough to permit relatively quick and inexpensive assessments to be made. As with products and processes, it is feasible to develop the assessment system with a 5 × 5 matrix in which one dimension consists of life cycle stages and activities and the other consists of environmental stressors (Graedel et al. 1995; Graedel 1998). For the two types of facilities described above, these matrices are shown in Tables 15.2 and 15.3.

Table 15.2. The environmentally responsible industrial facility matrix[a]

Facility Life Stage	Environmental Stressor				
	Ecological Impacts	Energy Use	Solid Residues	Liquid Residues	Gaseous Residues
Site development, facility					
Development and infrastructure	1,1	1,2	1,3	1,4	1,5
Principal business activity—Products	2,1	2,2	2,3	2,4	2,5
Principal business activity—Processes	3,1	3,2	3,3	3,4	3,5
Facility operations	4,1	4,2	4,3	4,4	4,5
Refurbishment, transfer, and closure	5,1	5,2	5,3	5,4	5,5

[a] The numbers are the matrix element indices i, j.

Table 15.3. The environmentally responsible office and residential facility matrix[a]

Facility Life Stage	Environmental Stressor				
	Ecological Impact	Energy Use	Solid Residues	Liquid Residues	Gaseous Residues
Site and infrastructure development	1,1	1,2	1,3	1,4	1,5
Facility development	2,1	2,2	2,3	2,4	2,5
Facility operations—indoors	3,1	3,2	3,3	3,4	3,5
Facility operations—outdoors	4,1	4,2	4,3	4,4	4,5
Refurbishment, transfer, and closure	5,1	5,2	5,3	5,4	5,5

[a] The numbers are the matrix element indices i, j.

To preserve consistency with product and process assessments, the facilities analyst studies the characteristics of the facility and of the activities that occur within it, and assigns to each element of the matrix an integer rating from zero (highest impact, a very negative evaluation) to four (lowest impact, an exemplary evaluation). She or he is guided in this task by experience, inspections of actual or planned facility characteristics, appropriate checklists, and other information. The process described here is purposely qualitative and utilitarian and provides a numerical end-point against which to measure improvement.

Once an evaluation has been made for each matrix element, the overall Environmentally Responsible Facility Rating is computed as the sum of the matrix element values:

$$\Sigma\Sigma M_{i,j}$$

Since there are twenty-five matrix elements, a maximum facility rating is 100. The assignment of a discrete value from zero to four for each matrix element implicitly assumes that the environmental impact implications of each element are equally important. An option for slightly increasingly the complexity of the assessment (but perhaps increasing its utility as well) is to utilize detailed environmental impact information to apply weighting factors to the matrix elements. For example, a certain facility might be thought to generate most of its impacts as a consequence of the processes used within it and few related to facility operations, so the processes row could be weighted more heavily than before and the facility operations row weighted correspondingly lighter. Similarly, a judgment that global warming constituted more of a risk than did liquid residues might dictate an enhanced weighting of the energy use column and a corresponding decreased weighting of the liquid residue column. To the extent that an appropriate weighting scheme is obvious and noncontentious, its use could provide an improved perspective on the environmental burden of the facility being evaluated.

The analyst needs to recognize that the life stages of Tables 15.2 and 15.3 are different from those for products or processes. For products, the five life stages that are considered are (1) premanufacture, (2) manufacture, (3) product delivery, (4) product use, and (5) recycling or disposal. For processes, the five life stages or activities are (1) premanufacture, (2) process implementation, (3) process operation, (4) complementary process operation, and (5) refurbishment, recycling, or disposal of the process equipment itself. For environmental stresses in the facilities assessment, four are the same as used for products and processes: energy consumption, solid residues, liquid residues, and gaseous residues. Materials choice is replaced with biodiversity, since facility development, operation, and closure have such direct and important effects on local ecosystems.

Assessing Generic Automobile Manufacturing Plants

As a demonstration of the operation of the tools described above, it is instructive to perform environmentally responsible facility assessments on facilities more or less familiar to all, at least in concept: generic automobile manufacturing plants of the 1950s and 1990s. Some of the relevant characteristics of the facilities, their products, and their processes are given in Table 15.4. Detailed assessments of the products (automobiles) and the processes by which they are made are presented elsewhere (Graedel 1998).

While it is fairly straightforward to picture and describe typical automobiles of different eras, and the processes by which they were made, there has historically been wide variation in the types of manufacturing sites and their development. Two extremes are employed to illustrate assessment ranking differences. The site chosen to represent the 1950s is an existing industrial site (a "brownfield site"), with already available commercial power, road networks, and other municipal services. The building itself is of brick, with steel framing and supports as required. Bus and trolley transportation are readily available to many of the employees. Heat-

Table 15.4. Salient characteristics of products, processes, and facilities for generic automobile manufacturing plants of the 1950s and 1990s

Characteristic	ca. 1950s	ca. 1990s
PRODUCT: THE AUTOMOBILE		
Material content (kg):		
Plastics	0	101
Aluminum	0	68
Metals	1,583	1,047
Rubber	85	61
Fluids	96	81
Other	137	76
Total weight (kg)	1,901	1,434
Fuel efficiency (miles/gallon)	15	27
Exhaust catalyst	No	Yes
Air conditioning	CFC-12	CFC-134a
PROCESS: AUTO MANUFACTURE		
Energy use	Enormous	Substantial
Painting	Organic, high volatility	Aqueous, low volatility
Recycling	Some	Extensive
Process hardware		
Welding	Frequent	Ubiquitous
Conveyer belts	Numerous	Numerous
Complementary processes		
Metal cleaning	CFCs	Aqueous detergents
FACILITY: AUTO MANUFACTURING PLANT		
Site	"Brownfield"	"Greenfield"
Worker transport	Bus, trolley	Private auto
Heating	Coal	Natural gas
Lighting	Incandescent	High-efficiency fluorescent
A/C fluid	None	CFC-12
Grounds	Fertilizer, pesticides	Natural areas
Building materials	Brick, steel	Concrete, composites
Recycling	No	Yes
Closure	Demolition	Reuse, adaptable

ing is provided by coal burning, and air conditioning has not yet become routinely available. Incandescent lighting is abundant. Much of the land is grassed, mowed, and regularly treated with fertilizers and pesticides. The building itself is "pur-pose-built," as the British say; it is not designed with the idea of ever using it for any purpose other than automobile manufacture. In contrast, the facility of the 1990s is built on a site new to commercial development: a "greenfield." Instead of modification or reconstruction of an existing building, natural land areas are devel-oped, together with the necessary infrastructure of roads, power lines, water and sewer services, and so forth. The structure is primarily concrete, but a wide variety of materials is used. Because the site is not near public transportation, private auto-mobiles are used by employees to go to and from work. Heating is provided by nat-ural gas, and modern air conditioning units with the potentially ozone-depleting refrigerant CFC-12 is used. In keeping with more enlightened modern practice, a substantial fraction of the grounds is maintained in a natural condition, and fertil-izer and pesticide use is minimized.

The assessment is begun by treating the first life stage, that of facility site selec-tion, development, and installation of infrastructure. The resulting ratings, and brief descriptions of the principal reasons for them, are as follows.

Site Selection, Development, and Infrastructure

Element Designation	Element Value and Explanation
1950s plant:	
Biodiversity (1,1)	2 (Brownfield site, but has biotic impacts)
Energy use (1,2)	3 (Few modifications to energy infrastructure)
Solid residue (1,3)	2 (Significant solid residues in site prep)
Liquid residue (1,4)	3 (Modest liquid residues in site prep)
Gas residue (1,5)	3 (Modest gaseous residues in site prep)
1990s plant:	
Biodiversity (1,1)	1 (Greenfield site, large biotic impacts)
Energy use (1,2)	0 (Complete new energy infrastructure)
Solid residue (1,3)	1 (Abundant solid residues in site prep)
Liquid residue (1,4)	3 (Modest liquid residues in site prep)
Gas residue (1,5)	3 (Modest gaseous residues in site prep)

The second stage of facility assessment is that of the environmental responsi-bility of the products made within the facility. For this stage, the previously per-formed assessment of generic automobiles of the 1950s and 1990s (Graedel et al. 1995) will be used. For incorporation into the facilities assessment, the integer rat-ings for each of these impacts were summed over all five life stages and then divided by five to put the rating on the same scale with the other facilities stages considered in this chapter. For example, the five materials choice ratings for the 1950s auto-mobile plant were 2, 0, 3, 1, and 3. Their sum is 9, and the sum divided by 5 is 1.8, which is entered into Table 15.5.

Principal Business Activity—Products

Element Designation	Element Value
1950s plant:	
Materials choice (2,1)	1.8 (CFC cleaning, virgin materials)
Energy use (2,2)	1.4 (Fossil fuel energy use is very large)
Solid residue (2,3)	2.2 (A number of components are difficult to recycle)
Liquid residue (2,4)	2.6 (Fluid leakage during operation)
Gas residue (2,5)	1.2 (No exhaust gas scrubbing; high emissions)

1990s plant:

Materials choice (2,1)	2.6 (Petroleum is a resource in short supply)
Energy use (2,2)	2.4 (Energy use during manufacture is fairly high)
Solid residue (2,3)	2.8 (Modest residues of tires and obsolete parts)
Liquid residue (2,4)	3.2 (Some liquid residues from cleaning and painting)
Gas residue (2,5)	2.6 (CO_2, lead [sometimes] emissions)

The third activity stage is processes, for which the rating scores of chapter 8 of Graedel (1998) are utilized.

Principal Business Activity—Processes

Element Designation	*Element Value and Explanation*
1950s plant:	
Materials choice (3,1)	2.0 (CFCs used for metal cleaning)
Energy use (3,2)	1.8 (Substantial process energy use)
Solid residues (3,3)	1.2 (No solid residue recycling)
Liquid residues (3,4)	2.0 (Liquid residues from metal processing)
Gaseous residues3,5)	2.0 (No control of paint shop emissions)
1990s plant:	
Materials choice (3,1)	2.6 (Few materials recoverable at facility demise)
Energy use (3,2)	2.0 (High energy needs for process removal)
Solid residues (3,3)	2.2 (Substantial solid residues at facility demise)
Liquid residues (3,4)	2.8 (Moderate liquid residues)
Gaseous residues (3,5)	3.0 (Few gaseous emissions concerns)

The fourth life stage, facility operations, has been described above; it encompasses any activities not directly related to products or processes. The ratings for the two generic facilities are as follows:

Facility Operations

Element Designation	*Element Value and Explanation*
1950s plant:	
Biodiversity (4,1)	0 (Pesticide use, all areas altered)
Energy use (4,2)	1 (Large energy use in facility operations)
Solid residue (4,3)	0 (No attempt to minimize solid residues)
Liquid residue (4,4)	0 (Extensive liquid discharges)
Gas residue (4,5)	2 (Moderate VOC emissions)
1990s plant:	
Biodiversity (4,1)	3 (Natural areas, no pesticides)
Energy use (4,2)	3 (Modest energy use in operations)
Solid residue (4,3)	3 (Extensive waste minimization and recycling)
Liquid residue (4,4)	3 (Extensive liquid residue treatment)
Gas residue (4,5)	3 (Efficient gaseous residue controls)

The final life stage assessment is for facility refurbishment, transfer, or closure. In the case of the 1950s facility, the design employed no consideration of reuse, so total demolition constitutes the only reasonable option available. For the 1990s facility, designed so that interior walls may be modified, wires, cables, and pipes added readily and inexpensively, and building services updated in modular fashion, reuse is a reasonable expectation.

Refurbishment/Transfer/Closure

Element Designation	Element Value and Explanation
1950s plant:	
Biodiversity (5,1)	1 (Major ecological impacts upon demolition)
Energy use (5,2)	1 (Major energy use in demolition and clearing)
Solid residue (5,3)	1 (Little reuse of materials possible)
Liquid residue (5,4)	2 (Significant liquid residues when demolished)
Gas residue (5,5)	2 (Significant gaseous residues when demolished)
1990s plant:	
Biodiversity (5,1)	3 (Little ecological impact when reused)
Energy use (5,2)	3 (Modest energy use when reused)
Solid residue (5,3)	3 (Extensive reuse—low demolition probability)
Liquid residue (5,4)	3 (Minor liquid residues when reused)
Gas residue (5,5)	3 (Minor gaseous residues when reused)

The completed matrices for the generic 1950s and 1990s automobile manufacturing plants are illustrated in Table 15.5. Examine first the values for the 1950s facility so far as life stages are concerned. The column at the far right of the table shows good environmental stewardship during site development and moderate environmental stewardship regarding product design, manufacture, and use. The ratings for facility closure are poor, and those for facility operations are abysmal. On the basis of the environmental stressors, shown by the column additions, the summed ratings for biodiversity and solid residues are particularly low. The overall rating of 41.2 is far below what might be desired.

In contrast, the overall rating for the 1990s facility is 64.2, much better than that of the earlier facility but still leaving plenty of room for improvement. The life stage that is particularly problematic is that of site selection and preparation. Energy use and solid residue generation receive the lowest ratings of the environmental stressors.

The target plots that complement Table 15.5 are shown in Figures 15.3 and 15.4. One instantly gets the sense of the areas in which improvement has occurred over the twenty-year interval, and also where modern approaches appear deficient.

Table 15.5. Environmentally responsible product assessments for generic 1950s and 1990s automobile manufacturing plants[a]

Life Stage	Environmental Stressor					
	Biodiversity, Materials[b]	Energy Use	Solid Residues	Liquid Residues	Gaseous Residues	Totals
1. Site selection development, infrastructure	2.0	3.0	2.0	3.0	3.0	13.0/20
	1.0	0.0	1.0	3.0	3.0	8.0/20
2. Principal business activity— products	1.8	1.4	2.2	2.6	1.2	9.2/20
	2.6	2.4	2.8	3.2	2.6	13.6/20
3. Principal business activity— Processes	2.0	1.8	1.2	2.0	2.0	9.0/20
	2.6	2.0	2.2	2.8	3.0	12.6/20
4. Facility operations	0.0	1.0	0.0	0.0	2.0	3.0/20
	3.0	3.0	3.0	3.0	3.0	15.0/20
5. Refurbishment, transfer, and closure	1.0	1.0	1.0	2.0	2.0	7.0/20
	3.0	3.0	3.0	3.0	3.0	15.0/20
Total	6.8/20	8.2/20	6.4/20	9.6/20	10.2/20	41.2/100
	12.2/20	10.4/20	12.0/20	15.0/20	14.6/20	64.2/100

[a] The upper numbers refer to the 1950s facility; lower numbers to the 1990s facility.

[b] The ratings in this column for life stages one, four, and five refer to impacts on biodiversity; for stages two and three on choice of materials

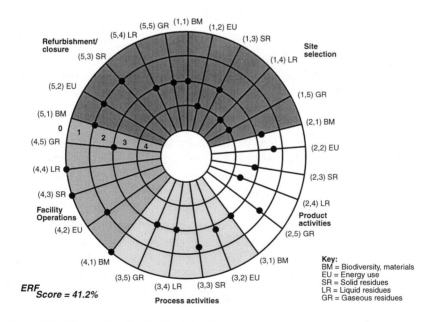

Figure 15.3. Target plots for the display of the environmental impacts of generic automobile manufacturing facilities of the 1950s.

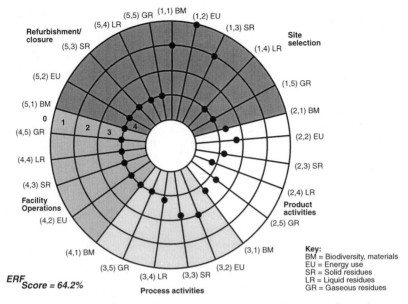

Figure 15.4. Target plots for the display of the environmental impacts of generic automobile manufacturing facilities of the 1990s.

Discussion

Corporations and individuals have traditionally been regarded as good citizens if they followed rules of behavior established by their societies. This reactive approach is now giving way to a proactive one. Processes were the first target of attention—emissions and energy use, for example. Products were next, as their environmentally related attributes were assessed and improved. Facilities are the third facet to receive attention. As techniques for facility assessment undergo further development, the construction and operation of green buildings will become an increasingly important aspect of environmental responsibility.

Two approaches to facility–environment interaction that are related to the discussion in this chapter are "green building design reviews" and "facility audits." Their scope can be appreciated from the perspective of the life-cycle diagram in Figure 15.1. In green building design, the emphasis is on life stage 1 and the energy-related aspects of life stage 2c. In facility audits, the emphasis is on life stages 2a and 2b, with less attention given to life stage 2c. Green building design rarely considers life stage 3, and facility audits universally ignore the final life stage.

Utilizing green building design reviews and facility audits for buildings is reminiscent of the traditional regulatory division of environmental monitoring and control into air, water, and waste. In each approach, practitioners tend to think only about their turf, and the system as a whole seldom approaches optimization. Facility evaluation and the improvement of facility environmental performance is made difficult by the long time scales involved and by the different parties (builders, owners, renters, and so on) in control at different phases of the process, but it is clear that optimization can only be approached if the facility evaluation is carried out from a systems perspective.

REFERENCES

Allenby, B.R., and T.E. Graedel. 1997. "Defining the Environmentally Responsible Facility." In *Proceedings of the Third National Academy of Engineering Workshop on Industrial Ecology*. Washington, DC: National Academy Press.

Callahan, M. 1994. "A Life Cycle Inventory and Tradeoff Analysis: Vapor Degreasing Versus Aqueous Cleaning." In *Proceedings of the Second IEEE International Symposium on Electronics and Environment,* Report 94CH3386-9. Piscataway, NJ: Institute of Electrical and Electronics Engineers, pp. 2115–2119.

Erlandsson, M., K. Mingarini, K. Nilver, K. Sundberg, and K. Odeen. 1994. *Life-Cycle Assessment of Building Components.* Report 35. Stockholm: Swedish Waste Research Council.

Graedel, T.E. 1998. *Streamlined Life-Cycle Assessment.* Upper Saddle River, NJ: Prentice-Hall.

Graedel, T.E., and B.R. Allenby. 1995. "Matrix Approaches to Green Facility Assessment." In *Second International Green Buildings Conference* (A.H. Fanney, K.M. Whitter, and T.B. Cohn, eds.). Special Publication 888. Gaithersburg, MD: National Institute of Standards and Technology, pp. 84–102.

Graedel, T.E., B.R. Allenby, and P.R. Comrie. 1995. "Matrix Approaches to Abridged Life Cycle Assessment." *Environmental Science and Technology* 20:134A–139A.

Lippiatt, B.C., and G.A. Norris. 1995. "Selecting Environmentally and Economically Balanced Building Materials." In *Second International Green Buildings Conference* (A.H. Fanney, K.M. Whitter, and T.B. Cohn, eds.). Special Publication 888. Gaithersburg, MD: National Institute of Standards and Technology, pp. 37–46.

Seiter, D., and W.L. Doxsey. 1995. *Sustainable Building Sourcebook.* Austin, TX: City of Austin Environmental and Conservation Services Department.

Tonooka, Y. 1992. "Emission Inventories in Japan and East Asia." In *Proceedings of the IGAC/GEIA Workshop.* Publication NILH-OR: 67/92. Lillestrom, Norway: Norwegian Institute for Air Research.

U.S. Green Buildings Council. 1995. *Green Building Rating Systems.* Bethesda, MD: U.S. Green Buildings Council.

Chapter 16

Environmental Performance of Buildings: Setting Goals, Offering Guidance, and Assessing Progress

Raymond J. Cole

Buildings are complex human creations. Their design involves the interaction and coordination of a wide range of professions, within a multitude of regulatory agencies and jurisdictions, and typically with demanding time and cost constraints. Their construction requires the involvement and phasing of numerous skills and trades, and their operation and use can compromise the initial design intentions. More confounding, unlike other artifacts that enjoy the benefits of prototype development, mass production, and subsequent correction and refinement, almost every building is a "one-off." Because of the scale and complexity of the building industry, the building delivery process is only capable of slow adaptation rather than sweeping overhaul. New emphases to building design are typically first captured by leading edge buildings. These are held up as exemplars of emerging priorities and typically enjoy considerably greater media coverage than their actual numbers represent. But the true measure of the significance of leading edge buildings lies in the extent to which mainstream practices are realigned in their wake. Superficial changes may occur to mainstream building practice with relative frequency, but the fundamental design and performance of buildings evolve relatively slowly.

For the second time within twenty-five years, environmental issues have become an explicit and prominent part of architectural discourse. If the late 1970s precipitated concern, the current debate has firmly entrenched environmental issues as an important consideration in building design. It is difficult to fully judge the change in the public awareness of environmental issues over the past twenty-five years. Since architecture does not typically change significantly unless the context in which it occurs changes (Ingersoll 1991), a clear direction of environmentally responsible building design remains to be charted—and will remain so for some time. A review of submissions to the 1997 Canadian Architect Awards of Excellence suggests that we are still very much in our infancy in understanding and practicing environmental responsibility and, more significantly, are far from developing the means to effect significant positive change (Cole et al. 1997).

During periods of relatively "mature" design criteria, one can expect a relatively close match between the specification of design criteria by clients and their subsequent interpretation by the design team. Such criteria typically become established as accepted design norms and do not need to be made explicit design criteria. By contrast, during this current period of environmental awareness, a common knowledge base is not yet established and issues of specification, interpretation, and implementation are less well defined. The overlaying of environmental considerations on the building design and construction process brings the inevitable difficulties of reassessing priorities, acquiring new skills, and developing and integrating new information into an existing project delivery process. The environmental agenda requires establishment of new performance goals and targets and provision of appropriate information to assist designers in reaching them. However, new emphases to design also inevitably carry with them the uncertainty of their acceptance or successful outcome. This can, to a degree, be alleviated by the use of assessment tools to establish whether new strategies are indeed effective in achieving expected levels of performance in these new areas of concern. The environmental agenda has significantly increased the potential number of performance criteria of relevance to design and precipitated a corresponding increase in interest and research activity to develop comprehensive building environmental assessment methods.

This chapter examines three mechanisms for making improvements in the environmental performance of buildings: setting and defining environmental goals, the formulation of effective information for design professionals, and development of methods for assessing progress toward the intended goals (see Figure 16.1). The chapter identifies some of the key characteristics and limitations of existing building environmental assessment methods and the requisite characteristics of emerging "second generation" methods and protocols.

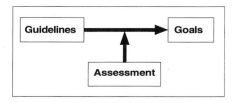

Figure 16.1. Goals, guidelines, and assessment.

Building Performance Goals

When new agendas such as environmental responsibility emerge, two distinct issues are either implicitly or explicitly included in the debate: the current state of affairs—the *benchmark*—and a notion of where we should be heading—the *goal* or target. This discussion occurs globally, nationally, communally, and, in the context of this chapter, at the level of the individual building performance.

The December 1997 Kyoto meeting on global warming and climate change depicted the immense political difficulties of arriving at consensus on performance targets at the international level. The total amount of greenhouse gases generated by human activity can be set against the currently acknowledged carbon sinks. Then, with varying degrees of confidence, the extent of this mismatch between emissions and assimilative capacity can be used as a legitimate basis for establishing appropriate target reductions (Houghton et al. 1990, 1996). There is widespread agreement that current rates of emissions will be catastrophic if unabated, and a picture is emerging regarding the extent to which various possible scenarios for reduction in greenhouse gas emissions will manifest as a stabilized concentration of carbon dioxide within the atmosphere (see Figure 16.2). Set against this ecological reality are the immense pressures of vested interest groups arguing that the cost of mechanisms to meet the proposed reductions would create severe economic hardship for industrialized nations. Desired goals are thereby compromised by the perceived "costs" of implementing effective change.

Within the Kyoto debates, the proposed notion that industrial countries might buy the carbon budgets from developing countries as a cheaper alternative to domestic reduction strategies raises important issues regarding the way and extent to which environmental burdens are apportioned. At this global level, however, the

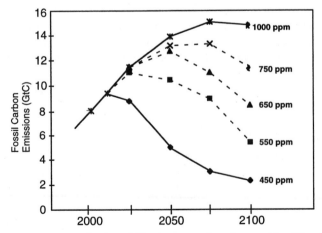

Figure 16.2. IPCC atmospheric stabilization scenarios. *Source:* After Houghton 1996.

limited assimilative capability of the earth's carbon sinks dictates that the amount of human output must stabilize at levels that will not trigger significant changes in global climate.

Buildings have considerable detrimental environmental consequences that must clearly be reduced. A significant amount of information exists on the energy and attendant greenhouse gas emissions for building operation, and information continues to emerge on the equivalent energy and emissions associated with building production—embodied energy and carbon dioxide. Similar to defining target emissions at the global scale, the question emerges as to what the target performance should be for energy and greenhouse gas emission for an individual building. Answering this seemingly simple question raises the important distinction between "green" and "sustainable" building design practice.

Emergence of Sustainability

Over the past decade, the terms *green* and *environmentally responsible* have been used to describe building design strategies that are less environmentally and ecologically damaging than typical practice. The assumption here is that by continually improving the environmental performance of individual buildings, the collective reduction in resource use and ecological loadings by the entire building stock will be sufficient to fully address the environmental agenda.

Following the publication of the Brundtland Commission's report, *Our Common Future,* in 1987, *sustainability* has emerged as a widely held and necessary notion to guide all future endeavors (WCED 1987). Sustainability will require that we become less wasteful of natural and human resources, take appropriate steps to maintain the functional integrity of the ecosphere so that it can remain resilient to human induced stresses and remain biologically productive, and place greater worth on the welfare of future generations. Agenda 21, as adopted at the 1992 UNCED summit meeting (United Nations 1992), has subsequently articulated many of the profound and far-reaching actions that are necessary in progressing toward this imperative. As a result, many local municipalities have been faced with developing local plans for implementing Agenda 21 and, if successful, developers and building designers can increasingly be expected to be faced with a local context containing sustainability features and criteria. However, although the social, political, and economic forces that will ultimately create the larger context for change are as yet unknown, the time frame over which any significant realignment is realistically possible will, in all certainty, be measured in generations.

In contrast to "green" design and construction, where the reference condition is typical current practice, developing environmental goals and information and making assessments of progress *toward* a declared, sustainable condition are profoundly more complicated. Sustainability embraces notions other than environmental performance. It has social and economic dimensions, embraces all facets of human activity (e.g., industry, transportation, and food production), and spans local actions through to redressing the major inequities that exist between developed and developing nations. The notion of a "sustainable building" is quite meaningless without reference to these broader contextual factors. More significantly, goal setting and assessment within the context of environmental sustainability requires an understanding of the *absolute* impact or stress that building design and operation place on ecological systems to ensure that it is within the assimilative capability of the local and global ecosystems. Similar to the global scale matching of sources and sinks, such an ideal would require an extensive understanding and quantification of the complex links between building decisions and ecological loadings.

Methods have been proposed that attempt to relate buildings and human activity to the absolute limits of the biosphere. The *ecological footprint*, for example, calculates the area of land required to biologically produce all the resources consumed by a community and to assimilate its wastes, indefinitely. It thereby provides a graphic view of the biological limits of the planet to support human activity (Wackernagel and Rees 1996). Applied to buildings, the procedure currently accounts directly for the land area required for the continued production of wood products, embodied and operating energy, and attendant carbon dioxide emissions. No account is made for the land area associated with the production of nonrenewable resources, except for the embodied energy and carbon dioxide, and methodological difficulties occur in assessing life-cycle impacts when combining the ecological footprint of the *initial* construction with the footprint associated with *recurring* impacts over the building life. *EcoCost* is a system that attempts to evaluate the impacts of producing building materials in *absolute* ecological terms, and in doing so attempts to bridge and synthesize environmental issues that are more readily quantifiable with those that continue to be elusive (Sainsbury 1995). The evaluation system considers the environmental impacts of producing building materials under the categories of land degradation, toxic impact, energy use impact, transportation impacts, longevity, itinerant impacts, and the recycled/reused nature of the product or process. *EcoCost* proposes reduction of the unimaginable complexity of ecological degradation to a few simple, linear equations producing a measure on a single, common Gaia scale defined between zero and one. A zero score implies a healthy functioning planet and the maximum impact of one is equivalent to the ecological devastation of the planet. Such a gross absolute scale of measurement requires that normal levels of material production impacts be subsequently measured in pico-picoGaias (i.e., one-trillionth of one-trillionth of a Gaia).

The ecological footprint and *EcoCost* approaches rely on a broad range of information and data sources to provide an assessment and the resulting performance indices are inevitably achieved at the cost of oversimplification. Reliable information for making judgments on the absolute impacts of buildings to evaluate alternative design choices and apportion the effects of building against the host of other stressors will not be attainable in the foreseeable future and may, in fact, never be completely possible. In the absence of this information, and because the focus is on individual building performance, environmentally responsible building design and assessment protocols implicitly accept the "ideal" performance goal as one of self-reliance or autonomy in energy, water, sanitary waste, and other performance areas. This notion denies the existence of community infrastructures and the potential variation in performance expectations between different buildings within a neighborhood or community.

Building Design Information

New emphases to building design are inevitably accompanied by a proliferation of information seeking to define the important issues and generate practical assistance to designers in making more informed decisions. The typical formats for environmental information are design "guidelines." These tend to be generic in nature, devoid of local or regional overlays, and by necessity give equal weighting to all aspects. They assume that designers will attribute relevance and priority in specific design situations.

The link between environmental "information" and "design" remains poorly defined. Most of the information contained in guidelines typically originates from the research community or those for whom the environmental issue is the primary interest. Such researchers are not typically directly involved or familiar with the building design decision-making process and the realities of the project delivery process. Moreover, the *reductive* techniques used in the development and definition of environmental criteria are different from the *integrative* processes necessary for their successful application and accommodation within a broad spectrum of other design issues and constraints. The products of research, such as prescriptive techniques, information, and subsequent design guidelines, have limitations in their applicability that are rarely, if ever, specified. Either a technique is, to an unknown extent, inapplicable and irrelevant to the design at hand, or the building design is limited by the requirement to apply the technique while remaining respectful to the conditions and assumptions for which it was initially developed (Wilson 1973). Both new knowledge and previous experience are used in design, but the structure of the knowledge depends on the specific project to which it is being applied and, as Wilson (1973) identifies, "the knowledge pushes out the object, but at the same time, the object pulls the knowledge into shape." Similar notions are presented by Papamichael and Protzen (1993), who argue that the design process is the "equivalent of exploring what is possible under the specific design context and adjusting performance criteria accordingly, since what is desirable may not be possible." Moreover, they show that design criteria are formulated throughout the design process and, depending on a host of issues, including the skills of the designer and greater or less time to explore issues, "the desired performance is either upgraded, improved, or degraded." These arguments reinforce the notion that the way in which individual design criteria are structured can affect the success with which they are accommodated in the design process.

The act of design links theory with the reality on which most of the complexity of architectural practice relies. The transfer of knowledge from theory into practice is often limited by the multiplicity of barriers and conflicts existing between the theoretical sources and their potential application (Cole and Lafreniere 1997). The context of a design project dictates the relevance and appropriateness of theoretical arguments. Whereas a proliferation of specific environmental criteria are being *pushed* from the research community, there is, to use Wilson's notion, currently no counter *pull* within design to receive and accommodate them. In the same way that efforts are currently being directed at the development of frameworks that organize environmental criteria in a coherent manner to convey interrelationships and priorities *for* design, it is necessary to establish parallel frameworks that facilitate a more effective integration of these criteria *into* design.

Research into the environmental performance and impacts of buildings aspires to an *inclusive* framework, which sees a total set of environmental considerations fully integrated into the design, construction, and operation of buildings. It implicitly assumes that environmental ideas and considerations can and will be readily assimilated within architectural design in their entirety. As Tschumi (1988) characterizes, "architectural and philosophical concepts do not disappear overnight" and "ruptures occur within an old fabric which is constantly dismantled and dislocated in such a way that its ruptures lead to new concepts or structures." Furthermore, he suggests that in architecture, "such disjunction implies that at no moment can any part become a synthesis or self-sufficient totality; each part leads to another, and every construction is off-balance constituted by the traces of another construction" (Tschumi 1988). This implies that environmental theory, information and strategies will only be assimilated *partially* and *selectively* within an existing design context.

Building Performance Assessment

As discussed earlier, setting environmental goals and developing information that is relevant to design raise a host of issues regarding "ideal" and "practical" increments of change. These also relate to the development of methods for assessing the environmental performance of buildings. Until the release of the *Building Research Establishment Environmental Assessment Method* (BREEAM) in 1990, little, if any, attempt had been made to establish comprehensive means of simultaneously assessing a broad range of environmental considerations in buildings (Prior 1993). Most environmental assessments were limited to single performance issues such as operating energy use. Environmental assessment methods are typically defined as those techniques developed to specifically evaluate the performance of a building design or completed building across a broad range of environmental considerations. By increasing the scope of considerations beyond energy use, building environmental assessment has made an immense contribution toward an understanding of the broader notion of whole building performance assessment. It is unlikely that any serious critique of buildings can return to single benchmarks of building performance. Since BREEAM, a host of other assessment methods have emerged including *Building Environmental Performance Assessment Criteria* (BEPAC) in Canada (Cole et al. 1993) and *Leadership in Energy and Environmental Design* (LEED) in the United States (U.S. Green Building Council 1996). More recently, a "second-generation" assessment method, *Green Building Assessment Tool* (GBTool), has been designed uniquely to generate detailed performance assessments of over thirty buildings (office buildings, schools, and multi-unit residential projects) from the countries participating in the Green Building Challenge '98 process (Cole and Larsson 1998).

Role of Building Environmental Assessment Methods

An environmental assessment of a building fills the dual role of identifying success at meeting a level of performance on the one hand and offering feedback to design and guidance for remedial work on the other. Furthermore, the assimilation of experience gained through environmental assessments can form part of a broader context for creating change within the building industry. Environmental assessment methods offer building owners the direct benefits of providing a common and verifiable set of criteria and targets so that those striving for higher environmental standards have a means of demonstrating and communicating that effort to prospective tenants. Gathering and organizing the requisite detailed information on the building for an assessment can itself be used by building management to lower operating, financing, and insurance costs as well as vacancy rates and to increase marketability (Cole 1998).

Environmental assessment methods also offer a means of structuring environmental information for new building designs and major renovations in a rapidly expanding field of knowledge and provide a reference by which building owners and design teams can formulate effective environmental design strategies. Moreover, the broad range of issues incorporated in environmental assessments requires greater communication and interaction between members of the design team and various sectors with the building industry (i.e., environmental assessment methods encourage greater dialogue and teamwork).

Structure of Environmental Assessment Methods

Range of Assessment Criteria

The range of environmental criteria that are relevant to buildings is potentially enormous and covers resource use, ecological impacts, and human health impacts. Any attempt to undertake a comprehensive assessment must be preceded by a declaration and characterization of this range. It is relatively straightforward to simply list environmental criteria, but organizing them into useful, related categories and prioritizing them for assessment is far more problematic (Cole and Campbell 1994). The number and organization of criteria and the rigor applied to the formulation in assessment methods are influenced by:

- The practicality and cost of making an assessment—the greater the number of criteria, the greater the effort required in collecting and analyzing the results.
- The ability to make assessments repeatedly and reliably by trained assessors or through self-assessment. The credibility of an assessment method within the marketplace is, in part, dependent on the consistency of the results (i.e., different assessors of the same building should produce essentially the same performance evaluation). Greater differences can be expected if the assessment methods include a large number of qualitative criteria involving personal judgment on the part of the assessor.
- Whether there is general agreement over the criteria, and therefore confidence, as to their significance. Although some aspects of building performance are widely accepted as critical environmental concerns and have clearly defined performance indicators (e.g., greenhouse gas emissions), others such as embodied energy or design for deconstruction are less understood at this time.
- The ability of users to fully comprehend the results of the assessment. Clearly, the comprehensiveness of an assessment is improved by increasing the number of assessment criteria that are included. However, the ability of building owners, users, and the public to interpret the results of an assessment diminishes with each additional criterion. Creating summaries of a wide range of criteria to make the results understandable becomes an increasingly important requirement but at the expense of making the overall process less transparent. This conflict between the need to be comprehensive on the one hand and the need for simplicity on the other is probably the most significant issue framing existing assessment methods.

Existing building environmental performance methods vary considerably in the number and range of criteria considered in an assessment. With varying degrees of rigor, all typically include criteria related to:

- *Resource consumption:* performance issues that relate to the depletion of natural resources—energy, land, water, and materials.
- *Ecological loadings:* performance issues that relate to the outputs from the build-

ing construction, operation, and demolition that place stress on natural systems—airborne emissions, solid waste, and liquid waste.

- *Indoor environmental quality:* performance issues that relate to the building characteristics that affect the health and comfort of building occupants—indoor air quality, thermal quality, lighting quality, and noise.

Beyond these *direct* environmental building performance issues, the various assessment methods include a broader set of performance issues, such as construction process and buildings, strategies to reduce automobile transportation, and sun and wind impacts on immediate surroundings. Several assessment methods also evaluate building operations and management practices where, for example, points are awarded for the appointment of an energy conservation officer or operations staff training programs. Although, these can be verified in the context of an existing building, assessment of such issues for new buildings is invariably one of assessing the *intentions* of building owners. It can be argued that it is not necessary to explicitly evaluate use patterns or management practices since they are implicitly captured within other performance measures (e.g., annual energy use). However, it will become increasingly important to be able to explain the performance improvements in terms of the relative contributions of physical improvements in the building envelope and systems and those resulting from changes in building use and operational practices.

Existing assessment methods were also developed to explicitly address environmental issues with little, if any, reference to other building performance concerns. While this single emphasis clearly draws greater attention to the emerging environmental agenda, such limitations will ultimately restrict their usefulness. Environmental assessment methods must be capable of logically expanding to embrace a broader range of performance issues so as to illustrate synergies and conflicts. The assessment protocol proposed by the Polish National Agency of Energy Conservation, for example, includes the broadest range of performance issues of all existing methods, extending the assessment into urban and architectural design (including building aesthetics) and, more significantly, economics. This relationship between environmental progress and costs remains a central issue in building design and construction and should be equally reflected in all assessment protocols.

Organization of Assessment Criteria

The way in which the performance issues are organized is equally important. BREEAM, for example, covers approximately eighteen performance criteria, organized in three categories—global, local, and indoor—thereby indirectly communicating that buildings have implications at a variety of scales. BEPAC includes approximately thirty criteria (with a much larger number of sub-criteria) organized in five major environmental topics—ozone layer protection, environmental impact of energy use, indoor environmental quality, resource conservation, and site and transportation—set in both building design and building management modules. LEED has a set of prerequisite criteria that must be met before the complete assessment is undertaken but does not use a discernible organizing framework or distinct categories for the balance of the performance criteria—these are simply listed in alphabetical order.

Voluntary Assessments

BREEAM, BEPAC, and LEED were developed to serve the specific requirements of the context in which they are used and have invariably been tempered by the necessity to meet the compromise of stakeholders and the practicalities of implementation. They are *voluntary* in their application and have the primary objective of stimulating market demand for buildings with improved environmental performance. Voluntary assessment protocols must serve two conflicting requirements—they must function as an objective and sufficiently demanding metric to have credibility within the environmental community while simultaneously being attractive to building owners who wish to have something positive to show for *any* effort that they have placed on environmental performance. Satisfying these twin requirements invariably compromises both the number of criteria that are assessed and where the benchmarks are set before performance points are earned. Moreover, the experience and subsequent evolution of voluntary environmental assessment methods as well as a broader understanding of building environmentally will be hindered by limited access to the detailed results of the individual assessments because they remain confidential unless the owners choose otherwise.

An underlying premise of voluntary assessments is that if the market is provided with improved information and mechanisms, a discerning building owner can and will provide leadership in environmental responsibility and others will follow suit to remain competitive. There is a clear distinction in the take-up of assessment methods for new and existing buildings by building owners. Whereas the cost of assessments for new buildings can be assimilated within the design and construction costs, assessing an existing building is an explicit cost with potentially profound implications for upgrading the building.

Handling Regional Variation

Existing assessment methods were not explicitly designed to handle region-specific issues. For example, although many countries are using BREEAM, the system was not originally designed to accommodate national or regional variations and the various customized versions do not emerge logically out of the source documents. Similarly, although BEPAC requires that the environmental impacts of energy use criteria be customized regionally to account for different fuel mixes and subsequent air emissions, the capability is neither simple nor generalizable to other performance areas. A framework intended to handle regionally specific issues in relation to a common core set of considerations must be designed from the outset to handle a wide range of parameters. GBTool provides an explicit declaration of a set of "core" performance criteria, the *intentions* of which are clearly stated so as to provide a common basis for developing customized criteria for specific geographic regions, as well as the logical addition of new criteria or the elimination of inapplicable ones.

Scoring Performance

Assessment implies measuring how well or poorly a building is performing, or is likely to perform, against a declared set of criteria. All existing methods assess *relative* performance and as such implicitly embody a scale of measurement as the basis for allocating performance points (see Figure 16.3). Ideally, an assessment scale would embrace current levels of performance and extend to a known and definable goal. Moreover, it would be more appropriate to maintain an open-ended scale, which could be logically extended as experience grows, and a clear set of goals. Given the difficulties of defining sustainability goals for each of the performance criteria discussed earlier, all existing assessment methods scale performance relative to current typical practice, with a fixed measurement scale. The primary difference among these methods lies in whether or not a common metric is used and whether the limits of the scale are explicitly defined.

There are two possible directions in which performance scores can be allocated, either offering an increased number of points for improved performance (i.e., the highest score would indicate the best possible performance) or offering a decreased number of points for improved performance. This would represent an approach that rewards the least impact. Given that most existing assessment methods are voluntary in their application, it is typical to use the former approach as a means of encouragement—"more" is still viewed as commensurate with "better."

Environmental assessment methods must accommodate both quantifiable performance criteria (such as annual energy use, water use, or greenhouse gas emissions) and more qualitative criteria such as the ecological significance of the site. Whereas the quantitative criteria can be readily evaluated on the basis of more

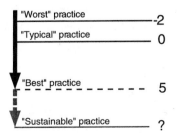

Figure 16.3. Defining assessment scales.

points awarded for better performance, the qualitative criteria can typically only practically be evaluated on a "feature specific" basis, where points are awarded for the presence or absence of desirable features.

Three characteristics of the assessment scale are of importance in establishing an appropriate measurement scale: the base or reference condition, the best condition, and the scaling increments.

Base or Reference Condition

The performance in a particular criterion is judged relative to a base or reference condition. A common, but often unstated, baseline for evaluation in assessment methods is a "typical" or "average" performance and, as such, recognition is given for better than industry norm performance. If scrutinized, this choice of benchmark is an extremely difficult one to both define and quantify across all assessment criteria in a consistent manner. BREEAM, for example, allocates one credit for carbon dioxide emission of $120-157$ kg/m^2/yr, two for $92-120$ kg/m^2/yr, three for $70-92$ kg/m^2/yr, four for $53-70$ kg/m^2/yr, and five credits for $40-53$ kg/m^2/yr. By extrapolation, these are implicitly related to a typical or average figure (zero credits) of approximately 200 kg/m^2/yr. Since these performance figures represent the combined effects of building design and building operation, their value as a meaningful reference is questionable if the operating schedule of the building is atypical. GBTool provides an explicitly stated benchmark for each criterion on which to determine the performance datum; in the case of carbon dioxide emission, for example, it requires the simulation of a "reference building" of the same size, type, and occupancy but designed according to regionally applicable energy code or standard.

Best Condition

All performance criteria in an assessment procedure embody the notion of an "ideal" or "best possible" performance, whether implicitly or explicitly stated. BREEAM, for example, presents the "best" carbon dioxide emission as being one that can currently be achieved, whereas GBTool proposes a significantly more demanding performance than current "best" practice as the upper end of the performance scale. The ability to clearly define a best possible performance again differs from one criterion to another. Whereas some criteria targets relate to a clearly defined and measurable condition, others are based on a host of compromises that include the anticipated difficulty and cost of incorporating strategies to meet the criteria.

Scaling Increments

Although all existing methods assign performance points to the various environmental criteria, there is typically no clearly logical or common basis for the way in which the maximum number of points that are attainable in each case are assigned.

BREEAM and LEED assign differing number of credits to each of the assessed performance criteria, thereby implying an indication of their significance. BEPAC and GBTool use a consistent scalar system for all performance criteria (e.g., 0–10, and –2 to +5, respectively), making the results of the assessment more comparable and comprehensible and, more significantly, facilitating the handling of both quantitative and qualitative data in an explicit manner.

Early versions of assessment programs adopted a simple linear allocation of points between the base and best performance benchmarks. Now, most assessment methods award an increasing number of points as the effort to achieve them increases. This nonlinear allocation of points recognizes that cost and effort typically increase dramatically the more industry norms are exceeded. Awarding a proportionally higher number of points for increased performance intervals is clearly most appropriate for voluntary programs where the objective is to encourage building owners to aspire to greater levels of performance. Indeed, given the incentive nature of many existing methods, only positive points are typically assigned (i.e., points are only given for features that are included but never deducted if they are not).

Presenting Assessment Results

A performance assessment is only a means to an end—it is the ability to make informed decisions based on the outcome of the assessment that is most critical. Although the field of environmental assessment continues to mature rapidly, it is seldom realized that the structure of these information sources is not neutral and can profoundly influence the outcome (e.g., the ability to comprehend linkages and conflicts). Although it is generally accepted that environmental criteria must be organized in ways that facilitate meaningful dialogue and application, the structuring of criteria within the assessment method is most important during the output of the performance evaluation. It is at this stage that the complete profile of the building is evident and when the "story" of the performance must be told in a coherent and informative way.

All the assessment methods generate a report on the performance of the building to provide guidance to the building owner or design team as well as to provide a summary or certificate of building performance. The notion of "environmental labeling" is often used in conjunction with environmental assessment as a logical outcome. These labels define the overall classification of the environmental merits of the building. Since environmental assessments cover an extremely wide range of criteria, presenting them in a manner that communicates an overall performance rating of a building clearly and succinctly, without compromising detail, is an important outcome.

There are two general approaches to summarizing the results of a performance assessment: *direct aggregation of scores* and *weighting of performance scores*.

Direct Aggregation of Scores

BREEAM and LEED use a simple designation of a number of points for achieved performance in each of the various environmental areas, employing a different scoring system for each and without concern for the significance of one criterion relative to the others except as indicated by the number of possible points or credits attainable. A simple aggregation is then used to provide a total score. In BREEAM, for example, the labels currently used are typically a classification of the performance according to descriptive categories such as *fair, good, very good,* or *excellent.* This categorization is further based on the variation in the number of credits possible for the particular building being assessed and the *balance* of the building's performance across the various categories of environmental issues covered within the assessment method (i.e., global, local, and indoor). Similarly, the summary of performance in the LEED program is judged as meeting a *bronze, silver, gold,* or, the best, *platinum* performance benchmarks through the simple addition of the various performance scores. In addition to the certificate that building owners can use as part of the leasing documents, BREEAM offers a comprehensive report identifying the basis of the assessment score that is, perhaps, the most valuable part of the overall process.

Weighting of Performance Scores

Some methods use a *common* scale as the basis for assessing all criteria (e.g., BEPAC uses a 0–10 scale for all criteria, and GBTool uses –2 to +5, with 0 representing the industry norm) and apply explicit weightings to acknowledge the different significance of each criterion prior to deriving the aggregate score. Weighting remains the most theoretically complex and controversial aspect of building performance assessment—the primary concern being the absence of an agreed theoretical and nonsubjective basis for deriving weighting factors. However, it will become an increasingly essential part of assessment protocols if they are to deal with environmental issues in a comprehensive way and still facilitate communication of the results in a simple manner.

Unlike BREEAM and LEED, which indirectly provide weightings by offering a higher number of potential credits for significant performance issues such as energy or carbon dioxide emissions, GBTool applies an explicit weighting factor to an attained performance score, thereby making "performance" and "significance" distinct.

The assessment criteria in GBTool are structured hierarchically in four levels: performance areas, performance categories, performance criteria, and performance sub-criteria, with the higher levels logically derived from the weighted aggregation of the lower ones (see Figure 16.4). The *nesting* principle of the four levels is a critical feature of the framework in that it enables a building performance to be described, and potentially assessed, at successively detailed levels. Consistency between levels of assessment and description is ensured since sub-criteria form the complete and logical subsets of the criteria, categories and performance areas

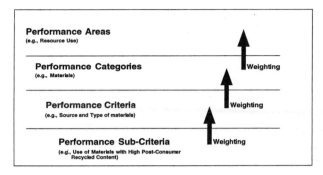

Figure 16.4. Nesting principle in GBTool.

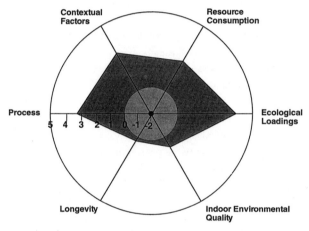

Figure 16.5. GBTool: Summary output of performance areas.

under which they are nested. The most important step in the process is the evaluation and assigning of an attained score for each performance sub-criterion and selecting appropriate weightings for it relative to other sub-criteria. Further, rather than summarizing overall building performance into a single rating, GBTool keeps the various performance areas distinct (see Figure 16.5).

Conclusions

BREEAM, BEPAC, LEED, and other existing assessment methods have individually and collectively made significant contributions to our understanding of building-related environmental issues. And, with varying degrees of success, they are fulfilling the current perceived needs and expectations for building environmental performance assessment in the context for which they were developed. Although

interest in environmental assessment protocols continues to increase, it is difficult
to fully anticipate their future role or the way they will ultimately evolve as an integral part of the building process. Their most significant contribution to date has
clearly been to acknowledge and institutionalize the importance of assessing buildings across a broad range of considerations beyond established single performance
criteria, such as energy.

There are two significant issues related to the way in which environmental
assessment methods may evolve, both related to their role as mechanisms for generating improvements in the environmental performance of buildings.

Voluntary to Mandatory

All first-generation assessment methods are voluntary in their application—an
emphasis that significantly compromises both their comprehensiveness and rigor.
Such methods will continue to become more sophisticated both in their structure
from an environmental standpoint as well as from their ability to find acceptance
with target markets. In this regard, positioning environmental issues that reflect
tangible value to building owners, and ideally at low cost, will dictate their overall
character and emphasis. However, the *acceptance* of existing assessment methods
also derives largely from the fact that they are voluntary. It is uncertain whether this
mechanism will be sufficient to create the necessary improvements in environmental performance of buildings needed to meet broader national environmental targets. The extent to which social and political forces will precipitate regulatory
reform is also currently unclear, as are the type of instruments that must (or will) be
introduced. Environmental assessment methods must be seen as one of several
mechanisms that will ultimately stimulate and produce change. They cannot easily
or logically be extended to form regulatory standards for building performance.
Whereas current environmental assessment methods only attempt to place a building's performance on a relative scale, if adopted within a general regulatory framework it would be necessary to achieve an agreed *level* of performance. Adoption of
such a mechanism would meet with considerable scrutiny and resistance by many
interest groups within the building industry and, through any consensus process,
would seriously challenge both the range of criteria as well as the basis for deriving
the overall required benchmark performance. Only *minimal* performance benchmarks across a broad range of environmental criteria would meet such acceptance.
Given the current political pressure surrounding global warming, if regulation is
introduced it will relate to the *specific* performance issues that affect a building's
greenhouse gas emissions.

Extension to Design Tools

A considerable amount of design-relevant information has emerged on a broad
range of environmental issues, far more than is currently incorporated in assessment methods. Selected criteria within assessment method documentation are cur-

rently being adopted as part of broader sets of design guidelines and specifications and are gradually diffusing through the design community in this form. However, since environmental assessment methods present an organized set of selected environmental criteria, by default they communicate to building owners and design teams what are understood to be the most significant environmental considerations. As such, existing assessment methods are used as design tools, even though they were not specifically designed to be. This, in combination with the fact that most assessment methods are voluntary, is deeply problematic, in that the methods may potentially institutionalize a limited definition of environmentally responsible building practices at a time when exploration and innovation must be encouraged (i.e., building owners may commit their designers to achieving a high performance score according to a specific assessment method). A tool designed to provide guidance on design requires the development of considerably more detailed information than one intended for simple, or even detailed, assessments. Moreover, given the issues associated with the different "structures" of information and their assimilation in design, different mechanisms are necessary to link the two. Future efforts will inevitably make the transition between building design and building assessment more seamless, possibly by providing either a parallel set of criteria or a further level of detail within a hierarchical structure logically related to the assessment criteria.

REFERENCES

Cole, R.J. 1998. "Emerging Trends in Building Environmental Assessment Methods." *Building Research and Information* 26:3–16.

Cole, R. J., and E. Campbell. 1994. "Translating Environmental Goals into Building Specific Strategies." In *Design and Technological Innovation for the Environment—Proceedings of 1994 ACSA Technology Conference* (C. Clipson and J. J. Kim, eds.). Ann Arbor: University of Michigan, pp. 63–67

Cole, R. J., and J. Lafreniere. 1997. "Environmental Information Frameworks—Linking Research with Building Design." *Proceedings of CIB Second International Conference on Buildings & the Environment* (June 9) 2:33–40.

Cole, R. J., and N. Larsson. 1998. "Green Building Challenge." *ASHRAE Journal* (May): 1–2.

Cole, R. J., D. Rousseau, and I. T. Theaker. 1993. *Building Environmental Performance Assessment Criteria: Version 1—Office Buildings.* Vancouver: The BEPAC Foundation.

Cole, R. J., B. Mackay-Lyons, and T. Scott. 1997. "Shades of Green." *Canadian Architect* 42:15–16.

Houghton, J. T., et al., eds. 1990. *Climate Change: The IPCC Scientific Assessment.* Cambridge: Cambridge University Press.

Houghton, J. T., et al. 1996. *Climate Change 1995: The Science of Climate Change.* Cambridge: Cambridge University Press.

Ingersoll, R. 1991. "Unpacking the Green Man's Burden." *Design Book Review* (Spring):19–26.

Papamichael, K., and J. P. Protzen. 1993. *The Limits of Intelligence in Design.* Energy and Environment Division, Lawrence Berkeley Laboratories, University of California, Berkeley, CA, Report # LBL-31742/UC-350.

Prior, J., ed. 1993. *Building Research Establishment Environmental Assessment Method (BREEAM),* Version 1/93 New Offices, Building Research Establishment Report, Second Edition.

Sainsbury, S. 1995. *EcoCost.* Thesis, Department of Architecture, University of Tasmania, Australia (unpublished).

Tschumi, B. 1988. "Parc de la Villette." *Architectural Design* 58:3–4.

United Nations. 1992. *Earth Summit '92: The United Nations Conference on Environment and Development.* Rio de Janeiro. London: Regency Press.

U.S. Green Buildings Council. 1996. *LEED (Buildings: Leadership in Energy and Environmental Design),* Environmental Building Rating System Criteria.

Wackernagel, M., and W. Rees. 1996. *Our Ecological Footprint: Reducing Human Impact on the Earth.* Gabriola Island: New Society Publishers.

WCED. 1987. *Our Common Future. [The Brundtland Report].* Oxford: Oxford University Press, for the UN World Commission on Environment and Development.

Wilson, C.B. 1973. "The Old Push-and-Pull: Two Problems in Design/Research Structures." *Edinburgh Architectural Research* 1:4–10.

Chapter 17

The Chicago Brownfields Initiative

William C. Trumbull

When Chicago was incorporated as a city in 1837, the city seal was inscribed with the motto *urbs in horto,* meaning "city in the garden." With that vision, the Chicago Department of Environment works to maintain a balance between environmental health and economic development, which are often viewed as distinct and competing goals. Our city is our environment, and continued economic prosperity requires a healthy environment, just as a sustainable environment depends on a healthy economy. In dense urban areas, residential communities, neighborhood parks, commercial areas, and industrial facilities relate to and depend on each other. Our garden is not just a place for flowers; it is our place to live, work, educate, and recreate.

The intrinsic relationship between the economy and the environment is best demonstrated by the brownfields movement, which focuses on environmental cleanup for economic development. In the past five years, Chicago and many other municipalities have demonstrated that environmental contamination is not an insurmountable liability but rather may be used as a tool to spur economic development in former industrial areas. This is the story of the Chicago Brownfields Initiative, which has grown from a small pilot project into an interdepartmental city program that cleans sites, creates jobs, and improves city neighborhoods.

From a regional land use perspective, efforts to preserve rural communities and productive farmlands, wildlife habitats and biodiversity have reinforced the need to limit urban sprawl by encouraging brownfields and infill development. The unfolding story of brownfields initiatives across the country will tell us much about how we value urban and rural landscapes, clean land, clean air, and our ability to access them.

The Beginning

The interactions of environmental contamination and economic development were first addressed at a 1991 conference in Chicago called New Uses for Old Buildings. The conference was prompted by several significant court rulings that had given rise to lender liability concerns. During one of the conference sessions, Charlie Bartsch of the Northeast Midwest Institute coined the term *brownfields* to describe industrial properties where environmental liabilities led to disinvestment and abandonment. The issues raised at that conference attracted national attention, and in January 1993 a Brownfields Congressional Field Hearing was held, again in Chicago. This hearing covered environmental barriers to redevelopment and the economic imbalance between previously used urban sites and the development of pristine greenfield properties. The hearing, which included a tour of an Archer Daniels Midland brownfield site, placed the brownfield issue onto the federal agenda for the very first time. Out of that hearing came the idea of modifying the federal tax law to allow clean-up costs to be treated as a deductible expense for redevelopment projects. A similar bill, with limited geographic applicability, was finally enacted in 1997. In the intervening years, several federal, state, and local laws as well as economic incentives have been developed to encourage private, public, and nonprofit brownfield activities.

An operating definition for a brownfield is "a vacant or underutilized property passed over for development due to real or perceived contamination." A brownfield can be the several hundred acres of a shuttered steel mill, a small abandoned factory, or a vacant service station. This is not just an urban issue, since one could probably be found in just about any community. At the most basic level, a brownfield is a real estate and economic development issue, complicated by environmental costs and liabilities as well as acquisition and development problems. The General Accounting Office (U.S. GAO 1995) estimates that there are over 500,000 brownfields across the country. Based on a compilation of several computer databases of land use and contamination parameters, the Army Corps of Engineers identified 711 potential brownfield sites in Chicago. Unless a more restrictive definition concerning environmental conditions, ownership, and land use is applied, brownfields are difficult to count. Consequently, a real inventory is not feasible.

The benefits of reusing brownfields are numerous and far-reaching. One obvious benefit is the environmental remediation and removal of harmful or hazardous materials that may otherwise not be treated. This leads to the elimination of blight in urban neighborhoods and can improve safety and curb illegal activities that often occur in poorly maintained buildings. Once a site is put back into productive use, the benefits become much more tangible. The creation of jobs and the generation of new property tax revenues are two direct benefits. Creating jobs in urban neighborhoods also limits the extent of suburban sprawl and the development of some of the country's most productive farmland. According to the Northeastern Illinois Planning Commission, between 1970 and 1990 the Chicago metropolitan regional population increased by only 4 percent, while the urban land area mushroomed by 46 percent. Creating jobs close to large groups of under- or unemployed persons will ease the welfare rolls, and ready access to public transportation will reduce the need for additional automobile traffic on already congested highways. For the past fifty years, the country has made significant infrastructure investments in urban areas. Roads, sewers, schools, hospitals, and other amenities are already in place and should not be abandoned only to be rebuilt to serve less densely developed suburban and rural areas.

The Chicago Brownfields Initiative was created to develop a series of programs to address environmental and redevelopment challenges. The process involves convening the Brownfields Forum to identify barriers to redevelopment, identifying funds for municipal redevelopment projects, and creating incentives for private-sector investments.

The Chicago Brownfields Forum

With support from the John D. and Catherine T. MacArthur Foundation, more than 100 representatives from government, business, finance, environmental, community and civic organizations gathered for two days in December 1994 and outlined the barriers to brownfields redevelopment in the city. The significant barriers were identified as: environmental liabilities, inflexible environmental regulations, uncertain costs and time lines, site control and access issues, availability of capital, community concerns, and the lack of data and channels of communication.

The forum was conceived as a broad-based, interdisciplinary task force to inform public policy on brownfield issues. For several months, smaller work groups met to draft recommendations. In May 1995, when the forum concluded, the groups had produced sixty-three recommendations that were then consolidated into nine project teams, each led by a public, private, or nonprofit entity. The Brownfields Forum Final Report and Action Plan was published in November 1995 and issued the following recommendations:

- Improve communications between stakeholders (property owners, developers, government agencies, lenders, lawyers, and communities)
- Strengthen nonprofit capacity
- Build city government capacity
- Streamline environmental regulations
- Encourage private-sector investment
- Improve public financing
- Support community involvement
- Prevent future pollution
- Influence regional planning

While the forum was in session, the city was undertaking the redevelopment of five pilot sites, which are presented in more detail later. It is important to note that the pilot projects and forum were mutually reinforcing; the sites informed the policy with real-life complications, while the expertise of the forum participants often served as a resource for moving the projects forward.

Many barriers have been addressed or eliminated, either by direct actions of forum participants or through the indirect influence of the recommendations. For example, while the forum was in progress, the Illinois legislature was debating amendments to the Environmental Protection Act to create the Illinois Site Remediation Program, which provides for the voluntary cleanup of sites based on end-use standards. Completing the program leads to a letter of No Further Remediation that provides liability protection from the state. The forum did not, as a group, participate in the legislative process, but the parallel activities kept a broader group informed of the issues and thus led to better legislation.

To address concerns by lending institutions reluctant to loan on contaminated property, forum participants produced a Model Lending Package that outlines a process for making loans on brownfield properties. To increase community capacity, the Chicago Association of Neighborhood Development Organizations established the Brownfields Institute. The institute developed an eight-course curriculum to educate community groups on the issues of cleaning up, marketing, and financing redevelopment projects. These are just a few of the many activities triggered by recommendations from the forum.

In 1998, with support from the U.S. EPA Region 5, the progress of the Brownfields Forum was formally evaluated. Just as the Brownfields Forum Final Report outlined the barriers to redevelopment, the evaluation tells us how successful we have been in overcoming them. The results of this evaluation reveal that 75 percent of the recommendations have been accomplished, through either direct or indirect actions of the forum. Areas that were identified as still needing attention are: financing of predevelopment activities, the involvement of public and community development corporations in redevelopment decisions, site control and land assembly processes, and pollution prevention incentives.

Brownfields Pilot Program

While the Brownfields Forum was identifying barriers, an interdepartmental work group from the City Departments of Environment, Planning and Development, and Law was demonstrating that environmental cleanup could lead to economic development. With $2.0 million of general obligation bond money, the group selected five sites (see Figure 17.1) based on (1) site access and control, (2) information on contamination, and (3) redevelopment potential. The thought was that the five sites could be investigated and, with any remaining money, one or two sites could be remediated.

As shown in Table 17.1, all five sites have been cleaned up for just over $1.0 million (excluding demolition costs, which were allocated from another city program.) One site has gone to the University of Illinois at Chicago for expansion, the other

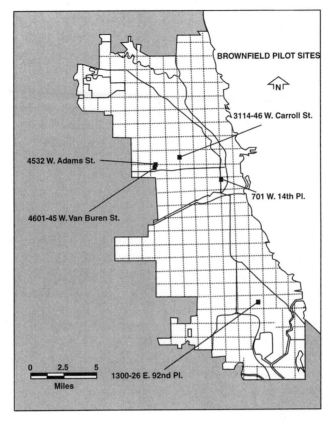

Figure 17.1. The City of Chicago Brownfields Initiative pilot sites.

four are now in productive reuse, having created 332 new jobs and retained another 950 in the city. One important lesson learned in the process came from the Madison Equipment site, which sat vacant for years because of perceived contamination. After an investment of $2,800 for an environmental assessment, the site was found to be clean. Formerly tax delinquent, the site will generate $340,000 in real estate taxes annually.

Another success story is the Verson Steel Company that is now expanding on the former Burnside Steel Foundry. The Burnside Company went into bankruptcy after an explosion shut down the plant in 1979. Over the years, scavengers removed everything of value, while midnight dumpers illegally dropped off truckloads of construction and demolition debris. The site was an environmental and health hazard to the community for almost twenty years. An adjacent company, Verson Steel, contemplated leaving the city, taking with them 500 jobs, in part because of the condition of the site next door. It took $760,000 of city funds to

Table 17.1. Chicago Brownfield pilot sites projects (1995–1997)

Project Name	Size (acres)	Demolition Costs ($)	Clean-up Costs ($)	Estimated Annual Tax Revenues ($)[a]	Jobs Created	Jobs Retained
Verson Steel	7.0	350,000	211,000	209,000 (ind)	125	500
Scott Peterson	1.8	400,000	303,000	23,500 (pk)	100	250
Blackstone Manufacturing	3.3	—	592,000	43,000 (pk)	7	200
Madison Equipment	2.1	—	2,800	62,000(wh)	7	NA
14th & Union	2.5	—	4,000	University of Illinois expansion	NA	NA
Total		750,000	1,112,800	337,500	239	950

[a] Tax revenue estimates based on a coverage ratio of 0.3 and assessments of $2.50/ft^2 for industrial (ind), $2.25/ft^2 for warehouse (wh), and $1.00/ft^2 for parking (pk).

demolish the remaining structures and remediate the seven-acre site. Last year, Verson Steel broke ground on a major expansion that will add 125 jobs, which will be available to community residents as part of the redevelopment agreement.

In addition to the original pilot sites, the Department of Environment has completed eight other remediation projects that are in various stages of redevelopment. Clean-up costs average $2.15 per square foot, which is within the range of the annual tax revenues received from the property after development. These costs have been minimized by carefully screening projects, remediating to industrial use standards, using engineered barriers and institutional controls, and competitively bidding projects to environmental consultants under term agreement contracts with the city.

Research Initiatives

The momentum developing for brownfield programs can be measured by the diverse fields of research that have shed light on the environmental, economic, and societal impacts associated with the issue. Some fundamental questions regarding the costs and benefits of brownfields efforts, community demographics, and estimates on the supply and demand of industrial real estate have been answered, and they are used to guide our program efforts. The following discussion will highlight the aspects of these studies that have been most relevant to our program.

The Cost of Sprawl

In a detailed analysis of the costs and benefits of inner city, inner suburban, and outer suburban developments (Persky and Wiewel 1996), a comparison was made to determine which scenario yields a greater overall economic benefit to the metropolitan region. The study found that the costs of an outer suburban development are high and are distributed among taxpayers, commuters, and city residents. The benefits are also high, but they accrue primarily to the businesses that locate in the outer suburbs. The reverse is true for an inner city development, where costs are also comparable to the benefits but the benefits are spread equitably among those who pay the costs. These findings suggest that the net benefits of sprawl are not shared by the region but are rather a redistribution of subsidies from the public to the private sector. The cost of urban sprawl—measured in terms of congestion, increased commute times and associated pollution, accident rates, new roads, sewers, and schools—are not paid for by the users of these services but by the region as a whole.

Urban Demographics

A study on the changing demographics and location of hazardous waste sites in Chicago (Baden and Coursey 1997) looked at population and hazardous waste facility data from 1960 and 1990. The study included an analysis of the sites in relation to the residential density, race, ethnicity, and income of the surrounding communities. The data show that, for both 1960 and 1990, waste sites tend to be located in low population density areas near commercial waterways. In 1960 these neighborhoods were predominately poor and white. In 1990 many of these neighborhoods were predominately Hispanic. In 1960 African-Americans were segregated in nonindustrial areas of the city, but by 1990 this group was more widely dispersed throughout the city. Under current market conditions, many riverfront industrial areas are being converted to high-end residential use, particularly on the city's north side. Curiously, this leads to an increased correlation between high income and proximity to historic hazardous waste handling facilities. The study found no evidence of environmental racism against African-Americans in the location of regulated hazardous waste facilities, and it suggests that the issue of environmental justice must be understood in terms of the complex social, historical, and economic forces that shape the urban landscape.

Industrial Demand

A recent study (Arthur Anderson 1998) defines the current and future demand for industrial real estate in Chicago. The results show that the decline in industrial real estate utilization has slowed and predicts an expansion through 2005. Future growth is predicted to be less in the manufacturing and more in the distribution and flexible service sectors. The economic benefits of the expansion include an estimated increase of almost $220 million in property tax revenues and the creation of 31,000 new jobs. The study also identifies 2,200 acres of industrial properties that could be brought back into service to accommodate some of the projected growth. Many of these sites are brownfields that will require coordinated environmental and economic development assistance.

Farmland Preservation

Two studies looking at the impacts of urban sprawl on rural communities and farmland preservation have been completed by the American Farmland Trust. The first study, called *Farming on the Edge* (Sorensen et al. 1997), identifies prime and unique farmlands threatened by development across the United States. The fertile farmlands surrounding the Chicago metropolitan area were ranked the third most endangered in the country. A second study, *Living on the Edge* (Sorensen and Esseks 1998), looks at areas of scatter development—meaning residential lots larger than one acre and more than a mile from an existing town—in relation to the cost of development and the access to municipal services. In most cases, the development costs for roads, water, sewers, and schools were subsidized by the nearby community. More importantly, the residents within the scatter development are at risk because of delayed emergency services. In one case, police response times were 600 percent greater than for an in-town resident, ambulance times were 50 percent higher, and fire response was 33 percent higher. In circumstances where response times in excess of five minutes can be fatal, these numbers are significant. Unfortunately, the only way to reduce these risks would be to build satellite emergency response facilities, again at a greater cost to the existing community.

Transportation Planning

Transportation planning models are frequently used to justify road construction and other large infrastructure projects, but they have often not been used to compare the impacts of alternative development scenarios. An initial study of transportation models (Anderson 1997) has demonstrated the economic, social, and environmental benefits of in-fill development. For example, a mixed-use infill development project in West Palm Beach, Florida, was compared to a similar greenfield development ten miles west of town. When compared to the greenfield site, the infill project resulted in a 58 percent reduction in household travel costs and a 61 percent reduction in average per capita vehicle miles traveled, a 100 percent increase in pedestrian connectivity and a 73 percent reduction in the loss of open space, and a 48 percent reduction in greenhouse gas emissions with a 28 percent decrease in ozone precursor emissions. These results suggest that from an environmental perspective, brownfields redevelopment programs will generate real clean air benefits, lower transportation costs, and improvements in quality of life for the region.

Future brownfields research could define baseline measures of unemployment, crime, drug use, and school test scores to better understand the relationship between environmental cleanup, economic development, and quality of life measures.

Building on the success of our Brownfields Initiative, the Chicago Department of Environment is undertaking a series of projects to assess the impact of federal Clean Air Act policies on urban redevelopment programs. The projects include modeling of economic and clean air measures, a regional dialogue for policy development, and a mayoral caucus to inform elected officials of the findings.

Chicago Brownfields Program Expansion

To this point we have demonstrated that (1) the Brownfields Forum, as a public–private policy process, has identified and reduced barriers to industrial redevelopment, (2) municipal site acquisition and cleanup can lead to economic development, and (3) there is a growing body of research that argues for a continued brownfields effort for environmental, economic, and social reasons.

Industrial Park Projects

The next phase of the program is to develop a process to fund and accelerate the land acquisition and clean-up process to meet the projected demands. This opportunity was provided when the Chicago Office of Management and Budget was awarded $54 million from the Federal Department of Housing and Urban Development (HUD) Section 108 Loan Guarantee Program. The loan guarantee secures a private bond placement that will provide the funds needed to undertake brownfields redevelopment projects to create modern urban industrial parks within the city. The obligation of the twelve-year note will be paid back by the proceeds of land sales, settlements for environmental litigation, and the revenues generated from tax increment financing districts that have been established along the city's industrial corridors.

Four large projects are now underway. The West Pullman Redevelopment Area on the far south side is the largest, with 140 acres being assembled while clean-up strategies are developed. Other sites range in size from 18 to 70 acres. Table 17.2 provides estimated cost and revenue data for these large industrial park projects. These are complex, three- to five-year projects that involve legal, environmental, and real estate development challenges.

A team of real estate consultants, architects, and market specialists has been brought in to assist in the assembly, to create development guidelines, and to develop market strategies for these sites. The number of jobs created and the increased tax revenues generated will measure the success of these projects.

Table 17.2. Chicago Brownfield Industrial Parks (1997–2000)

Industrial Park Developments	Area (acres)	Demolition Costs ($)	Clean-up Costs to Date ($)	Estimated Annual Tax Revenues ($)
West Pullman	140	400,000	110,000	4,600,000
Roosevelt & California	70	NA	135,000	2,300,000
Roosevelt & Kildare	18	NA	207,500	550,000
Sacramento Crushing	18	NA	2,500,000	NA

Supplemental Environmental Project

Other resources of funding have also been used for the program. In coordination with the Federal Department of Justice (DOJ) and the Environmental Protection Agency (EPA), we have negotiated the first Supplemental Environmental Project for a settlement between a paint manufacturer and the federal agencies. In this case, a paint manufacturer settled with the DOJ/EPA for alleged environmental violations on their site. In addition to a penalty, the city has reached an agreement with the company for $950,000 to clean up a nearby brownfield site under the terms of the federal consent decree. The significance of this agreement is that the money remains in the community where the pollution allegedly occurred rather than being sent back into a general fund.

EPA Regional Pilot Grant

With a grant from the U.S. EPA Region 5 we are developing guidelines for community participation in the clean-up and redevelopment process. We have found that there are opportunities for public participation in the planning process and for the establishment of tax increment financing districts, zoning designations, and other land use decisions. We are looking for ways to incorporate the communication of environmental information into existing public processes.

Brownfields and Wetlands

The Illinois/Indiana SeaGrant Program of the Department of Commerce is funding another project. The Lake Calumet Region of Chicago and Northwestern Indiana is composed largely of degraded wetlands, abandoned and active industrial areas, and landfills. There has also been a long history of dedicated environmental activism in the area. We are looking for opportunities in the Lake Calumet region for brownfield sites adjacent to wetlands in need of restoration. The objective is to package them as a single project so that the brownfields cleanup can spur economic development while the wetland restoration will lead to ecosystem and habitat improvements. Four project areas have been identified and environmental assessments are now being completed.

Public Policy Initiatives

Because of the Brownfields Forum, several policy initiatives were begun to encourage private-sector investment in redevelopment and to build city capacity to develop sites that would not be developed otherwise. The Illinois Site Remediation Program potable groundwater prohibition, tax incentives, environmental loan program, and an emissions reduction trading bank have been established to encourage private redevelopment. City capacity has increased through various funding sources, eminent domain reform, and the creation of an environmental lien, which all give the city tools to spur redevelopment.

Illinois Site Remediation Program

The Illinois Site Remediation program, like many other state voluntary clean-up programs, encourages private-sector remediation projects by providing clean-up objectives based on the future use of the property industrial/commercial versus residential) and provides for a No Further Remediation Letter (NFR) from the state at the completion of the process. The NFR letter provides liability protection for meeting specified clean-up objectives. In Illinois, the NFR letter is further supported by a Memorandum of Understanding with the U.S. EPA Region 5, which essentially states that the federal government will have no interest in sites cleaned up under the state program. The clean-up objectives in the state program can be obtained directly from a table or can be site-specific and determined from risk-based calculations that take into account the contaminants, exposure routes, and the possible receptors.

In the year since the program rules were finalized, seventy sites in Chicago have been voluntarily remediated under the state program, demonstrating that, given the opportunity for certainty in the clean-up process, responsible land owners will undertake environmental projects that result in economic redevelopment.

Potable Groundwater Prohibition

Using a risk-based approach in the Illinois Site Remediation Program can mean turning to institutional barriers or engineering controls that can be invoked to mitigate the risk of exposure. For example, Lake Michigan is the potable water supply for Chicago and the surrounding metropolitan area. Much of the shallow groundwater in the city is contaminated, some of it by the residue from the Great Chicago Fire of 1871. Establishing a prohibition on the drilling of potable water wells in the city creates an institutional control that effectively eliminates the need to consider ingestion of groundwater as a pathway. As a result, a remediation project in the city must only demonstrate protection of human health and the environment but does not have to remediate groundwater to the most stringent drinking water standards. In addition, if contamination extends under a city roadway, the Department of Environment can enter a right-of-way agreement that allows contamination to remain in place but tags the location to the city permitting process so its presence will be communicated to anyone requesting a permit to dig in the right-of-way.

Tax Incentives

Redevelopment projects in the city of Chicago may be eligible for three tax incentive programs. The federal tax credit allows clean-up costs to be deducted in the year they occur but is limited to Federal Empowerment Zones and other designated areas. The Illinois state tax credit allows eligible remedial expenses to be credited against state income tax. A special Cook County property tax classification lowers the assessed valuation to 16 percent of market value and can be added to other programs for up to eighteen years. Taken in combination, a theoretical brownfields development project that meets all three criteria could recover 50 percent of remediation costs through tax incentives in the first year.

Chicago Brownfield Tax Incentives

Industrial real estate developers in Chicago may be eligible for three tax incentives enacted to encourage remediation and redevelopment projects. There are eligibility requirements for each program that limit their applicability to specific projects and certain costs. The federal tax incentive is a deduction against taxable income for remediation costs in targeted areas. The Illinois tax incentive is a transferable 25 percent tax credit against eligible remediation costs, and the Cook County property tax incentive reduces assessment rates to 16 percent of market value for up to five years resulting in 55 percent annual tax savings. In conjunction with other programs, the county incentive can be extended an additional ten years.

DEVELOPMENT SCENARIOS. A hypothetical development is presented to demonstrate the applicability of these incentives. The following assumptions were used in evaluating the potential tax savings for a redevelopment project in Chicago.

Land acquisition	$100,000
Remediation costs	$500,000
Redevelopment expenses	$1,000,000
Taxable income (34% tax bracket)	$5,000,000

In the first scenario, the site is located in a Federal Empowerment Zone or other targeted area within Cook County, Illinois. Therefore, it is eligible for the federal, state, and county incentives. The federal deduction is $170,000, the state tax credit is $40,000 in the first year, and the property tax savings are $41,500 per year, for a maximum of eighteen years. Taken together, the developer could realize a 50 percent tax savings in the first year of the project.

In the second example, the site is not eligible for the federal deduction but can take advantage of the state income tax credit, for a total of $40,000 in years one and two, and $20,000 in year three. Again, the county incentive is worth $41,500 per year for up to eighteen years. Because of limitations in the state program, the developer would realize a 16 percent tax savings in the first year. However, both incentives are transferable and could be included in future property transactions.

	Federal Deduction	State Tax Credit	County Property Tax Savings	Total First-Year Tax Savings	Percentage of Remediation Costs
Scenario 1: Federal/state/ county	$170,000	$40,000	$41,500	$251,500	50%
Scenario 2: State/county	Ineligible	$40,000	$41,500	$81,500	16%

Environmental Loan Program

The Chicago Department of Treasury has established a Linked-Deposit Environmental Loan Program whereby city funds in a ratio of 3 to 1 are deposited in participating banks for loans made to small or minority/women-owned businesses for environmental compliance projects.

Emissions Reduction Trading Bank

Another creative incentive for encouraging redevelopment is the Emissions Reduction Trading Bank, established with a donation of 300 tons per year of volatile organic carbon emissions by the 3M Corporation. The Wheatland Tube Company was undertaking a brownfield project but would not have been able to expand their operations if they could not obtain emissions credits. Their project involved a $2.0 million cleanup and a $12 million expansion that will create twenty-five new jobs. As part of the package, they received ninety-nine tons per year from our trading bank, and we retired 30 tons per year as an emissions reduction. The Department of Environment is now formulating methods to convert future emission reduction activities into credits that can be used for additional development opportunities.

Land Acquisition Tools

In 1997 two statutes that improve municipalities' ability to acquire brownfield properties were signed into law in Illinois. The eminent domain statute was revised so that environmental costs could be deducted from the determination of fair market value in condemnation proceedings. Without this provision, municipalities were faced with paying a price based on a clean parcel of land and then having to pay again for the cleanup. The environmental lien was created so that abandoned properties that are more that two years tax delinquent can be investigated and remediated by the city, and the cost of remediation creates a foreclosable lien on the property. This statute follows the demolition lien provisions used to tear down unsafe structures within the city.

Federal Brownfields Agenda

Despite years of debate over the Federal Superfund Program, there has been very little progress on legislative reform, and consequently there is no federal legislation that recognizes brownfields. As long as Superfund and brownfields are bundled together in Congress, the brownfields-specific legislation will not likely move through Congress. The U.S. EPA Brownfields Agenda has focused on administrative reforms, liability clarifications, and the creation of programs that fit under the existing Superfund mandate. To date, 121 municipalities have received pilot grants of up to $200,000 to inventory and assess brownfield sites. Unfortunately, the money cannot be used for cleanup but can be used only for site assessments and inventories. The agency has also piloted a revolving loan fund for cleanup to selected communities, but the results of the program have not yet been evaluated. In February 1998, sixteen communities, including Chicago, were designated as "Showcase Communities" for their accomplishments. The designation carried the coordinated commitments of fifteen federal agencies to bring multiple resources to these programs. This is viewed as an opportunity to bring other agencies, such as the Departments of Commerce, Justice, and Labor, and the Small Business Administration, into the brownfields arena so that their programs can focus on the brownfield redevelopment projects.

Until the brownfields agenda is recognized by federal legislation and supported by appropriations, agencies will have to rely on existing programs to fund brownfield projects.

Conclusions

The Chicago Brownfields Initiative has built a solid foundation for urban redevelopment by conducting the Brownfields Forum, remediating sites, and looking at economic research for support of our policies. The Chicago Brownfields Forum provided the framework for making meaningful changes to the way brownfields are perceived and pursued in the city. The Pilot Program has demonstrated that it is economically desirable to acquire brownfields, leading to a significant expansion of the program. An emerging field of economic and social research is validating the sustainability and cost efficiencies gained by urban redevelopment.

Over the past few years we have learned a few lessons. All brownfields are local, and the true cost has to be measured in terms of the economic degradation and the lost opportunities to communities blighted by brownfield properties. Brownfields are as much a real estate transaction and economic development issue as they are an environmental problem. Consequently, successful projects require multiple resources from a broad range of participants. With adequate tools, other municipalities can use land acquisition authorities, enforcement actions, environmental litigation, and condemnation effectively to spur redevelopment.

The Chicago Brownfields Initiative has taken an aggressive position on turning environmental liabilities into economic assets, and we do this to clean up properties, create jobs, and improve neighborhoods. Based on successful projects, sound policies and relevant research will continue to break new ground in urban redevelopment.

REFERENCES

Anderson, Arthur LLP. 1998. *City of Chicago Industrial Market and Strategic Analysis.* Chicago Department of Planning and Development.

Anderson, Geoffrey. 1997. *Transportation and Environmental Impacts of Infill Versus Greenfield Development.* Criterion, Inc., Planners Engineers for U.S. Environmental Protection Agency, Washington, D.C.

Baden, Brett, and Don Coursey. 1997. *The Locality of Waste Sites Within the City of Chicago: A Demographic, Social, and Economic Analysis.* Chicago: University of Chicago.

Esseks, J., et al. 1998. *Fiscal Costs and Public Safety Risks of Low-Density Residential Development of Farmland: Findings from Three Diverse Locations on the Urban Fringe of the Chicago Metropolitan Area.* DeKalb, IL: American Farmland Trust.

Persky, Joseph, and Wim Wiewel. 1996. *Central City and Suburban Development: Who Pays and Who Benefits?* Chicago: Great Cities Institute.

Sorensen, A. Ann, and J.D. Esseks. 1998. *Living on the Edge: The Risks and Costs of Scatter Development.* DeKalb, IL: American Farmland Trust.

Sorensen, A. Ann, Richard P. Greene, and Karen Russ. 1997. *Farming on the Edge.* DeKalb, IL: American Farmland Trust.

U.S. GAO. 1995. *Community Development: Reuse of Urban Industrial Sites.* Washington, DC: U.S. General Accounting Office.

Chapter 18

Sustainable New Towns™ and Industrial Ecology

Ernest A. Lowe

Patterns of urban development are a particular focus of concern in the search for a path to a sustainable world. The majority of world cities are vortices of unsustainability, concentrating environmental threats and social and economic distress (see Figure 18.1).

- As magnets of hope, cities have drawn rural populations who, in most developing countries, live in sprawling urban slums, shanty towns, colonias, or townships.
- Their economies reflect the growing global inequality of wealth and income distribution.
- Cities concentrate industrial development and its pollution.
- Urban production and consumption extracts resources from around the planet and deposits massive volumes of waste, creating a bloated "urban footprint" (Wackernagel and Rees 1994).
- Motor vehicles dominate urban transportation systems, producing gridlock, excessive use of valuable land, local air pollution, and greenhouse gases.
- Cities' massive and inefficient energy consumption wastes resources and generates greenhouse gases.
- Economic globalization lacks an effective model for sustainable local development.

By 2000, some 50 percent of the world's population will be in cities and megacities (cities with ten million or more residents) (Girardet 1995, 1996). So urban planners, architects, environmentalists, social activists, and many others have focused their quest for sustainability on the transformation of cities and towns. Existing communities have enlisted in a sustainable community movement, forming visions, action strategies, and urban sustainability indicators.

Planners and designers have created major new town development projects that

Figure 18.1. A densely settled area of Alexandra, a township northwest of Johannesburg, South Africa. Here, 600,000 people are concentrated on a square mile of land.

feature more advanced ecological design and land use, including Coffee Creek in Indiana, Haymount in Virginia, and Abacoa in southern Florida. While excellent in terms of ecological design, such projects do not begin to address the economic development and social issues of sustainable development, particularly in developing countries.

The proposed Televillages project in London integrates high-tech economic development, education, housing, and ecological design in a form that may be adaptable to some developing countries but can play only a modest role in filling their employment deficits (Ledgerwood 1997). Malaysia's Multimedia Development Corridor is a large-scale project offering powerful telecommunications infrastructure, incentives, and entry into Asian markets. Developing countries generally lack the capital and skill base required to mount such a project.

Sustainable community initiatives in established cities have achieved successes in waste reduction, pollution prevention, formation of environmental industry economic development strategies, development of eco-industrial parks, and ecological restoration. However, such initiatives, after forming bold visions, often suffer from "creeping incrementalism," moving forward in a fragmented, unsystemic fashion. The greatest energy often goes to increasing efficiency of resource use, only one of the many requirements for sustainability. *The environmental side of sustainable community work must also deal directly with issues of biodiversity, the viability of local ecosystems, and the land area reserved for all other species.*

Researchers such as Richard Levine and Ernest Yanarella at the University of Kentucky's Center for Sustainable Cities argue that an incremental path alone is unlikely to achieve true sustainability. They fear that some incremental solutions may lock in major errors and generate unforeseen outcomes that further damage social, economic, and environmental systems. (For instance, the change of present automobile designs to decrease pollution and increase fuel efficiency ignores the enormous land surface consumed by road transportation. Incremental improvements in autos may actually delay the transition to really sustainable public transportation systems and urban plans.). Levine and Yanarella (1998) call for sustainable community designers to shift from piecemeal approaches to whole systems solutions.

The issues of urban sustainability are profound for developed and developing countries alike. A particularly high priority should be development and testing of systems solutions applicable to meeting the massive needs of urban populations in developing countries.

Sustainable New Towns™

We have evolved our concept of the Sustainable New Town™ (SNT) as a systems solution to be tested in the context of post-apartheid South Africa. This vision integrates economic development, job creation, education/training, design of the built environment, community development, and ecological stewardship. We propose that SNTs could provide quality low-cost housing in economically and socially viable communities that function with minimal environmental impact.

Planners and designers of SNTs will view their outcome as a whole system rather than as a patchwork of separate initiatives and incremental development decisions. The fragmented approach is inherently inefficient and ultimately costly in economic, social, and political terms. We believe that an integrated approach will be more cost-effective and will lower the financial and environmental risks of urban development. Synergy among the five design elements of an SNT will enable creation of communities that can evolve and adapt as economic and social conditions change.

Meeting South Africa's profound and interrelated needs for housing, jobs, and education is the immediate context for applying the SNT concept. However, the basic model could apply in many other developed countries and the underdeveloped regions of industrialized countries like the United States.

The SNT model seeks full integration among five basic elements of community:

1. *Green urban planning and design of infrastructure and buildings:* The town plan, building design, and infrastructure will support the formation of a secure and creative society with easy access to jobs, training and educa-

tion, and culture. Utilizing an innovative and proven construction process, the physical development itself will have *affordable housing* that is far superior to and less expensive than most houses built for low-income people. In South Africa, government subsidies cover costs of basic shelter and infrastructure for families with an annual income below 3,500 rand (about $580). Additional overseas and domestic finance will provide larger units to families able to qualify for a mortgage. The design of the built environment of SNTs will fit them to their local conditions and preserve a healthy natural environment.

2. *A strong, diverse local economy:* Diversified economic development strategies will provide jobs, grow and maintain businesses aligned to South Africa's development goals, and ensure financial support for business and community development.

3. *Community life-long learning:* Formal and informal structures for education and training will develop capable citizens and administrators, skilled entrepreneurs and employees, and caring stewards of the town's social and ecological systems.

4. *A self-governing, self-organizing society:* A strong and participatory local political system and civic organizations will enable the community to evolve its governance, civil society, and processes of conserving its common wealth.

5. *Environmental stewardship as foundation:* Ecological principles will guide all other levels of design to establish a lasting foundation for the long-term physical health of the residents and the protection of local and global natural systems.

As system planners work to integrate these five aspects for creating a sustainable community, they will build in processes that promote the participation of the town's citizens to adapt the community designs and plans to the needs of the people. Architects sometimes speak of "cowpath" design to illustrate this principle of adaptation to local desires and cultural context. Rather than rigidly laying out all walkways on a piece of property, they may enable its inhabitants to establish the routes through it before setting down pavement. Similarly, though the wise planner provides the physical, financial, and intellectual infrastructure necessary for a sound foundation, creating sustainable communities is mostly about setting the conditions in which self-organization and societal learning can unfold. This is the essence of the SNT.

SNTs will become vital urban laboratories for testing answers to the difficult dilemmas of sustainable urban development. The SNT can be a greenfield development, occupying appropriate undeveloped land and recruiting its residents from townships, shantytowns, or colonias. Or designers can use it to guide planning of "implants" into existing townships, enabling voluntary relocation from very densely populated areas. Another major option is redeveloping existing facilities with infrastructure and housing, such as closed factories, military bases, or power plants.

A typical SNT module will provide approximately 3,000–5,000 housing units and buildings for industry and commercial and municipal services. A sequence of modules at this scale could become a major town constructed in phases within an SNT master plan. From the beginning, physical planning will interrelate with design of the economic, sociopolitical, learning, and ecological communities. A community learning center will be the first structure built to serve as the locus of citizen participation in design as well as the urban laboratory studying the process.

The SNT's integration of the five elements required for viable communities will inform design of policies, redevelopment of townships, strategies for economic development and industrialization, and the practice of participatory governance.

The Challenge of Designing SNTs

Sustainability of the built environment depends on the sustainability of the socio-economic systems in which design and management decisions are made and it depends on the people inhabiting the houses, offices, and industrial facilities that are built. The design of the built environment, in turn, conditions the behavior of the decisionmakers and inhabitants.

This means that designers of the built environment seeking sustainable out-comes must work in terms of the whole system that evolves living communities. Their work must be integrated with that of economic development strategists, educators, administrators in government and civil society, and ecological stewards. The architects, the urban planners, and the construction, civil, and ecological engineers must work with synergy among themselves and then with those responsible for the socioeconomic and natural environments.

In the past two decades, green building projects have prompted increased collaboration among design professionals. To plan and design successful SNTs will call for a new quality of integrative design, which this recent experience of multidisciplinary design will support. Industrial ecology and information technologies are among the emerging foundations for this new level of integration.

South Africa as Context for SNTs

South Africa offers both familiar urban needs and unique opportunities for demonstrating new solutions for the design of sustainable cities. Under apartheid, black, colored, and Asian populations were uprooted and relocated in townships, tribal "homelands," or other special areas. There is a three million unit shortfall in housing. Millions of township residents live in shacks, crowded together and often without basic infrastructure for power, water, and sewerage (see Figure 18.2). Half of the population has no access to electricity. A high national level of unemploy-

Figure 18.2. Behind a poor township in the Cape Flats, west of Cape Town, stands Table Mountain, home of over 5,000 unique native plant species. This image highlights the intersection of environmental and economic interests in sustainable development. (Photo by David Weisman.)

ment—33 percent overall, with 75 percent in some township areas—makes acquisition of housing difficult. Education and training is inadequate to overcome the profound gaps left by apartheid (South African Department of Housing 1995).

The new South African Constitution and governmental strategies place a high priority on meeting all of these needs. The country's two-tier economy offers unique opportunities because there is industrial infrastructure and well-developed resource and basic manufacturing industries. The liberation movement created local leaders and civic organizations that are playing a strong role in community and economic development. Thousands of township microentrepreneurs include many candidates for becoming owners and managers of larger firms. Many black and white South Africans are moving into a new future with enthusiasm, vision, creativity, and openness to new ideas (Lowe 1998).

The Five Elements of the SNT

The following sections describe the five basic elements of community that SNTs attempt to integrate: the built environment, strong local economy, community lifelong learning, governance, and environmental stewardship.

The Built Environment

Other contributors to this volume have covered many design options for a sustainable built environment in detail, including sustainable urban planning and land use, water and energy infrastructure, architecture, landscaping, and construction. We will primarily discuss three major strategic issues relating to design of SNTs—the need for gaining the density required by sustainable land use in a "full world"; additional options for ecological infrastructure; and the role of full-cost accounting in managing trade-offs among financial, environmental, and social values.

More Compact Towns

The New Urbanist movement in urban planning has started a trend away from urban sprawl and fragmented neighborhoods with "innovations" such as transit-oriented development (TOD) and traditional neighborhood development (TND). In common with New Urbanists like Peter Calthorpe and Andres Duany, designers of SNTs will create more compact communities. We will integrate economic and social activities with living space in a socially agreeable living environment. Wherever possible, patterns of traditional South African cultures will inspire habitat and community design. For instance, round houses and village layouts are typical and could guide contemporary design.

Developments will offer a variety of affordable multi-unit and single-family dwellings, enabling different levels of density and mixed use. Residential areas will connect closely with commercial zones and community services (schools, clinics, parks, and municipal offices), providing easy access and minimizing motor transport. This pedestrian- and bicycle-oriented environment will enhance quality of life as well as public safety. (Small vehicles will still be available for the elderly and others with limited mobility.) The town plan will maintain abundant open space in the community for play and relaxation as well as community gardens.

The New Urbanists have demonstrated the majority of these design choices in U.S. new towns developed in recent years or now on the drawing board. However, we believe that meeting the need for housing in developing countries (and for many areas in the United States) will require a more compact model of urban planning than this school of planning has projected.

The Limits of New Urbanist Developments

Some leading New Urbanist projects include the Coffee Creek Center in Indiana (William McDonough + Partners, Conservation Design Forum, and J.F. New & Associates working with Lake Erie Land Development), Andres Duany's Seaside resort in Florida, and Peter Calthorpe's Laguna West in California.

Duany and Calthorpe's Abacoa project in southern Florida is a useful example of the limits of New Urbanism. The excellent master plan for this new town on 2,000 acres calls for a 5,000-student university satellite campus, a baseball training center, and, ultimately, homes for 15,000 residents. The urban plan and building design meet high environmental standards and will preserve over half of the land in its natural state (Kibert 1998).

In the township of Alexandra, adjoining Johannesburg, 600,000 people now live (the great majority in shacks) on roughly a square mile, or 640 acres of land. It would take 40 Abacoas on 125 square miles to provide Alexandrans with new towns at the level of density planned in the Florida development. The most famous township, Soweto, houses over four million inhabitants to the south of Johannesburg. Creating quality, secure, affordable, and ecologically sound communities for such large numbers demands a more compact urban model *with higher densities* than the New Urbanists offer.

Still, the traditional neighborhood development model appears to generate a level of sprawl that is not sustainable in the long run. Some urban and regional planners and architects are committed to learning how to accommodate the housing and community needs of growing populations in a more compact manner. Land use planning must meet the competing needs of urban development, land required for healthy ecosystems, and preservation of farmland needed to feed increasing numbers of people and to provide new bio-materials (*The Built Environment* 1992; Tilman 1997). The goal of achieving more compact cities while maintaining quality of life is critical to the design of SNTs.

The New Urbanists gain greater compactness with their emphasis on walkable communities, mixed neighborhoods with nodes of shops and services, a variety of residence forms (including modest multistory structures), and preservation of natural lands and parks. We must develop other strategies for gaining livable higher density.

One option for increasing density and affordability—cohousing—has been demonstrated in Denmark, the United States, and other countries. In early stages of planning, future residents will be consulted on the appropriateness of this model for South Africa. In cohousing units, families share common work, cooking, and recreational areas, while having private family spaces and greater flexibility in the use of space. This significantly reduces space and costs per family and may fit well with traditional cultures (*Cohousing Resource Guide* 1998; The Cohousing Company 1998).

A broader approach to compact planning is really a reversion to earlier urban models in which quality public space typically reduced the need for space in the home. For centuries Viennese coffeehouse culture, for instance, has provided many citizens with a vibrant setting for social and cultural life. In South African townships, street culture, churches, and shebeens (taverns) play a similar role that could be extended into new town development.

Compact Urban Design for Durban

A 1996–1997 design competition in South Africa generated many plans for compact cities to meet the country's need for quality affordable housing (Tilman 1997). The winning submission, Urban Generator, was created by the Cape Town and Durban team of Suzanne du Toit, Theresa Gordon, Joanne Lees, and Barbara Southworth. The 30-hectare (74-acre) site is part of Cato Manor in Durban. The competition called for at least 100 housing units per hectare. The winning plan varies from 95 to 225 units per hectare (38 to 90 per acre) laid out according to a "collective approach to subdivision, construction, and allocation which can achieve higher densities, greater affordability and better urban qualities."

The designers propose that public acceptance of this higher density would be supported by a communal approach to financing and management emphasizing the role of a community housing association. Row houses and apartments (ranging from two- to four-story walk-ups) share good access to transport, the marketplace, and an urban resource center. The site's border with a nature reserve would maintain public spaces for "meetings, ceremonies, entertainment, religious events and commemorations." The jurors said this entry was the one that, "fully recognizes that the housing problem in South Africa is not only about shelter, but is also about the creation of highly livable, total living environments" (Tilman 1997).

For three decades, Paolo Soleri has been the most ambitious proponent of compact cities that offer quality of life and lower ecological impact. In the late 1960s his visionary arcologies (architecture + ecology) were a manifesto for building up, not out, in order to preserve the health of both natural and social systems. Hundreds of planners and designers have learned from participation in the planning and very gradual construction of Arcosanti, a 7,000-person arcology north of Phoenix (Soleri 1987; Arcosanti 1998). Some key themes in Soleri's vision include:

- Plan the town or blocks of buildings as integrated solar systems, not just as individual buildings with solar.
- Humanize the larger scale of buildings by diversity of use in the neighborhoods within them and by access to light, fresh air, and interior gardens.
- Balance smaller space for individuals and families with safe and convivial social space and commercial services close at hand.
- Balance the concentration of human habitat with parkland and gardens within easy walking distance.
- Where feasible, locate spaces for office, light industrial, and craft employment close to residential areas, providing ease of access and adding variety to the life of the community.

The combination of population growth, unmet need for housing, and competition for land generates a demand that we learn how to live together in a much more compact pattern. Designers of SNTs will need to build on the work of New Urbanists, Soleri, South African planners, and many others trying to achieve high density joined with quality of life. We will need to remember the bitter lessons of the Great Society public housing program in the 1960s that built "ghettos in the sky," such as Cabrini Green in Chicago and Geneva Towers in San Francisco. The latter's buildings, with nearly 600 units, were dramatically imploded on May 16, 1998, after becoming a notorious crime-ridden vertical slum. Its twenty stories were reduced to flattened rubble in ten seconds, demonstrating the unsustainability of this old model of urban density.

Ecological Infrastructures

SNTs in areas with electricity will employ a combination of grid power and renewable systems as energy sources for buildings. Renewable sources might include wind, passive solar, building components with embedded photovoltaics, wind generators, and fuel cells. Half of South Africa's population lives in areas without electricity, offering an opportunity to demonstrate the potential cost-competitiveness of renewable systems when the cost of new fossil fuel generation and transmission capacity is avoided. The selection of all materials, construction techniques, lighting, and equipment will promote high energy efficiency.

Stephen Strong's chapter on renewable energy (Chapter 6) focuses on photovoltaic solar with brief discussion of hydroelectric, wind, geothermal, and solar thermal technologies. Fuel cell technology is now being piloted at a number of utilities and, with flywheel storage, could conceivably be used as a distributed energy source. Recent breakthroughs in solar hydrolysis of water as well as conversion techniques for natural gas suggest that this renewable source could become commercially feasible earlier than generally expected. Heavy investments in fuel cell technology by Daimler Benz and other auto manufacturers could hasten technology breakthroughs in energy areas.

Industrial ecology encourages SNT designers to view energy infrastructure as a whole system. This implies designing lighting, cooking, heating, and cooling—in the context of building design—as an integrated system and seeking opportunities for cascading energy from one use to another. A compact urban plan would make it easier to view the town itself or perhaps neighborhoods as solar units.

Water and sewage systems will use proven ecologically based treatment systems that enable highly efficient use and reuse of this scarce resource. Where environmentally feasible, landscaping and gardens will utilize industrial and other water by-products (see Chapter 8).

The design of transportation infrastructure will avoid dominance of automobile transport by emphasizing access to effective public transit systems. Economic development funding will encourage efficient and safe private transport businesses with links to public transit.

Telecommunications infrastructure will enable entrepreneurs and students to tap into national and global information systems. SNTs will incorporate features of Televillage developments now underway in the United States, the United Kingdom, and other countries. For instance, Grant Ledgerwood describes a Greater London project that will integrate green housing, telecommunications infrastructure, economic development, and educational resources in an ecological planning context. The University of Greenwich is partnering with several local housing associations in the proposed development. The goal is to lower the environmental impacts of housing and transportation and to enhance business and educational opportunities for residents (Ledgerwood 1997).

John Lyle's vision of regenerative landscapes reflects the approach we recommend in SNTs (see Chapter 9). Designers will view the site as an ecosystem to be restored and continually renewed, with all other elements of the built environment designed in terms of its unique character. Residents will enjoy wetlands, ponds, and streams; native trees, shrubs and grasses; and community gardens.

Quality Affordable Construction That Creates Jobs

In South Africa, SNTs will use an innovative, cost-effective, and environmentally sound construction technology for building attractive and affordable homes as well as community, commercial, and industrial facilities. For instance, systems using forms and poured mixes could significantly lower construction costs and time. Most workers need only brief training to become competent craftsmen in this method. This training will enable people to build their own homes and participate in community construction, to the extent that self-help housing is demanded. The workers will learn a skill that could gain them continuing employment in the building trades.

The first SNTs will also include demonstrations of other alternative building materials and construction methods as part of a Sustainable Community Learning Center that serves visitors from South Africa and around the world.

Calculating the Life-Cycle Costs and Benefits of Green Design

Financing of SNT construction will require a budgeting process that demonstrates the costs and benefits of design choices over the full life-cycle of buildings and infrastructure. This mode of budgeting will support designers in making trade-offs between various environmental and social options. Financial institutions will need to understand the advantage of spending more on some initial costs in order to accrue substantial long-term savings in the operation of buildings.

Designers have most frequently used life-cycle costing in energy retrofits or new building energy systems. Many utilities, such as Southern California Edison, work with customers to calculate the benefits of energy-efficient windows, insulation, and heating, ventilating, and air conditioning systems over the full life of the building. They offer incentives based on a life-cycle cost analysis of the energy savings over time (often in the form of a loan repaid from those savings.) A number of software tools, such as DOE-2, enable simulation of a building's energy performance in order to determine life-cycle cost and payback on the higher initial investment (National Audubon Society/Croxton Collaborative 1994). Sustainable architectural and engineering teams have pioneered this systems view of the economics of construction in many green buildings, such as the Audubon House.

However, life-cycle costing tools are not usually used in civilian projects beyond energy cost analysis. This apparent gap may be filled by adaptation of tools created for military projects. Logistics engineering has developed sophisticated life-cycle cost analysis (LCCA) tools and integrated them into a more comprehensive approach. LCCA is one segment of the entire logistics support process. Here the tools are always used as an integrated system. This approach to life-cycle costing may be adapted to budgeting of SNTs as whole systems as well as their infrastructure and individual buildings (O'Dea and Freeman 1995).

A Strong Local Economy

In Chapter 5 of this book, Herman Daly challenged orthodox development economics with a proposal that sustainable development must be based in strong local economies. He argues that attempts to compete in a global economy degrade natural systems and communities when low wages and weak regulations set the terms for winning (Daly 1996). SNTs will be urban laboratories for evolving and testing models for successful local economic development.

Economic development for SNTs will seek to create local economies with the strength and diversity needed to serve unmet local needs and to compete in provincial, national, and global economies. An economic infrastructure and training programs will support new microenterprises and creation of larger businesses by successful microentrepreneurs. Environmental and social standards will be high for new ventures and recruited firms. A central question that SNT development planners will need to answer is, *How can we turn the threats of economic globalization into opportunities?* This challenge is one that local economies are facing around the world.

Economic Infrastructure

In order to build and sustain a strong local economy, SNTs will incorporate effective business support structures, financing institutions, revolving loan funds, and education and training accessible to local entrepreneurs. These comprehensive and integrated services will provide the support that steadily builds peoples' skills and confidence to be successful. Microenterprise models, like the Grameen Bank, and mid-scale business development models, like the Ecumenical Community Development Trust, have demonstrated that this comprehensive infrastructure can produce high success rates for start-up businesses in developing countries.

The Ecumenical Development Co-Operative Society mobilizes investment capital in order to provide loans to business enterprises in poor countries. Finances originate from churches and others who subscribe to the promotion of development as a liberating process, aiding economic growth, social justice, self-reliance, and respect for creation. Based in Europe, it has supported business startups in

Africa, Eastern Europe, Brazil, Southeast Asia, the Caribbean, the Middle East, and India. In Bangladesh, Grameen Bank has a microenterprise and self-help housing loan portfolio of over $400 million. It has served a client base of over 2.3 million borrowers and has become a model for similar microenterprise banks in other countries, including the United States.

The community's learning center will provide education and training to develop managerial, technical, and basic work skills that match the needs of employees and entrepreneurs for the whole range of businesses being created in the town.

While supporting bottom-up microenterprise development, economic development infrastructure will focus on attracting and developing small or mid-scale companies. To this end, the town will feature business incubators. An incubator or hive is the home for developing businesses that are collocated and receive support services to nurture them to a point that they can take off and be sustainable. The design of SNT incubators will draw on South African successes as well as innovative models in the United States. The SNT's incubators will help entrepreneurs by providing:

- Support in venture financing, marketing, accounting, organization design, and other business capabilities.
- Access to common legal, secretarial, bookkeeping, information systems, and office equipment.
- Collaboration among businesses in a shared facility.
- Access to timely information on markets and emerging technical opportunities, including support for technical transfer from small to mid-size entrepreneurial enterprises in other countries.
- Access to training in business basics through the town's learning center.

A mix of public and private sources may provide incubator start-up funding. Local utilities and banks have significant self-interest in seeing new businesses succeed and often help seed the development of incubators. Moreover, potential investors see participation in an effective incubator as a factor that will increase the success rate of new ventures in which they invest. Incubators can range from profit-making entities allied with venture capital funds to public institutions with no financial interest in the incubator's businesses. The latter model may be preferable for SNTs. Here the developer, business, government, and the community (especially environmental and labor interests) can cooperate in incubator planning.

In the United States, incubators often focus on attracting firms within an industrial cluster such as renewable energy, telecommunications, or environmental technology. Another focus may be firms addressing common markets with complementary goods and services. In either case, this clustering opens opportunities for synergy in marketing and research.

Microenterprises

A microenterprise support structure will assist small-scale start-up activities as well as help established ones become more viable as they move into the new community. Public and private partnerships between government agencies, NGO programs, and businesses will help with start-up financing, entrepreneurial mentoring, and referrals. Community housing associations, community banks, and trade unions are three sources of local capital for forming a revolving loan fund. SNT planning will include a variety of physical settings for microenterprises, such as a microenterprise mall, craft workshops, and combined living and working spaces.

South Africa's existing microenterprise economy will be a rich source of business people ready to start small and mid-size firms. Under apartheid the informal economy was often the only place for blacks to gain entrepreneurial skills. A person selling from an open-air food stall might evolve into an owner of a small shop and then into the operator of a chain of township markets. Another source of entrepreneurs are surplus managers in large companies laying off employees.

Eco-Industrial Parks

SNT development can focus economic development with eco-industrial parks (EIPs), a development innovation sparked by industrial ecology. The basic premise of the EIP is that companies can improve their economic performance while minimizing environmental impact by collocating and linking their environmental management and resource use (Lowe et al. 1995). One dimension of collaboration is that businesses can utilize normally wasted by-products of other firms. For instance, a brick and tile manufacturer could use by-product fly ash from a power plant, coal gasification facility, or steel mill.

An EIP adjacent to a major manufacturing plant or a power station would create markets for presently unmarketed and wasted energy and materials by-products. These new companies might help the major facility gain higher efficiency of energy and materials use, generate new revenues, and lower disposal costs.

A broader mission for an EIP would be resource recovery—recruiting and creating firms to do recycling, remanufacturing, reusing, and composting. The inputs would be materials, used products, and energy from the outputs of residential, industrial, agricultural, and municipal sectors in a region. By closing the loops in regional metabolism such a park would increase the efficiency and competitiveness of the local economy (Lowe 1997).

Some other industrial clusters that could play a role in EIPs or broader SNT economic development strategy include:

- *Energy efficiency cluster:* Firms providing consulting services and products to promote energy efficiency in South African industry, municipal operations, and residences.

- *Renewable energy cluster:* Renewable energy products and services, especially firms offering integrated energy solutions.
- *Green chemistry cluster:* Companies creating solvents, catalysts, and other products from bio-materials and benign chemical processes.
- *Telecommunications cluster:* Products and services that help link all elements of the SNT and its EIP to provincial, national, and global markets and sources.

Sustainable Farming and Food Processing

The importance of this sector of green business will vary from one SNT to another. In more urban settings it might simply be a matter of community gardens and edible landscaping for EIPs. Where farmland and water is available, a promising option would be organic farms developed on the model of U.S. community-supported agriculture. South Africa's large supply of unemployed workers makes the higher labor requirements of organic farming a desirable job creation strategy. Intensive organic farming can increase food output dramatically over that of large-scale factory farming.

A particular farming niche with worldwide markets is growing medicinal plants, which are native to South Africa in great abundance. This would be of great value ecologically as many medicinals are threatened by overharvesting in the wild. In order not to compromise their healing properties, organic farming is the only acceptable practice for these crops.

A Case Study: Full Belly Farm

Four partners operate an organic farm on 120 acres in a small valley northwest of Sacramento, California. They hire twelve full-time farm workers and five apprentices, paying a wage several dollars over the usual minimum wage and including full benefits. Full Belly supplies a wide variety of fruit and vegetables to 520 families each week (through drop sites in urban neighborhoods) as well as to three farmers markets and a halfway house for women with cancer. The average price of this organic produce is much lower than that usually charged in markets. Organic farmers in many states are working in this model of community-supported agriculture, demonstrating the business and ecological value of organic farming (Full Belly Farm 1996–98).

The Role of Large Corporations

Transnational corporations can play a creative role in building strong local economies when they recognize the value to themselves of business diversity, quality of workforce, local markets, and other benefits of such communities. Strategies for development of SNTs will seek balance and the strength required to set environmental, social, and economic criteria for entry by large corporations. Maintaining such a filter will require support for SNT recruitment policy by economic development agencies at other levels of government, unions, and NGOs in order to avoid the typical recruit-at-all-costs strategies local governments often follow.

Community Life-Long Learning

In addition to addressing the economy, infrastructure, and buildings of the community, an important long-term process for SNTs is the development of the community's citizenry. Existing schools and newly created community learning centers can help develop the administrators and entrepreneurs that are badly needed by South African towns.

Schools as Learning Communities and Centers of Community Learning

The SNT's schools and adult learning centers will prepare all residents to be effective citizens and stewards of their common wealth. This mission is the platform on which citizens will learn the skills needed for employment, health, creativity, and continuing learning. Training for entrepreneurs, managers, and employees will be closely tied to the community's economic development objectives.

Educational system designers will incorporate proven practices for developing and implementing innovative learning models. They will draw on traditional and new approaches to learning being developed in South Africa and other countries, including:

- The creation of high-performance learning communities, within low-income communities, that draw on principles of successful organizations.
- Charter schools that allow educators and local communities to work with greater autonomy.
- Distance learning that uses technology to enable people and students to learn in their homes or communities from experts and resources throughout South Africa and the world.
- A more holistic understanding of the diversity of human intelligence.

South African educators will be recruited to create and adapt the education and training approaches to the needs of the SNT. Parent and community involvement will be key to defining the educational vision that schools will pursue so that all students can reach high levels of learning and be prepared for their future and South Africa's future.

Facilities for education and training activities will be the first of the town's buildings to be constructed. As they are helping to create the new town, future citizens will begin entrepreneurial and work skills training and local authority staff will gain new capabilities.

The Community Learning Center

The first SNTs will become models of sustainable community development processes for South Africa and the developing world. To capitalize on this potential for sharing its learning, early SNTs will create community development learning centers. Such centers will have information and communication systems for sharing with other communities what is learned in the town about planning, economic and community development, construction processes, and environmental protection. Citizens, planners, business people, and administrators will be able to improve their capability to work on sustainable community development here. The center could offer courses and workshops that cover real estate finance, urban planning and design, leadership of effective citizen involvement processes, and other skills important to speeding the progress of community development and housing.

The curriculum could also include a training program for building trades skills, including managerial training, with a focus on sustainable, affordable construction techniques. It will coordinate with the university and technikon (South African technical colleges) training programs as well as with other organizations that conduct research on housing, economic development, community development, and environmental protection. Through the center the SNT will be a living test bed for policy and program design.

The learning center itself could be a source of income and job creation that would pay for its own operations. Moreover, the presence of a learning center will create a demand for commercial and hospitality services for hosting visitors and students from other communities around South Africa and from other countries. The stream of visitors will open opportunities for a hotel or inns, restaurants, cafes, and entertainment establishments.

Governance and Civil Society

The success of a community depends on a properly functioning local government to protect and nourish its citizens and social capital, provide stewardship for its natural capital, and foster the positive evolution of its people. A self-organizing and self-governing community will provide the foundation for a healthy political system and governance. Local community housing associations can act on behalf of the residents of its housing stock and contribute to the development of the community.

A Self-Governing and Self-Organizing Community

An enduring quality of life depends not only on economic capital, jobs, homes, and possessions. It requires the social capital represented by strong families and ties of kinship, effective civic organizations, capable governance, and trust in one's neighbors and public servants. The solid economic base of SNTs will be interdependent with the institutions of governance, civic society, conflict resolution, and stewardship. However, such institutions have to grow in a self-organizing fashion; they can not simply be designed and implanted.

What *can* be designed and set up in an emerging SNT are the conditions for a healthy sociopolitical community to evolve. These include:

- Respect for traditional forms of governance and conflict resolution.
- An inclusive process of shared decision making, including the full involvement of women in all processes of community development.
- An open communication and participation process that provides full information about the SNT development's proposed plans and actual results;
- Learning and organizing resources—training in local authority administration, in citizen involvement, and in economic development, including case studies of successful community development elsewhere.
- Public–private partnerships including nongovernmental and community-based organizations.

Though it is too early to specify how local self-governing structures might operate, the community housing association is one institution to facilitate and ensure that these conditions prevail.

Community Housing Association

A community housing association (CHA), representative of community residents and other participants, could act as a "codeveloper" and property manager. It might be a cooperative society or a public corporation. The CHA would own and manage housing stock until residents redeem their mortgages. Its governance and professional staff should reflect the interests of residents as well as sources of project financing. The CHA could be the recipient of subsidy block grants, when available.

The CHA would support residents in adopting the full responsibilities of home ownership. It would manage property-related issues, including collections and dispute resolution, thus avoiding the difficulties of intervention by outside authority. It would also handle property sales and property management. The CHA's share of profits from the SNT could be fed into local economic development and provision of community services.

Community Participation in Design

Citizen participation in design of all five elements of SNTs is a crucial facet of our development strategy. In South Africa the constitution and housing policy insist on citizen input. The input and guidance of future residents of the town will ensure evolution of a civil society strong enough to manage many issues of security, welfare, and both ecological and community stewardship. We envision design as a dialogue between the professionals and the future inhabitants. We discuss some of the methods for doing this later in the section titled "Integrative Planning and Design."

The Town as Steward of Its Natural Environment

An understanding of the nature of local ecosystems and the ecological constraints—from local to global levels—will be the foundation for designing the SNT.

All aspects of this development must support long-term biodiversity and health of earth, water, air, and human systems. Without this, there is no economic or social sustainability. (South Africa still has very high biodiversity. Its Bill of Rights uniquely guarantees the right to a healthy environment.)

Unlike one-size-fits-all international design, SNT planning will integrate the community into its immediate natural setting. Design will be guided by keen appreciation of the aspects of the site, its contours, its wind and solar exposure, and its hydrology, flora, and fauna. Design of buildings and infrastructure, construction practices, and landscaping will all seek to maintain and utilize these natural features.

Awareness of potential impacts of the emerging community on planetary systems will be another level of stewardship. Building and infrastructure design will minimize resource consumption and generation of greenhouse gases in materials and in operation of buildings. Healthy materials will help keep residents well.

Economic development will seek to create and recruit new businesses that are nonpolluting and eco-efficient. Candidates will include several clusters of businesses in environmental and energy technologies.

In terms of concrete environmental planning methods, the mandated environmental impact assessment will be only the beginning. Active participation of ecologists and environmental nongovernmental organizations will highlight options for ecologically preferable solutions at every stage of design and construction, including an ecological site survey and identification of opportunities for restoration of native ecosystems.

Industrial ecology will provide a systemic framework and methods to SNT residents and professionals for assessing alternative options for design of the built environment and for economic development. For instance, industrial metabolism studies build a picture of the information, energy, and materials flows that constitute a community's urban footprint. Clear perception of the broader hinterland a town draws on can enable its residents to limit their impact.

The SNT's social norms, education, and political institutions will establish and maintain these requirements for environmental stewardship while helping residents understand the full range of values the environment serves in their lives. Stephen Kellert's contribution to this volume (Chapter 3) helps expand our understanding of stewardship beyond the utilitarian focus often assumed. He eloquently evokes the aesthetic, humanistic, symbolic, moralistic, and naturalistic rewards that complement the utilitarian and scientific values we derive from a healthy mutual relationship with the natural systems that are our home.

Varieties of Sustainable New Towns™

The name "Sustainable New Town" suggests a greenfield development, starting from scratch. It is, of course, less than ideal if the town displaces farmland or nature reserves. In South Africa, about 600,000 people live in the township of Alexandra, northeast of Johannesburg. To the southwest, Soweto includes over four million residents. West of Cape Town, the Cape Flats townships sprawl for miles. In these and many other urban settlements, most people live in crowded, substandard houses or shacks. Comparable settlements exist around every major city in other developing countries. Can the SNT's integrated approach be used in the redevelopment of such areas?

Community leaders in South Africa's townships and urban planners supporting them believe a path of redevelopment is possible. In Alexandra, for instance, the politics of liberation have evolved into a strong set of civic institutions implementing new housing and economic development. At least a thousand microenterprises and dozens of larger firms provide a source of entrepreneurs prepared to create larger businesses. When visiting this crowded township, one senses a notable liveliness and spirit that suggests great potential.

Phased redevelopment of townships can readily utilize the five elements of the SNT model for creating fully viable communities. However, this will have to be coordinated with greenfield developments to provide desirable voluntary relocation opportunities as the very high density is reduced. Greenfield developments will be important for the next decade in rural areas to provide an alternative to country townships and to decrease the migration into the large cities. The process must also enable business and job development in areas beyond the township boundaries, including creation of eco-industrial parks.

Another potential variant of the SNT would utilize the major property holdings, housing, and infrastructure of the military or of state-owned companies. These companies acknowledge that their assets need to be converted from company towns to independently sustainable communities. Using them as the foundation for integrated SNT redevelopment would create a network of communities distributed through several provinces and provide an alternative for urban township dwellers.

Rural SNTs and student housing and entrepreneurial centers are two more varieties to be explored. All of these forms show good potential for synergistic interaction, supporting each other's role in the transformation of South Africa.

Integrative Planning and Design

The concept of the SNT calls for integration across the work of planners and designers in many disciplines and a wide variety of companies and public agencies. The process must also include significant participation by the future residents of such communities. The evolution of each of the five elements of an SNT must reflect all of the other elements in a synergistic fashion. From the start of planning, all participants must be engaged in a learning process that enables correction of errors and amplification of successes. Otherwise the concept is unlikely to be effectively realized.

This combination of requirements appears to conflict with the dominant mode of development, which maintains high walls between professions, between agencies, and between designers, clients, and the public. However, since the 1980s ecological design projects have been demonstrating that integrative design is not only possible but highly pragmatic. While much of this work has focused on teamwork among design professions for the built environment, the teams are becoming increasingly comprehensive in scope.

In addition, the emerging field of industrial ecology offers a highly integrative framework and methods. Logistics engineering, concurrent engineering, the learning organization, and information technologies further add to our capability for integrating complex systems design processes.

Integration in Ecological Design Projects

As designers of the built environment began to address issues of energy and materials efficiency, healthfulness of materials, and impacts of construction, they found they had to end old fragmented design habits. To effectively meet environmental goals and keep budgets within limits, they started to evolve more integrative design processes. An early case is the planning of a headquarters building for Nederlandsche Middenstandsbank (NMB) in Amsterdam, the Netherlands. The bank instructed its team to work across their disciplines—architecture, construction engineering, landscape architecture, energy, and art—and to incorporate employees in the design process.

> The bank stated that human and environmental concerns were as important as economic criteria such as flexibility, efficiency, and low operating costs. Engineers, landscape designers, and artists on the design team all were invited to contribute their ideas from the start, rather than being called upon, as is customary, after the architects and clients had settled upon a scheme. All the participants in the design process were encouraged to stray into one another's areas of specialization in order to encourage a more holistic integration of design factors. The result is an extraordinarily expressive building shaped by a remarkable synthesis of aesthetic, social, economic, and scientific principles. (MacClean 1990)

The NMB bank designers worked for three years in this integrative fashion, with construction beginning in 1983 and completed in 1987.

One process used a great deal for ecological planning is the charrette. At one time design charrettes were strictly intensive architectural design sessions to meet tight project deadlines. Integrative designers of sustainable or green projects have adopted the term for meetings to build project vision and integrate design ideas from various disciplines. Usually a charrette is a two-to-three-day intensive session including the project core team, agency personnel, design consultants, and local citizens. A team at Green Development Services, the consulting organization spawned by Rocky Mountain Institute, has written a useful guide to green development, including many project case studies and guidelines for integrative design (Wilson et al 1997).

Real Estate Developers as Integrators

The real estate developer is inevitably a system integrator, needing to coordinate many agencies and professions to transform an investment in land into infrastructure and buildings that will provide a competitive return on investment. To ensure filling commercial and industrial spaces in mixed-use projects, the developer must gain support of economic development agencies as well as the usual planning/zoning, public works, and environmental agencies. This is done through basic business skills and networking, no particular methodology. Similarly, the developer integrates the work of a professional team that usually includes urban planners, architects, landscapers, a variety of engineers, and marketing people.

The Cost of Whole Systems Design

Some designers and clients assume that integrated design inevitably costs more. Developer John Clark of Washington, D.C., put the question of design costs in a larger framework:

> Is it more expensive? In using this type of holistic planning we spend a lot of money in a short time in the beginning. My Haymount project cost $600,000 in planning. But the data that came out of that planning was never questioned for its scientific objectivity and accuracy. The development plan itself was not changed from the day it was drawn to the day it was approved. A sister project planned with a regular process cost "only" $175,000 to plan. In the course of approval it was changed repeatedly and the design changes cost 8 million dollars before we could go ahead. At the end the plan was unrecognizable, densities were reduced, and locations shifted. What I bought for $600,000 at Haymount allowed me to move through without the plan suffering, costing me less than a tenth of what the other project cost. So good upfront planning is really more economical. (Lowe et al. 1995)

Industrial Ecology

In Chapter 2, Charles Kibert surveyed industrial ecology (IE) as it focuses on the efficiency and environmental quality of resource flows in our economies (the presently dominant mode of IE). Thomas Graedel (Chapter 15) supports the relevance of this level of IE for sustainable construction. The present author and many others have worked toward a broader view of this emerging discipline (Lowe et al. 1997). We see IE as a branch of systems science and practice with particular strengths for supporting multidisciplinary processes and integrating design in SNTs, EIPs, and other complex systems. Its values and methods guide designers to:

- View the human system under consideration as part of its ecosystem and larger natural systems.
- Coordinate planning and action across time and space (local to global; short to long term).
- Coordinate design choices with emerging understanding of environmental challenges (global to local).
- Balance economic, social, and environmental considerations (human needs and ecological needs and constraints).
- Balance efficiency and resilience in system design.

Industrial Ecology as Design Framework

The discipline of industrial ecology will be central to integrating design of SNTs. This is a dynamic systems-based framework that enables management of human activity on a sustainable basis by:

- Minimizing energy and materials usage.
- Ensuring acceptable quality of life for people.
- Minimizing the ecological impact of human activity to levels natural systems can sustain.
- Maintaining the economic viability of systems for industry, trade, and commerce.
- Viewing these systems within natural systems.

IE methods offer processes for finding a balance between ecological, economic, social, and technical interests, a balance defined by natural constraints. A particular strength of this branch of systems science and practice is its emphasis on evaluating design options across scales of time and space (Lowe et al. 1997).

Earlier in this book Herman Daly (Chapter 5) and Sarah van Gelder (Chapter 4) argued that an economy is inevitably a part of nature, embedded in a network of ecological interactions. IE amplifies this concept with the view that all of the instruments of economy and society are similarly embedded and subject to the constraints imposed by natural systems. By heeding this obvious but still uncommon notion, designers of educational programs as well as development strategies or physical infrastructures can gain an essential context for coordinating their work.

For instance, John Todd's "living systems" demonstrate a remarkable strategy for cutting waste of the increasingly valuable resource of water through ecological and agricultural processing of sewage, essentially viewing this aspect of infrastructure as part of nature (Chapter 8). This approach to infrastructure design supports economic development planners in creating green job opportunities and augmenting organic food production. It would also connect well with ecological landscaping that creates wetlands for purifying stormwater runoff. IE assumes that all infrastructure issues at a site can best be handled as whole systems embedded in natural systems.

IE encourages coordination of planning across time and spatial scales. Deciding between a living system plant and a standard sewage treatment plant would require evaluating costs and benefits over the life-cycle of the two systems, not simply estimating upfront construction costs. The first implementation of Todd's design in a region would yield an added benefit through the demonstration of a valuable technology for sewage treatment, water conservation, and economic development. For an arid region this could have broad implications for water use strategy, helping to avoid conflict locally and even internationally.

IE's long-term perspective brings another essential dimension to design integration—understanding emerging environmental challenges. Current examples of this are research on endocrine system disruption caused by many chlorinated substances and study of synergistic interactions among toxic substances. Company and economic planners are developing strategies for the sunsetting of chlorinated substances. Manufacturers of building materials and designers of the built environment are searching for alternative materials.

Planning of a major SNT development will require both internal integration of the design team and coordination with regional strategies for sustainable development. IE planning steps might include an inventory of the area's ecological conditions and constraints (ecology); a survey of the flows of materials and energy in human systems (industrial metabolism); methods for improving industrial, commercial, and household use of energy (energy efficiency) and materials (pollution prevention and recycling); and a means of assessing alternative strategies (design for environment and dynamic input–output modeling). The effort would integrate these IE methods with urban planning, economic and community development, education, and citizen input.

Industrial Metabolism

One IE method, industrial metabolism (IM), traces materials and energy flows from initial extraction of resources through industrial and consumer systems to the final disposal of wastes. This analysis at a community and regional level enables planners and residents to understand energy and materials flows through a local economy as a whole system. (The analysis can be expanded to include information and money flows.) Community metabolism studies enable planners to create strategies for increasing efficiency of resource use, for developing new businesses and jobs, for creating education and training programs, and for extending the life of major municipal infrastructure investments. This firm foundation for SNT planning would help build a strong closed-loop economy operating with high resource efficiency and low pollution. In William Rees' language, it would have a relatively small urban footprint (Lowe et al. 1997).

Other IM studies could focus on the flows within the construction industry. Models of construction metabolism would suggest strategies for reducing waste and otherwise lowering environmental impacts.

Design for Environment

Architects and engineers seeking to apply green design principles in their work have a growing range of environmental options, specifications, and data available. A work like the American Institute of Architects' *Environmental Resource Guide* (five inches thick and growing) provides a wealth of possibilities. With so much data, designers need better tools to support their complex decision-making process. Design for environment (DFE) offers such a method of decision support for designers. It has evolved out of concurrent engineering and product life-cycle analysis as a vital stream of industrial ecology.

Two AT&T executives, Braden Allenby and Thomas Graedel, have extended their application of DFE from electronics manufacturing to industrial facility design. They recommend a largely qualitative rather than quantitative approach. They believe the design task is generally too complex to lend itself to effective quantitative analysis. In complex design situations, they state, "Quantitative models simply eliminate too much information that could be valuable to the designer in reaching design decisions." In addition, too many value judgments are buried in the data; and the data itself is too incomplete to drive a quantitative system.

Allenby and Graedel offer tools to help designers compare alternative options in a more systemic way and to graphically demonstrate those aspects of design that would most improve the environmental performance of a facility. DFE matrices provide a design team speaking many different professional languages with a common framework for seeing the whole project and the place of each part in the whole (Allenby and Graedel 1995; Chapter 15 of this volume).

Webs of Integration

Telecommunications and information technology is rapidly enhancing capabilities for integrative design and citizen involvement. Sophisticated 3-D graphics and virtual reality systems, computer assisted design (CAD) programs, geographic information systems (GIS), geographic positioning systems (GPS), teleconferencing, and the World Wide Web are some of the key tools enabling multidisciplinary teams to coordinate planning and design processes. While electronic tools cannot replace face-to-face design sessions, they can support continuing communication and co-creation once a team spirit is established.

A project operations center for SNT planning could enhance integration across the many disciplines and languages involved. This room would have computers, graphic projection equipment, faxes, and whiteboard and corkboard on all walls. In this facility, any working team would be able to reference a graphic model of the whole project and all of its subsystems. It could also display project timelines, budgets, GIS data, site photos and renderings of the site plan, and other conceptual maps of the work they are doing. This level of access to easily absorbed information would enable project teams to better integrate their work and to communicate with future residents. This operations center would continue to function through all phases of project development and then serve as a hub for community governance.

The Learning Organization

To achieve the breakthroughs needed for integrating the diverse elements of community design, the SNT project team will function as a learning community or organization. The learning organization model will be especially important in early projects, in which fast recovery from inevitable design errors will be imperative. The openness, flexibility, and systems view of the learning organization are the qualities needed for success in the SNT development process.

Some essential attributes of a learning organization include :

- As a group, it uses both failures and successes as opportunities to build the strength of its effort.
- The team is willing to check members' underlying assumptions and beliefs to break through apparent conflicts.
- It explores how the pieces each member manages come together into a whole system.
- The group observes its learning and communication processes to continually improve its collective ability to learn.
- The learning organization is able to sustain a rapid pace of change as necessary to adapt to changing conditions in the environment.

The foundations for learning organization design were laid by noted systems scientists such as Stafford Beer, Peter Senge, and Chris Argyris (Beer 1979; Senge 1990; Senge et al. 1994).

Citizen Involvement

> . . . it is not possible to design or operate cities on a sustainable basis without the ongoing participation of the citizenry of the city. It's not just a question of democracy or equity. In order to operate on a sustainable basis, a city needs to be able to take advantage of the collective genius of the people who live there. (Levine 1997)

Citizen participation in design of SNTs is not just political expediency. Development of highly complex systems really demands a high degree of self-organization, as does the post-apartheid political culture of South Africa. SNT projects must evolve their way to successful completion, with the collective genius defining the terms of success and measuring its achievement. Professional planners and designers then must form a partnership with the future residents of the town, respecting their culture, their forms of communication, and their needs.

The webs of integration can include public web pages, citizen input meetings, displays in public spaces, a series of printed project reports, and focus groups. The SNT learning center will be a hub for this citizen involvement process.

Guidelines for Team Integration

Case studies of integrative design suggest a number of basic guidelines:

- Assemble the full team early in the process, even before site selection, to ensure that all points of view guide the design process.
- Brief the team on the whole system being designed, with a focus on the needs of and benefits to the ultimate users/residents.
- Establish incentives that reward teamwork and cost savings that derive from integrative planning.
- Encourage input from specialists on all aspects of the project. When contributing outside of their area of expertise, they may conceive innovative design solutions more readily than those directly responsible.
- Keep channels open for input throughout the project. Consider a project intranet and other electronic tools to keep the whole system in view, to keep the team informed, and to encourage communication across disciplines and interests.
- Be sure the general contractor participates from the beginning to help designers understand implications of their choices for cutting cost, minimizing waste, and reducing environmental impact in the actual construction.

Conclusions

The Sustainable New Town™ concept is a systems approach to achieving local sustainable development that is being applied initially in South Africa but is of potential relevance to developing countries around the world. There is no SNT in existence at the time of writing, but funding is still being secured for the first demonstration project in South Africa. The global economic crisis at this writing is making investors cautious, but socially responsible investors are continuing to fund development projects there. Preparations are also underway for a first U.S. new town along the lines described in this chapter.

Each of the elements of this vision has been demonstrated separately. There are model new town projects with excellent integration of building, infrastructure, and landscaping design suited to the constraints and features of their sites' ecological character. Eco-industrial parks and industrial resource exchanges are under development in the United States, South Africa, Australia, Europe, and Asia. Breakthroughs in education and workforce training are creating learning communities in disadvantaged communities. Sustainable farming has demonstrated its productivity as well as its healthfulness. Economic development planners are implementing institutions for building strong local economies in many communities. Some actors in the global economy are beginning to face the need to balance globalization with the strengthening of communities.

The only thing new in the SNT is the evolution of all five elements of a viable community as a whole system. Designers will integrate tested innovations from around the world into a community plan created with intense attention to the unique cultural, economic, and natural systems of each site.

Designers and planners have been gaining experience in synergistic design processes. They can draw on tested methods and tools to support their integrative teamwork. The complexity of their challenge in planning SNTs is manageable as long as they remember the critical balance between design and self-organizing evolution, between their professional expertise and the genius of the people who will live and work and play in SNTs.

None of this is any more complex than the prospect of living in a dying habitat for humanity. We now are learning how to live within a living world.

REFERENCES

Allenby, Braden, and Thomas Graedel. 1995. *Industrial Ecology*. Englewood Cliffs, NJ: Prentice-Hall, pp. 285–289; and "Defining the Environmentally Responsible Facility." Paper from 1994 Woods Hole Workshop on Industrial Ecology, National Academy of Engineering.

Arcosanti. 1998. Web site: www.arcosanti.org

Beer, Stafford. 1979. *The Heart of Enterprise*. New York: John Wiley and Sons.

The Built Environment. 1992. Special issue on the "Compact City," vol. 18, no. 4.

The Cohousing Company. 1998. Web site: http://www.cohousingco.com/links.htm

Cohousing Resource Guide. 1998. Web site: http://www.cohousing.org/CRG/toc.html

Daly, Herman. 1996. *Beyond Growth: The Economics of Sustainable Development*. Boston: Beacon Press.

Full Belly Farm. 1996–98. Weekly newsletter provided in the boxes of organic produce it delivers in San Francisco Bay Area cities.

Girardet, Herbert. 1995. *The Urban Age: Sustainable Cities in an Urbanising World*. Web site: http://www.oneworld.org/overviews/cities/girardet_urbanage.html

Girardet, Herbert. 1996. *The Gaia Atlas of Cities, New Directions for Sustainable Urban Living*. London: Gaia Books Limited.

Kibert, Charles. 1998. A three-volume sustainability code based on the Abacoa project—The Sustainability Rationale, the Sustainable Development Code (SDC) and the Sustainable Construction Code-Residential (SCCR). Center for Construction and Environment, University of Florida, Gainesville.

Ledgerwood, Grant. 1997. *Enterprise Televillages and Social Housing Innovation: Strategic Community Design, Market Testing, and Business Planning of Sustainable Residential Communities for Entrepreneurs*. Proposal produced by the University of Greenwich, London.

Levine, Richard S. 1997. "Design as the Operative Model for Generating Sustainable Cities." *Annual Conference Proceedings of the American Solar Energy Society*, Washington, D.C. (Draft is on web site of Center for Sustainable Cities, College of Architecture, University of Kentucky, Lexington, Kentucky, at http://www.uky.edu/Classes/PS776/cscinfo.html)

Levine, Richard S., and Ernest J. Yanarella. 1998. "Don't Pick the Low-Lying Fruit: Sustainability from Pathway to Process." *Annual Conference Proceedings of the American Solar Energy Society*, Washington, D.C. (Draft paper is on the Internet: http://www.uky.edu/Classes/PS776/cscinfo.html)

Lowe, Ernest. 1997. "Regional Resource Recovery and Eco-Industrial Parks: an Integrated Strategy." Paper presented at a conference on industrial recycling networks, Karl-Franzens-Universitat Graz, Austria, April 28–29.

Lowe, Ernest A. 1998. These statements are based primarily on personal conversations with several hundred innovators in the new South Africa.

Lowe, Ernest, Stephen Moran, and Douglas Holmes. 1995. *Fieldbook for the Development of Eco-Industrial Parks*. Prepared for U.S. EPA under a cooperative agreement with Research Triangle Institute. (Released by Indigo Development as *Eco-Industrial Parks Handbook*, Indigo Development, Oakland, CA.)

Lowe, Ernest, John Warren, and Stephen Moran. 1997. *Discovering Industrial Ecology: An Executive Briefing and Sourcebook*. Cleveland, OH: Battelle Press.

MacLean, Henry. 1990. "Banking on Nature's Power and Poetry." *Design Spirit* (Winter/Spring):9–14.

Nathan, Joe. 1996. *Charter Schools: Creating Hope and Opportunity for American Education*. San Francisco: Jossey-Bass.

National Audubon Society and the Croxton Collaborative. 1994. *Audubon House*. New York: John Wiley & Sons.

O'Dea, Katherine, and Gregg Freeman. 1995. "Environmental Logistics Engineering: A New Approach to Industrial Ecology." *Total Quality Environmental Management* (Summer) 4:73–86.

Senge, Peter. 1990. *The Fifth Discipline: The Art and Practice of the Learning Organization*. New York: Doubleday/Currency.

Senge, Peter, et al. 1994. *The Fifth Discipline Fieldbook: Strategies and Tools for Building a Learning Organization.* New York: Doubleday/Currency.

Soleri, Paolo. 1987. *Arcosanti: An Urban Laboratory?*, 2nd ed. Santa Monica, CA: VTI Press.

South African Department of Housing. 1995. *A New Housing Policy and Strategy for South Africa.* Pretoria: South African Department of Housing.

Tilman, Harm. 1997. *Integration or Fragmentation: The Housing Generator Competition for South African Cities.* Rotterdam: Academie van Bouwkunst. Available on the Internet: http://www.africaserver.nl/hg

Wackernagel, Mathis, and William Rees. 1996. *Our Ecological Footprint: Reducing Human Impact on Earth.* Philadelphia: New Society Publishers.

Wilson, Alex, Jenifer L. Uncapher, Lisa McManigal, L. Hunter Lovins, Maureen Cureton, and William D. Browning. 1997. *Green Development: Integrating Ecology and Real Estate.* Snowmass, CO: Rocky Mountain Institute. Web site: http://www.rmi.org

About the Contributors

RANDALL ARENDT is a land use planner, site designer, author, lecturer, and an advocate of conservation planning. He is vice president of conservation planning at the Natural Lands Trust in Media, Pennsylvania. He coauthored the award-winning volume *Dealing with Change in the Connecticut River Valley: A Design Manual for Conservation and Development* and is the principal author of *Rural by Design: Maintaining Small Town Character*.

RAYMOND J. COLE is currently a professor in the School of Architecture at the University of British Columbia, where he has been teaching environmental issues in building design for the past twenty years. Dr. Cole heads the Environmental Research Group (ERG) at the School of Architecture, which undertook the development work on the Building Environmental Performance Assessment Criteria (BEPAC) program, the first comprehensive method of assessing the environmental performance of office buildings in Canada.

HERMAN E. DALY is currently senior research scholar at the University of Maryland School of Public Affairs. He is cofounder and associate editor of the journal *Ecological Economics*. His interest in economic development, population, resources, and environment has resulted in over one hundred articles in professional journals and anthologies, as well as numerous books, including *Toward a Steady-State Economy* (1973), *Steady-State Economics* (1977, 1991), *Valuing the Earth* (1993), and *Beyond Growth* (1996). He is coauthor, with theologian John B. Cobb Jr., of *For the Common Good* (1989, 1994), which received the 1991 Grawemeyer Award for Ideas for Improving World Order.

THOMAS E. GRAEDEL is professor of industrial ecology in the School of Forestry and Environmental Studies at Yale University, a position he assumed in 1997 after twenty-seven years at AT&T Bell Laboratories. He was the first atmospheric chemist to study the atmospheric reactions of sulfur and the concentration trends in methane and carbon monoxide. As a corrosion scientist, he devised the first computer model to simulate the atmospheric corrosion of metals. One of the founders of the newly emerging field of industrial ecology, he coauthored the first textbook in that specialty and has lectured widely on its implementation and implications.

STEPHEN R. KELLERT is a professor at the Yale University School of Forestry and Environmental Studies. Much of his work has focused on the value of biodiversity and its conservation. He is the author of over one hundred publications, including *Kinship to Mastery: Biophilia in Human Evolution and Development* (Island Press, 1997); *The Value of Life: Biological Diversity and Human Society* (Island Press, 1996); *The Biophilia Hypothesis* (coedited with E.O. Wilson, Island Press, 1993); and *Ecology, Economics, Ethics: The Broken Circle* (coedited with F.H. Bormann, Yale University Press, 1991).

CHARLES J. KIBERT is the director of the Center for Construction and Environment at the University of Florida, a CSR/Rinker Professor in the M.E. Rinker School of Building Construction, and a University of Florida Research Foundation Professor. He founded the Cross Creek Initiative, a nonprofit organization for transferring sustainable building methods and technologies to the construction industry. He organized and coordinates Task Group 16 of Conseil International du Batiment (CIB), an international research body that promotes sustainability principles in the creation and operation of the built environment. He is the primary author of *Turning Brownfields into Vital Community Assets, Greening Federal Facilities,* and over ninety papers on the sustainable built environment.

GAIL A. LINDSEY is the founder and president of the Raleigh, North Carolina, firm Design Harmony, Inc., a leader in environmentally conscious architecture. She is currently the chair of the American Institute of Architects' Committee on the Environment (COTE) and chair of the North Carolina Green Building Council. She is on the advisory board of *Environmental Building News.* She has been involved with "The Greening of the White House," "The Greening of the Pentagon," and "The Greening of Habitat for Humanity." She has also been instrumental in "The Sustainable Initiative for the National Park Service" at the Grand Canyon and Yellowstone National Park. Her firm's work has been published in *Green Architecture, The Ecology of Architecture,* and in the Japanese magazine *BISES.*

ERNEST A. LOWE is director of the Indigo Development Division of RPP International and one of the pioneers in applying industrial ecology to sustainable community development. He served as project manager and lead author of *Discovering Industrial Ecology,* an executive briefing and sourcebook on industrial ecology, as well as *Eco-Industrial Parks: A Handbook for Local Development Teams.* Mr. Lowe has conducted a strategic review of an eco-industrial park for Sasol Chemical Industries (South Africa), supported Northern California economic development agencies in the planning of a resource recovery based eco-industrial park, and worked on the Baltimore eco-industrial Empowerment Zone project. His current work is focused on the design and development in South Africa of a Sustainable New Town™ incorporating an eco-industrial park.

JOHN TILLMAN LYLE was professor of landscape architecture at the California State Polytechnic University in Pomona. He was the founder of the Center for Regenerative Studies and guided its development until 1994. Professor Lyle taught and practiced ecological planning and design, emphasizing the essential roles of natural evolved processes in the human environment. He practiced architecture as part of the landscape. He is the author of *Design for Human Ecosystems* (1985), *Regenerative Design for Sustainable Development* (1994), and numerous articles published in *Landscape Architecture, Landscape Journal, Nikkei Design, Biocity,* and other periodicals. In 1996, he received the ASLA Medal, the highest award for professional achievement of the American Society of Landscape Architects.

NADAV MALIN is a principal of E Build, Inc., and coeditor of *Environmental Building News,* where he researches and authors many of the product reviews and feature articles on materials used in construction. Malin consults on material choices for green building projects and is leading the assessment effort of a project for the international Green Building Challenge '98. Malin is also leading an E Build project to develop green building decision-making software for designers. Before joining the team that started *Environmental Building News,* he was a home builder in southern Vermont.

DAVID ORR is currently professor and chair of the Environmental Studies Program at Oberlin College. He is best known as an environmental educator and for his pioneering work on environmental literacy and campus ecology. His present work is focused on ecological design and specifically the design and construction of an environmental studies center at Oberlin College. He is the author of *Earth in Mind* (1994), *Ecological Literacy* (1992), and over ninety published articles.

STEPHEN J. STRONG is president of Solar Design Associates, Inc., a group of architects and engineers dedicated to the design of environmentally responsive, sustainable buildings and the engineering and integration of renewable energy systems that incorporate the latest in innovative technology. In 1985, working with New England Electric, he completed the world's first photovoltaic-powered neighborhood in central Massachusetts. His firm provides technical support to the Sacramento Municipal Utility District solar program. He is the author of *The Solar Electric House.*

JOHN TODD is president of Ocean Arks International, visiting professor of ecological design at the University of Vermont, principal of John Todd Research and Design Inc., and cofounder and director of Living Technologies, Inc. His work on ecological design, including energy, architecture, waste, food, and ocean transport has been published in many books, including *The Village as Solar Energy* (1980), *Tomorrow is Our Permanent Address* (1980), *Reinhabiting Cities & Towns: Designing for Sustainability* (1981), *Bioshelters, Ocean Arks, City Farming: Ecology as the Basis for Design* (1984), and *From Eco-Cities to Living Machines: Principles of Ecological Design* (1994).

WILLIAM C. TRUMBULL is the assistant commissioner in the Chicago Department of Environment responsible for the city's Brownfield Initiative, which links environmental remediation with economic development. Mr. Trumbull is on the board of directors of the National Association of Local Government Environmental Professionals and of the Chicago Brownfield Institute Advisory Council, and he is active in several other environmental and economic development organizations.

SARAH VAN GELDER is editor-in-chief of *Yes! A Journal of Positive Futures* and the founder and executive director of Positive Futures Network. *Yes!* magazine and the network advocate a just, compassionate, and sustainable future. Sarah has written, spoken, consulted, and developed journal issues on the themes of the built environment, voluntary simplicity, win-win politics, ecological business, future studies, community-based economics, sexuality, and sustainable communities. Sarah was previously editor of *In Context*, which during her tenure was awarded the 1994 Alternative Press Award for best coverage of emerging issues.

DANIEL WILLIAMS has practiced sustainable green architecture and regional planning since 1976. His work in regional and community design includes The New South Dade Planning Charrette, a post–Hurricane Andrew regional planning project; The WIN Plan, Watershed Interactive Network, a community involvement project of the South Florida Water Management District concerned with a sustainable water supply for Dade County; The South Dade Watershed Project, a greenways–blueways regional planning study for the South Florida Water Management District; and the Miami River Watershed Plan, an infill-retrofit of the communities within the Miami River watershed. Presently he is research associate professor at the Center for Urban and Community Design at the University of Miami School of Architecture and is investigating the relationship between greenways/blueways, hydrology, and community planning.

PETER YOST is assistant director of the Structures and Environmental Systems Division of the National Association of Home Builders (NAHB) Research Center in Upper Marlboro, Maryland. As a former remodeling contractor of seven years, he brings practical field experience in residential construction to complement his academic training in resource efficiency issues. Mr. Yost's work at the NAHB Research Center currently includes project management of construction and demolition waste management studies.

Index